THE
SIOUX
IN
SOUTH DAKOTA
HISTORY

S**THE**OUX

IN SOUTH DAKOTA HISTORY

A TWENTIETH-CENTURY READER

EDITED BY RICHMOND L. CLOW

SOUTH DAKOTA STATE HISTORICAL SOCIETY PRESS

Pierre, South Dakota

The articles in this anthology originally appeared in:
South Dakota History
South Dakota State Historical Society
900 Governors Drive, Pierre, SD 57501-2217

This publication is funded, in part, by the Harold S. Shunk Memorial Fund
and Dakota Authors, Inc. Additional funding provided by the Great Plains
Education Foundation, Inc., Aberdeen, S.Dak.

Library of Congress Cataloging-in-Publication data
The Sioux in South Dakota history : a twentieth-century reader / edited
by Richmond L. Clow.
p. cm.
Includes index.
ISBN 978-0-9777955-4-3
1. Dakota Indians—History. 2. Dakota Indians—Social life and
customs. 3. South Dakota—History. 4. South Dakota—Social life
and customs. I. Clow, Richmond L.
E99.DIS6172 2007
978-004′975243—dc22
2007033598

11 10 09 08 07   1 2 3 4 5

Design by Rich Hendel

To Ginny and Tad, my friends on this journey

CONTENTS

INTRODUCTION

· · ·

W hile the story of the Sioux people in the nineteenth century has long been documented and discussed, the experiences of the Sioux in the twentieth century are less well known but equally important. Accounts of their role in annihilating Custer's troops on the banks of the Little Greasy, their confinement on the Great Sioux Reservation, and their fate at the hands of soldiers at Wounded Knee have found their way into print and stood as icons of Sioux history for generations. The names of Sitting Bull, Crazy Horse, Red Cloud, Drifting Goose, Struck-by-the-Ree, and Little Crow are also widely known. Gradually, however, there has been a scholarly effort to leave the shadow of the nineteenth century and uncover the history of the Dakota, Lakota, and Nakota Sioux people in the twentieth century.

For nearly four decades, the editors of *South Dakota History* have encouraged research into these important stories in order to reveal the changing lives, perspectives, problems, and opportunities the twentieth century created for the Sioux. The essays in this volume have been gleaned from past issues of the peer-reviewed quarterly journal, established by the South Dakota State Historical Society in 1970. Over the years, *South Dakota History* has achieved a strong reputation for publishing high-quality scholarship, winning numerous national awards for excellence, including three prestigious Ray A. Billington awards from the Western History Association. Several authors whose works appear in this anthology are both award-winning writers and recognized authorities in their fields of scholarship. The collection is not intended to be a comprehensive examination of twentieth-century Sioux history but, rather, a sampling of the best essays *South Dakota History* has to offer on a variety of facets and themes in Sioux history since 1900.

The twentieth century witnessed the effects of many ill-conceived nineteenth-century federal policies directed toward tribal people. By the mid-1800s, the nation's leaders had formulated the concept of reservations in an effort to civilize and Christianize tribes. The completion of a treaty with the Yankton Sioux in 1858 created the first reservation in southern Dakota Territory. The Sisseton-Wahpeton reservation in the northeastern corner of what would become South Dakota followed in 1867. Expanding on the Fort Laramie Treaty of 1851 that defined western boundaries for the Sioux, the Fort Laramie Treaty of 1868 created the Great Sioux Reservation from the lands west of the Missouri River. In 1877, the Black Hills Agreement withdrew the Black Hills from the Great Sioux Reservation.[1]

The reservation concept produced results contrary to the policy makers' stated goals. Instead of prosperity, there was poverty; instead of self-sufficiency, there was dependency on the federal government. Reformers and Congress pushed harder toward the goal of making American Indians self-supporting members of society. The General Allotment Act of 1887 provided for private property and eventual citizenship. Congress gained further land cessions through the Sioux Agreement of 1889 that opened millions of acres in western South Dakota to non-Indian homesteaders and defined boundaries for the Crow Creek, Rosebud, Pine Ridge, Cheyenne River, Lower Brule, and Standing Rock reservations.[2]

Land allotment began on the Yankton reservation in 1888 and quickly moved to the other Sioux reserves. Instead of creating self-supporting citizen-farmers, however, allotment drove the Sioux deeper into poverty, creating an anomaly whereby the Sioux were citizens, but the United States government held their property in trust. Most Sioux on the reservations lacked the means to farm and were forced to lease or sell their allotted property, further reducing their standard of living in the process.[3]

As the disaster of land allotment unfolded, Congress sought new policy directions and by the 1930s postulated that increasing tribal self-governance would free the Sioux from federal dependency. The passage of the Indian Reorganization Act (IRA) in 1934 encouraged the reorganization of existing tribal governments. Most South Dakota Indians accepted the idea of self-governance but were divided over the provisions of the legislation. Eventually all South Dakota tribes except the Yanktons, who favored their current business-committee form of governance, adopted charters or constitutions based on the IRA model.[4]

After World War II, the pendulum of federal policy swung back toward eliminating tribal status. "Termination," as it was called, was not as strong in South Dakota, however, as it was in other states where Indian communities were perceived as more affluent and therefore ready to be released from federal overlordship. By the 1960s, a focus on tribal self-rule reemerged as tribal leaders pushed for greater self-determination and government-to-government relations with Washington. From these wide-ranging changes in federal Indian policy, many twentieth-century Sioux stories have emerged.[5]

These stories are as diverse and as varied as the land where they unfolded. Arising from the array of policies that have affected the lives of the Sioux in South Dakota are issues such as the Black Hills land claim, conflicts over state and tribal jurisdiction, taxation of tribal interests, tribal participation in state elections, and the development of public schools on reservations. The Great Depression and drought, fair treatment of tribal members in state courts, and the role of the Native American Church in shaping Sioux identity are among countless other possible topics in any discussion of events of the twentieth century. The authors of the essays in this collection tell many of these stories but leave the door open for other scholarly research.

In Part 1, "The Struggle for Land," Frederick Hoxie's "From Prison to Homeland: The Cheyenne River Indian Reservation before World War I" discusses the 1889 Sioux Agreement that ceded portions of the Great Sioux Reservation to the United States, created the Cheyenne River reservation and five other smaller reservations, and initiated preparations to allot land in severalty to individuals. These events melded the Blackfeet, Sans Arcs, Two Kettles, and Minneconjous into the Cheyenne River Sioux. Fusion of the bands continued with the establishment of a tribal police force, court, and, in 1903, a twelve-member business committee that replaced the bands' former government. Once allotment had been completed, part of the reservation was opened to homesteading in 1909, and government schools intensified their efforts to assimilate the Indians. Hoxie argues that these events produced cultural change, not assimilation. Rather than eliminating Lakota culture, the government's policies instead created new "cultural homelands" where native identity could survive.

Harry H. Anderson to some extent counters Hoxie's vision of an emerging reservation nationalism in describing the divisions between mixed-blood and full-blood Sioux in "The Waldron-Black Tomahawk Controversy and the Status of Mixed Bloods among the Teton Sioux." During the nineteenth century, mixed-blood individuals were an integral part of the Lakota world, serving as interpreters and marrying Sioux spouses, but the process of land allotment placed the two groups on a collision course. In 1890, two enrolled members of the Cheyenne River Sioux, mixed-blood Jane Waldron and full-blood Black Tomahawk, both claimed the same 320-acre allotment. The Department of the Interior declared ʻhat Waldron was not, in fact, an Indian, forcing her to sue for her right to receive an allotment. Anderson analyzes the case, which was decided in Waldron's favor in 1905. This legal conflict was a precursor to subsequent political conflicts between these groups in Indian country throughout the twentieth century.

The process of allotting a reservation proved to be simpler than administering the allotted lands through the years, as Michael L. Lawson describes in "The Fractionated Estate: The Problem of American Indian Heirship." Tribal members often died without wills, forcing estates into probate. Under official policy, the land was divided among the heirs equally on paper but remained in federal trust. The parcels were soon reduced to fractions of the original estates, and heirs often leased out the land in order to gain some economic benefit. This division of shares became more acute with the passing of each generation, thus reducing the heirs' ability to work their land or derive income from it.

Like all communities, the Sioux experienced both joy and hardship, as the essays in Part 2, "Reservation Life" show. Allison Fuss Mellis explores the importance of rodeo as a twentieth-century tribal institution in "Cowboys on the Reservation: The Growth of Rodeo as a Lakota National Pastime." Sioux cowboys had ridden bison or bucking horses in Wild West shows and worked on cattle ranches since the 1880s. Focusing on the Pine Ridge and Cheyenne River reservations, Mellis argues that after World War I, greater opportunities arose for Lakotas to compete in rodeos and fairs off the reservation. At the same time, rodeos on the reservation became important social gatherings and contributed to the reservation economy, as well.

While the rodeo represented a positive facet of pre-World War II tribal life, the Great Depression and drought of the 1930s brought suffering and hunger. On 15 July 1933, Rosebud Superintendent William O. Roberts provided a glimpse of this calamity, noting, "Yesterday was the toughest day at an Indian agency that I ever experienced. There were more people clamoring for food than I have ever seen."[6] Following the election of Franklin D. Roosevelt as president, Congress enacted legislation organizing direct and indirect relief programs for the unemployed on and off reservations. Roger Bromert examines some of this legislation in his article, "The Sioux and the Indian-CCC." The Civilian Conservation Corps-Indian Division (CCC-ID) work-relief program took on the difficult assignment of improving reservation sanitary conditions, rehabilitating homes, growing community gardens, and building water facilities. Despite its shortcomings, which Bromert also outlines, the CCC-ID provided jobs and helped to prevent starvation during a period of extreme duress.

As adults struggled to find work during the depression, their children often attended either day schools or boarding schools where idealistic philosophies outstripped available resources. In "The Diaries of a Day-school Teacher: Daily Realities on the Pine Ridge Indian Reservation, 1932–1942," Laura Woodworth-Ney tells the story of Marion Billbrough Dreamer, who taught for ten years at a day school on Pine Ridge. In addition to instructing the students at Day School

Number Five near the small community of Oglala, she provided them with medical care and clothing and acted as recreation director and confidant to the local population. Through her marriage to tribal member George Dreamer in 1935, she gained insights into reservation life that helped her in her work.

The theme of physical and mental well-being continues in Part 3, "Health on the Reservation." Perhaps no reservation-based medical professional is better known to contemporary anthropologists and historians than James R. Walker, MD. In "James R. Walker's Campaign against Tuberculosis on the Pine Ridge Indian Reservation," Don Southerton examines Walker's efforts to improve tribal health by fighting the disease known as the "white death." Remembered today primarily for his ethnographic field work,[7] Walker was equally important as a physician who sought innovative ways to treat and prevent tuberculosis.

Scott Riney addresses mental illness and its accompanying violence and hopelessness in "Power and Powerlessness: The People of the Canton Asylum for Insane Indians." For the first three decades of the twentieth century, this unique institution housed tribal members who had been judged mentally unfit to remain on the reservation. Despite the shroud of privacy covering many records, Riney gives voice to those individuals committed to the asylum. Poorly trained and overworked staff contributed to deplorable conditions at the institution, which was closed in 1934.

In Part 4, "Changes in Government Policy," several authors chronicle the major Indian policy shifts that occurred in the years following the two world wars. Richmond L. Clow, in "Tribal Populations in Transition: Sioux Reservations and Federal Policy, 1934–1965," describes the deteriorating economic conditions that stalked the reservations before the passage of the Indian New Deal. Hailed as one of the most important congressional policy decisions in tribal history, the Indian Reorganization Act (IRA) of 1934 was intended to increase tribal home rule. The IRA escalated political participation on the reservations as tribal members debated the strengths and shortcomings of the proposed tribal government reorganization, which included provisions for ratifying constitutions and corporate charters. Following World War II, the debate centered on the tribes' role in reservation governance and the administration of antipoverty programs.

In the immediate postwar years, tribal members on South Dakota reservations suffered from scarce economic opportunities. Steven C. Schulte's essay, "Removing the Yoke of Government: E. Y. Berry and the Origins of Indian Termination Policy," unravels the complex relationship between Congressman Berry and his tribal constituents on the Standing Rock reservation. Berry advocated trading government relief for a weekly paycheck and pushed his "Operation Bootstrap" as the mechanism to put Sioux people to work. While some labeled Berry a terminationist, his stand against the Bureau of Indian Affairs resonated with many tribal members who desired freedom from government control.

The economic impact of the 1930s drought and periodic downstream flooding forced many to consider new uses for the Missouri River, which formed the boundaries of several South Dakota reservations. The 1944 Pick-Sloan Plan intruded on numerous tribal communities and lands. Upon construction of four main-stem dams in the state, the Missouri flooded large sections of the Standing Rock, Lower Brule, Crow Creek, Cheyenne River, and Yankton reservations. In "'We lost our way of living': The Inundation of the White Swan Community," Michael L. Lawson recounts how the massive Fort Randall Dam project disrupted the lives of the Yankton people at White Swan. As Lake Francis Case filled in behind the dam, Yanktons lost firewood, berries, grazing lands, and graves to the rising water. Instead of benefiting the community, the project destroyed it by ending subsistence practices that depended on a free-flowing river, forcing residents to disperse.[8]

The loss of subsistence lifestyles often served as a stimulus for twentieth-century resistance and protests. Just as Blue Water Creek, the Little Bighorn, and Wounded Knee became symbols of Sioux resistance in the nineteenth century, so, too, did points of confrontation in the twentieth century as the Red Power movement and the American Indian Movement (AIM) gained strength. In Part 5, "Confrontation and Radical Action," Akim D. Reinhardt describes the reasons behind Wounded Knee II in "Spontaneous Combustion: Prelude to Wounded Knee 1973." He chronicles the incidents that led to AIM's seventy-one-day takeover of the church and village of Wounded Knee on the Pine Ridge reservation. Two events, the murder of Raymond Yellow Thunder in Gordon, Nebraska, and the election of Richard Wilson as chair of the Pine Ridge council, provided the match and the gasoline that ignited the largely spontaneous takeover at Wounded Knee.

Joshua Garrett-Davis examines another confrontation in the final essay in this collection, entitled "The Red Power Movement and the Yankton Sioux Industries Pork-processing Plant Takeovers of 1975." In the spring of 1975, small groups of Yankton tribal members twice occupied the white-owned and white-managed pork plant at Wagner, South Dakota. Members of AIM organized the first takeover in March to protest poor working conditions and the lack of Yankton involvement in the plant's management. The second, more volatile, occupation took place in May when seven armed Yankton tribal members occupied the facility. Although neither occupation succeeded in creating stable economic opportunities for tribal members, both episodes helped to raise the tribal community's political consciousness.

An anthology such as this one helps readers explore the mutual history of contemporary Sioux communities and their nontribal neighbors and understand why relationships between them are often strained. The imposition of ill-conceived policies toward the Sioux in the nineteenth century produced contrary and even disheartening results for the twentieth-century reservation population. Reservation life brought a measure of security, but it was accompanied by dependency, further erosion of land bases, and traumatic cultural change. The trials and triumphs that the Sioux in the twentieth century experienced provide fertile terrain for further research as historians, anthropologists, and others seek to understand the Sioux role in a changing world.

NOTES

1. 11 Stat 743, 749; 15 Stat 505, 635; 19 Stat. 254.

2. 24 Stat 88; 25 Stat 888; Herbert T. Hoover, "The Sioux Agreement of 1889 and Its Aftermath," *South Dakota History* 19 (Spring 1989): 58–59. For a study of the evolution of reservation policies at mid-century, see Robert Trennert, *Alternative to Extinction: Federal Indian Policy and the Beginnings of the Reservation System, 1846–51* (Philadelphia: Temple University Press, 1975).

3. U.S. Department of the Interior, Office of Indian Affairs, *Annual Report of the Commissioner of Indian Affairs, 1888* (Washington, DC: Government Printing Office, 1888), xxxvi, 69–70. For an examination of the land allotment and fee-patenting process, consult Janet McDonnell, *The Dispossession of the American Indian, 1887–1934* (Bloomington: Indiana University Press, 1991), especially chapter one, "Allotment: The Land Divided," and chapter two, "Allotment: Policy Implementation." See also her work on competency commissions that issued fee patents to tribal members on South Dakota reservations in "Competency Commissions and Indian Land Policy, 1913–1920," *South Dakota History* 11 (Winter 1980): 21–34.

4. There are numerous studies on the Indian New Deal. For one, see Graham D. Taylor, *The New Deal and American Indian Tribalism: The Administration of the Indian Reorganization Act, 1934–45* (Lincoln: University of Nebraska Press, 1980).

5. For a study of the termination period, see Larry W. Burt, *Tribalism in Crisis: Federal Indian Policy, 1953–1961* (Albuquerque: University of New Mexico Press, 1982). See Thomas Clarkin, *Federal Indian Policy in the Kennedy and Johnson Administrations, 1961–1969* (Albuquerque: University of New Mexico Press, 2001), for an investigation of changing policies in the 1960s.

6. W. O. Roberts to John Collier, 25 July 1933, File 101, Policy Rosebud Office, General Correspondence, 1930–1950, Box 565, Rosebud Agency, Records of the Bureau of Indian Affairs, Record Group 75, National Archives-Central Plains Region, Kansas City, MO.

7. See James R. Walker, *Lakota Belief and Ritual*, ed. Raymond J. DeMallie and Elaine Jahner

(Lincoln: University of Nebraska Press, 1980); James R. Walker, *Lakota Society*, ed. Raymond J. DeMallie (Lincoln: University of Nebraska Press, 1982); and James R. Walker, *Lakota Myth*, ed. Elaine A. Jahner (Lincoln: University of Nebraska Press, 1983).

8. For a broader study of the effect of the Missouri River main-stem dams on tribal life, see Michael L. Lawson, *Dammed Indians: The Pick-Sloan Plan and the Missouri River Sioux, 1944–1980* (Norman: University of Oklahoma Press, 1982). For a study of the Standing Rock reservation alone, see Michael L. Lawson, "The Oahe Dam and the Standing Rock Sioux," *South Dakota History* 6 (Spring 1976): 203–28.

1

THE
STRUGGLE
FOR LAND

FREDERICK E. HOXIE

FROM PRISON TO HOMELAND

THE CHEYENNE RIVER INDIAN RESERVATION
BEFORE WORLD WAR I

. . .

There should be no doubt that the Sioux Agreement of 1889 was designed to destroy what remained of the Teton, or Lakota, bands' traditional way of life. The eastern reformers who drew up the agreement and the politicians who approved it were committed to replacing the old ways with new ones. Hunting, living in bands, accepting the rule of elders, following the wisdom of religious leaders, and traveling in an annual cycle across a large territory—these were all targets of the new law. Senator Henry L. Dawes, the author of the 1887 General Allotment act that bore his name and the principal architect of the 1889 agreement, believed there was no alternative. As he wrote, "We may cry out against the violation of treaties, denounce flagrant disregard of inalienable rights and the inhumanity of our treatment of the defenseless . . . but the fact remains. . . . Without doubt these Indians are to be somehow absorbed into and become a part of the 50,000,000 of our people. There does not seem to be any other way to deal with them."[1] By 1889, Dawes was convinced of his own wisdom. South Dakota had become a state. New rail lines were snaking across the plains, and thousands of settlers—some of them freshly arrived from Europe—were traveling west to share in America's last great land boom.[2]

Dawes promised that the new land would satisfy white land hunger while it started the Sioux on the road to total assimilation. The agreement provided that (1) the tribes would cede 11 million acres west of the Missouri River to the United States; (2) six reservations would be established on the remaining lands (Standing Rock, Cheyenne River, Lower Brule, Crow Creek, Rosebud, and Pine Ridge); (3) the government would create a fund to provide individuals with

This essay originally appeared in *South Dakota History* 10 (Winter 1979): 1–24. It was presented in slightly different form at the 1978 Council on the History of the Northern Plains Indians sponsored by the Center of Indian Studies, Black Hills State College, Spearfish, South Dakota. The author thanks Ellen In the Woods for her research assistance.

farming equipment, supplies, and schools; and (4) each reservation eventually would be allotted among the people who lived there.[3]

Secretary of the Interior John Noble welcomed these steps. He wrote that "the breaking up of this great nation of Indians into smaller parts and segregating . . . separate reservations for each of said parts marks a long step toward the disintegration of their tribal life and will help them forward to . . . civilized habits."[4] Like Dawes, the secretary believed that the pace of white settlement in South Dakota made it impossible for the Teton bands to maintain their old ways. The 1889 law would force the tribes into the modern world.

Not surprisingly, tribal leaders among the Sioux did not agree with Senator Dawes and the secretary. Still angry over the theft of the Black Hills and the government's refusal to live up to the 1868 Fort Laramie Treaty, tribal headmen wanted no part of additional land cessions. To them it was obvious that further reductions in the size of their nation would mean the arrival of still more whites, along with increased pressure from missionaries and educators, and more demands that they turn to farming.

The 1868 treaty had stipulated that three-fourths of the adult male members of the tribes must approve all future land sales. Seven years and four different congressional delegations were required before the tribes approved this new agreement. While several leaders won significant concessions during these negotiations, the 1889 agreement was a major defeat for the tribes.[5] Its ratification was met with anger and depression. It is probably no accident that the announcement of the 1889 agreement and the fighting at Wounded Knee occurred within a year of each other.

But the events of 1889 and 1890 did not mark the last days of the Sioux Nation. Surprisingly, Lakota culture survived the programs designed to kill it. The 1889 agreement failed to destroy all the old ways. It failed to turn red men into white men. It failed to achieve the complete "disintegration" of tribal life. And the supreme irony: the reservations forced on the tribes did not become vehicles for "civilizing" and assimilating them; instead, they became cultural homelands, places where a native identity could be maintained and passed on to new generations. Rather than graveyards for culture, the reservations created in 1889 eventually became centers for awareness and even for hope. To describe this paradox is to beg the question—Why? How did the prisons of the nineteenth century become the cultural homelands of the twentieth?

When the Cheyenne River Indian Reservation was established in 1889, it contained four distinct Lakota bands whose ways of life had not changed fundamentally for generations. Prior to 1889, the Indians living near the Cheyenne River had been confined to the area around old Fort Bennett and urged to farm and adopt Christianity. But despite these restrictions and demands, there was little direct pressure on them to break up their camps and leave the protected river bottoms where they had made their winter homes.[6]

The bands had little contact with one another. Minneconjous lived on Cherry Creek in what would become the western end of the reservation. Sans Arc communities could be found along the Moreau River at places such as White Horse and On the Trees, running near what would become the northern border of the reserve. The Blackfeet and Two Kettle bands hugged the Missouri, spreading out between Fort Bennett and the Moreau. Most of these camps had a headman and some sort of government day school that operated sporadically during the year. Of course, allotment had not yet begun.[7]

While game was growing scarce and the government's rations were not always reliable, farming and stockraising had not yet become essential to the people's livelihood. Five district farmers visited the various communities, but as the superintendent reported in 1890, "they usually [had] very little to show for their work."[8] People at the Cheyenne River Agency survived on a combination of rations, money from odd maintenance and freighting jobs, and whatever they could hunt or gather on the prairie.

The 1889 agreement undermined this peaceful routine. The government stepped up its efforts at the agency and broadened the scope of its activities. As Senator Dawes had promised, the campaign to "absorb" the Sioux into American society began in earnest. First, the Cheyenne River Agency was moved from Fort Bennett—which lay outside the new reservation—to Charger's Camp on the Missouri River. While the Minneconjous living on Cherry Creek were further than ever from the superintendent's office, the Blackfeet and Two Kettle bands on the Missouri and the Sans Arcs on the Moreau were now close at hand. Second, a large boarding school was built next to the new agency. By 1904, this school had space for 130 students. In addition, up to 200 children began to be sent to Bureau of Indian Affairs (BIA) schools in Pierre and Rapid City and to the mission school at Oahe. These institutions, coupled with the day schools at Cherry Creek, Thunder Butte, Green Grass, On the Trees, and White Horse, could accommodate all of the approximately 650 school-age children on the reservation. Consequently, the agency could now step up its campaign to force all young people to attend school. By the early 1900s, it was almost impossible for a family to avoid sending its children away for an education, the principal goal of which was to separate the children from their traditions and their past.[9]

School attendance also increased in response to the expansion of the Indian police and the Courts of Indian Offenses. In 1890, when the reservation was

Students gathered for this 1909 photograph
in front of the boarding school at Cheyenne Agency.
State Archives Collection,
South Dakota State Historical Society

being organized for the first time, the superintendent at Cheyenne River noted that "many of the best Indians will not serve" on the police force. Whether this was because of the low pay offered them (as the superintendent thought) or because of the controversy surrounding the arrest and killing of Sitting Bull at nearby Standing Rock is unclear. What is certain, however, is that within ten years the Indian police were active in every part of the reservation. In 1896, policemen began to be selected from the districts, and police stations were erected at Cherry Creek and White Horse. The tribal courts, with judges selected from the four bands, met regularly and passed judgments on all but five major crimes.[10]

A third feature of the government's activism on the new reservation was the practice of stationing farmers in each district. During the 1890s, subagencies were constructed at Cherry Creek and White Horse. Thunder Butte was added in 1909. These installations were permanent homes for the farmers who supervised individual family gardens and monitored the cattlemen who leased tribal pastureland. Through the efforts of these men, the area being cultivated at Cheyenne River began to grow. In 1895, only 700 acres had been planted in crops. Two years later that figure had nearly doubled, and by 1907 the superintendent reported that "at no time has there been so much farming . . . [on] this reservation." The gains in stock raising were equally impressive. In 1890, 500,000 pounds of Indian cattle were sold to the agency for rations. In 1899, that figure had doubled.[11]

The year 1900 marked the beginning of allotment at Cheyenne River. Crews of surveyors worked methodically across the entire reservation. By 1909, they had made more than twenty-one hundred homestead assignments.[12] This process not only pushed families out onto their own land, but it brought home to each member of the reservation the fact that a new era had begun and that the government was determined to change their old way of life. The new reservation environment demanded that the Indians respond or perish.

Changes in Indian ways of life were apparent almost from the beginning of the government's assimilation drive. One of the most obvious of these was the dispersal of the population across the reserve. Rather than camping in concentrated areas and keeping to the place where their band had originally settled, young people began moving out on their own. For example, a man born near Fort Bennett in 1885 remembers that "they allotted land to us and wherever our land was, was our homestead."[13] As a result, he moved to faraway Iron Lightning and began farming his allotment. Men like him thus opened up new areas of the reservation. In addition to Iron Lightning, Thunder Butte in the extreme northwest and Red Scaffold in the southwest were both settled during these years. People lived near their land and began to think of themselves as part of something new—the Cheyenne River Sioux Tribe. As the superintendent reported in 1897, "The Indians of this reservation, while composed of what were formerly known as the Blackfeet, Sans Arc, Minneconjou and Two Kettle bands of Sioux, are now regarded as one people, without any distinction as to band."[14] While the superintendent was overstating things—band designations are important even today—his perception was accurate. People on the reservation were now being defined as a single tribe. It was logical that they would begin defining themselves in the same way.

The second area of change involved the organization of reservation life. The Indian police and courts functioned as a unified whole and helped foster the idea of a reservation unit. Whether they were admired or hated, the policemen affected everybody, and they made it clear that Cheyenne River was a single place.

Another feature of this new tendency to organize the four bands into a single structure was the creation in 1903 of a twelve-man tribal business council. Prior to 1903, two kinds of councils had operated. The first was a general council open to all adult males assigned to the agency. This was the group that had been assembled to approve the 1889 agreement. The second council was an executive body made up of principal headmen. The new business council changed the old pattern in significant ways. First, members of the business council were elected from different parts of the reservation. Four men were chosen from each of the districts: White Horse, Cherry Creek, and the Agency District. (Thunder Butte was added in 1909.) And second, each councilman was elected by a local council, meeting at the subagency. These district councils also had to ratify all decisions involving money or the leasing of tribal property. While elders and traditional band leaders could still be chosen, this new system allowed younger people to rise to positions of influence. Nineteen hundred three marked an important step in the gradual shift of leadership away from band leaders and toward people chosen for their ability to represent their constituents in a unified tribal government.[15]

As the reservation neared its twentieth anniversary in 1908, the people of Cheyenne River were surviving in their new environment. They were farming and raising cattle, relying less and less on government rations. Their children were attending school. Many of them were living in new settlements, and all of them were gaining a fresh image of themselves. They were a part of the Cheyenne River Tribe. While the members of this new tribe were themselves responsible for the changes that were taking place, it was clear that the government's programs had started the process.

But did the presence of these new institutions and new ways of life signify rapid assimilation? Does the fact that the tribe's adaptation began with the creation of the reservation mean that the Cheyenne River people were straying from their traditions and giving in to the white man? How did they respond to the erection of schools, the spread of allotment, and the rising power of the tribal police? Were the councilmen, the farmers, and the policemen all people who had been absorbed into the modern world? The behavior of the tribe during the remainder of the period before World War I reveals that answers to these questions should not be taken for granted. While first accepting a number of changes in their tribal organization and way of life, the people of Cheyenne River soon demonstrated that there were limits to their flexibility. They intended to remain a tribal people.

For the non-Indians of South Dakota, the twenty years following the passage of the 1889 Sioux Agreement brought unprecedented growth. White population in the state rose by over 60 percent. New branch lines linked small towns to major railroads, putting cattlemen and farmers within easy reach of eastern markets. South Dakota's boosters imagined that soon the state would finally live up to its publicity. This feeling intensified as the region emerged from the depression of the 1890s, and wheat and beef prices began to climb to new heights. After bottoming out at fifty cents in 1895, wheat rose to almost a dollar a bushel in 1908.[16]

Good times and the prospect of future prosperity brought new demands that the Teton reservations be reduced in size. Rosebud was the first to feel this pressure. In 1901, the tribe agreed to sell a large portion of its reservation to the government. The territory was not opened immediately, however, because a dispute arose in Congress over whether or not the government should pay for it. Some legislators argued for ratification of the agreement (and payment of the amount promised) while others suggested that they simply seize what they needed for settlement. The two groups were deadlocked until 1903 when the Supreme Court decided *Lone Wolf v. Hitchcock* and specifically authorized the national legislature to exercise its "plenary authority" in the disposition of all Indian lands.[17] There was now no legal reason for Congress to pay the Rosebud tribe the money it had been promised. Armed with this invitation, the advocates of seizure won out, and a large portion of the Rosebud reservation was soon open to white settlement.[18]

With Rosebud behind them, it did not take long for South Dakota's merchants and farm speculators to turn their attention to Cheyenne River. Opening this reservation to settlement would—in the words of one Pierre newspaper— be "the impetus of the development of Central South Dakota." "It means," the editorial continued, "the building of a great city right at Pierre."[19] On 9 December 1907, Senator Robert Gamble (whose South Dakota backers called him "the empire builder") introduced a bill to take a portion of the Cheyenne River reserve for homesteading. At the same time, Philo Hall, the state's lone congressman, introduced a second bill that proposed to open all of the reservation's unallotted land.[20] Both bills were forwarded to the secretary of the interior for his comments. Within a few days, the secretary had instructed James McLaughlin, a thirty-five-year veteran of the Indian Service, to go to South Dakota and convince the residents of Cheyenne River to approve the idea.[21]

But people on the reservation did not wait for McLaughlin before they let their feelings be known. Less than a month after the two bills were introduced, the tribe's general council met and spoke out against them. The group also appealed to the Indian Rights Association (IRA) for help. Writing on behalf of the general council, James Crow Feather noted that "we . . . consider ourselves incapable of plunging into the whirl of citizenship."[22] The business council sent a second letter to the IRA that listed four reasons for opposing Gamble's and Hall's bills:

1. Our consent was never asked.
2. In our reservation we think the lands are rich in mineral deposits.
   We want these lands to be examined before opening for settlement.
3. The bill is not satisfactory to us.
4. What former treaties promise is not fully carried into effect yet.[23]

After approving the texts of these two letters, the tribe's leaders decided to chose one delegate from each district to visit Washington. They selected Allen Fielder (Agency District), Percy Phillips (White Horse), and Ed Swan (Cherry Creek).

While willing to accept the government's schools and farming campaigns, the council rejected further land cessions out of hand. When Inspector McLaughlin arrived at Cheyenne Agency on 16 March 1908, he found James Crow Feather, the chairman of the business council, there to meet him. Bad weather kept most people from attending the conference with McLaughlin, but the inspector (with his BIA orders in his pocket) presented his case anyway. Crow Feather, speaking for the council, responded sharply, "There are many more of us people than are here today, . . . and we have a way of doing business in matter of this kind. . . . It is our business council. . . . This matter is of interest to the whole tribe. I am chairman of the business council and we have rules regarding this matter, and I would like to carry them out. . . . I would like to have all the people together when we do business regarding land."[24] McLaughlin ignored Crow Feather. He told the group that "Congress has the right to open the Indian reservations by legislative enactment without obtaining the consent of the Indians" and that they would be better off if they agreed to the change.[25] After two days of fruitless speechmaking, the inspector returned to Washington.

McLaughlin's prediction that Congress would act on its own quickly came true. Less than two weeks after he left South Dakota, the Senate Indian Affairs Committee endorsed a bill to open nearly half the reservation to white homesteaders. Again, James Crow Feather protested. In a letter to the commissioner of Indian Affairs, he minced no words, "I do not like this way of doing business, because it is not according to the rules of the Indian Office, both here and in Washington. Mr. McLaughlin made a story of my people that did not represent them correctly. . . . As the bill now is it [is] against our will. This is not honest."[26]

The tribal business council immediately dispatched the delegation they had selected in January. These men argued their case at the Indian Office, offering to open a small portion of the reserve but demanding the retention of mineral rights on whatever lands were taken. Unfortunately, their efforts were in vain. They arrived in Washington during the first week of April. On 15 April, the homestead bill passed the full Senate; five days later, it was approved by the House Indian Affairs Committee. At that point, its ultimate passage was a foregone conclusion. President Roosevelt signed the bill on 29 May 1908.[27]

Despite their defeat, the tribal leadership continued to protest the new law. At its next meeting, the general council adopted a resolution declaring that "the members of this reservation have been treated unjustly in the opening of a portion of this reservation."[28] A year later, the superintendent reported that "the people of this reservation cannot become reconciled to the idea that they did not have a proper voice in the recent ceding of the lands of this reservation to the United States."[29] The tribe had lost a battle, but it was gaining valuable experience in dealing with assaults on its territory. Tribal spokesmen had met the government's agents with effective arguments. Delegates representing the three districts on the reservation had presented their case in Washington. The business council had responded quickly to the crisis and presented a unified position to opponents. If the tribe had more time to organize when the next attempt was made to push a homestead bill through Congress, perhaps then their protests would be heard.

The people at Cheyenne River did not have long to wait for a new attack. In 1909, within a few months of the arrival of the first homesteaders on the freshly opened lands, South Dakota's merchants and politicians began lobbying to open still more territory to white settlement. This time they wanted all of the remaining tribal lands. Their goal was nothing less than the "final absorption" that Senator Dawes had predicted. South Dakota's Senator Robert Gamble introduced his bill to authorize the sale of all unallotted land on the Cheyenne River Reservation in December. The politicians' argument was by now familiar: "It is a matter of the utmost importance to the development of the state."[30] While no one in Washington immediately opposed the idea, it was soon apparent that the new bill would not be rushed through as quickly as the first one had been. Homesteads opened by the 1908 law were only beginning to be settled, and it was obvious that they would go slowly. By the end of 1911—two years after the first filing—only one-quarter of the available land had been claimed.[31] Neither Congress nor the Indian Office felt any overriding need to go along with Gamble and his backers.

This time the tribe would have more time. The general council began its resistance by passing a unanimous resolution opposing the measure and authorizing a delegation of eight to go to Washington. Before this group left, Inspector McLaughlin reappeared but got nowhere. Only thirty-six people showed up for the "council" he summoned.[32] With Congress eager to adjourn for the 1910 elections and the tribe unified in its opposition, it seemed clear that the bill would not come up for a vote. Gamble decided to put off the battle until 1911.

When the legislators reassembled in the fall of 1911, the senator was ready with a new version of his bill. Once again resolutions were passed at Cheyenne River condemning the idea, and once again Major McLaughlin appeared to argue his case. But the tribe refused to continue this now familiar charade. Percy Phillips, who had represented the White Horse district in trips to Washington in 1908 and 1910, was the first to speak when the representative from Washington arrived. "A delegation went to Washington concerning this same bill a year ago last winter," he exclaimed. "We went down there and we . . . would not have anything to do with the bill."[33] Why, he asked, should the tribe discuss it again? Others spoke up. Charles La Plant, who was aware that the meeting was being recorded, protested that from McLaughlin's speech someone reading the transcript might get the impression that an official council was taking place. He reminded the inspector that "this is not what we call a general council."[34] John Last Man was the most eloquent. Turning to McLaughlin, he said, "This bill has been before Congress for the last four years and you come every time to present it to us. . . . It seems like this bill called for the rest of our reservation being sold and the money to be used for the benefit of the whites. . . . [With the bill] this reservation is opened up and gone and used to the benefit of the white men and for them until the Indians die of starvation."[35]

The 1910 Cheyenne River Reservation delegation
to Washington, DC included (standing, from left)
James Crow Feather, Justin Black Eagle, Fred LaPlant,
and Percy Phillips. Seated, from left, are Patrick Miller,
Roan Bear, No Heart, and Runs the Enemy.
State Archives Collection,
South Dakota State Historical Society

Finally, after listening to the inspector's familiar arguments, Chairman James Crow Feather announced that the business council had decided that "a delegation should be sent to the Indian Office . . . to discuss this matter with them face to face. . . . We are all well acquainted with you," he told McLaughlin, "and . . . we have come to the conclusion of sending a delegation to the Indian Office and that is our answer to this bill."[36] Immediately after Crow Feather spoke, the meeting was adjourned. The next day, 23 November 1911, McLaughlin left the reservation. Three weeks later a new delegation was appointed by the tribe's general council. It consisted of representatives from each of the reservation districts. What is more, the tribe enlisted the support of the Cheyenne River superintendent and the head of the local boarding school. Both men wrote to Washington opposing the new bill, the school principal arguing that its passage would "be disastrous to these Indians."[37]

In early April, the tribal delegation arrived at the Indian Office to make its case in person. It consisted of Ed Swan from Cherry Creek (who was making his third trip to the capital); Oliver Black Eagle from Thunder Butte; Bazille Claymore from the Agency District; Straight Head, probably from White Horse; and Charles Jewett. The group not only opposed Gamble's bill, but it also presented six counterproposals to the commissioner. These ranged from a suggestion that he join them in fighting against further homesteading bills, through requests that full payment be made for lands already opened, to demands that the Indian Office improve health care, education, and administration on the reservation.[38]

Whether they realized it or not, the delegation's elaborate statement succeeded in so confusing the situation that passage of Gamble's bill was now almost impossible. The BIA would have to study their counterproposals and review the current management of the reservation before the commissioner could recommend that Congress pass the measure. And with so little pressure from potential settlers, Congress would not pass the bill unless the BIA approved it. The slow pace of the BIA bureaucracy now became an asset to the tribe. By the time an opinion could be offered, Congress was eager to adjourn and the proposal was buried. In the years to come, more attempts would be made to pass this bill, and while a similar effort was successful at Standing Rock in 1913, it never succeeded at Cheyenne River.

There is no written record of the tribe's reaction to its victory over Senator Gamble and South Dakota's boosters. In fact, because the bill was simply delayed and not voted down, reservation leaders might not have realized that they had won. For many, it must have taken a winter without a visit from Major McLaughlin to convince them of their success. Less obscure were the dramatic changes that had occurred during the last generation in the tribe's style and system of leadership. Leaders were now chosen by districts and picked—at least in part—for their ability to deal with the business and political details that confronted them. In this respect, it is significant that the 1910 and 1912 delegations to Washington both included men like Ed Swan and Percy Phillips who had been to the capital before. Experience and familiarity with "white ways" had become another qualification for leadership. The business council, with four representatives from each district, had become an effective and flexible body. It could respond quickly to crises and speak credibly for the entire tribe.

Few would claim that the 1908 law that opened nearly half the Cheyenne River reservation to white settlement was a blessing to the tribe, or that the struggle to retain their remaining unallotted lands was beneficial. But what should be recognized in these events is the way they sparked people on the reservation to organize themselves to respond. The conflict heightened their commitment to the reservation and forced them to produce effective leaders. Senator Gamble's campaign to abolish the Cheyenne River reserve had a unifying and strengthening impact on the people who lived there. Equally significant, resistance to the Gamble bills was led by the business council—an institution created by white men. The white men had created it, but the tribe was now operating it.

Disputes over homesteading were not the only source of conflict between the tribe and the outside world during this period just prior to World War I. Law and order, education, and agriculture were also areas in which the hostility of outsiders allowed (and sometimes forced) the people at Cheyenne River to develop and maintain their own way of life. The final disposition of these issues was also a measure of the tribe's adaptation to their reservation environment.

Prior to the arrival of white homesteaders, the Indian police and the tribal courts had exclusive responsibility for law and order on the reservation. Policemen patrolled the entire reserve, keeping intruders and unauthorized cattle out and enforcing the superintendent's orders in Indian communities. The court met monthly in each of the four districts and heard cases involving violations of regulations (drunkenness, adultery) and disputes between individuals (conflicting claims to property, settlement of estates, and so forth). Once the homesteaders began arriving in 1909 and 1910, many people believed that the tribe would come under the jurisdiction of the new counties that would be organized on the opened lands. Some even expected the reservation institutions to disappear. The *Pierre Daily Capital-Journal* promised that with the new law "another district is unfolding to civilization. . . . No doubt good towns will spring up in this valley which is not so famed, but much larger than the renowned valley of the Mohawk."[39] These predictions proved incorrect. Drought and dust storms accompanied the homesteaders to their claims. Instead of prosperous new farms and bustling boom towns, the open lands produced stunted crops and shattered dreams. In the summer of 1913, Farming Superintendent Charles Davis reported that "the reservation is the worst burned I have about ever seen. . . . At present there is no market for agricultural lands."[40]

Because of their many hardships, the white settlers had no interest in policing Indian communities. As a result, few reservation residents were prosecuted in the state courts.[41] In addition, the scattered non-Indian communities made law enforcement more difficult. As Superintendent King wrote in 1912, "The opening of the . . . reservation . . . created . . . a community without law . . . this was quickly taken advantage of by bootleggers, gamblers, horse thieves, cattle rustlers and soldiers of fortune generally."[42]

Because the state did not act in the face of this rising crime rate, the duties of the Indian police and the tribal courts did not disappear but became even more important. While obviously an arm of the superintendent and not always popular, the reservation's law enforcement officers were respected in the community. Elderly members of the Cheyenne River Tribe recalled the effectiveness of the Indian courts during these years. For example, a man from Cherry Creek remembered, "They had a tribal court (when I was young). . . . That judge he didn't go to school, he have no education, but just a little. . . . and they'll have a court there. And a real court too, them days. . . . and there's a policeman, didn't go to school, he stands there. . . . That's the kind of law and order we had, them days, they were pretty strict. . . . But that's a real court they have."[43]

A similar point can be made about the government schools on the reservation. Here again many people felt that the new county governments would accept Indian children into their schools and, as a consequence, that the BIA schools would disappear. The agency superintendent reported in 1914, for example, that he expected three day schools to "likely be abandoned for the next year, and the public schools organized in their place." This idea was killed in 1915 when South Dakota repealed a law that had opened its schools to Indians.[44] From that time forward, only children whose tuition was paid by the government would be allowed to attend local white schools. As a result, most Indian children continued to be educated together, either in their own communities or in boarding schools. As in the area of law enforcement, rejection by white society caused tribal members to maintain their ties with each other.

Finally, the presence of boss farmers in each of the four districts helped hold the communities together. The farmers lived at the subagencies and were primarily responsible for supervising individual farms and acting as ombuds-men for all BIA business. Boss farmers were involved in arranging leases, dis-tributing rations, assisting the tribal courts, and hearing complaints. Once the white homesteaders arrived, a new duty was added to this list: keeping settlers off of tribal land and away from Indian cattle. Disputes arose almost as soon as the reservation was opened. The boss farmer was in a unique position. He was a white man, but he was a federal official. He knew the Indians well and was responsible for their government-issue property. Cheyenne River may have been unusual, but most of its farmers seem to have been honest and willing to challenge local whites if they felt there was a reason. They did this, for example, in 1915 when Dewey County tried to tax the assets of allottees and when the South Dakota herd law was being used to capture and steal Indian cattle.[45]

Through all of their activities, the boss farmers were living reminders to the native people on the reservation that they were a distinct community that could expect certain kinds of help and protection. Some of the flavor of the district life that focused around a boss farmer was conveyed by an elderly resi-dent who remembered Cherry Creek in the years before World War I: "Cherry Creek used to be something like a town. They had a restaurant, a warehouse, . . . and a police headquarters, court house, and doctor's office, and carpenter shop and blacksmith shop—[they had] everything."[46] "Everything" was at the subagency. It was where people went for their ration and lease money; it was where court was held; it was a place for visiting and keeping in touch with each other.

These patterns, established in the years prior to World War I, persisted through the 1920s. The tribal council continued to block congressional attempts to open more land or reduce their power. The Indian police and the tribal courts both functioned despite the influx of white settlers. County and state officials still had little interest in extending their jurisdiction to tribal members, and the Cheyenne River courts continued to be respected. (This situation was not affected by the 1924 citizenship act.[47]) Reservation day schools and the boss farmer system remained important measures of the tribe's separation from the state government. In all of these areas, it was clear that the new reservation culture that had emerged at Cheyenne River would continue into the future.

Why did the 1889 Sioux Agreement, designed to "absorb" the four Lakota bands at Cheyenne River, fail? Why did this reservation—which was supposed to be a focus of government efforts to assimilate native people—remain an Indian reserve? The preceding discussion of events of the early twentieth century on the reservation has suggested some answers. The reservation became the set-ting for a new kind of culture, one that adopted certain non-Indian institutions but which used these to defend traditional values and goals. The reservation was a new environment for the people of Cheyenne River. It placed new restrictions on their activities and made new demands on them, and pressure from the outside world forced them back on themselves. As a result, they used many of the new reservation institutions as vehicles for self-defense and cultural survival. The tribal council, which the government had thought would be useful only when there was property to be sold or leases to be signed, became an effective force in the struggle to hold on to unallotted tribal lands. The courts and police system emerged as the only protection available against lawless homesteaders or errant fellow tribesmen. The schools—while bleak and often cruel—gave native children an alternative once they had been rejected by the white community. And the boss farmers, with all of their duties, created a focus for life in each district and served as a reminder of the kind of protection federal power could provide. All of these institutions—even though they were inventions of the government—were used to serve the interests of tribal members.

It would be incorrect to interpret this narrative as a simple defense of the Indian police or the tribal council or the BIA schools. For it is important to remember that each of these institutions was forced on the tribe. What is more, they benefited the tribe only because the people at Cheyenne River had rich traditions and a continuing loyalty to their culture. Those feelings of identity and strength, which overrode the horrors of the past, shaped the activities of those who were drawn to the new reservation institutions. The council opposed land openings, the policemen chased off cattle rustlers, and the people gathered at the subagencies because they never stopped feeling that they belonged to a special group and that they had an obligation to each other that was greater than the sum total of outside pressure. Thinking back to these early years, one of the tribe's oldest members recalled, "In 1912 they had a fair in Dupree [a town on the opened portion of the reservation] and I remember one white man, Congressman Henry L. Gandy, he said forty years from now there won't be no Indians. . . . He come near make it. . . . But we Indians will be Indians all our lives, we never will be white men. We can talk and work and go to school like the white people but we're still Indians."[48] Beginning with that feeling, many of the people who participated in government-sponsored institutions worked to make those institutions serve the interests of the group. Without a sense of identity within the tribe, these institutions might have served their original purpose. And the reverse is true: if the traditions had remained without the new institutions, they alone might not have succeeded in keeping the tribal culture alive. The Gamble bill would have passed, law and order would have vanished, and reservation life would have had no focus.

Every culture is constantly changing. Values and traditions may persist, but ways of life are never static. The creation of the Cheyenne River reservation caused dramatic changes in the lives of the people who were forced to live there. But despite these upheavals, the culture of those people survived. Thus, we should view the early twentieth century not as a period of assimilation but as a time of rapid cultural change. The councilmen, the tribal judges, the policemen, and the rest were caught up in this process. They faced great pressures, but all through the crises they worked to maintain their culture rather than to surrender it. For this reason, the early history of the Cheyenne River Reservation should be understood not as a time of defeat and hopelessness but as a crucial period of adaptation and survival. Forced into a strange new world, these people used the tools available to them to protect and preserve the place they now call their homeland.

NOTES

1. Henry L. Dawes to Secretary of the Interior Teller, quoted in Loring B. Priest, *Uncle Sam's Stepchildren: The Reformation of United States Indian Policy, 1865–1887* (New Brunswick, NJ: Rutgers University Press, 1942), 194–95.

2. See Howard R. Lamar, *Dakota Territory, 1861–1889: A Study of Frontier Politics* (New Haven, CT: Yale University Press, 1956), chaps. 8–9; and Everett Dick, *Sodhouse Frontier, 1854–1890: A Social History of the Northern Plains from the Creation of Kansas & Nebraska to the Admission of the Dakotas* (New York: D. Appleton-Century Co., 1937).

3. See 25 Stat 888–99.

4. John Noble, quoted in Francis Paul Prucha, *American Indian Policy in Crisis: Christian Reformers and the Indian, 1865–1900* (Norman: University of Oklahoma Press, 1976), 186–87.

5. See Prucha, *American Indian Policy in Crisis*, 169–87. Congress authorized the first version of this agreement in 1882.

6. See U.S. Department of the Interior, Office of Indian Affairs, *Annual Report of the Commissioner of Indian Affairs to the Secretary of the Interior, 1890* (Washington, DC: Government Printing Office, 1890), 42.

7. U.S. Public Health Service, Public Health Indian Hospital, Eagle Butte, South Dakota, *History of the Cheyenne River Reservation*, 1–5.

8. *Report of the Commissioner of Indian Affairs, 1890*, 42.

9. Ibid., 323.

10. Ibid., 45; *Report of the Commissioner of Indian Affairs, 1896*, 284; *Report of the Commissioner of Indian Affairs, 1899*, pt. 1, 328.

11. *Report of the Commissioner of Indian Affairs, 1895*, 282; *Report of the Commissioner of Indian Affairs, 1897*, 263; Thomas Downs to Commissioner of Indian Affairs, 26 Aug. 1907, General Correspondence, Cheyenne River, File 031, Records of the Bureau of Indian Affairs, Record

Group (RG) 75, National Archives (NA), Washington, DC; *Report of the Commissioner of Indian Affairs*, 1899, pt. 1, 328.

12. Tabulation based on unpublished allotment schedule, Cheyenne River Agency Realty Office, Eagle Butte, South Dakota. See Frederick E. Hoxie, "Jurisdiction on the Cheyenne River Reservation: An Analysis of the Causes and Consequences of the Act of May 29, 1908," a report prepared for presentation in U.S. v. Dupris, No. CR77-30056-01, U.S. District Court, District of South Dakota, app. 2.

13. Hoxie, "Jurisdiction on the Cheyenne River Reservation," app. 2.

14. *Report of the Commissioner of Indian Affairs*, 1897, 262.

15. See Ira A. Hatch to Commissioner of Indian Affairs, 11 Feb. 1903, Letters Received #10772, 1903, RG 75, NA.

16. See U.S. Bureau of the Census, *Historical Statistics of the United States, 1789–1945* (Washington, DC: Government Printing Office, 1949), 106.

17. Lone Wolf v. Hitchcock, 187 U.S. 565 (1903).

18. For a detailed description of the effects of the Lone Wolf decision on land openings at Rosebud and elsewhere, see Frederick E. Hoxie, "Beyond Savagery: The Campaign to Assimilate the American Indians, 1880–1920" (PhD diss., Brandeis University, 1977), 380–92.

19. *Pierre Daily Capital-Journal*, 13 Apr. 1908.

20. Gamble's bill was S 1385 and Hall's was HR 10527. Both were presented in the 60th Congress, 1st session.

21. Acting Secretary of the Interior Frank Pierce to James McLaughlin, 26 Dec. 1907, General Correspondence, Cheyenne River, File 308.1, RG 75, NA.

22. "Proceedings of the General Council of the Cheyenne River Sioux Tribe, 6, 7, and 8 January 1908 at Whitehorse, South Dakota," enclosed in Superintendent to Commissioner of Indian Affairs, 23 Jan. 1908, General Correspondence, Cheyenne River, File 054, RG 75, NA.

23. Ibid.

24. Senate Committee on Indian Affairs, *Sale of Portion of Surplus Lands on Cheyenne River and Standing Rock Reservations*, 60th Cong., 1st sess., 1908, pt. 2, S. Rep. 439, 19.

25. Ibid., 2:18.

26. James Crow Feather to Commissioner of Indian Affairs, 25 Apr. 1908, General Correspondence, Cheyenne River, File 308.1, RG 75, NA.

27. 35 Stat 460. The area was opened by a presidential proclamation dated 19 August 1909. See 36 Stat 2500.

28. "Proceedings of the General Council of the Cheyenne River Sioux Indians, 3 June 1909," Folder 63023-09, General Correspondence, Cheyenne River, File 054, RG 75, NA.

29. L. F. Michael to Commissioner of Indian Affairs, 2 Aug. 1909, General Correspondence, Cheyenne River, File 054, RG 75, NA.

30. Robert Gamble to Richard A. Ballinger, 14 Dec. 1909, General Correspondence, Cheyenne River, File 308.1 (No. 99923-09), RG 75, NA.

31. *Report of the Commissioner of Indian Affairs*, 1911, 113.

32. James McLaughlin to Secretary of the Interior, 10 Feb. 1910, General Correspondence, Cheyenne River, File 308.1 (No. 99923-09), RG 75, NA.

33. "Minutes of Council Held by James McLaughlin, Inspector—Department of the Interior, with the Indians of the Cheyenne River Agency, South Dakota, Relative to the Sale and Disposition of the Surplus Lands of their Reservation as Contemplated by Senate Bill 108, 62d Congress, 1st session," 6, attached to James McLaughlin to the Secretary of the Interior, 23 Nov. 1911, Legislation, File 5-1: Cheyenne River—Opening (pt. 1: 62d Cong.), Records of the Office of the Secretary of the Interior, RG 48, NA.

34. Ibid., 7.

35. Ibid., 8.

36. Ibid., 10.

37. Superintendent of Cheyenne River Agency School, quoted in Secretary of the Interior to R. J. Gamble, n.d., Legislation, File 5-1, RG 48, NA. The agency superintendent's views were expressed in Thomas J. King to Commissioner of Indian Affairs, 27 Feb. 1912, General Correspondence, Cheyenne River, File 308.1 (No. 99923-09), RG 75, NA.

38. Edward Swan to Hon. William H. Taft, 1 Apr. 1912, Legislation, File 5-1, RG 48, NA.

39. *Pierre Daily Capital-Journal*, 4 June 1908.

40. Charles Davis to Superintendent, 14 Aug. 1913, General Correspondence, Cheyenne River, File 916, RG 75, NA.

41. A search of the criminal court records of Dewey and Ziebach counties for 1910–1920 revealed that only four tribal members were prosecuted for violations of state law during that period. One of the four was an adopted white man. For details, see Hoxie, "Jurisdiction on the Cheyenne River Indian Reservation," 117–28 and apps. 97–114.

42. Thomas J. King to Commissioner of Indian Affairs, 25 Mar. 1912, Response to Circular #612, Special Series A, Box 1, RG 75, NA.

43. Hoxie, "Jurisdiction on the Cheyenne River Indian Reservation," app. 75.

44. "Superintendents' Annual Narrative and Statistical Report from Field Jurisdictions of the Bureau of Indian Affairs, Cheyenne River, 1914," Sec. 3: Schools, pt. 2, RG 75, NA; South Dakota, Session Laws (1915), chap. 168.

45. See U.S. v. Pearson, 231 F. 270 (8th Cir. 1916); and Thomas J. King to Commissioner of Indian Affairs, 25 Mar. 1912.

46. Hoxie, "Jurisdiction on the Cheyenne River Indian Reservation," app. 12.

47. See Charles Burke to Charles D. Munro, 2 Mar. 1923, General Correspondence, Cheyenne River, File 173, RG 75, NA; and J. Henry Scattergood to W. F. Dickens, 11 Feb. 1932, General Correspondence, Cheyenne River, File 175, RG 75, NA.

48. Olney Runs After, interview, Cherry Creek, SD, 25 Aug. 1977.

HARRY H. ANDERSON

THE WALDRON-BLACK TOMAHAWK CONTROVERSY AND THE STATUS OF MIXED BLOODS AMONG THE TETON SIOUX

. . .

Events of recent years on the Teton, or Lakota, Sioux reservations in the western Dakotas have emphasized the influence the mixed-blood population exercises in the political and economic lives of Indian communities. The participation of descendants of white-and-Indian parents in tribal affairs is not a new phenomenon. Neither are the keen rivalries that exist between this element and their full-blood cousins. Today, however, the classifications of mixed blood and full blood are based as much upon cultural characteristics as they were, historically, upon biological factors.[1]

The emergence of the Sioux mixed bloods as an influential force having distinctive economic and political interests began to take place during the last decade of the nineteenth and the early years of the twentieth centuries. A lengthy dispute over an allotted tract of Indian land highlighted this development and eventually appeared on the docket of the Circuit Court of the United States, District of South Dakota, Central Division, as *Jane E. Waldron, Complainant, v. The United States of America, Black Tomahawk, and Ira A. Hatch, as Indian Agent at Cheyenne River Indian Agency, Defendants.* The decision, handed down in 1905 in favor of the plaintiff, established in broad and virtually unassailable terms the full and equal status of Sioux mixed bloods in all legal aspects of their tribal affiliation.[2]

An examination of the circumstances surrounding the case provides important historical perspective on the position of mixed bloods in modern Sioux political life. The one thousand-odd pages of printed testimony upon which the court ultimately based its decision describe in considerable detail the status of mixed bloods during the early reservation period and identify the roots of the mixed-blood–full-blood rivalry existing today. In addition, this case was unique in that the court formally recognized the authority of tribal custom and

This essay originally appeared in *South Dakota History* 21 (Spring 1991): 69–83.

tradition at a time when official government policy called for the destruction of almost every vestige of traditional Sioux life.

The basic outline of the Waldron and Black Tomahawk controversy can be simply sketched. The principals in this landmark dispute, Jane E. Van Meter Waldron, a mixed blood married to a white man, and Black Tomahawk, a full-blood Teton of the Two Kettle band, were both enrolled at the Cheyenne River Sioux Agency located on the Missouri River in north-central South Dakota. Both sought to receive an allotment covering the same tract of land on a portion of the former Great Sioux Reservation that had been ceded under the Sioux Agreement of 1889. That document provided for the creation of five smaller reservations west of the Missouri River: the Rosebud, Pine Ridge, Lower Brule, Standing Rock, and Cheyenne River. The territory not included in these new reservations was opened for white settlement and for allotment to individual Indians such as Jane Waldron and Black Tomahawk.[3]

The tract of land claimed by the two parties consisted of 320 acres on the west bank of the Missouri River immediately north of the frontier community of Fort Pierre. Waldron established residence on the property in early July 1889, and Black Tomahawk did the same later that month. They filed their allotment declarations at the Cheyenne River Agency on 10 September and 4 October 1890, respectively. Both erected structures in which to live and added other improvements as their means permitted. After receiving their conflicting claims, the Department of the Interior asked for a ruling on the issue through the Justice Department. The opinion by an assistant United States attorney general favored Black Tomahawk, stating that as the child of a white father and a mixed-blood Indian mother, Waldron was not, in fact, an Indian and was not entitled to be enrolled at Cheyenne River or eligible to take an allotment. The foundation for this opinion was the common-law rule that a child born to a white man and his Indian wife follows the condition of the father and is a citizen of the United States rather than an Indian. Citizens, as non-Indians, were not entitled to receive allotments under terms of the 1889 agreement.[4]

When the Interior Department denied the Waldron allotment application, the Waldron family tried political influence to obtain a reversal but without success.[5] Waldron continued, however, to reside on the disputed tract without serious legal opposition until 1899. In March of that year, the government issued Black Tomahawk a trust patent and shortly thereafter ordered Agent Ira Hatch to remove Waldron, by force if necessary, from the disputed claim.[6] When she subsequently filed suit in federal court, her case hinged on proving, first, that as a mixed blood she was, in fact, an Indian, and second, that she had a right to file for an allotment at Cheyenne River Agency.

Jane E. Van Meter Waldron won a landmark suit
against the federal government, thus establishing the
full and equal status of mixed bloods in all legal aspects
of their tribal affiliation.

Faye Longbrake, Dupree, SD

After procedural delays, hearings finally began before a special court examiner in December 1902. Seven sessions, totaling twenty-six days, were held over a period of seven months at Pierre, the South Dakota state capital, at Cheyenne River Agency, and at the Yankton Sioux Agency at Greenwood, South Dakota, where a number of older members of Waldron's mother's family were enrolled. In all, 114 witnesses testified (some being summoned for both sides), the majority of whom were Indians who required the services of an interpreter. This Indian testimony, together with the evidence provided by other mixed bloods and whites closely associated with the Sioux, gave the case its unique character and greatly influenced the decision handed down by District Judge John E. Carland on 1 July 1905. The decision was a complete victory for Waldron, reversing the initial ruling and ordering the revocation of Black Tomahawk's trust patent. The court stated that historic precedent and Sioux custom respecting the status of mixed bloods were the determining factors in recognizing them as Indians with full legal rights, including participation in allotment.[7]

In one respect, at least, Waldron was ideally suited to bring the legal action that resulted in such a far-reaching affirmation of mixed-blood rights. Through her mother, she was descended from one of the oldest mixed-blood families among the Sioux. One maternal great-grandfather, Augustine Aungie, himself part Indian, is generally recognized as one of the three founders of Prairie du Chien, Wisconsin, a primary trading center on the upper Mississippi River in the late eighteenth and early nineteenth centuries. Another great-grandfather played an even more prominent role in the early history of the Old Northwest. He was Robert Dickson, the Scottish fur trader through whom the British enlisted support among the western Indians during the War of 1812. Both Dickson's and Aungie's wives were full-blood Sioux women. Their granddaughter, Mary Aungie, married Arthur C. Van Meter, a white man, and it was from this union that Jane Waldron was born. By Waldron's evaluation of her ancestry, her mother was five-eighths Indian and she was five-sixteenths. Culturally, however, she and her family claimed roots deep in the traditional ways and lifestyle of her mother's people, and it was evidence of this heritage that ultimately influenced the court in her favor.[8]

The Fort Laramie Treaty of 1868 that had created the Great Sioux Reservation also acknowledged that the white men then residing with Sioux wives and families among the Teton bands were full-fledged members of the tribe. By the late 1880s, the sons and daughters of these old fur traders and other whites had literally as well as figuratively "come of age." In earlier years, the numbers and influence of this group had been small. In 1876 and 1877, for example, when the army took control of the Cheyenne River Agency following the Custer disaster and other hostilities of that period, a military census disclosed that less than two dozen mixed-blood families were then living on that part of the reservation.[9] When the Sioux Agreement of 1889 was negotiated, however, 107 white and mixed-blood males over the age of eighteen signed the document. More than 50 percent of these signers were under thirty years of age, and over 70 percent were less than forty years old.[10] Paralleling this numerical growth was the government's institution in the 1880s of acculturation policies that suited the interests, needs, and capabilities of the mixed bloods and served to further increase their stature.

At the same time, however, the position of the mixed bloods within the tribal structure and under existing treaty provisions was not clearly defined. Agency administrators generally recognized the right of mixed bloods to equal shares of ration issues and annuity goods, primarily because tribal custom permitted mixed bloods to be included. Even though the Fort Laramie Treaty of 1868 had recognized white men living with the Teton bands as tribal members, that document made no provision for officially identifying, either then or later, exactly who was included among these so-called 68-ers and their privileged offspring.[11]

Like the 1868 treaty, the Sioux Agreement of 1876, which ceded the Black Hills, made no specific reference to the mixed bloods. One section did indicate, by implication at least, that they were not of equal standing with the full bloods. Article 7 provided that persons then residing among the Sioux who were considered to be of objectionable moral character could be excluded from benefits and even removed from the reservation. The only person to whom these penalties could not be applied was "an Indian of full blood." Thus, a mixed blood (or even a "68-er") could be deprived of both rations and annuities and expelled from the reservation if the commissioner of Indian affairs decided his presence was not "conducive to the welfare" of the Sioux.[12]

The record of councils between chiefs of the Sioux agencies and the two government land commissions that met with Indian leaders in 1888 and 1889 shows that even at that late date the position of the mixed bloods was not one of full equality. In their speeches, the tribal chiefs expressed a definite concern over the status of the mixed bloods. Swift Bird, a Two Kettle chief from Cheyenne River, expressed a typical attitude when the tribal delegations visited Washington, DC, in the fall of 1888: "It is hard to tell on which side [the mixed bloods] belong, to the whites or to the Indians, but we take them and want them confirmed as our people."[13] The persistence with which Sioux leaders pursued this issue indicates that they, and presumably the rest of their people, recognized the inferior position the mixed bloods occupied in relation to the full bloods in tribal affairs.

The mixed-blood issue cropped up even more frequently in 1889 during councils at the Sioux agencies with the commission headed by General George Crook. This time, however, the appeals for a greater voice in reservation matters came directly from the mixed bloods and white men themselves. The Crook commission was only too happy to encourage this development, for the vast majority of mixed bloods and reservation whites solidly supported the proposed land cession, and the commission needed all the votes it could muster to secure the required three-fourths affirmative majority. At Cheyenne River Agency, the question of mixed-blood eligibility to vote came up a number of times, both in formal council and in private. While not fully certain about the right of the mixed bloods and younger whites to vote, the commission allowed them to do so and let the legality of their actions be determined later. At Cheyenne River, mixed bloods and white men cast over 35 percent of the first 270 votes for the 1889 agreement. There is no way to determine how many of their full-blood relatives they influenced during the key early stages of balloting. Significantly, when the court handed down the decision in the Waldron case fifteen years later, it gave as one of its reasons for deciding in Waldron's favor that many mixed bloods, including two of her brothers, had voted in support of the 1889 agreement and its provisions for taking land by allotment. The court said it could not now, by ruling against Waldron, deprive the mixed bloods of a benefit that had been promised them in exchange for their vote.[14]

It was against this background, then, that Jane Van Meter Waldron sought to establish her rightful status as an enrolled mixed-blood Indian at Cheyenne River Agency. The evidence submitted by both sides in her suit illuminates at least three important aspects of the mixed-blood problem: their legal and cultural position within the Sioux tribes; the complexity of relationships on the reservation, including the impact of intertribal friction and personal animosity; and the economic advantages mixed bloods frequently derived from their position within both the white and Indian worlds.

Waldron's case was materially strengthened by the knowledge and ability of her attorney, Charles E. DeLand, a Pierre lawyer whose scholarly interest in the history of the upper Missouri River, particularly its Indian inhabitants, had uniquely equipped him to try such a suit.[15] Page after page of testimony shows that DeLand's preparation and presentation of evidence was efficient and systematic. After establishing the qualifications of his witnesses, he launched into a series of basic questions: Are you acquainted with the laws, customs, and practices of the Sioux concerning mixed-blood families? What are these customs? Is there a custom with respect to the heads of families? Who is the head of the family when the father is white and the mother a mixed or full-blood Indian? Through whom do the children derive their tribal rights? Are such customs applicable to families living outside reservation boundaries?

After establishing that customs regarding mixed-blood families did exist and that the head of the family was clearly the Indian woman, through whom the children derived their treaty rights whether residing on or off the reservation, DeLand posed more specific questions regarding Waldron's family history. Had they received benefits at the Yankton and Cheyenne River agencies? Were they regarded as Indians by both whites and Indians? Was this status affected by the family's migration from one place to another or the education of the children off the reservation?[16] Over and over again, the responses were uniformly favorable to DeLand's client. The defense counsel, Assistant United States Attorney W. G. Porter, regularly challenged his opponent's questions as immaterial and finally, at one point, stated in frustration that his objection was "cumulative, all [of these questions] having been asked of about 25 witnesses."[17] The massive impact of their testimony was apparent even to him.

Under DeLand's direction, the portrait of Jane Van Meter Waldron's life as an Indian was broadly and skillfully drawn. As a young girl, she dressed, played, and lived like a full-blood Sioux, not learning to speak English until the age of eight. Her mother sat in the Yankton tribal circle with other family heads and drew rations and annuities for herself and her children. Waldron's white father had no official status whatever in these tribal matters. When Waldron attended school at Ripon College in Wisconsin, her expenses were paid from a government fund administered through the Sioux mission school at Santee, Nebraska. One of her younger brothers attended Lincoln Institute in Philadelphia and in 1888 represented the American Indian people at Queen Victoria's jubilee. Her mother's funeral featured two services, one conducted by Christian Indians in their native tongue, after which her father held a "give-away" ceremony, distributing presents to all in attendance. As a married woman, Waldron held a ration ticket at Cheyenne River for herself and her relations. They regularly received annuities and other treaty benefits, and, in 1891, a government agent allowed Waldron to select an allotment for her oldest son on lands ceded under the 1889 agreement. And so on it went.[18]

Against this overwhelming evidence, defense attorney Porter attempted to present the other side of the coin—the white lifestyle in which the Van Meters, Waldrons, and their children also shared. The testimony resulting from his efforts is more useful today in supplementing Waldron's biography than it was in 1903 in defending against her suit, for on several occasions Waldron used

Drawing on his scholarly knowledge of American Indians,
Charles E. DeLand skillfully and systematically established
Waldron's rightful status as an enrolled mixed-blood Indian.
State Archives Collection, South Dakota State Historical Society

Porter's questions to aid her cause materially. During cross-examination, the defense established that Waldron had lived for most of her life in frame or log houses like other whites in the region; that she and her husband had been married by a white clergyman; that she and her children had adopted the dress, manners, and customs of whites; and that she had been appointed to a state regulatory board by two governors of South Dakota.[19] Waldron then completely negated the effect Porter had been seeking, observing, "Well I tried to imitate the customs of the white race as fast as I could learn them, I think that is the aim of the government."[20] On another occasion, when Porter continued to emphasize her adoption of white ways, she replied with some feeling, "I presume if we had been aware that we were going to have everything taken away from us the minute we began to be white we would not have striven so hard to be anybody."[21] Waldron displayed the same vigor and conviction on the witness stand that had enabled her to battle for fifteen years to affirm her allotment rights. This ability to overcome adversity was apparently part of her character. As a young girl, she was so frequently sick that one of her Indian names had been Suta Sni, meaning "not strong." Yet, she was described in later life as "small & wiry; tough as a boot; could handle horses better than most men."[22] It might be added that she could handle United States attorneys quite well, too.

In addition to its far-reaching legal implications, the Waldron case is useful for identifying the development of political or cultural factions among the Sioux people. The distinction between mixed bloods and full bloods that was almost entirely biological in Waldron's day has now become more descriptive of a way of life without regard to blood fractions. The pattern for this cultural realignment had already begun to emerge in the early 1900s, as is evident from even a superficial look at the witnesses who gave evidence in the Waldron case. Testifying in support of Waldron were eight non-Indians (seven white men and one black) married to Sioux women as well as a number of the more acculturated members of the mixed-blood community. Of the nine identifiable mixed bloods called on behalf of the plaintiff, eight testified in English without an interpreter. The full bloods who gave evidence in favor of Waldron included a number who were generally recognized as Christian Indians. Four of these were actually employed as native missionaries on the Cheyenne River reservation.

In contrast, the witness list for Black Tomahawk included primarily what today would be called "traditionalists." It contained no whites who had married into the Sioux tribe, and only three of the mixed bloods could communicate in English well enough to dispense with the interpreter. Only one native mission worker was included among the many more full bloods testifying for the defense. This full-blood group included all the surviving chiefs of the tribal council, plus a number of leading conservatives, commonly referred to then as "non-progressives" or "kickers." This group had been active in the 1890 Ghost Dance movement, lived far from the agency, and strongly opposed land cession and allotment.

Her long, intimate association with the Sioux people through her mother's family greatly strengthened Waldron's efforts to establish the primacy of Sioux traditions and practices among mixed bloods as the foundation of her case. At the same time, it was precisely her mixed-blood background that caused much of the opposition to her suit on the part of many Cheyenne River reservation full bloods. In addition, part of the testimony taken by both sides was influenced or obscured by prior disputes and personality clashes the Waldrons and their mixed-blood and white relatives had had with the full-blood element, agency officials, and even off-reservation whites.

The Department of Justice ruling that Waldron was not an Indian was, for the defense, a convenient bit of legal fiction; few who knew Waldron, even among her opponents, would have seriously argued the issue of her Indian background. What her full-blood opposition found objectionable was that she was the *wrong kind* of Indian. Her tribal heritage was that of a Santee, or Eastern, Sioux mixed blood rather than Teton, or Western, Sioux. Waldron's family had been adopted by part of the Teton Two Kettle band, which resided on the Cheyenne River reservation along with the Miniconjou, Sans Arc, and Blackfeet bands, but many Tetons refused to recognize this adoption. The lands being ceded and allotted under the 1889 agreement were Teton lands and, according to the Cheyenne River spokesmen, the Santees had no right to any benefits under that document. Teton mixed bloods could, and did, take allotments without tribal leaders uttering a word of objection. However, the chiefs repeatedly voiced their opposition to the participation of the Santee and Santee mixed bloods in the lengthy negotiations of 1888 and 1889. They argued that the Santees had long ago sold off their lands in Minnesota with no Teton ever receiving a dollar's worth of benefits. Moreover, the Santees had forfeited much of the money they should have received for their lands by going to war against the whites in 1862. After their defeat in the Dakota Conflict of 1862, they had been exiled to a small reservation in Nebraska.[23] Now, "those poor people" were demanding a share of the Teton lands.[24]

The Waldron and Van Meter families were easily identifiable as Santees, despite their convenient adoption by some of the Two Kettles. "I can tell them by the talk that they are Santees," said one member of the Sans Arc band, referring to the Santee dialect, which used a "d" in place of the Teton "l."[25] Anti-

Santee sentiment on the Teton reservations was at its height at the time of the Waldron-Black Tomahawk dispute, and it was not surprising that this issue played an important part in the case.

Violation of tribal custom was another issue raised by the defense as, one after another, the old tribal chiefs of the early reservation period testified that the tribal council had never approved placement of the Van Meter-Waldron families on the ration and annuity rolls. Council approval, they maintained, was necessary for all mixed bloods who were not a part of the four Teton groups residing at Cheyenne River. The old chiefs also testified that not only had Waldron, her parents, brothers, and sisters never been recognized by the tribal leaders, but at one council in June 1889 a unanimous vote had been taken to request the agent to have them removed because as Santees they did not properly belong on the reservation.[26]

Underlying some of this opposition was a strong personal dislike for certain male members of the Van Meter-Waldron clan. One witness for the defense testified regarding John W. ("Buck") Williams, the husband of Waldron's aunt, Helen, that the Indians "hate him the worst kind."[27] Others told that the full bloods suspected Arthur Van Meter of stealing and butchering their cattle because hides had been seen floating in the Bad River near his ranch. One of the Van Meter sons, John, became embroiled with a tribal policeman during the 1889 land councils and a few years later had a dispute with a Two Kettle chief over ownership of an abandoned agency building.[28] Many of the full-blood leaders who testified against Waldron had not forgotten that her father had been an active leader in rounding up support for the 1889 agreement, which they vehemently opposed. It hardly helped improve their attitude when at one point Waldron's attorney tried to impeach their testimony by characterizing them as former "renegades and floaters" who forfeited any rights at Cheyenne River because they had fought against Custer and gone into Canadian exile with Sitting Bull.[29]

This position was without merit, but there was another accusation that the Waldrons were able to prove to the satisfaction of the court so that it was accepted as a finding of fact. Black Tomahawk was, in effect, a tool of off-reservation white interests who had directed his selection of the land in question so that they could acquire it for their own purposes at a later date. The white men involved were identified as residents of the city of Pierre, on the east bank of the Missouri opposite the disputed allotment, but the motivation for their interest was never clearly stated in the court proceedings. Years later, Waldron maintained that railroad interests were behind the whole affair and that her successful court action had forced the Chicago & North Western Railroad to locate its division point and roundhouse in Pierre rather than west of the Missouri as it had desired.[30]

The allotment question, likewise a central issue in the Waldron case, also provides some insight into the economic aspects of the mixed-blood–full-blood relationship. More perceptive mixed bloods sometimes took allotments in particular geographic patterns designed to give them long-range economic advantage. One allotting agent, for example, was willing to locate 640 acres due the Waldrons in adjacent forty-acre parcels strung out along the Bad River. Such an arrangement would have provided control of water access — essential to a growing range economy — for a large portion of grazing land. Economic advantages like these became particularly important after 1901, when the government ended the free-ration system and required the Sioux to become self-supporting or participate in reservation improvement projects to earn their food supplies.[31]

Full bloods frequently resented the ability of certain mixed bloods to take full advantage of the opportunities offered through government policies. The Waldron case offered several other early examples. In particular, the Indians on the Cheyenne River reservation complained that the Van Meters and Waldrons obtained more farm implements from the agency than did the full bloods who belonged on the reservation. The full bloods also resented Jane Waldron's grazing of fifty head of cattle on tribal lands in 1897 while she also occupied the disputed allotment tract off the reservation. The reservation agent ruled the practice perfectly legal, but the full bloods still regarded it as an example of mixed bloods getting the best of both worlds.[32]

These matters, like others touched upon in the Waldron case, have a familiar ring. Mixed bloods today, particularly those more closely attuned to the standards of white society, frequently take advantage of whatever opportunities contemporary reservation life affords. They do so for reasons that the full bloods or cultural traditionalists choose either not to respond to or reject completely. As in the past, some full bloods resent the results of the mixed bloods' actions. Then, too, the influence of outsiders continues, with the white reservation rancher or town merchant replacing the railroad promoters of Black Tomahawk's day in attempting to manipulate one side or the other in tribal decision making. Finally, old personal rivalries, some handed down through families from generation to generation, remain a part of the modern reservation situation. If nothing else, the case of Waldron v. United States et al. shows that the roots of these conditions go deep into the history of the Teton Sioux and are far more complex than superficial studies of the mixed bloods have led us to believe.[33]

NOTES

1. For material on the contemporary mixed-blood–full-blood relationship, see Ethel Nurge, ed., *The Modern Sioux: Social Systems and Reservation Culture* (Lincoln: University of Nebraska Press, 1970), especially Robert E. Daniels, "Cultural Identities among the Oglala Sioux," 198–245; and Vine Deloria, Jr., *Behind the Trail of Broken Treaties: An Indian Declaration of Independence* (New York: Delacorte Press, 1974), 40–41, 187, 198.

2. Oral testimony and depositions taken during court-ordered hearings in Waldron v. United States et al. were printed in two paper-covered volumes containing 1,037 pages (N.p., 1904). The volumes are deposited with the South Dakota State Historical Society, Pierre, and are hereafter cited as *Testimony*. The decision of the court is found in Waldron v. United States et al., 143 F. (8th Cir. 1905): 413–20.

3. A convenient summary of the basic facts in the initial phase of this dispute can be found in U.S. Department of the Interior, Office of Indian Affairs, *Sixty-first Annual Report of the Commissioner of Indian Affairs to the Secretary of the Interior, 1892* (Washington, DC: Government Printing Office, 1892), 31–33.

4. Ibid.

5. A. C. Van Meter to Charles Foster, 13 Dec. 1892, and Foster to the Secretary of the Interior, 13 Dec. 1892, *Testimony*, 1025–26. Foster had been a member of the 1889 government commission that secured Sioux approval for sizable land cessions and the initiation of allotment. These communications stressed the vital role Waldron's father, Arthur C. Van Meter, other white husbands of Indian women, and mixed bloods had played in securing approval of the 1889 agreement at Cheyenne River Agency.

6. Trust Patent, *Testimony*, 1028–29; Waldron v. United States et al., 416.

7. Special Examiner's Report, *Testimony*, 1–4; Waldron v. United States et al., 414–20.

8. Peter Lawrence Scanlan, *Prairie du Chien: French, British, American* (N.p.: By the Author, 1937), 70–71; *Testimony*, 39–40 (Jane E. Waldron), 685–86 (John P. Williamson), 696–97, 704 (Harriet Aungie).

9. Register of Indians at Cheyenne Agency, Fort Bennett, vol. 54, 60, Records of the United States Army Continental Commands, 1821–1920, Record Group 393, National Archives, Washington, DC. For background on both the establishment of the agency and its military takeover, see Harry H. Anderson, "A History of the Cheyenne River Indian Agency and Its Military Post, Fort Bennett, 1868–1891," *South Dakota Historical Collections* 28 (1956): 390–551.

10. Senate, *Reports Relative to the Proposed Division of the Great Sioux Reservation, and Recommending Certain Legislation,* 51st Cong., 1st sess., 1890, Ex. Doc. 51, 288–96.

11. For more information on the relationship of these "68-ers" to the negotiation of the

Fort Laramie Treaty of 1868, see Harry H. Anderson, "Fur Traders as Fathers: The Origins of the Mixed-Blooded Community among the Rosebud Sioux," *South Dakota History* 3 (Summer 1973): 245–52.

12. Senate, *Report and Journal of Proceedings of the Commission Appointed to Obtain Certain Concessions from the Sioux Indians*, 44th Cong., 2d sess., 1876, Ex. Doc. 9, 22.

13. Senate, *Report Relative to Opening a Part of the Sioux Reservation*, 50th Cong., 2d sess., 1888, Ex. Doc. 17, 236. Wizi, a Crow Creek Yanktonais, and Hollow Horn Bear, a Brule, from Rosebud, made similar appeals in September of 1888. Ibid., 224.

14. *Reports Relative to . . . the Great Sioux Reservation*, 48–49, 82–83, 173, 288–91; *Testimony*, 119–20 (William P. Oakes), 213–14 (John T. Van Meter), 324–25 (Rev. Edward Ashley); Waldron v. United States et al., 418.

15. DeLand published two lengthy ethnological studies of the Arikara and Mandan Indians in volumes three (1906) and four (1908) of the South Dakota State Historical Society's *South Dakota Historical Collections* series. While these studies are now badly outdated, DeLand's detailed treatment of the Sioux Wars (1868–1891), which appeared in volumes fifteen (1930) and seventeen (1934) of the same series, is still useful.

16. For examples of DeLand's technique, see *Testimony*, 79–83 (Rev. Thomas L. Riggs), 94–95 (William Benoist), 101–04 (Louis LaPlant), and 181–83 (D. F. Carlin).

17. *Testimony*, 720 (Long Foot).

18. These and other details concerning Waldron's background are found scattered throughout *Testimony*, 5–37 (Arthur C. Van Meter), 38–77 (Jane E. Waldron), 420–41 (Helen Williams), and 693–704 (Harriet Aungie).

19. *Testimony*, 69–70, 73–74 (Jane E. Waldron).

20. Ibid., 63.

21. Ibid., 69.

22. Flora Ziemann to Harry H. Anderson, 1 Sept. 1975. Ziemann, long a resident of the Fort Pierre area, kept in contact with Jane Waldron after the family moved to Canada in 1912. She provided much useful personal information about Waldron and her family for this study.

23. *Testimony*, 780, 788–90, 792 (John Yellow Owl), 815–16 (Black Eagle), 858 (Charging Eagle); *Reports Relative to . . . the Great Sioux Reservation*, 161, 169, 174, 183; *Report Relative to . . . the Sioux Reservation*, 234.

24. *Reports Relative to . . . the Sioux Reservation*, 210.

25. *Testimony*, 817 (Black Eagle). The Sioux nation consists of three principal divisions: Santee, or Eastern (Dakota); Yankton and Yanktonais, or Middle (Nakota); and Teton, or Western (Lakota). Nurge, *The Modern Sioux*, xiii. The languages of these groups, while essentially the same, contain definite variations in pronunciation, particularly for consonants and occasionally in the meaning of words. For example, the directive "go home!" would be *kihda* in Santee, *kikda* in Yankton, and *kigla* in Teton speech. Thomas Lawrence Riggs, "Sunset to

Sunset: A Lifetime with My Brothers, the Dakotas," *South Dakota Historical Collections* 29 (1958): 160–63.

26. Testimony, 387–88 (Swift Bird), 406–7 (Four Bears), 466–69 (Little No Heart), 783, 787–88 (John Yellow Owl), 803–4 (Henry Takes His Blanket), 822 (Hump).

27. Testimony, 843 (Moses Spotted Eagle).

28. Testimony, 604 (John Holland), 786 (John Yellow Owl), 804 (Henry Takes His Blanket); *Reports Relative to . . . the Great Sioux Reservation*, 178.

29. Testimony, 949 (Soloman Yellow Hawk). After hearing DeLand's statement, defense counsel Porter commented that DeLand should "be sworn if he is going to testify in this case" (ibid.). Charles Foster, a member of the Crook Commission, had made a similar accusation against these conservative full bloods in 1889. Angered because they refused to sign the agreement and threatened physical harm to any Indian who did, Foster called them "outcasts on the face of the earth" (*Reports Relative to . . . the Great Sioux Reservation*, 185).

30. Waldron v. United States et al., 16; Testimony, 939–40 (Black Tomahawk), 942–43 (William Benoist); Ziemann to Anderson, 19 July 1975.

31. Testimony, 58 (Jane E. Waldron); *Report of the Commissioner of Indian Affairs*, 1901, 1: 6.

32. Testimony, 617, 619 (Dennis Buck), 990 (Felix Benoist), 1013 (Jane E. Waldron).

33. For example, the index to James C. Olson's important and detailed study entitled *Red Cloud and the Sioux Problem* (Lincoln: University of Nebraska Press, 1965) contains only two brief references to the mixed bloods. One is a lengthy quotation from Pine Ridge Agent Valentine T. McGillycuddy, who blamed the white "squaw-men" and mixed bloods for the failure of the Sioux to progress toward self-support (293). McGillycuddy's statement typifies his widely circulated and highly prejudicial view of these people—a view that has probably done more than any other historical source to create a general but erroneous image of the Sioux mixed bloods as worthless, shiftless troublemakers. While George E. Hyde's *A Sioux Chronicle* (Norman: University of Oklahoma Press, 1956) presents a more understanding treatment, even Hyde does not devote any attention to the development of the mixed bloods as an influential force among the Tetons. Finally, the contemporary studies contained in *The Modern Sioux*, edited by Ethel Nurge, all but ignore historical background on the subject. Some of the best insights into modern reservation politics can be obtained from a careful analysis of Robert Burnette's *The Tortured Americans* (Englewood Cliffs, NJ: Prentice-Hall, 1971).

MICHAEL L. LAWSON

THE FRACTIONATED ESTATE

THE PROBLEM OF AMERICAN INDIAN HEIRSHIP

. . .

The most problematic legacy of federal Indian land policies of the nineteenth century has been their peculiar rules and policies regarding inheritance. Because physical partitioning of land allotments upon the death of an allottee was deemed to be inconsistent with the policy goal of establishing individual farms and ranches on reservations, allotted estates were merely divided on paper and continued in federal trust for the benefit of heirs, or they were sold out of trust, almost always to non-Indians, with proceeds being distributed among the decedent's family. These probate practices led eventually to the disuse or alienation of millions of acres of Indian land. The exponential growth of the so-called undivided interests (or, more accurately, unpartitioned interests) in trust allotments rapidly made it infeasible for most heirs to make practical use of the land themselves. They soon found they could only derive economic benefit from their inherited interests by agreeing, in unanimity with all other heirs to a given allotment, to lease out the land and/ or its resources (most often, again, to non-Indians). Thus, allotment and its escalating heirship problem not only reduced thousands of tribal members to the status of petty landlords but created as well an administrative conundrum for the federal trustee that may well be without parallel in all the vastness of this nation's bureaucracy.

The federal government recognized Indian heirship as a growing administrative problem even within the first generation following passage of the General Allotment Act of 1887. In 1910, Congress found it necessary to authorize more clearly defined procedures for the determination of heirs and the administration of trust estates, and in 1934, it finally repealed the allotment policy and appropriated funds for tribal land consolidation. Yet, the government provided little else in the way of general mitigation of the heirship problem prior

This essay originally appeared in *South Dakota History* 21 (Spring 1991): 1–42. A summarized version of the essay was presented in slightly different form at the annual meeting of the American Society for Ethnohistory in Toronto on 3 November 1990.

to enactment of the Indian Land Consolidation Act of 1983 (ILCA). The most controversial aspect of this statute, passed with only token tribal consultation, provided that certain minimal interests of Indians who died intestate (without a will) would revert to the ownership of the tribe having jurisdiction over the land, through the legal procedure known as escheat, rather than be divided further among heirs. Congress amended the ILCA in 1984, and the United States Supreme Court ruled in its 1987 decision in Hodel v. Irving, a case originating in South Dakota, that the escheat provision of the original statute was unconstitutional.[1] The purpose of this article is to provide a summary history of Indian heirship and to offer at least an interim analysis of the legislation that now represents the federal government's primary solution to this longstanding problem.

Land has been the primary source of conflict and confrontation between American Indians and the European Americans whose culture gained dominance over this nation. One of the most easily discernible differences between these peoples and their respective cultures has been in their concepts of land-ownership. The American Indians' long tradition of communal use of land and resources, with all of its interwoven cultural and religious significance, proved to be incompatible with the European notions of "civilization" held by those of the dominant culture who formulated federal Indian policy during the latter half of the nineteenth century. Despite the rapid rise of industrialism in the post-Civil War era, the agrarian ideal, as personified by the yeoman farmer, remained deeply ingrained in the national psyche of the United States. Just as the equally strong European notion that no people should hold more land than they could make practical use of led to the practice of extracting huge land cessions from America's native tribes,[2] the universal belief in the supremacy of private landownership led to experiments in granting separate plots of tribal land to individual Indian families for the purpose of establishing agricultural homesteads.[3]

Although the allotment of Indian lands had been tried as early as 1633, these model experiments in social engineering reached their apex as an expression of national policy with the passage in 1887 of the General Allotment Act. This legislation also represented a culmination of the assimilationist efforts of the Protestant Christian reformers who dominated Indian policy making during that era, and it is often called the Dawes Act, after its principal architect, Senator Henry L. Dawes of Massachusetts, or merely the Severalty Act. It provided, in effect, that tribal members would be allotted individual tracts of land either within their tribe's common lands or reserved areas or within the public domain lands and would thereupon become citizens of the United States. The

VERY ROSEBUD INDIAN OWNS A FARM

This Bureau of Indian Affairs photograph of Sioux Indians
from the Rosebud reservation and non-Indian officials emphasizes the
United States policy of imposing European landownership patterns
on the natives of the American West.

State Archives Collection, South Dakota State Historical Society

heads of families were entitled to allotments of 160 acres, while single persons over eighteen years of age and orphans under eighteen could qualify for forty-acre allotments. The reservation lands remaining after all eligible tribal members received allotments were to be opened up for non-Indian settlement, at least initially with the consent of the tribe, rather than reserved for future generations of Indian families.[4]

In order to ease the Indians' transition into all the rights, privileges, and responsibilities of propertied citizenship, the General Allotment Act provided that title to these allotments would be held in trust by the United States for at least twenty-five years, during which time the land could not be sold, leased, taxed, mortgaged, devised by will, or otherwise encumbered without the consent of the federal government. It was hoped that by the end of this probationary period, the individual allottee, who would then be eligible to receive the usual fee simple title to the land, would have learned how to make productive use of the acreage, to know its market value, and to be ready to assume full responsibility for it, including the payment of taxes. If this was found not to be the case, the law gave the president discretionary power to extend the trust period.[5]

The General Allotment Act was not based on any familiarity with the tribes and their cultures or on an investigation of actual conditions. It rested solely on a theoretical belief in the inferiority of common landownership. The suitability of the Indians and their lands and environments for agriculture was never questioned. The legislation was enacted because of the support it drew from two rather polarized interest groups: eastern theoreticians and humanitarians apparently sincere in their motives to integrate tribal members into the mainstream of the dominant American culture; and land-hungry frontiersmen who saw allotment as an opportunity to acquire more land inexpensively, through the purchase of either the "surplus" lands that would be left after the reservations were allotted or the allotments themselves once their restrictions were removed.[6]

The legislators who supported the General Allotment Act admitted that the government's earlier experiments in severalty, which had resulted in the issuance of some twelve thousand allotments, had been fraught with failure because most of the land had passed quickly into the hands of white traders and land companies. These experiments had been initiated in a number of early removal treaties, such as those negotiated with the Cherokee, Chickasaw, and Potawatomi tribes between 1816 and 1818. These treaties allowed certain individual tribal members to select tracts of land within the tribal territory ceded to the United States and remain there after the rest of the tribe was removed to the

West. By mid-century, allotment had become part of the tactical arsenal aimed at terminating tribal existence. By accepting fee simple title to lands (with or without restrictions against alienation) and full national citizenship, allottees under the provisions of treaties such as those ratified in the spring of 1854 with the Oto, Missouri, Omaha, and Shawnee tribes were separated from both the tribal estate and their legal status as tribal Indians.[7]

The proponents of the General Allotment Act blamed these earlier failures on the alienability of the land titles and asserted that the results would differ substantially if the lands were protected more strongly from alienation. The practice of allotting tribal land by conveyance to the United States to be held in trust for individual Indian allottees and beneficiaries began in 1882 and, with the passage of the General Allotment Act, became the primary form of tenure for allotments.[8]

The General Allotment Act did not change or amend previous treaties or agreements and did not apply to all reservations (certain tribes in Oklahoma and New York and what was known as the Sioux Strip in Nebraska were exempted). Neither was it sufficient by itself to allot all Indian lands. Additional legislation was needed to apply its provisions to specific reservations and individuals. For example, legislation in 1888 enabled some residents of the Lake Traverse reservation of the Sisseton-Wahpeton Sioux in Dakota Territory to become the first in the nation to receive allotments under provisions of the general act.[9]

The controversial act of 2 March 1889, which partitioned the Great Sioux Reservation into six separate tribal reserves in North and South Dakota and eventually opened nine million acres to white settlement, also extended the 1887 allotment provisions to the Lakota people but doubled the acreage to 320 acres for each head of family. Previously, a limited number of Sioux had established family farmsteads under provisions of Article 6 of the Fort Laramie Treaty of 1868. During the legislative debate over partitioning, Congressman Thomas G. Skinner of North Carolina calculated that if the Great Sioux Reservation were divided equally among the approximately twenty-five thousand tribal members, each man, woman, and child would receive an allotment of around 880 acres. Even after the partition, an equal division would have resulted in allotments of approximately five hundred acres.[10]

In 1902, a joint resolution in Congress imposed the provisions of the General Allotment Act on all allotments except those in Oklahoma. The general statute of 1887 and subsequent enabling legislation provided that if an allottee died while the property was still in federal trust status, the estate would be divided among heirs according to the laws of descent and partition in the state or territory in which the land was located. However, state courts were precluded from having any probate jurisdiction over these allotments. The secretary of the interior assumed the power to determine heirs, and federal district courts also exercised jurisdiction over allotment inheritance cases. Tribal customs for settling such matters involving property were ignored, although later statutes applied tribal law to certain heirship determinations. The act of 28 February 1891, for example, provided for the legitimization of the children of parents married according to Indian custom and declared children born out of wedlock to be the legitimate issue of their fathers. Although this statute was silent regarding the rights of illegitimate children to inherit from their mothers, the law has been interpreted as meaning that this kind of inheritance would be governed by local statutes.[11]

In the tradition of Anglo-Saxon law, the probating of an estate was usually resolved either by dividing property physically among heirs, so that each parcel then became a separate estate, or by selling the property and dividing the proceeds, all in accordance with the local laws of succession or the instructions of the decedent's will. The restrictive provisions and agrarian considerations on which the federal allotment policy was built, however, combined to create a much more complex situation for the probating of Indian trust estates. Those who implemented early probate decisions determined that physical partitioning was impracticable because it placed the estates in conflict with the goals of the allotment policy. Indians commonly had large families, and decision makers concluded that a subdivision of the allotted tracts would render them inefficient as practical agricultural units, either for the heirs or for the non-Indians who might come to use or purchase the property in the future. Instead, it was decided that the inherited interests in the allotments would merely be divided on paper and continued in trust for the heirs, who would then be placed in a position similar to tenants-in-common. Unlike heirs who inherited interests in fee-simple lands, the beneficiaries of Indian trust land did not possess the right to file suit for a portion of an estate.[12]

The long-term effect of these peculiar probate policies has been the progressive fractionalization of those estates for which the initial federal trust period was extended. During the more than ninety years between the General Allotment Act and the Indian Land Consolidation Act, most of the original allotments were divided numerous times on paper, the equities grew smaller proportionately as the number of heirs increased, and individual tribal members, many of whom had no land for their own use, accumulated minimal interests in several scattered estates, sometimes within a number of separate reservations. This heirship problem mushroomed to the point where thousands of

Indians were helpless to make effective use of their inherited interests. Thus it was that allotment as a program to eradicate communal land holdings succeeded, ironically, only in creating a bizarre and much less efficient form of common landownership.

The drafters of the General Allotment Act apparently gave little thought to the specific, practical problems of inheritance or generally to the rights and needs of married women or future generations of tribal members. So quickly did both the early allottees and the Indian agents in the field find the general allotment policies to be deficient that Congress was compelled within just four years to begin its nearly half-century effort to modify the original provisions.

By providing allotments of 160 acres to heads of households and forty acres to minors, the allotment act failed to provide married women with separate rights to land. An Indian woman turned out of her house by her husband, for example, was not entitled to an allotment of her own. Those critical of this omission, including anthropologist Alice Fletcher, demanded the equalization of allotments to men, women, and children, arguing that the young and able-bodied who received only forty acres should not have less land than the old and infirm. In response, Congress enacted an amendatory statute in 1891 that provided entitlement for allotments of at least eighty acres of agricultural land and 160 acres of grazing land to each Indian.[13]

The policy of selling the reservation lands that remained after allotment ignored the resource needs of future tribal members. Many tribes readily agreed to sell their surplus lands, and many such agreements were approved by Congress. The process was hastened after the United States Supreme Court ruled in the 1903 case of *Lone Wolf v. Hitchcock* that Congress possessed the power to dispose of Indian lands without tribal consent. In 1904, the pattern for nonconsent sales was subsequently set through legislation that opened up 416,000 acres of the Rosebud Sioux reservation in South Dakota. By 1934, some sixty million acres of Indian land had been liquidated in this manner; most of it at the price of $1.25 per acre, the proceeds of which were distributed on a pro rata basis to tribal members or used to offset agency appropriations.[14]

For a variety of reasons, the allotment policy did not succeed in transforming many Indians who were not already farmers into productive agriculturalists. A seminal cliometric analysis of the General Allotment Act by economic historian Leonard A. Carlson in 1981 concluded that tribal members were generally less successful as farmers on their own individual tracts than they had been previously on their communal lands. This study also demonstrated how the allotment program, through the sale of surplus reservation lands and the eventual opportunities to lease or purchase allotments, served best the economic interests of white settlers rather than Indians. A provocative evaluation of Congress by the Finnish scholar Markku Henriksson concluded that this was generally true of all Indian legislation enacted between 1862 and 1907.[15] Nevertheless, the allotment policy did have its effect on tribal culture over the long term, to the extent that farming and ranching are now major enterprises in Indian country, albeit rather fragile ones.[16]

On many reservations the granting of land in severalty and the almost simultaneous pro rata distribution of the proceeds of surplus land sales combined to have a negative effect. Land money erased incentive for farming activities, and, with the encouragement of unscrupulous merchants, its rapid dissipation often left the Indians with little or no funds for farming or ranching equipment. Many allotted lands had less than favorable soil and climatic conditions, and many allottees, including the old and infirm and students attending boarding schools and other minors, were unable to establish even a homestead on their tracts. As a result, much of the land was not only unfarmed but was unused for any productive purpose.[17]

Hoping to generate some kind of income from undeveloped allotments, tribal leaders began pleading with Congress in the early 1890s to lift the restrictions against the leasing of allotted lands. Western settlers also pressured the legislators to permit them to gain access to the "wasted land." The proponents of leasing argued that allottees would benefit from observing the successful operations of non-Indian farmers and ranchers on a portion of their land, and that lease income would allow the tribal members to make improvements on the remainder of their allotments. They also reasoned that leasing revenues might also justify a reduction in the federal appropriations for Indians.[18]

Despite the statutory resolve of Senator Dawes and the other reformers in 1887 to keep allotments absolutely unencumbered and inalienable, these same policy makers were easily swayed just four years later by the arguments favoring leasing. Thus, in the same 1891 statute that provided for the equalization of allotments, Congress agreed to authorize leasing on a limited scale. Any allottee who was found by reason of age or "other disability" to be unable to occupy or improve their land was permitted, with the consent of the secretary of the interior, to enter a lease agreement, the terms of which were limited to three years for farming and grazing lands and ten years for mining lands. Because few leases were approved under these terms, public pressure soon brought about a liberalization of the leasing provisions. Congress alternately eased and tightened the restrictions until finally enacting legislation in 1910 that reduced the constraints to the point where any allotment could be readily leased for up to five years. By 1921, such leases required only the approval of the superintendent of the reservation. By 1934, more than 13.9 million acres of allotted lands were being leased.[19]

Leasing compromised the best interests of the allotment policy. In common with treaty rations and pro rata distributions, it tended to encourage idleness. The leasing out of a majority of allotments on some reservations transformed allottees or their heirs into "a race of petty landlords" whose only nongovernment subsistence depended on the meager unearned income derived from their allotment interests.[20]

Leasing also served early to make Indian agents aware of complications emerging from the extraordinary policies regarding the inheritance of trust lands. The leasing of an allotment in heirship status required the consent of all the heirs. As the heirs themselves died and equities in the estates grew ever smaller, leasing often became the only viable option for deriving income from the inherited interests. Yet, potential lessees often shied away from heavily fractionated tracts because of the difficulty of obtaining the consent of all the heirs. As a result, thousands of acres of allotted lands still remained idle. For those heirship lands on which leases were negotiated successfully, the burden of distributing the proceeds of the lease among the heirs according to their fractional interests in the estate fell upon the Office of Indian Affairs (which did not officially become the Bureau of Indian Affairs until 1947). By the 1930s, the government's cost in managing a lease often exceeded the value of the lease.[21]

Between 1899 and 1904, the federal government again contradicted the intentions of severalty land and complicated its own allotment record keeping, passing legislation that provided the secretary of the interior with the general discretion to grant rights-of-way and easements through Indian reservations and allotted lands. This authority allowed railroads, telephone and telegraph lines, gas and oil pipelines, and electrical power lines to crisscross allotments, often decreasing their agricultural potential.[22]

Another modification of the allotment policy evolved from a demand for the sale of allotted lands on the part of both tribal members and non-Indian settlers. For those allotments that could not be easily utilized, leased, or partitioned in any beneficial way, the solution seemed to be to lift the trust restrictions against outright alienation. To this end, legislation in 1902 authorized the secretary of the interior to sell allotments in heirship status and divide the proceeds among the heirs. Under this law, a single "competent" heir could petition for the sale of an entire allotment. Four years later, Congress authorized the secretary to allow original allottees to dispose of their land. Since tribal members seldom had the means to purchase the allotments approved for sale,

The problems of the realty offices of the Bureau of Indian Affairs in obtaining the signatures of heirs on land sales and lease forms are dramatized in these companion cartoons, which appeared in one of the many federal studies of the heirship situation.

House Committee on Interior and Insular Affairs, *Indian Heirship Land Study: Analysis of Indian Opinion as Expressed in Questionnaires*, vol. 1, 86th Cong., 2d sess., 1960 (Washington, DC: Government Printing Office, 1961) the land passed inevitably into non-Indian ownership. By 1934, approximately 3.7 million acres of allotted land had been alienated from Indian ownership through the vehicle of supervised sales.[23]

The selling and leasing of allotted lands and inherited interests gradually turned the Indian Office into a giant real-estate and banking enterprise. The broad powers of the secretary of the interior over Indian lands and funds were delegated to agency superintendents, and proceeds from the lease or sale of allotments were also maintained under federal trust and deposited in Individual Indian Money (IIM) accounts at agency banks. Proceeds from the sale of an allotment were sometimes used to purchase other tracts for allottees or heirs. Because these lands were held in fee-simple title by the Indian owners but were subject to restrictions against alienation, they became known as "restricted fee allotments" as opposed to "trust allotments" held in trust for individual tribal members. As has often been the case throughout its history, the Indian Office had neither the manpower nor resources to perform its administrative tasks adequately. The demand for the lease or sale of allotted lands became so brisk by 1913 that the agency reported a backlog of forty thousand requests involving sixty million dollars worth of land.[24]

Escalating criticism of the trust and citizenship provisions of the General Allotment Act led to further legislative revisions in 1906. It had become apparent by then that the citizenship conferred with allotments had proven to be a disadvantage to many tribal members because it created the incongruous situation of placing their persons, but not their allotments, outside the protection of federal courts at a time when many local authorities were reluctant to enforce state laws where Indians were concerned. The Indian Office discovered that citizenship greatly retarded its program to mitigate liquor trafficking on reservations. The issue was brought to the fore in 1905 when the United States Supreme Court in *Matter of Heff* overturned the conviction of a man who had sold liquor to an allotted Indian because the allottee, as a citizen, was "outside the reach of police regulations on the part of Congress."[25]

In reaction to the Heff decision, Congressman Charles H. Burke of South Dakota, who later became commissioner of Indian affairs, introduced legislation that would postpone citizenship for future allottees until the end of the twenty-five-year trust period, during which time the federal government would maintain exclusive jurisdiction over them. The Burke Act of 1906 also authorized the president to extend the initial trust period on allotments if conditions so warranted, further delaying citizenship. For those allottees judged to be sufficiently competent to manage their lands and other affairs, however, this statute authorized the secretary of the interior to issue fee patents for their allotments, and personal citizenship thereby, even before the expiration of the initial trust period.[26]

In common with so many other of the well-intentioned revisions of allotment policy, the implementation of this law opened yet another avenue for the rapid alienation of allotments. While those who desired citizenship could apply for a determination of their competency, federal officials proceeded to force about ten thousand allottees or their heirs to accept fee patents without their application or consent. This work was done either through the use of commissions, which purported to establish the competency of individuals, or by the arbitrary issuance of fee patents to tribal members whose Indian blood quantum was one-half or less. Most of those who received fee patents, with or without consent, either sold their lands or lost them through the foreclosure of a mortgage within a short time. The practice of issuing the so-called forced fee patents was halted in 1921, and legislation in 1927 and 1931 authorized the cancellation of such patents under certain conditions. However, because these laws stipulated that the patentee could not have sold or mortgaged the land in the interim, only about 470 of the forced fee allotments were ever restored to trust status. By 1934, the issuance of fee patents, forced or otherwise, had accounted for the loss of about twenty-three million acres of Indian land.[27]

The allotment policy not only alienated tribal members from their land, but it also became a rationale for taking away their given names. In order that Indian family members might all be known by the same surname on agency allotment and probate records, the government set about to replace the customary Indian system of personal name-giving, substituting either English family names or loose English translations of Indian names for those in the native language and then introducing Christian first names. By 1909, for example, the famous Santee Sioux physician, Charles A. Eastman, who had himself been known as Ohiyesa previously, had revised the names of some twenty-five thousand Sioux people as part of his role as a special Indian agent.[28]

Finally coming to the realization that allotment could not be implemented uniformly in all Indian communities, Congress sought to correct deficiencies in the administration of allotted lands and inherited estates through a major revision of the General Allotment Act in 1910. Among the many provisions of a law signed on 25 June of that year was one that permitted tribal members, for the first time, to devise their trust estates by will, subject to the approval of the secretary of the interior. This act also specified the secretary's authority to determine the heirs of those allotment interest holders who died intestate. This authority was established as being exclusive of state courts and legislatures, except in Oklahoma and Arkansas, and of primary federal court jurisdiction, although this power in relation to tribal courts has never been defined clearly. In addition, the 1910 statute delineated more clearly the power of the secretary to administer trust estates, including the power to sell or purchase heirship lands and grant fee patents to heirs.[29]

Following this legislation, the secretary of the interior issued the first orders regulating the determination of heirs and the approval of wills. More comprehensive regulations were issued in 1915, and these were revised in 1923, 1935, and 1938. The commissioner of Indian affairs appointed hearing examiners to conduct probate hearings. Agency superintendents were authorized to assist tribal members in the drafting of wills and to conduct probate hearings in the absence of a hearing examiner. Each will and probate required the preparation of a complete case report, which was transmitted with recommendations regarding approval to the commissioner, who in turn reported the case to the secretary. The secretary then issued an order determining heirs or approving or disapproving of a will. Until 1943, the secretary issued an order in every Indian probate case.[30]

After 1910, any Indian who still held an interest in a trust allotment, which might have initially been inalienable under any circumstance, could seek approval to sell, lease, or even partition that interest, to devise it by will or make a gift conveyance of it to other family members, or to receive fee-simple title to it. About the only transaction that an Indian owner could not initiate was the execution of a mortgage of the trust interests. Alas, in 1956, Congress also eliminated this restriction and thus created yet another possible means of alienation through foreclosure by creditors.[31]

All of the legislative tinkering with the original provisions of the General Allotment Act did little to halt the exponential growth of fractionated interests in the allotments that remained in trust. Consequently, federal policy makers spent much of the twentieth century searching for an adequate solution to the problem of Indian heirship. In 1926, heirship was one of the problems focused on in the comprehensive investigation of reservation conditions and federal Indian administration commissioned by Interior Secretary Hubert Work. The Institute for Government Research, an independent organization that later became the political branch of the Brookings Institution in Washington, DC, conducted the study. Because the nine researchers involved in this project were directed by political analyst Lewis Meriam, the results of the study, published in 1928 as The Problem of Indian Administration, has become more commonly known as the Meriam Report.[32]

As a solution to the heirship problem, the Meriam Report recommended that the government establish a revolving fund that would permit tribes to purchase inherited interests and consolidate fractionated allotments into units that would be workable economically. It suggested that revolving loans to individuals should have liberal repayment terms in order to prevent any further loss of trust land and to halt the use of revenues from inherited interests as a means of sustaining tribal members in a life of "irresponsible idleness." The study also urged that tighter restrictions be placed on the sale of inherited lands. Recognizing the escalating burden borne by the government in the management of heirship lands, Meriam's report discouraged further allotments because it found that they resulted in "an enormous increase in the details of administration without a compensating advance in the economic ability of the Indians."[33] In response to these recommendations, the Herbert Hoover administration considered a proposal to allow tribes to purchase heirship lands on a deferred payment basis, with the federal government holding the mortgages. Even though this plan would have cost only one hundred thousand dollars per year, the fiscal constraints of the Great Depression precluded its implementation.[34]

The Meriam Report set the stage for the major policy reforms of the New Deal era that were established under the auspices of President Franklin Roosevelt's Indian commissioner, John Collier. This former social worker and activist did not consider the expectation of inheritance to be a vested right and concluded that Congress had the authority to modify the rules of descent pertaining to Indian trust land. Thus, Collier's original draft of what became the Indian Reorganization Act of 1934 (IRA) provided for the exchange of inherited interests for a proportional share in the tribal estate through the medium of "certificates of interest." These certificates, which could be issued with or without heir consent, would guarantee use rights to certain tracts and could be subject to division by inheritance, although the land units themselves would remain in tribal ownership. However, the storm of protest that arose from allottees and heirs, who saw this plan as a scheme to confiscate their interests for the benefit of landless tribal members, soon forced Collier to modify his proposals. In the end, Congress also proved unwilling to test its authority either to limit inheritance or to provide for involuntary land exchanges.[35]

Although the major thrust of the IRA, which is also known as the Wheeler-Howard Act, was to provide for the partial restitution of tribal sovereignty through the establishment of federally approved constitutional governments, it also implemented and, in some cases, expanded the recommendations of the Meriam study regarding allotted lands. Sections 4 and 5 of the statute prohibited further allotments, extended indefinitely the trust periods and alienation restrictions on existing allotments, and provided for the restoration to tribal ownership of surplus lands on which there had been no settlement. The IRA also provided for the voluntary transfer of individual allotments to tribal ownership and appropriated limited funds for tribal land consolidation and the purchase of additional lands for reservations. Similar provisions were also extended to the Oklahoma tribes through the Oklahoma Indian Welfare Act of 1936.[36]

Although various circumstances prevented the government from realizing the IRA's full reform potential, the repeal of the allotment policy, in and of itself, represented a legislative watershed. "The allotment system with its train of evil consequences," proclaimed Commissioner Collier, "was definitely abandoned as the backbone of the national Indian policy," and the concept of common landownership was "reaffirmed."[37] This policy shift came after a total of 246,569 allotments had been made, accounting for 40,848,172 acres of land, and after the Indian trust-land base, which had approximated 138 million acres at the time of the General Allotment Act, had been reduced to around 52 million acres.[38]

The end of allotment did not stop the further compounding of heirship interests through the passage of time, and the IRA proved ultimately to be deficient in providing for the consolidation of either reservation lands "checkerboarded" by non-Indian holdings or individual allotments fractionated by the ever-growing number of heirs. The promise of the "Indian New Deal" was crippled by chronic underfunding of its programs and the IRA's limited applicability. In their devotion to tribal self-determination, Collier and other architects of the legislation established that the law would apply only to those tribes that voted to accept its provisions. For a variety of reasons, not the least of which was Indian distrust of the government, a number of tribes, representing nearly 40 percent of the nation's Indians, rejected the IRA.[39]

In August 1938, a group of Indian New Deal policy makers, including Commissioner Collier and Associate Solicitor Felix S. Cohen, convened in Glacier Park, Montana, for a three-day conference on Indian land problems. A committee instructed to review probate procedures made a number of specific recommendations, which included restricting the sale of heirship lands to heirs, other tribal members, or the tribe itself and limiting the right of inheritance to those interests that would comprise a viable economic unit and then only to lineal descendants, thereby excluding collateral relatives. It was suggested further that the right to devise property by will also be limited to allotments that were economic units and that the designated beneficiaries of such wills be restricted to heirs or tribal members. Regarding spousal inheritance, the committee recommended that the rights of nonmember spouses be limited to either life use or a designated interest and that the inherited property rights of all surviving spouses be terminated upon remarriage. The conference rejected a recommendation to limit inheritance to those having an Indian-blood quantum of one-half or more and voted to give further consideration to a proposal to restrict the inheritance rights of Indians who already possessed an economic unit.[40]

The recommendations of the Glacier Park conference were never implemented. The Great Depression continued to place financial restraints on government programs, and the exigencies of World War II soon distracted federal attention from Indian affairs. Although the Interior Department took little action to resolve the heirship problem in the 1940s, it did revise its administration of Indian probates. By orders issued in 1943 and 1944, the secretary of the interior delegated to the commissioner of Indian affairs the authority to determine heirs and probate the estates of all Indians except those belonging to the Osage tribe in Oklahoma. The secretary retained only the prerogative to review the commissioner's decisions upon appeal. This change created a procedure of initial and appellate probate decisions similar to that which is still in place.[41]

Under new regulations issued by the secretary in 1947, examiners of inheritance within the Bureau of Indian Affairs (BIA) were empowered to make the initial decisions regarding estates and heirs, and their judgments were appealable only to the secretary, thus eliminating the role of the commissioner. These probate examiners operated out of eight district offices under the direct administrative supervision of the BIA's chief counsel in Washington, DC. Because of the large number of allotments in the north-central section of the country, nearly half of the Indian probate offices were located in that region (at Minneapolis, Minnesota; Bismarck, North Dakota; Pierre, South Dakota; and Billings, Montana). The other offices were at Carson City, Nevada; Phoenix, Arizona; Portland, Oregon; and Shawnee, Oklahoma. Finally in 1949, the secretary's authority regarding the review of appeals was delegated to the solicitor, the legal officer of the Department of the Interior.[42]

While Congress failed to enact any general legislation dealing with the heirship problem for nearly a half-century following the IRA, it did pass several laws, beginning in the 1940s, which provided for the establishment of land consolidation programs and tribal inheritance codes on particular reservations. Among the nine tribes that sought and received such special legislation were the Sisseton–Wahpeton (1974, 1984), Standing Rock (1980), and Devils Lake (1983) Sioux in North and South Dakota. Some tribes also developed their own successful programs, including the Cheyenne River and Rosebud Sioux in South Dakota.[43]

Disparaging of government efforts to deal with the problem of fractionated allotments, the Rosebud Sioux Tribe launched its own innovative land consolidation program in 1943, establishing the Tribal Land Enterprise (TLE) as a sub-chartered corporation of the tribe with its own board of directors. The TLE was authorized to purchase the inherited interests of tribal members. However, the payments were not to be made in cash but rather in stock certificates in the corporation, which were initially valued at one dollar per share and were to be adjusted periodically to reflect the appraised value of the TLE's total purchased land base. Tribal members could then use their stock certificates to purchase or lease land assignments from the corporation, hold them as investments, or sell them to others, including nonmembers and non-Indians (although TLE voting rights and land assignments were limited to Rosebud tribal members.)[44]

In order to control future heirship problems, the TLE provided that land assignees could designate only one beneficiary for each 160-acre tract. If an assignee died with more than one heir and had not made such a designation, then the heirs had to decide among themselves who would take the assignment. In cases where no heirs were found eligible to assume the assignment, the stock certificates or deposits for the land were to be distributed to the heirs. The certificates themselves could also be devised by will or otherwise passed on to heirs. Although the Rosebud TLE has had problems, including periods when the corporation paid no dividends and lacked sufficient capital to redeem outstanding certificates, it has been touted as being the best tribal land-exchange program in the nation. By 1979, the corporation had acquired over four hundred thousand acres of inherited lands and issued nearly 1.9 million shares.[45]

The 1950s witnessed one of the most confused eras of Indian administration as a vocal element in Congress strove to terminate federal services to tribes. Proposals to resolve the heirship problem were also introduced in every legislative session throughout the decade, but none were given serious consideration. While withdrawal policies were being discussed and implemented on Capitol Hill, an understaffed and underfunded Indian bureau was losing ground in its effort to manage the heirship burden. In 1952, the BIA reported that out of the 115,130 allotments that remained in trust, 54,674 had been fractionated as a result of the death of the original allottee. A special outside survey team reported in 1954 that the agency faced a backlog of 2,987 probate cases and 11,000 unapproved land transactions. The probate backlog was growing at a rate of approximately 11 percent each year.[46]

As an example of a complicated heirship situation, this report cited a case where the estate of an allottee who had died in 1891 had still not been fully probated (this may have been the infamous Lake Traverse Allotment No. 1305, which this article describes more fully later). Because the process was not initiated until 1921, twenty-nine of the fifty-eight originally determined heirs had themselves died during the course of the prolonged probate procedures. As a consequence, the BIA had only managed to probate the estates of twenty-five of these decedents by 1952. By that time, the cost of the probate proceedings had doubled the appraised value of the estate. The survey team also provided examples of how minimal values and multiple interests had combined to create absurd probate situations in the case of estates left in the form of personalty, such as IIM accounts, rather than real property. In one case, a decedent left $38.22, which was divided among fifty-six heirs. Ten of the heirs received ten cents, twenty-one received three cents, and the rest received varying amounts ranging up to nine dollars.[47]

Congress enacted legislation in 1956 that permitted individual owners of allotted Indian trust land to execute a mortgage or deed of trust to such lands, subject to the approval of the secretary of the interior. This act was created to encourage Indian landholders to use commercial credit to the maximum extent possible, with the supervision of the federal government. Yet, coming after a generation of efforts focused on consolidation, this statute had the effect of reintroducing the specter of potential land loss. Tribal members eagerly took advantage of the law, mortgaging more than eight hundred fifty thousand acres in Montana and the Dakotas alone by 1986, mostly for agricultural loans. However, many of these mortgages are now in default, and the affected Indian farmers and ranchers face the danger of losing the land to their creditors through foreclosure.[48]

In 1959, the General Accounting Office (GAO), the government's independent auditing agency, found that the annual cost of managing heirship lands exceeded one million dollars. In keeping with the termination mentality of the era, the GAO blamed the problem on the government's trust relationship with the tribes and recommended the automatic issuance of fee patents to all competent heirs.[49] One agency spokesman offered that Indians were "sufficiently competent to realize the [monetary] benefit of being incompetent."[50]

In 1960, the House Committee on Interior and Insular Affairs, as it prepared to formulate corrective legislation, initiated what remains as the government's most comprehensive investigation of Indian heirship. Based on a survey of nine thousand heirs, tabulated by the Bureau of the Census, and analyzed by consultants from the Library of Congress, this study was published in two volumes in 1961. This research brought the problem into focus for congressional review and enunciated what was called the "rule of heirship land," i.e., that increased fractionalization equals increased federal costs and decreased heir income.[51]

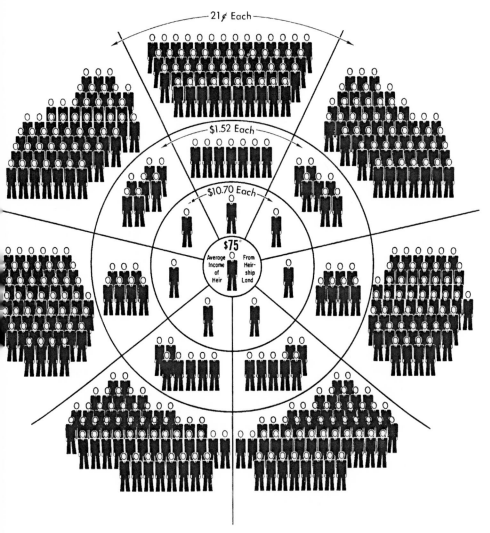

As individual income from heirship land decreases over the years,
the federal government's administrative problems increase. Estimating an
average of seven heirs per probate, this chart projects that a sole owner's income
of seventy-five dollars would diminish to twenty-one cents per heir by the
fourth generation. At the same time, the number of signatures needed
by the Bureau of Indian Affairs to lease the land would increase from
one to three hundred forty-three.

House Committee on Interior and Insular Affairs, *Indian Heirship Land Study:*
Analysis of Indian Opinion as Expressed in Questionnaires, vol. 1, 86th Cong.,
2d sess., 1960 (Washington, DC: Government Printing Office, 1961)

The committee survey found that half of the more than twelve million acres then in heirship status was owned by six or more heirs, that an equal amount of the acreage was being used by non-Indians, and that 3 percent of the land was not being used at all. An analysis of the heirs who responded from the states of North and South Dakota and Nebraska, where the largest number of allotments had been made, found that a majority did not live on a reservation. Less than one-third lived on any trust land and less than one-fifth farmed or ranched on their own heirship land. The average heir held an interest in between three and four estates, from which they received a total annual income of between fifty and one hundred dollars; the majority were also found to have interests on more than one reservation.[52]

With the Indian heirship land study in hand, Congress tried throughout the 1960s to enact legislation that might help mitigate the problem that Senator Frank Church of Idaho described as an "unconscionable mess."[53] Beginning with Church's introduction of a new heirship bill in 1961, there ensued a long round of proposals and counter-proposals between Congress and the BIA. The participants in this prolonged debate tried without success to find a solution that might balance the concerns of heirs in safeguarding their individual property rights and of tribes in preventing the further erosion of trust lands with the government's need to relieve its administrative burden. The House Subcommittee on Indian Affairs wanted to increase the constraints on individual property rights and expand administrative discretion in the issuance of fee patents. The Senate Subcommittee preferred to increase the scope of private property rights and provide increased funding for land consolidation.[54]

The BIA failed ultimately to endorse any of the congressional initiatives. Commissioner Philleo Nash proposed instead that the secretary of the interior be given wide discretion to allow tribes to purchase title to idle or unproductive heirship tracts without heir consent. Such purchases would be made on an installment plan through the issuance of "certificates of indebtedness," reminiscent of John Collier's proposed certificates of interest, that would evidence the tribe's obligation to pay heirs their proportional share of the appraised value of the allotments. The BIA's posture was that tribal and public interest in maintaining Indian ownership should not be secondary to the maximization of individual wealth. The Senate doubted the efficacy of this plan and argued that the certificates would also become a part of the heirship tangle. The Justice Department also ruled that the scheme would violate the vested property rights of individual owners by failing to provide full and just compensation prior to divesting them of their title equities.[55]

The BIA had long advocated a rule of primogeniture, which would eliminate the inheritance rights of all heirs who did not have an interest above a certain minimum and permit estates to pass to a single heir or escheat to the tribe, but it declined to support such legislation when it was introduced in 1966. Instead, it proposed an alternative primogeniture policy based on a minimum fraction of ownership, the involuntary exchange of certain interests, and the establishment of an increased loan fund for land consolidation. Unable to agree with this approach, Congress made no discernible progress toward solving the heirship problem until the 1980s.[56]

As the 1960s came to a close, Indian Commissioner Robert L. Bennett listed heirship lands among the six basic problems affecting the BIA's relations with Congress that were "of longstanding duration with little prospect of immediate solution."[57] Remedies proposed from various quarters during this period included limiting inheritance to a spouse or other single heir in a prescribed order, or to a limited number of heirs (not more than fifteen), or to just lineal descendants, or to members of the same tribe, or to those with a certain minimum Indian-blood quantum (at least one-quarter). Other proposals restricted inheritance to those heirs who had a certain minimal interest in an estate as measured by either acreage (two and one-half acres), percentage (16 or 32 percent), or appraised cash value ($100), with a provision that all interests below these thresholds would escheat to the tribe.[58]

Many observers suggested the reduction of the unanimous consent requirement for the partition or sale of allotments. Indian claims attorney Marvin J. Sonosky, for example, proposed in 1961 that the consent requirement be lowered to 50 percent of the owners in cases where there were less than ten heirs, and to 25 percent where there were ten or more interest holders. This same formula was incorporated in separate bills that were introduced in 1969 by Senators George S. McGovern of South Dakota and Henry M. Jackson of Washington. Sonosky also urged that the consent requirements for leasing heirship lands be dropped in cases where extreme fractionalization prevented effective use of the land.[59]

Several critics proposed that the federal revolving fund for tribal land consolidation be increased to as much as $55 million and that either the federal or tribal governments be empowered and funded to condemn heirship lands for consolidation purposes. Stephen Langone, a legislative analyst who studied the problem for the Joint Economic Committee of Congress in 1969, suggested that individual land consolidation programs be initiated in conjunction with tribal programs to permit the free exchange or purchase of interests between individual owners, tribes, and the government and thereby maximize the full potential for consolidation. He also proposed that heirs either be compelled to pay the administrative costs of land transactions and probates out of their estate revenues or to forfeit their proportional interests.[60]

In a 1971 study of the heirship problem in the *Washington Law Review*, Ethel J. Williams sketched the components that an ideal solution to the Indian inheritance dilemma would have to include. First, it would have to protect the equity of all heirs and guarantee the realization of a fair market value for their vested property right. An ideal solution would likewise need to safeguard tribal control over the land and at the same time permit it to be put to its most productive use. From the standpoint of federal administration, an optimum solution would also reduce the costs of managing trust land, thereby saving the taxpayers money.[61]

While Congress tried to grapple with possible solutions to the heirship problem, the Department of the Interior once again revised the administrative structure for Indian probates. On 1 July 1970, the Office of Hearings and Appeals was created and, as part of it, the Interior Board of Indian Appeals (IBIA) and the Hearings Division. The Hearings and Appeals Office was made independent of the Office of the Solicitor (it now functions under the assistant secretary of the interior for policy, management, and budget). The IBIA was established as a three-member, quasi-judicial tribunal to review appeals of final decisions made by the BIA. The function of the former examiners of inheritance was transferred from the BIA to the Hearings Division. The hearing examiners, who now have the title of administrative law judges for Indian probate, continued their authority to conduct public hearings and make initial decisions, which were then made appealable to the IBIA.[62]

The authority to approve Indian wills was brought under this new structure on 1 March 1971 when the secretary of the interior delegated to the departmental solicitor the duty of examining wills and issuing reports on them to Indian agency superintendents. This authority was further delegated to regional and field solicitors. It included the power to approve the form of wills pertaining to trust property only. The department also issued guidelines in 1971 for the drafting and approving of such wills. Indians who wished to devise both fee and trust property were encouraged to have a single will drawn up by a private attorney because government agents do not have the authority to approve wills involving fee property and the wills of trust property do not require their approval as long as they are valid otherwise. However, two separate wills are permissible in some jurisdictions.[63]

Indian agency superintendents continued to be the first link in the probate chain, functioning in a manner similar to executors or administrators of estates under state law, by preparing essential data on decedents and their trust property for the administrative law judges in their region. This information generally includes an inventory of property, a family history, and a listing of any claims against the estate. The gathering of these data is assisted by the BIA's regional computerized title plants, which store information on all federal Indian realty. At present, there are seven regional administrative law judge offices and five regional BIA title plants. The reservations in the Dakotas, for example, are served by administrative law judges in Rapid City and Minneapolis and by the title plant in the Aberdeen Area Office of the BIA. If the decedent died intestate leaving a small estate of less than one thousand dollars in an IIM account, the agency superintendent has the authority to hold an informal hearing to determine heirs and to make what is called a "summary distribution" of the property.[64]

In 1980, Congress provided for a limited expansion of the class of people to whom an Indian could devise property by will. Because various states had changed their laws to provide for spousal inheritance of the entirety of an estate in cases of intestacy (to the exclusion of other descendants), this statute permitted tribal members to will their property not only to immediate heirs but also to any lineal descendant or to any other Indian person who might be eligible to hold an interest in trust property.[65]

Three of the smaller Sioux reservations in South Dakota provide examples that illustrate the extreme level to which fractionalization and administrative complexity had risen by the early 1980s. In 1982, Allotment No. 1305, consisting of eighty acres on the Lake Traverse reservation of the Sisseton-Wahpeton Sioux Tribe, was found to have 439 heirs. The lowest common denominator (LCD) used to determine fractional interests in this tract was 3,394,923,840,000. A forty-acre portion of the allotment was then being leased at a rate of $1,080. A breakdown of the lease distribution, which cost the BIA an estimated $17,560 per year to administer, revealed that more than two-thirds of the heirs received less than one dollar per year from their interest in the property. Approximately one-third realized less than five cents, and the interest of one hundred of the heirs entitled them to a fraction of one cent. The largest interest holder received $82.85, but the value of the smallest owner's share was $.0000564. At that rate, it would have taken 177 years for the smallest heir to earn one cent, and 88,562 years to accumulate five dollars, which was the minimum amount for which the BIA would issue a check. If this forty-acre parcel could have been sold at its appraised value of eight thousand dollars, the share of the smallest owner would have been $.000418, and if it had been physically partitioned, this heir would have received title to approximately thirteen square inches.[66]

A survey of thirty of the most heavily fractionated allotments on the Lake

Traverse reserve, conducted by this writer in 1982, revealed that the average estate had 196 heirs and that the average heir had interests in fourteen other allotments. If these tracts would have been sold in that year, the average payment to the smallest heir would have been thirty-six cents, and if partitioned, the smallest heirs would have been entitled to an average of 174 square feet. At the average 1982 lease rate, it would have required these heirs an average of 1,344 years to realize five dollars from these estates.[67]

In 1983, a forty-acre allotment on the Yankton Sioux reservation (No. 10326A) was found to have 1,075 owners, including 13 non-Indians who held interests in fee title (2 of them as life estates, meaning they had the right to ownership throughout their lifetimes). The Indian heirs were from thirteen different reservations, most (640) from the Pine Ridge Sioux reserve. The LCD for this allotment was 1,030,382,265,600, and only 8 of the owners had a share of 2 percent or more. The tract was not being leased, but if it had been it would have cost the BIA approximately forty-three thousand dollars to distribute the annual lease income, which may not have been more than one thousand dollars. Although this allotment had more than twice as many heirs as Lake Traverse Allotment No. 1305, the proportional share of the smallest heirs was much greater. Nevertheless, if the tract had been leased for one thousand dollars, it would have taken 16,340 years for the smallest owners to earn five dollars. The allotment would have to have been sold for $30,334 in order for these owners to receive one cent. If the tract had been physically partitioned, these owners could have claimed only sixty-seven square inches or less than one-half square foot.[68]

As a final example, Allotment No. 56-A, a seventy-two-acre tract on the Crow Creek Sioux Reservation, had 502 heirs in 1983, only 6 of whom owned a share of 2 percent or more. The LCD for this allotment was fifty-seven digits long:

422,928,436,064,611,462,839,873,060,573,527,180,037,703,675,438,
004,160,000.

Expressed as a fraction, the share of the smallest owners was
685,843,200/1,375,139,991,799,967,953,796,391,435,811,164,924,408,
493,364,411,150.

Yet, these minimal heirs owned a greater proportional share of this tract than did the smallest owners of either Lake Traverse Allotment No. 1305 or Yankton Allotment No. 10326-A.[69]

Interest among legislators in providing a general solution to the heirship problem, which had languished throughout the 1970s, peaked again in 1982.

A bill (HR 5856) introduced by Congressman Morris K. Udall of Arizona on 23 February of that year moved at surprising speed through Congress without much public attention. Staff members of the House Committee on Interior and Insular Affairs, of which Udall was chairman and Franklin Ducheneaux, a member of the Cheyenne River Sioux Tribe of South Dakota, was chief counsel, drafted the bill. Apparently, the legislation was proposed with little or no outside initiative, either from the tribes or the Interior Department.[70]

Aimed primarily at providing the first general authority for tribes to establish land consolidation programs and the adoption of tribal inheritance codes, the Udall bill, without proposing any additional appropriations, contained several provisions for at least an initial mitigation of the heirship problem. Of these, the one that would prove the most controversial was also the only one that was involuntary on the part of the tribes. It provided that upon the death of an owner of Indian trust land, any interest in the decedent's fractionated estate that amounted to 2 percent or less of the total acreage of a given tract and which had not earned at least one hundred dollars in income within the year prior to death, would escheat to the tribe having jurisdiction rather than descend to such minimal heirs. It provided further that these small interests would escheat whether or not they had been devised previously to the heirs by a will.[71]

The House interior committee held a hearing on the Udall bill on 20 May 1982 to which it invited representatives from only three tribes to testify, all of which were from the Southwest, a region with relatively few allotted reservations. The committee then attached the bill to one that had been introduced on 19 February 1981 by Senator Quentin N. Burdick of North Dakota (S 503) to establish a land consolidation plan and tribal inheritance code for the Devils Lake Sioux Tribe of the Fort Totten Reservation in his home state. The House then passed its amended version of the combined bills on 6 December 1982 and sent it to the Senate. Because it was so late in the extended "lame duck" session of the Ninety-seventh Congress, the Senate passed the legislation without referring it to its Select Committee on Indian Affairs. Reportedly, this procedure was followed at the urging of the committee members themselves, who were afraid that they might not again have an opportunity to enact such important legislation regarding Indian lands. Yet, in fact, the whole strategy of the architects of the bill appears to have been to pass the measures with a minimum of debate. Apparently, they concluded that it would be better to get some kind of solution in place, and correct its weaknesses later through amendatory legislation, rather than to run the risk of having these proposals bog down in controversy as so many previous heirship bills had done. Thus, with President Ronald

Reagan's signature on 12 January 1983, the Indian Land Consolidation Act of 1983 (ILCA) became law.[72]

Beyond its escheat provision for minimal estate shares, the ILCA extended to all federally recognized tribes the provisions of Section 5 of the Indian Reorganization Act regarding the exchange of lands, whether or not a tribe had originally voted against the IRA. The consent requirement for the tribal purchase of allotted lands was lowered from 100 percent to more than 50 percent of the owners or more than 50 percent of the undivided interests in any tract where there were fifteen or more owners. Exempted from this provision was any tract for which the acquisition was objected to by those owners who held 50 percent or more of the total interests. Any Indian owner who was in actual use and possession of the tract was given the right to purchase it by matching the tribal offer. Finally, the statute authorized tribes to adopt their own inheritance codes to provide more restrictive limitations than were previously found in general federal law on the rights of nonmembers and non-Indians to inherit trust land within the tribe's jurisdiction. However, the right of non-Indian and nonmember spouses and children to retain inherited interests in a life estate was protected. In cases where an Indian decedent devised interests by will to persons ineligible to inherit under the new tribal codes, the law gave the tribe an opportunity to purchase such interests prior to probate. Such devisees were given the option of either accepting the money or retaining a life estate in their interests.[73]

The BIA endorsed the ILCA generally, even though it had recommended several technical amendments. For example, it suggested an escheat provision that would have affected owners of less than a 2 1/2 percent interest whose total interest was determined to be worth less than two hundred dollars. However, attorneys within the Indian division of the Interior Department solicitor's office, and particularly Wayne Nordwall who represented that office at the congressional hearings, favored the legislation more enthusiastically.[74] After the legislation was enacted, John W. Fritz, the deputy assistant secretary of the interior for Indian affairs, who functioned in the position previously titled the commissioner of Indian affairs, lauded the ILCA as a "legislative milestone."[75]

While preparing the final amended version of the Udall bill for floor votes, the printers made several transcription errors. As a result, two sections of the actual document that the House and Senate passed, and which the president signed into law, were garbled beyond comprehension. Although the printing was corrected by those responsible for codifying the statute, those members of the House and Senate committees who had supported the measure felt obliged to have Congress enact corrective legislation. Accordingly, Representative Udall introduced a joint resolution (H.J. Res. 158) to make technical corrections in the ILCA on 23 February 1983, just six weeks after the original bill had been signed.[76]

In the meantime, the ILCA had become effective immediately upon its being signed into law. The estates of tribal members who died after 12 January 1983 were thus made subject to the escheat provisions of the statute, which had been set forth in Section 207 of the act. On 3 March 1983, the BIA issued a memorandum to its area directors advising them of the escheat provisions and providing them with instructions to follow until such time as regulations implementing the law could be promulgated fully. Tribal members concerned that their tribe would take away their interests were advised to either purchase additional shares from co-owners to bring their ownership above 2 percent, convey their interests to co-owners or relatives and reserve a life estate in the tract, or, if feasible, partition the tract in such a way as to enlarge the owner's proportional share.[77]

The joint resolution to clear up garbled wording in the ILCA passed the House on 19 April 1983 without further hearings and was referred to the Senate Select Committee on Indian Affairs for consideration. Prompted by adverse tribal reactions to the ILCA, the Senate committee held a hearing on the bill on 26 July 1983, at which time a number of amendments were proposed.[78] Most tribal representatives who testified at the Senate hearing were critical of the ILCA and the manner in which it was enacted. Norman Hollow, chairman of the Assiniboine and Sioux tribes of the Fort Peck reservation in Montana, for example, criticized Congress for not providing greater consultation with the tribes when the ILCA was first being considered in 1982. He called for the repeal of the act and the scheduling of a series of field hearings in order "to grant the opportunity for reservation people to appear and express their concern."[79]

Of all the sections of the land consolidation law, tribal leaders and their attorneys were most vociferous in their objections to the involuntary escheat provisions. "We do not want what it gives us," stated Paul Iron Cloud, a member of the Oglala Sioux Tribe of the Pine Ridge reservation in South Dakota. "We, as a tribe, do not want to take over people's land without compensation."[80] On Pine Ridge, the nation's most allotted Indian reserve, the BIA estimated that approximately 51 percent of the 95,019 owners who held interest in the reservation's 11,330 allotted tracts would be subject to the 2-percent restriction embodied in Section 207 of the ILCA.[81]

Oglala Sioux tribal members Mary Irving, Patrick Pumpkin Seed, and Eileen Bissonette each had parents or uncles who died within six months of the enactment of the ILCA to whom they or their children were potential heirs or named devisees. After being notified that a probate hearing had been scheduled for the week of 24 October 1983 to determine if the Oglala Sioux Tribe had the right to escheat to interests in the Chester Irving estate that might otherwise have descended to her, Mary Irving filed suit against Secretary of the Interior James Watt in the United States District Court for South Dakota on behalf of herself and the interests represented by Pumpkin Seed and Bissonette. The complaint claimed that Section 207 of the ILCA represented a taking of property to which tribal members had a vested right without just compensation in violation of the Fifth Amendment to the United States Constitution. It also requested both preliminary and permanent injunctions against enforcement of the escheat provision by the Department of the Interior.[82]

This case was bound to break new legal ground, for no previous decisions had ever addressed a sovereign's attempt to abolish inheritance completely and require certain property to escheat at death. After deliberating over the possible precedents, Judge Andrew W. Bogue articulated, probably unknowingly, the same view of Indian inheritance that John Collier had expressed a half-century before. He ruled that the plaintiffs had only a mere "expectancy of heirship" rather than a vested property right entitled to constitutional protection. He concluded further that since Congress had the plenary power to enact statutes affecting heirship, the escheat provision of Section 207 did not violate the taking clause of the Constitution.[83]

In a footnote to his opinion, Judge Bogue disagreed with the policy implemented by the ILCA. He stated that the argument that tribal ownership of heirship land would "benefit the Indian population as a whole is simply not valid in this court's experience" since the benefits derived from tribal lands "do not filter down to the vast majority of the Indian people" on the reservations. Because in his view land consolidation would not function as contemplated, he opined that Congress "would be well-advised to examine closely the practical effect of legislation such as [the ILCA]."[84]

Attorneys for the plaintiffs began immediately to plan an appeal of the Bogue decision. In the meantime, Congress had suspended further consideration of the joint resolution to amend the ILCA until the summer of 1984. On 31 July, the Senate select committee held a second hearing in order to measure views of the ILCA after it had been implemented for some time. In response to concerns raised during its hearings, the committee recommended several changes in the original legislation. The House and Senate agreed to the new language in early October, and President Reagan signed the amended and comprehensible ILCA on 30 October 1984.[85]

The new legislation loosened the restrictive language of Section 207, permitting minimal interests to be devised by will to other owners of the same tract and allowing for a rebuttal of the statutory presumption that a minimal interest was without significant economic value. While the 2-percent cutoff was maintained, the valuation requirement of the interests was changed from having earned less than one hundred dollars in the year preceding the decedent's death to being "incapable" of earning less than one hundred dollars in any one of the five years from the date of the decedent's death. This new language was aimed at protecting minimal interests in mineral or timber lands, where revenue values were subject to wide fluctuation. Where the minimal interest had earned less than one hundred dollars in any of the five years preceding death, the statute presumed, subject to rebuttal, that it was incapable of earning one hundred dollars in any one of the five years following death. In addition, the new language allowed tribes to adopt codes providing for the disposition of minimal interests that could take precedence over the escheat provisions of Section 207, provided these tribal laws prevented the further descent or fractionalization of such minimal interests.[86]

The amended ILCA permitted tribes to purchase one or more interests in an allotment without having to buy an entire tract and revised the consent requirement for such purchases. Whereas the original law required the consent of a simple majority of the owners of the undivided interests in any tract where there were fifteen or more owners, the amended statute permitted the tribal purchase of "any tract" with the consent of the ownership, regardless of how many interest holders there were. The right to match a tribal offer for purchase of such a tract was limited further to owners who had been in actual use and possession of the tract at least three years prior to the tribal initiative. If within five years of a purchase by an actual user the tract was offered for sale or proposed for removal of its trust restrictions, the law now provided that the tribe would have 180 days in which to acquire the property by paying the owner the fair market value of the tract. Finally, the new language further restricted the right of nonmembers or non-Indians to receive a life estate in their inherited interests. This right was limited to a spouse and/or children whose interest equaled 10 percent or more of a tract of land or who actually occupied the tract as a home at the time of the decedent's death.[87]

Just eleven days prior to the enactment of the ILCA amendments, President Reagan had signed legislation approving a new inheritance code for the Sisseton-Wahpeton Sioux Tribe of the Lake Traverse reservation in North and South Dakota. This statute was remarkable, not only because of its restrictive provisions, but also because it established the precedent that tribes might ignore the general provisions of the ILCA and continue to seek specific legislation for their heirship problems. The new Lake Traverse code was much stricter than the ILCA, limiting inheritance to enrolled tribal members and providing for the escheat to the tribe of parcels of two and one-half acres or less regardless of value. Yet, the BIA had opposed the legislation. Because the ILCA was enacted, in part, to eliminate the necessity of individual tribes having to obtain congressional approval for their land consolidation and tribal inheritance programs, the bureau felt strongly that the tribe should adopt its code through the ILCA provisions. However, the Sisseton-Wahpeton Tribe deserved credit for taking the initiative in attempting to solve the heirship problem on what has historically been one of the worst fractionated reservations. It also merited praise for managing to convince its membership that strict measures were necessary. Tribal attorney Bertram Hirsch and former tribal chairman Jerry Flute credited this success to strong tribal leadership and to a series of public forums that the tribal government held to discuss proposals.[88]

Within a few days of the enactment of the ILCA amendments, the plaintiffs in the Irving case appealed the district court's decision to the Eighth Circuit Court of Appeals in Saint Louis. The appellants did not assert that their own property rights had been taken unconstitutionally, but rather that their decedent's right to pass the property at death had been taken. Almost six months later, on 29 March 1985, Circuit Judge John R. Gibson rendered his decision in the case of *Irving v. Clark* (Secretary of the Interior William Clark). In common with Judge Bogue, Judge Gibson also held that the plaintiffs had only an expectancy of heirship and not a vested property right at the time that the ILCA was enacted and that Congress had the power to alter and condition rights that had not been vested in individual tribal members. However, he concluded that since Section 207 did not provide for compensation to the estates of the decedents for the interests that were subject to the escheat provision, it was in violation of the Fifth Amendment. Without explanation, Judge Gibson went on to declare that not only was the original version of Section 207 unconstitutional, but the 1984 version was also, even though the amended provisions were not an issue before the court in this case.[89]

The federal government, in the name of Secretary of the Interior Donald P. Hodel, then proceeded to appeal the circuit court's decision to the United States Supreme Court. On 8 May 1987, Justice Sandra Day O'Connor delivered the opinion of the court in the case of *Hodel v. Irving*, in which all of the other justices concurred in three separate written opinions. The court ruled that the original version of Section 207 amounted to a taking of the property of the decedents without just compensation. Although it held that the collective economic impact of the escheat provision could be substantial, even though the income generated by any single estate might be minimal, the court found dubious the argument that the original plaintiffs had any "investment-backed expectations" in the estates of the decedents.[90]

The court found further that the character of the government's regulation in this case was "extraordinary" because it amounted to "virtually the abrogation of the right to pass on property to one's heirs, which right has been part of the Anglo-American legal system since feudal times." Even the government as defendant conceded that the total abrogation of the right to pass property was unprecedented and probably unconstitutional. In his concurring opinion, Justice John Paul Stevens chided Congress for the "abruptness and lack of explanation" with which it enacted Section 207 without adequate hearings or floor debate. He stated further that because the escheat provision was effective immediately upon enactment of the ILCA, the government deprived the decedents in this case of the due process of law required under the Fifth Amendment by failing to provide for an adequate "grace period" in which they would have had fair opportunity to arrange for a consolidation of their interests or otherwise avoid the consequences of escheat.[91]

Finally, the court expressed the view that the circuit court's ruling that the 1984 amended version of Section 207 was also unconstitutional was "at best, dicta," since none of the property scheduled to escheat in this case would have done so pursuant to the amended statute. While the court offered no opinion as to the constitutionality of the amended Section 207, it did discuss appropriate methods for resolving the heirship problem. It suggested that the further compounding of interests could be minimized by establishing regulations that would abolish the descent of such minimal interests by rule of intestacy, thereby compelling owners to designate an heir by will in order to prevent an escheat.[92]

Fourteen months after the Irving case was decided, the amended Section 207 escheat provisions were also challenged in federal court. On 26 July 1988, Sonya Curley, a member of the Navajo Nation, filed suit in United States District Court in New Mexico against Secretary of the Interior Hodel. As an heir whose potential inherited interests in five allotments were found to be subject to escheat to the Navajo Nation, Curley claimed that the escheat provisions of the amended ILCA also violated the due process clause of the Fifth Amendment by not allowing an adequate grace period in which to arrange for the consolidation of fractionated interests. She also claimed that escheat violated the taking clause by depriving decedents of their property without payment of just compensation. The federal government agreed eventually to an out-of-court settlement of this case, largely because it surmised that it could not receive a favorable decision on the issue of a grace period, which in this case amounted to the five months between the enactment of the 1984 amendments and the death of Curley's father.[93]

Although the amended Section 207 would appear to be ripe for further legal challenges, and a BIA memorandum of 16 June 1988 even anticipated such litigation, no further suits have been filed. Factors of money and time may now inhibit additional court action. No economic incentive exists for potential heirs of minuscule property interests to pursue such litigation, and as more time passes, the issue of a grace period becomes less subject to challenge. However, as more escheats take place under the law and reluctant tribes are more often placed in the position of becoming involuntary owners of an increased number of fractional interests, the tribes may question whether the United States as a sovereign has the authority to dictate to other sovereign entities (the tribes) regarding the kinds of property to which they must accept ownership.[94]

The BIA held the escheat provisions in abeyance between October 1985 and June 1988 pending the outcome of the Irving case and a ruling by the Justice Department regarding the constitutionality of the amended statute.[95] In a memorandum of 4 March 1988, John O. McGinnis, the deputy assistant attorney general, opined that the new Section 207 would survive a constitutional challenge under both the taking and due process clauses as long as owners of inherited interests "had an adequate opportunity to adjust their affairs to avoid forfeiture of their interests."[96]

Between June of 1988 and the spring of 1991, more than twenty-one thousand inherited interests were escheated under the provisions of the amended Section 207. It is estimated that through this number of escheats the BIA has avoided the addition of between thirty-five and fifty thousand new heirs. Thus, the ILCA appears to be making an incremental dent in the heirship problem. As is evident from the previous example of Yankton Allotment No. 10326-A, all but 8 of the 1,075 interests in that tract in 1983 would now be subject to escheat. Yet, BIA agency realty personnel have indicated that the escheat provisions have served to increase their administrative workload. They must now provide additional data to the administrative law judges before estates can be probated, including the amount, in both the fractional and decimal form, of the decedent's ownership in each tract in which an inherited interest was held. For each tract in which the decedent held a 2 percent or less interest, they must also determine the amount of income that might have accrued to that interest during the five years preceding death.[97] While the escheat provisions should eventually reduce the workload of agency staff (since the interests that escheat and the new heirs that are avoided both mean that there will less division of estates on paper in the future), for the time being they represent an increased burden on personnel who are already overworked.

For their part, tribal leaders have been reluctant to implement the voluntary provisions of the ILCA. As of 1991, no tribe has yet adopted an inheritance code under the act, and only two tribes, the Cherokee Nation of Oklahoma and the Pueblo of Nambe in New Mexico, have had land consolidation programs approved under the law. In neither case, however, did the desire or necessity to reduce heirship interests motivate the tribes, for neither has serious problems in this regard.[98]

In 1988, Margo S. Miller, a graduate student at Harvard University's Kennedy School of Government, conducted an analysis of tribal responses to the ILCA. She found that tribal leaders were generally confused or uninformed about the law, largely because the BIA had been slow to disseminate information and guidelines pertaining to the statute. Miller also discovered that the tribal leadership, for a variety of reasons, had chosen not to take any action. Some tribes had no need for the law, since they either had no allotments or had already adopted inheritance codes and/or consolidation programs. Others had chosen to focus on other priorities, such as the development of natural resources or the purchase of land within their reservation. While several tribal leaders felt that land consolidation programs and tribal laws limiting inheritance would serve to stir up conflict and alienate their members, others stated that their tribes did not have sufficient means to purchase fractionated interests, especially since the legislation did not provide funds for that purpose. Several leaders expressed both their continued frustration with the magnitude of the heirship problem and its seeming insolubility and their skepticism of the incremental solution offered by the ILCA.[99]

As of this writing, the BIA has yet to publish regulations implementing the ILCA, but it currently has four task forces working on various aspects of heirship and probate problems. Among the goals of these task forces is the development of a program that would allow the BIA, for the first time in its history, to provide estate planning and administration as part of its technical assistance to tribes and tribal members. Another goal is to develop a model code of inheritance that would allow tribes to conform with the movement of the states toward the development of uniform inheritance codes. The BIA also hopes eventually to provide improved guidance regarding such matters as life estates, gift conveyances, and alternatives to escheat.[100]

The Indian Land Consolidation Act falls short of the ideal solution to the heirship problem postulated by Ethel Williams in 1971. Although it gives tribes a greater opportunity to retain control and make more productive use of trust lands, it neither protects the equities of all owners of heirship land interests nor offers a short-range reduction of federal costs. The potential for further legal challenges and the reluctance of tribal leaders to implement the statute now casts a cloud over the future of both this solution to the historic heirship problem and the tribal land consolidation efforts it was designed to encourage.

NOTES

1. 24 Stat 388; 36 Stat 855; 48 Stat 984; 96 Stat 2515; 98 Stat 3171; Hodel v. Irving, 107 S. Ct. 2076 (1987).

2. For a further explanation of this notion, which is attributed to an hypothesis of the philosopher Emer de Vattel, see Herbert T. Hoover, "The Sioux Agreement of 1889 and Its Aftermath," *South Dakota History* 19 (Spring 1989): 73–74.

3. Markku Henriksson, *The Indian on Capitol Hill: Indian Legislation and the United States Congress, 1862–1907* (Helsinki: Finnish Historical Society, 1988), 165–67.

4. J. P. Kinney, *A Continent Lost—A Civilization Won: Indian Land Tenure in America* (Baltimore: Johns Hopkins Press, 1937), 82; 24 Stat 388. For a detailed description and analysis of the General Allotment Act and the reform environment in which it was enacted, see Henry E. Fritz, *The Movement for Indian Assimilation, 1860–1890* (Philadelphia: University of Pennsylvania Press, 1963); Robert Winston Mardock, *The Reformers and the American Indian* (Columbia: University of Missouri Press, 1971); Francis Paul Prucha, *American Indian Policy in Crisis: Christian Reformers and the Indian, 1865–1900* (Norman: University of Oklahoma Press, 1976); Francis Paul Prucha, *The Great Father: The United States Government and the American Indians*, 2 vols. (Lincoln: University of Nebraska Press, 1984), 2:659–86; Wilcomb E. Washburn, *The Assault on Indian Tribalism: The General Allotment Law (Dawes Act) of 1887* (Philadelphia: J. P. Lippincott Co., 1975); D. S. Otis, *The Dawes Act and the Allotment of Indian Lands*, ed. Francis Paul Prucha (Norman: University of Oklahoma Press, 1973); and Loring Benson Priest, *Uncle Sam's Stepchildren: The Reformation of United States Indian Policy* (1942; repr., Lincoln: University of Nebraska Press, 1975).

5. 24 Stat 388.

6. Henriksson, *Indian on Capitol Hill*, 170, 177.

7. *Felix S. Cohen's Handbook of Federal Indian Law, 1982 Ed.* (Charlottesville, VA: Michie, Bobbs-Merrill, 1982), 130, 616; Stephen A. Langone, "The Heirship Land Problem and its Effect on the Indian, the Tribe, and Effective Utilization," in Joint Economic Committee, Subcommittee on Economy in Government, *Toward Economic Development for Native American Communities, a Compendium of Papers*, Joint Committee Print, vol. 2 (Washington, DC: Government Printing Office, 1969), 522; 7 Stat 150, 156, 185; 10 Stat 1038, 1043, 1053.

8. Otis, *Dawes Act*, 50–51; Prucha, *American Indian Policy in Crisis*, 241–44; Priest, *Uncle Sam's Stepchildren*, 178–79; 22 Stat 341; *Cohen's Handbook of Federal Indian Law*, 616.

9. Henriksson, *Indian on Capitol Hill*, 173, 178; Leonard A. Carlson, *Indians, Bureaucrats, and Land: The Dawes Act and the Decline of Indian Farming*, Contributions in Economics and Economic History, no. 36 (Westport, CT: Greenwood Press, 1981), 64; Stanley Norman Murray, "A Study of Indian Land Relations as Illustrated through the History of the Lake Traverse Reservation Sioux" (master's thesis, University of Wisconsin, 1953), 187; 25 Stat 611.

10. 15 Stat 637; 25 Stat 890; Henriksson, *Indian on Capitol Hill*, 183.

11. 32 Stat 744; 26 Stat 794; U.S. Department of the Interior, Office of Hearings and Appeals, *Digest of Federal Indian Probate Law*, 1972, 17; *Cohen's Handbook of Federal Indian Law*, 633–34, 634n.15.

12. House Committee on Interior and Insular Affairs, *Indian Heirship Land Study: Analysis of Indian Opinion as Expressed in Questionnaires*, 2 vols., 86th Cong., 2d sess., 1960 (Washington, DC: Government Printing Office, 1961), 1:1; Langone, "Heirship Land Problem," 525; Burt Edward Powell, "Land Tenure on Northern Plains Indian Reservations" (PhD diss., Duke University, 1975), 338.

13. *Cohen's Handbook of Federal Indian Law*, 133; Prucha, *American Indian Policy in Crisis*, 257; Prucha, *Great Father*, 2:668n; 26 Stat 794.

14. Lone Wolf v. Hitchcock, 187 U.S. 553 (1903); 33 Stat 254; U.S. Department of the Interior, Natural Resources Board, "Indian Land Tenure, Economic Status, and Population Trends," pt. 10 of *The Report on Land Planning* (Washington, DC: Government Printing Office, 1935), 6.

15. See Carlson, *Indians, Bureaucrats, and Land*; and Henriksson, *Indian on Capitol Hill*.

16. John Fredericks III, "Indian Lands: Financing Indian Agriculture: Mortgaged Indian Lands and the Federal Trust Responsibility," *American Indian Law Review* 14, no. 1 (1989): 105–06.

17. Prucha, *Great Father*, 2:671; Michael L. Lawson, "Indian Heirship Lands: The Lake Traverse Experience," *South Dakota History* 12 (Winter 1982): 218–19.

18. Lawson, "Indian Heirship Lands," 219; *Cohen's Handbook of Federal Indian Law*, 134–35; Otis, *Dawes Act*, 107–08; U.S. Department of the Interior, Office of Indian Affairs, *Annual Report of the Commissioner of Indian Affairs to the Secretary of the Interior for the Year 1886* (Washington, DC: Government Printing Office, 1886), xix.

19. Prucha, *Great Father*, 2:672; 26 Stat 794; 28 Stat 286; 30 Stat 62; 31 Stat 221; 36 Stat 855; 41 Stat 1225; "Indian Land Tenure, Economic Status, and Population Trends," 7.

20. "Indian Land Tenure, Economic Status, and Population Trends," 2, 7.

21. Roy W. Meyer, *History of the Santee Sioux: United States Indian Policy on Trial* (Lincoln: University of Nebraska Press, 1967), 327, 332; Powell, "Land Tenure on Northern Plains Indian Reservations," 338.

22. 30 Stat 990; 31 Stat 790; 31 Stat 1083; 33 Stat 65.

23. 32 Stat 245; 34 Stat 182; "Indian Land Tenure, Economic Status, and Population Trends," 6, 15–16.

24. *Cohen's Handbook of Federal Indian Law*, 615–16, 631; Prucha, *Great Father*, 2:874.

25. In re Heff, 197 U.S. 488, 509 (1905).

26. 34 Stat 182.

27. Richmond L. Clow and Janet McDonnell, Institute of Indian Studies, University of South Dakota, "A Report on the Bureau of Indian Affairs' Fee Patenting and Cancelling Policies, 1900–1942," prepared for the Bureau of Indian Affairs, Aberdeen Area Office, Branch of Rights Protection, 1 June 1981, 11–13, 18, 27–28, 31, 39–40, 43–44; 44 Stat 1247; 46 Stat 1205; "Indian Land Tenure, Economic Status, and Population Trends," 6.

28. Prucha, *Great Father*, 2:673-74; Raymond Wilson, *Ohiyesa: Charles Eastman, Santee Sioux* (Urbana: University of Illinois Press, 1983), 120–28.

29. 36 Stat 855; Ethel J. Williams, "Too Little Land, Too Many Heirs—The Indian Heirship Land Problem," *Washington Law Review* 46 (1971): 723–24; *Cohen's Handbook of Federal Indian Law*, 634–35.

30. *Digest of Federal Indian Probate Law*, vii–viii.

31. 70 Stat 62.

32. Frank C. Miller, introduction to Lewis Meriam, et al., *The Problem of Indian Administration* (1928; repr., New York: Johnson Reprint Corp., 1971), ix. See also Donald T. Critchlow, "Lewis Meriam, Expertise, and Indian Reform," *Historian* 43 (May 1981): 325–31.

33. Meriam, et al., *Problem of Indian Administration*, 40–41.

34. Powell, "Land Tenure on Northern Plains Indian Reservations," 339–41; Senate Committee on Interior and Insular Affairs, *Purchase of Allotments of Deceased Indians*, 72d Cong., 2d sess., 1933, S. Rep. 1203.

35. Powell, "Land Tenure on Northern Plains Indian Reservations," 341–43.

36. 48 Stat 984; 49 Stat 1967.

37. *Report of the Commissioner of Indian Affairs*, 1934, 78–80.

38. Langone, "Heirship Land Problem," 525; "Indian Land Tenure, Economic Status, and Population Trends," 6.

39. Lawson, "Indian Heirship Lands," 226.

40. "Resume of Proceedings," Conference on Indian Allotted and Heirship Land Problem, 14–17 Aug. 1938, Glacier Park, MT, Department of the Interior, Natural Resources Library, Washington, DC.

41. *Digest of Federal Indian Probate Law*, viii.

42. Ibid.; House Committee on Interior and Insular Affairs, *Survey Report on the Bureau of Indian Affairs* (Washington, DC: Government Printing Office, 1954), 15.

43. 88 Stat 1468; 98 Stat 2411; 94 Stat 537; 96 Stat 2515.

44. Frank Pommersheim and Anita Remerowski, *Reservation Street Law: A Handbook of Indian Rights and Responsibilities* (Rosebud, SD: Sinte Gleska College Press, 1979), 145.

45. Ibid., 145–49; Williams, "Too Little Land, Too Many Heirs," 731.

46. *Survey Report on the Bureau of Indian Affairs*, 14, 16, 33.

47. Ibid., 14–15.

48. 70 Stat 62; Fredericks, "Indian Lands: Financing Indian Agriculture," 106–07.

49. Powell, "Land Tenure on Northern Plains Indian Reservations," 346–47, 346n.

50. John R. Kurelich, speaking to Senate Committee on Interior and Insular Affairs, 9–10 August 1961 in *Indian Heirship Land Problem: Hearings before the Subcommittee on Indian Affairs on S 1392*, 87th Cong., 1st sess. (Washington, DC: Government Printing Office, 1961), 84.

51. *Indian Heirship Land Study*, 1:xiii–xv.

52. Ibid., 1:53-54; Williams, "Too Little Land, Too Many Heirs," 712.

53. *Indian Heirship Land Problem*, 72.

54. *A Bill Related to the Indian Heirship Land Problem*, 87th Cong., 1st sess., 1961, S 1392; Powell, "Land Tenure on Northern Plains Indian Reservations," 348–50. The separate approaches of the House, Senate, and BIA are evident in the Senate Committee on Interior and Insular Affairs hearings entitled *Indian Heirship Land Problem*.

55. Powell, "Land Tenure on Northern Plains Indian Reservations," 349–50; John A. Carver, Jr., Assistant Secretary of the Interior, to Senator Clinton P. Anderson, Chairman, Committee on Interior and Insular Affairs, 10 July 1961, and Byron R. White, Deputy Attorney General, to David E. Bell, Director, Bureau of the Budget, 8 Aug. 1961, both in *Indian Heirship Land Problem*, 7–9, 12–14.

56. Powell, "Land Tenure on Northern Plains Indian Reservations," 350; House Committee on Interior and Insular Affairs, *Indian Fractionated Land Problems: Hearings before the Subcommittee on Indian Affairs on HR 11113*, 89th Cong., 2d sess. (Washington, DC: Government Printing Office, 1966).

57. Robert L. Bennett, quoted in Prucha, *Great Father*, 2:1100.

58. Williams, "Too Little Land, Too Many Heirs," 726–27; Langone, "Heirship Land Problem," 543; Bertram E. Hirsh, "Draft of a Bill Pertaining to the Inheritance of Trust or Restricted or Fee land on the Lake Traverse Reservation, North Dakota and South Dakota, and for other Purposes" (Floral Park, NY, 1981).

59. *Indian Heirship Land Problem*, 161–62; *A Bill Relating to the Indian Revolving Loan Fund and the Indian Heirship Land Problem*, 91st Cong., 1st sess., 1969, S 522; *A Bill to Provide for the Resolution of the Indian Fractionated Ownership Problem, and for other Purposes*, 91st Cong., 1st sess., 1969, S 920.

60. *Bill Relating to the Revolving Loan Fund*; Williams, "Too Little Land, Too Many Heirs," 733–34; Hirsh, "Draft of a Bill Pertaining to Inheritance"; Langone, "Heirship Land Problem," 543–44.

61. Williams, "Too Little Land, Too Many Heirs," 724–25.

62. *Digest of Federal Indian Probate Law*, viii–ix; *Cohen's Handbook of Federal Indian Law*, 636–37.

63. *Cohen's Handbook of Federal Indian Law*, 636–37; Howard Piepenbrink, Chief, Branch of Titles and Research, Division of Real Estate Services, Bureau of Indian Affairs, interviews, Washington, DC, 10–11 Oct. 1990.

64. *Cohen's Handbook of Federal Indian Law*, 636; Piepenbrink, interviews; Pommersheim and Remerowski, *Reservation Street Law*, 136. Other offices for administrative law judges of Indian probate are in Albuquerque, Billings, Phoenix, Sacramento, and Tulsa.

65. 94 Stat 1207.

66. Title Status Report No. 347-1352 (1982), Title and Records Section (TRS), Aberdeen Area Office (AAO), Bureau of Indian Affairs (BIA), Aberdeen, SD (hereafter cited as TRS, AAO, BIA); Lease No. 35205, Allotment No. 1305, Realty Records, Bureau of Indian Affairs, Sisseton Agency, SD; Shirley De Couteau, Realty Specialist, Bureau of Indian Affairs, interview, Sisseton Agency, SD, 9 Feb. 1982.

67. Calculations are based on data drawn from Land Indexes, Title Status Reports, and Probate Records maintained by TRS, AAO, BIA.

68. Title Status Report No. 346-10326-A (1983), TRS, AAO, BIA.

69. Title Status Report No. 342-56-A (1983), TRS, AAO, BIA.

70. *A Bill to Provide for the Consolidation of Indian Lands, for the Elimination of Small Fractional Interests in Indian Lands, and for other Purposes*, 97th Cong., 2d sess., 1982, HR 5856; Piepenbrink interviews.

71. House Committee on Interior and Insular Affairs, *Authorizing the Purchase, Sale, and Exchange of Lands by the Devils Lake Sioux Reservation, North Dakota, and for Other Purposes: Report on S 503*, 97th Cong., 2d sess., 1982, H. Rep. 97-908 (hereafter cited as H. Rep. 97-908).

72. Margo S. Miller, "Tribal Responses to Federal Land Consolidation Policy," Policy Analysis Exercise, Master in Public Policy Program, Harvard University, Kennedy School of Government, 12 Apr. 1988, 15; Gerald Anton, President, Salt River Pima-Maricopa Indian Community, Sacaton, AZ, 26 July 1983, in Senate Select Committee on Indian Affairs, *Amendments to the Indian Land Consolidation Act: Hearing on H.J. Res. 158*, 98th Cong., 1st sess., (Washington, DC: Government Printing Office, 1983), 31–32; *A Bill to Authorize the Purchase, Sale, and Exchange of Lands by the Devils Lake Sioux Tribe of the Devils Lake Sioux Reservation, North Dakota, and for Other Purposes*, 97th Cong., 1st sess., 1981, S 503; "Indian Land Consolidation," Public Law 97-459, *U.S. Code Congressional and Administrative News*, 97th Cong., 2d sess. (1982), Bd. vol. 4, *Legislative History*, 4415–25; Miller, "Tribal Responses to Federal Land Consolidation Policy," 10; Piepenbrink, interviews; 96 Stat 2515.

73. 96 Stat 2515.

74. Kenneth L. Smith, Assistant Secretary, Indian Affairs, to Morris K. Udall, Chairman, House Committee on Interior and Insular Affairs, 9 Sept. 1982, H. Rep. 97-908, 12–19; Piepenbrink, interviews.

75. John W. Fritz, Deputy Assistant Secretary, Indian Affairs, 26 July 1983, in *Amendments to the Indian Land Consolidation Act*, 5.

76. Miller, "Tribal Responses to Federal Land Consolidation Policy," 12; House, *Joint Resolution to Make Technical Corrections in the Act of January 12, 1983 (Public Law 97-459)*, H. J. Res. 158, 98th Cong., 1st sess., 1983; Senate Select Committee on Indian Affairs, *To Make Technical Corrections in the Act of January 12, 1983 (Public Law 97-459)*, 98th Cong., 2d sess., 1984, S. Rep. 98-632, 2 (hereafter cited as S. Rep. 98-632).

77. John W. Fritz to All Area Directors and Superintendents, 2 Mar. 1983, in *Amendments to the Indian Land Consolidation Act*, 12–14.

78. S. Rep. 98-632, 2.

79. *Amendments to the Indian Land Consolidation Act*, 35.

80. Ibid., 38.

81. Ibid., 10.

82. Irving v. Watt, *Indian Law Reporter* 11 (Mar. 1984): 3009–10; Irving v. Clark, 758 F 1260 (8th Cir. 1985).

83. Irving v. Clark, 1262n; Irving v. Watt, 3009–10.

84. Irving v. Watt, 3010n.

85. Senate Select Committee on Indian Affairs, *To Amend the Indian Land Consolidation Act of 1983: Hearings on H. J. Res. 158*, 98th Cong., 2d sess., (Washington, DC: Government Printing Office, 1984); "Indian Land Consolidation Act, Amendment," *U.S. Code Congressional and Administrative News*, 98th Cong., 2d sess. (1984), Bd. vol. 5, *Legislative History*, 5470–81; 98 Stat 3171.

86. 98 Stat 3171.

87. Ibid.

88. 98 Stat 2411; Sidney L. Mills, Director, Office of Trust Responsibilities, Bureau of Indian Affairs, 21 June 1984, in Senate Select Committee on Indian Affairs, *Pertaining to the Inheritance of Trust or Restricted Land on the Lake Traverse Indian Reservation, North and South Dakota, and for Other Purposes*, 98th Cong., 2d sess., 1984, S. Rep. 98-607, 6–7; Lawson, "Indian Heirship Lands," 213–31; Miller, "Tribal Responses to Federal Land Consolidation Policy," 27.

89. Irving v. Clark, 1260–69.

90. Hodel v. Irving, 2076–77.

91. Ibid., 2078, 2083, 2085–86, 2092.

92. Ibid., 2080n, 2084.

93. Curley v. Hodel, Civil No. 88-0886 JC (10th Cir. 1988); Piepenbrink, interviews.

94. Piepenbrink, interviews.

95. Ibid.

96. John O. McGinnis to Ralph W. Tarr, Solicitor, Department of the Interior, 4 Mar. 1988, Files of the Branch of Titles and Research, Bureau of Indian Affairs, Washington, DC.

97. Piepenbrink, interviews; Alice Harwood, Realty Specialist, Bureau of Indian Affairs, interview, Washington, DC (formerly at Fort Berthold Indian Agency, ND), 11 Oct. 1990; John W. Fritz to All Area Directors, 14.

98. Lee Maytubby, Realty Specialist, Division of Real Estate Services, Bureau of Indian Affairs, interview, Washington, DC, 11 Oct. 1990; Miller, "Tribal Responses to Federal Land Consolidation Policy," 14.

99. Miller, "Tribal Responses to Federal Land Consolidation Policy," 14–27.

100. Piepenbrink, interviews; Deputy to the Assistant Secretary, Indian Affairs (Trust and Economic Development) to All Area Directors, 31 July 1986 and 28 Jan. 1988, to Aberdeen, Anadarko, Billings, and Portland Area Directors, Field Solicitor, Twin Cities, Minnesota, and Director, Office of Hearings and Appeals, 17 May 1990, and Howard Piepenbrink, Chief, Branch of Titles and Research, to Deputy Assistant Secretary, Indian Affairs (Trust and Economic Development) 6 Oct. 1987, 16 Aug. 1989, and 1 June 1990, all in Files of the Branch of Titles and Research, Bureau of Indian Affairs, Washington, DC.

2

RESERVATION LIFE

COWBOYS ON THE RESERVATION

THE GROWTH OF RODEO AS A LAKOTA NATIONAL PASTIME

. . .

In the two decades following World War I, rodeo became an increasingly popular national pastime for both European Americans and American Indians.[1] During those years, many Lakotas, or western Sioux, living on the Pine Ridge and Cheyenne River Indian reservations in South Dakota enthusiastically participated in and staged rodeos both on and off the reservation. By 1920, most Lakotas were products of their reservation environments, where many had worked as cattle ranchers and farmers and performed in rodeos in various settings. At the same time, government officials and missionaries eased assimilationist efforts initiated in the 1880s. Authorities had begrudgingly come to realize that they could do little to prevent Lakota citizens from celebrating as they pleased on or off the reservations. Thus, subtle changes in the Office of Indian Affairs' policies, combined with a steady flow of dollars from land leases, allowed many Lakotas to experience greater freedom of cultural expression.[2] In response, Lakota men and women from the Pine Ridge and Cheyenne River reservations accelerated their excursions on and off their reservations to participate in Wild West shows, professional rodeos, and county and tribal fairs. During the 1920s and 1930s, events like the Pine Ridge Sioux Rodeo became important community celebrations, generating outside attention for the reservation and involving Indians at every level from managers to competitors to spectators.

The roots of rodeo in Indian culture reach as far back as the eighteenth century when Plains Indians acquired horses. Historian Richard W. Slatta noted that throughout North and South America "many cowboy cultures evolved from a blending of the Spanish heritage of the conquistadors and pre-existing Indian cultures."[3] From the Spanish, who had introduced horses to America, Indian cowboys in Mexico and the American Southwest inherited games such as pialar, in which a rider on horseback ran a gauntlet of cowboys who attempted to lasso the animal's legs and throw the rider to the ground. In the corrida del

This essay originally appeared in South Dakota History 29 (Fall 1999): 211–27.

gallo, the chicken or rooster pull, riders galloped toward a chicken who had been buried up to its neck and attempted to wrench the unfortunate bird from the ground. Both activities required skills later used in rodeo events. Horsemen on the Northern Great Plains competed in their own bucking bronc contests and horse races, developing skills later transferred to ranching and rodeo. Such contests were waged within war societies, with other native groups, and with white traders.[4]

As the northern Plains Indians made the transition from traditional to reservation life between 1880 and 1920, many began to incorporate cattle ranching and rodeo into their economic and social lives. During those four decades of aggressive assimilationist policy, Plains peoples were settled permanently on reservations, saw their lands allotted, sold, and leased, and were encouraged to become farmers and stockmen. Yet, Plains Indians did not so much assimilate as they allowed for intense cultural change. They experimented with new economic, social, and political practices, based on what their cultures and the Indian Office would allow.[5] They selectively adopted and adapted activities such as rodeo into their reservation lives and economies as they realized that they "could be like white men and not be white men."[6]

By 1889, the Lakotas, who once commanded an area that included much of the Northern Great Plains, had been reduced to living on six reservations in central and western South Dakota: the Pine Ridge, Cheyenne River, Crow Creek, Lower Brule, Rosebud, and Standing Rock. In the 1890s, Indian agents like Charles G. Penney of Pine Ridge and Charles E. McChesney of Cheyenne River actively encouraged cattle ranching on tribal lands. Stock raising appeared to be a viable alternative to farming on the semiarid reservations, and agents hoped such activities would distract the Indians from traditional activities like sun dances and scalp dances, which the government had restricted in the 1880s. For the Lakotas, the occupation not only suited the Office of Indian Affairs but also allowed for continued contact among themselves, horses, and the outdoors. By 1901, the Pine Ridge herd had grown to nineteen thousand head, increasing by more than one-third the following year. As ranchers, Lakotas gained more of the roping, riding, and wrestling skills that they would soon display in competition.[7]

Many Lakota cowboys first participated in rodeo while working reservation herds, just as non-Indian cowboys had done to pass time on cattle drives. Not until 4 July 1882, however, did rodeo performed for paying crowds arrive on the scene. William F. ("Buffalo Bill") Cody's "Old Glory Blow-Out," staged in North Platte, Nebraska, featured cowboy games like bronc riding in addition to Indians on horseback reenacting the Battle of the Little Bighorn. The per-

Indian cowboys drew on their native roots and adapted their
skills as horsemen to life on the reservation. These men
worked on a Pine Ridge reservation ranch.
State Archives Collection,
South Dakota State Historical Society

formance also served as the prototype for Cody's "Wild West," which began touring the following year. Over the next several decades, Oglala Lakotas from Pine Ridge made up the largest group of Indians traveling with the show, which performed for large American and European audiences.[8] During one month in 1911, 230 Oglalas joined five different companies touring the world in what one observer termed "the annual wild west exodus."[9]

During the same time period, northern Plains Indian cowboys and audiences also traveled to off-reservation county and state fairs, where, donning headdresses and riding buffaloes, they served as tourist attractions.[10] In 1910, Lakotas from the Cheyenne River, Standing Rock, and Pine Ridge reservations attended a four-day-long Independence Day celebration at Dupree on the Cheyenne River reservation. There they staged a parade and mock attack on the town before competing in horse races. They participated over the objections of the Cheyenne River agent, who had sought to keep the Indians from associating with "the bad men of Dupree."[11]

As they gained rodeo experience, Lakota cowboys went on to compete in professional rodeos. David Blue Thunder from the Rosebud reservation and George Defender from the Standing Rock reservation made notable appearances. After winning first place at the Miles City (Montana) Roundup in 1914, Defender went on to compete in big-time events all the way to Madison Square Garden.[12] Lakotas from Pine Ridge also competed in the Cowboy Tournament in Denver, Colorado, in 1911; the Mid-West Stampede in Hot Springs, South Dakota, in 1921; the Old Range Round-Up in Sutherland, Nebraska, and the United States Championship Cowboy Rodeo in Denver in 1924; and the Frontier Days rodeo in Cheyenne, Wyoming, in 1929.[13]

As early as 1905, the Indian Office had begun to institute fairs on the reservations as a way to foster enthusiasm for agriculture and to keep Indians closer to home. In 1911, Indian fairs were held on fourteen reservations; six years later, fifty-eight reservation fairs took place.[14] Agents like John R. Brennan of Pine Ridge, however, soon found these gatherings, originally organized on a district-by-district basis, to be as distracting as the off-reservation events. In 1912, he urged reservation residents to "get together and agree to discontinue the district fairs and . . . hold but one fair on the Reservation each year."[15] The editor of the *Oglala Light*, a publication produced at the United States Indian Training School at Pine Ridge, concurred. "These small fairs are a detriment in a way to more and better farming," the editor wrote, "and also, as these fairs are held all through the month of September and (this year) to the middle of October, the Indian, with his roving disposition, has no trouble in following each fair from its start to its finish."[16] Two years later, the government insti-

George Defender (second from left) was one of several
Lakota cowboys who won fame as a regional rodeo
champion and went on to compete in national events.
State Historical Society of North Dakota,
Bismarck (image no. 1952-4286)

tuted a single, reservation-wide fair with the stated purpose of "encouraging the people of the Pine Ridge reservation to grow more and better crops and to improve the quality of their cattle and increase their herds."[17] The annual reservation-wide fair, which the Indians themselves helped to organize and manage under the agent's direction, also provided an opportunity for Indians to compete in their own rodeos. The Pine Ridge Indian Fair schedules for 1917 and 1919, for example, listed rodeo events such as a barrel-roping contest and "a cowboy race by riding bronchos."[18]

Despite the emergence and popularity of the government-sponsored reservation fairs, Lakotas continued to leave their homes to attend fairs and rodeos off their reservations. Frederick Hoxie, writing of the Crow tribe in Montana, called such celebrations twentieth-century "cultural innovations" that enabled Indians to continue to gather as a people, although in ways that local whites would accept.[19] In addition, many Indians had more freedom to attend such gatherings. Following the turn of the last century, federal agents who had initially supported tribal ranching efforts bowed to pressure from non-Indian ranchers and approved the leasing of individual reservation allotments to outsiders. By 1917, large non-Indian companies dominated reservation grazing lands. On Pine Ridge, for example, John Glover, foreman of the Quarter Circle 71 outfit of the Newcastle Land and Livestock Company, acquired five hundred thousand acres of lease land at the center of the reservation.[20] Taking advantage of a meager but steady income from such lease payments, many Lakotas spent part of the 1920s traveling off their reservations to summer fairs and rodeos.

Just as the Office of Indian Affairs had both encouraged and discouraged ranching, it likewise treated the Lakotas' participation in rodeo with ambivalence. Rodeo perpetuated the image of Indians as cattle ranchers making productive use of the land. On the other hand, the Indians' traveling to rodeos often resulted in their neglecting reservation homesteads and crops for prolonged periods. Under the leadership of Commissioner of Indian Affairs Charles H. Burke, agents became more amenable to the prospect of Indians traveling to off-reservation fairs where they could benefit from competition with white farmers. In 1927, Cheyenne River Superintendent William O. Roberts informed the president of the Faith, South Dakota, fair and rodeo association: "The Indian Department is agreeable to the matter of Indians participating in County fairs in a competitive effort and to observe the quality and production in white communities. Our restrictions in matters of this kind hinge on the economic condition of the individual Indian. You, of course, know that there are Indians who will be gone a week before fair and stay a week after, thus injuring himself through long absence from his garden and poultry."[21] That year, the organizers of the Faith Fair and Rodeo encouraged the presence of Cheyenne River Lakotas by offering "four free beeves" to Indians who attended.[22] There, they competed in rodeo events such as bronc riding, goat roping, and wild horse racing.[23]

While government officials may have relaxed their attitudes toward Indian participation in some off-reservation events, they continued to have misgivings about the professional rodeos that took Indians far from home. In 1927, Superintendent Roberts reprimanded five Cheyenne River residents traveling with the King Brothers Rodeo Circus who found themselves stranded near Detroit when a sheriff seized the show's property.[24] Showing little sympathy for their request for transportation home, Roberts informed Commissioner Burke that Archie Did Not Go Home, Black Man, Felix Dog Arm, and Mr. and Mrs. George Hunter had "left the reservation strictly on their own responsibility." Roberts continued, "It is also very reasonable to assume that the Indians were fully acquainted with the advisability of arranging contracts through the office. . . . When [an Indian] takes matters into his own hands in this respect, it seems to me advisable to permit him to reap the rewards of such a contract if he has been successful, and to make other arrangements if his judgement was in error."[25]

Despite such incidents, Lakotas remained involved in rodeo both on and off their reservations. Shows such as Texicole-Charley's Troupe of Wild West Performers and the Sells-Floto Circus "wanted Indians who could perform as fancy ropers and bronco riders."[26] Joe Yellowhead of Cheyenne River was one of those who answered the call, working for the Miller Brothers 101 Wild West Show in the late 1920s. Yellowhead rode both broncs and buffaloes, recalling that his employers had him "paint up as a Indian with the war bonnet." He preferred riding the show's tame buffalo over busting broncs, which he recalled as "too tough—just like riding a big barrel you know."[27]

By the mid-1920s, Indian agents had become dissatisfied with the reservation-wide fairs, the focus of which had shifted from agricultural displays to equestrian contests. This sentiment led to the discontinuance of the annual Pine Ridge Indian Fair in 1925 in favor of "local industrial exhibits [to] be held in the various districts."[28] Two years later, forty-six Lakota men petitioned Commissioner Burke for the resumption of the Pine Ridge Fair, which, they said, had "been an incalculable value to the Indians from the aspect of advertising and demonstrating the industry and farming produce of the Indians, to the outside communities from which vast numbers of white people attend the celebration."[29] Although officials maintained that the district agricultural displays should meet this need, many Lakotas did not find the local exhibits socially gratifying.

The subsequent reaction of a group of Pine Ridge men illustrated the extent to which the Lakotas had embraced rodeo and incorporated it into their lives. In 1928, the Oglala Lakotas themselves formed the Pine Ridge Sioux Rodeo Association to offer reservation Indians an opportunity to gather and compete, as cowboys and community members, in an activity that formed part of their heritage. On the Pine Ridge reservation, all eight districts—Oglala, Allen, Kyle, Manderson, Porcupine, Wakpamni, Red Shirt Table, and Wanblee—were represented at the rodeo. Similarly, an Indian-organized reservation-wide fair and rodeo held on the Cheyenne River reservation united the Promise, White Horse, Eagle Butte, Cherry Creek, and Thunder Butte districts.[30]

The new Pine Ridge superintendent, James H. McGregor, expressed fear that the annual rodeo "would take many away from their homes and have them camped here for a week, when they would need to be at work on their farms and gardens."[31] Still, he and other Indian Office officials tolerated the rodeo in the hope that it would slow the trend of Indians leaving to participate in off-reservation shows, fairs, and rodeos. They also expressed optimism that the rodeo would indirectly promote animal husbandry by glorifying the skills of cattlemen.[32]

In the absence of either government interference or assistance, the Pine Ridge Rodeo Association took full responsibility for public relations, financial affairs, facilities construction, policing, and staging. At an organizational meeting on 6 February 1928 in the Pine Ridge Young Men's Christian Association (YMCA) building, the group elected five officers: Hermus Merrival, president; Charles Yellow Boy, vice-president; James La Pointe, corresponding secretary; Frank G. Wilson, recording secretary; and Godard Cottier, treasurer. A three-member board of directors consisted of Philip Romero, John Colhoff, and Ben Janis. Another seventeen Lakota men signed on as members.[33] The association set forth its objectives early on. Through its annual reservation-wide rodeo, the group intended to generate outside attention, raise revenue, and promote Lakota pride and camaraderie. According to its organizers, the rodeo's primary aim was to "put Pine Ridge on the map. Let the people know where it is; let them know what kind of country it is; show them the wonderful farmlands [and] natural resources."[34]

During its decade-long existence, the Pine Ridge Rodeo Association publicized itself to large non-Indian audiences. Newspaper advertisements, feature articles, and word-of-mouth accounts inspired numerous inquiries from throughout South Dakota and as far away as Haxton, Colorado, and Rochester,

During the 1920s and 1930s, Lakotas sponsored,
staged, and competed in rodeos much like this one at Interior,
near the Pine Ridge reservation.
State Archives Collection,
South Dakota State Historical Society

New York.[35] In 1929, Francis Case, then editor of the *Hot Springs Evening Star* and a future United States senator from South Dakota, contacted association president Hermus Merrival to request "a write-up of the Rodeo and perhaps some paid advertising."[36] Reporters for area newspapers wrote glowingly of their rodeo experiences. A Rushville, Nebraska, newspaper deemed the 1931 "bucking contests, bull-dogging and calf roping contests . . . especially good," concluding, "People in this part of the country always look forward to the Pine Ridge Rodeo."[37] The publicity attracted an eclectic group of spectators. Captain A. E. King, commander of the Fourth Field Artillery Regiment at Fort Robinson, Nebraska, arranged for 250 men to hike sixty-five miles to the 1929 rodeo in a training exercise that combined work and pleasure.[38]

Throughout the late 1920s and 1930s, the rodeo associations on both the Pine Ridge and Cheyenne River reservations subsidized their events through ticket sales, concession sales, and fund-raising dances. Once the receipts were counted and expenses paid, the rodeos rarely made a profit, even when gate receipts were as high as $114 per day, as at the 1927 Cheyenne River Sioux Rodeo. Supplies, including posts, poles, lumber, and miscellaneous hardware, were costly.[39] In 1933, Pine Ridge Rodeo Association secretary Frank Goings calculated that the organization's treasury was fifteen dollars in the red, due in part to unanticipated expenses. "All had authority to hire this man and that man," he complained. "One bill I didn't know was paid which I objected to was $8 given some cowboys who didn't have any way of getting out of town."[40] Clearly, the demands of staging such an event sometimes strained the association's budget and tried the tempers of its members.

Although white cowboys were allowed to compete in the Pine Ridge Sioux Rodeo, the association consistently sought to employ Lakotas in as many rodeo-related jobs as possible. It also purchased beef for the event from Lakota cattle ranchers and charged non-Indian vendors a concession fee of five dollars per day to sell their wares, which ranged from nectar drinks to blankets and novelties. In addition, the association secured donations from local non-Indians, such as the seventy-five dollars Richard Talmadge of Rushville gave for the purchase of beef in 1928.[41] "Rabbit dances," proposed at the first meeting of the rodeo association in 1928, provided the most steady flow of revenue. An appointed committee attended the dances, held every Saturday night in the months leading up to the rodeo, to collect "voluntary gifts toward the good cause."[42] They proved to be profitable ventures, for the musical entertainment received just five dollars per night to perform.[43]

In addition to enriching the social environment of the reservation, the Pine Ridge Rodeo Association used its treasury to improve the reservation's built environment. At their second meeting on 16 November 1928, the directors discussed work on the existing rodeo grounds, including the track and dance hall.[44] In 1929, they began building a bigger hall to accommodate the large crowds of rodeo-goers and evening revelers. The association predicted the new dance hall would provide "a continual source of revenue," envisioning its use as a "town hall, community hall, a place for government officials to meet Indians, a council hall, exhibit hall for the district fair and any number of things."[45] The United States government did, in fact, use the building to house Emergency Conservation Workers on the reservation in 1933. The association also built a sun shade, or dance pavilion, and maintained all of the structures well, reporting damage from vandalism only in 1932.[46]

With funding and buildings in place, the Pine Ridge Rodeo Association was left the tasks of staging and policing the annual event. The organization's by-laws required the group to arrange for patrolling the grounds and "take care of all relief cases arising from attendance at the rodeo."[47] The directors also devised a set of "Official Rules" banning "liquor, rowdyism and quarreling."[48] In 1930, Superintendent Jermark reported one incident of illegal alcohol consumption to the commissioner of Indian affairs and expressed concern that rodeo "not infrequently attracts an undesirable element."[49] The following year, however, Pine Ridge field agent B. G. Courtright assessed the association's regulation positively. "So far as I can learn from the records and inquiry," he reported, "there have heretofor [sic] been no disorder or trouble in connection with policing the grounds and no unruly or objectionable element has been encouraged to enter the reservation on account of the Rodeo."[50]

Finally, the Pine Ridge Rodeo Association determined the program and prizes for the event, usually held for three days during the first week of August. Most of each day was devoted to bronc riding, steer wrestling, and horse racing, but the program also featured activities such as battle reenactments, baseball games, parades, and traditional dances. Noticeably absent from the published program was the premium list for agricultural contests that had been a feature of government-sponsored Indian fairs.[51] While non-Indians were invited to participate, the rodeo contestants were predominantly Lakotas, who relished the opportunity to display their skills as horsemen and compete for such prizes as bridles and Navajo blankets. The three thousand Lakotas who attended the 1931 Pine Ridge Rodeo attested to its popularity, and the *Shannon County News* declared the event "a genuine Sioux Rodeo."[52]

In 1933, Hermus Merrival resigned as rodeo association president to devote more time to farming, and the local American Legion chapter stepped in to assist with fundraising, conducting the dances, and sharing in the profits.

The involvement of the American Legion provoked some dissent among association members. Tensions climaxed in 1934, when the Legion requested use of the dance hall for its own July rodeo and then proposed that it take over management of the Pine Ridge Sioux Rodeo, as well. Rodeo association secretary Frank Goings, with support from Superintendent McGregor, entreated the other members to accept the offer, but in the end the board refused to relinquish either the rodeo or the dance hall.[53] The Pine Ridge Rodeo Association persisted as directors of the annual Pine Ridge Sioux Rodeo until it was replaced later in the decade with a reincarnation of the reservation-wide agricultural fair and rodeo.

Beginning in 1934, Indian New Deal funds, available principally through the Wheeler-Howard or Tribal Organization Act, inspired a resurgence of Lakota ranching. Ironically, the period also marked the end of the autonomous rodeo as officials sought to replace the entertainment-oriented gatherings with "educational" tribal fairs.[54] Although the days of the independent Lakota rodeos of the 1920s and 1930s were at an end, rodeo itself had become a cultural celebration for organizers and participants alike. An activity with native roots and official acceptance, rodeo gave Lakotas an opportunity to gather as a people and an arena in which to display skills acquired before and during the transition to reservation life. When the tribal fair reemerged at Pine Ridge, Cheyenne River, and elsewhere as the reservations' primary gatherings, rodeo remained a centerpiece of those events.

NOTES

1. Kristine Fredriksson, *American Rodeo: From Buffalo Bill to Big Business* (College Station: Texas A & M University Press, 1985), 21–22; L. G. Moses, *Wild West Shows and the Images of American Indians, 1883–1933* (Albuquerque: University of New Mexico Press, 1996), 252.

2. Frederick E. Hoxie describes a similar cultural phenomenon on the Crow Reservation in Montana after World War I. He suggests that "the shift in frequency and content of the Crow fairs during the 1920s was a reflection of the tribe's declining economic power as well as of its resilient, determined commitment to community values and cultural independence" (Hoxie, *Parading through History: The Making of the Crow Nation in America, 1805–1935* [Cambridge: Cambridge University Press, 1995], 308).

3. Richard W. Slatta, *Cowboys of the Americas* (New Haven: Yale University Press, 1990), 128. See also Richard W. Slatta, "Cowboys and Gauchos," *Américas* 33 (Mar. 1981): 3–8; Richard W. Slatta, "Cowboys, Gauchos, and Llaneros: Horsemen of the Americas," *Persimmon Hill* 12 (1983): 8–23; and Mary Lou LeCompte, "The Hispanic Influence on the History of Rodeo, 1823–1922," *Journal of Sport History* 12 (Spring 1985): 21–38.

4. Slatta, *Cowboys of the Americas*, 129–39; Jill P. Sweet and Karen E. Larson, "The Horse,

Santiago, and a Ritual Game: Pueblo Indian Responses to Three Spanish Introductions," *Western Folklore* 53 (Jan. 1994): 75–76; Laurence Flatlip, Crow oral historian, interview, Western Heritage Center, Billings, MT, 23 Feb. 1995; Glendolin Damon Wagner and William A. Allen, *Blankets and Moccasins: Plenty Coups and His People, the Crows* (Caldwell, ID: Caxton Printers, 1933), 193–95.

5. Frederick E. Hoxie explores the emergence of a new reservation culture on the Cheyenne River Indian Reservation in "From Prison to Homeland: The Cheyenne River Indian Reservation before WWI," *South Dakota History* 10 (Winter 1979): 1–24.

6. Peter Iverson, *When Indians Became Cowboys: Native Peoples and Cattle Ranching in the American West* (Norman: University of Oklahoma Press, 1994), 84.

7. Ibid., 53; Herbert T. Hoover, "The Sioux Agreement of 1889 and Its Aftermath," *South Dakota History* 19 (Spring 1989): 58; Iverson, *When Indians Became Cowboys*, 53, 67–70; Moses, *Wild West Shows*, 253.

8. Barbara Williams Roth, "The 101 Ranch Wild West Show, 1904–1932," *Chronicles of Oklahoma* 43 (Winter 1965–1966): 416; Fredriksson, *American Rodeo*, 4, 140; Joseph J. Arpad and Kenneth R. Lincoln, *Buffalo Bill's Wild West* (Palmer Lake, CO: Filter Press, 1971) 9; Moses, *Wild West Shows*, 25.

9. *Oglala Light* 1911 (Apr. 1911): unpaged.

10. Castle McLaughlin, "The Big Lease: Confined-Range Ranching on the Fort Berthold Indian Reservation, 1910–1950," *North Dakota History* 61 (Fall 1994): 19.

11. *Dupree Leader*, 7 July 1910. Although agents often sought to restrict the Indians' travel to such gatherings, a federal case in 1879 involving the Ponca leader Standing Bear had established that peaceable Indians were free to move about as they pleased. Moses, *Wild West Shows*, 63.

12. *Reservation Round-Up: Stories of Pioneer Days in the Settling of the Pine Ridge Reservation Area* (Porcupine, SD: Big Foot Historical Society, 1968), 9; Iverson, *When Indians Became Cowboys*, 74.

13. Contract between Stockmen's Club of Denver and eighteen unnamed Indian performers, 5 Apr. 1911, Paul Martin, Secretary, Mid-West Stampede, to Superintendent Tidwell, 9 June 1921, Program, Old Range Round-Up, Sutherland, NE, 28–30 Aug. 1924, James A. Buchanan, Committeeman, Cheyenne Frontier Days, to E. W. Jermark, 20 May 1929, Contract between William T. Roche, General Manager, United States Championship Cowboy Rodeo, and E. W. Jermark, 1924, all in Local Fair and Rodeo Correspondence (FRC), Pine Ridge Agency (PRA), Main Decimal Files 047–049, Box 166, Records of the Bureau of Indian Affairs, Record Group (RG) 75, National Archives-Central Plains Region (NA-CPR), Kansas City, MO.

14. Moses, *Wild West Shows*, 207; Thomas C. Maroukis, "Yankton Sioux Tribal Fairs: The Early Twentieth Century," *Institute of American Indian Studies Bulletin* 127 (Aug. 1992): 39.

15. *Oglala Light* 1912 (Sept.–Oct. 1912): 9.

16. Ibid., 10.

17. Program, Fourth Annual Pine Ridge Indian Fair, 26–28 Sept. 1918, FRC, PRA, NA-CPR.

18. *Oglala Light* 1917 (Oct. 1917): unpaged; Program, Fifth Annual Pine Ridge Indian Fair, 25–27 Sept. 1919, FRC, PRA, NA-CPR.

19. Hoxie, *Parading through History*, 363.

20. Iverson, *When Indians Became Cowboys*, 70.

21. Roberts to McCormack, President, Faith Fair and Rodeo, 24 Aug. 1927, 1925–1945 Correspondence (FRC), Cheyenne River Agency (CRA), General Records Main Decimal Files 047:1922–1928, Box 185, RG 75, NA-CPR.

22. McCormack to Roberts, 8 Aug. 1927, FRC, CRA, NA-CPR.

23. Program, Faith Fair and Rodeo, 31 Aug.-2 Sept. 1927, FRC, CRA, NA-CPR.

24. Roberts to Commissioner of Indian Affairs (CIA), 11 July 1927, and CIA Charles Burke to William Williamson, 5 July 1927, FRC, CRA, NA-CPR.

25. Roberts to CIA, 11 July 1927, FRC, CRA, NA-CPR.

26. Moses, *Wild West Shows*, 255.

27. Joe Yellowhead, interview by Steve Plummer, Eagle Butte, SD, 8 June 1971, Tape no. 695, American Indian Research Project, South Dakota Oral History Center, University of South Dakota, Vermillion, SD.

28. Charles H. Burke to E. W. Jermark, 23 June 1927, FRC, PRA, NA-CPR.

29. Petition to Honorable Charles H. Burke, composed by James Ryan, Martin, SD, 23 June 1927, FRC, PRA, NA-CPR.

30. Minutes, Pine Ridge Rodeo Association (PRRA) 6 Feb. 1928, FRC, PRA, and W. O. Roberts to Farmers, Cheyenne River Reservation, [1928], FRC, CRA, NA-CPR.

31. McGregor to Frank Goings, 2 June 1932, FRC, PRA, NA-CPR.

32. E. W. Jermark to CIA, 25 June 1930, FRC, PRA, NA-CPR.

33. Minutes, PRRA, 6 Feb. 1928.

34. Ibid., 22 Jan. 1929.

35. Lou Walker to Pine Ridge Agency, 20 July 1929, E. W. Jermark to Mrs. H. B. Billingley, 29 July 1929, W. O. Roberts to William Center, 27 July 1937, P. L. Hallam to W. O. Roberts, 28 July 1938, and R. Walter White to Pine Ridge Agency, 24 May 1938, all in FRC, PRA, NA-CPR.

36. Case to Merrival, 29 July 1929, FRC, PRA, NA-CPR.

37. "Pine Ridge Rodeo a Success," Rushville, NE, newspaper clipping, 1932, FRC, PRA, NA-CPR.

38. King to E. W. Jermark, July 1929, FRC, PRA, NA-CPR.

39. Notice of receipt of $114 from Rodeo Association, Cheyenne River Agency, 23 Sept. 1927, FRC, CRA, E. W. Jermark to Hermus Merrival, 12 Sept. 1929, FRC, PRA, Frank Goings

to James H. McGregor, 16 Sept. 1933, FRC, PRA, and Dempster and O'Connell Hardware, Gordon, NE, to Pine Ridge Agency, 26 July 1930, FRC, PRA, all in NA-CPR.

40. Goings to James H. McGregor, 30 Aug. 1933, FRC, PRA, NA-CPR.

41. B. G. Courtright, Field Agent in Charge, to Hermus Merrival, 18 June 1931, Merrival to E. W. Jermark, 4 Aug. 1928, Dorothy Arnold to James H. McGregor, 7 Aug. 1933, E. E. Kobernusz to Mayor of Pine Ridge, 17 June 1929, and Anonymous to Mr. President, Pine Ridge, 19 Jan. 1929, all in FRC, PRA, NA-CPR.

42. Minutes, PRRA, 12 Feb. 1928, FRC, PRA, NA-CPR.

43. Anonymous to Mr. President, 19 Jan. 1929.

44. Minutes, PRRA, 16 Nov. 1928, FRC, PRA, NA-CPR.

45. Ibid., 22 Jan. 1929.

46. McGregor to Merrival, 11 July 1933, Jermark to Charles Yellow Boy, 22 July 1930, McGregor to Goings, 17 May 1932, all in FRC, PRA, NA-CPR.

47. Minutes, PRRA, 6 Feb. 1928.

48. "Consideration on Basis for Pine Ridge Rodeo," 1928, FRC, PRA, NA-CPR.

49. Jermark to CIA, 25 June 1930.

50. Courtright to Merrival, 18 June 1931.

51. Program, Pine Ridge Sioux Rodeo, 2 Aug. 1929, and Official Rules, Pine Ridge Sioux Rodeo, 1928, FRC, PRA, NA-CPR.

52. Program, Pine Ridge Sioux Rodeo, 2 Aug. 1929; *Shannon County News*, 6 Aug. 1931.

53. Merrival to Pine Ridge Rodeo Association, 21 July 1933, McGregor to Charles Gerber, 15 Aug. 1933, and Goings to McGregor, 10, 28 May 1934, all in FRC, PRA, NA-CPR.

54. Iverson, *When Indians Became Cowboys*, 140; R. E. Coulter, Pine Ridge Agricultural Extension Agent, to Guy McDonald, Agricultural Extension Service, Brookings, SD, 30 Aug. 1939, FRC, PRA, NA-CPR.

THE SIOUX AND THE INDIAN-CCC

· · ·

The federal government initiated some significant legislation and relief programs for the Indians during the 1930s, designed primarily to
reverse traditional policies of Indian-white relationships. Reaction to
these efforts varied and thus caused officials to alter objectives from time
to time to accommodate various tribes, including the Sioux. One well-known
legislative measure, the Wheeler-Howard Act, paved the way for the enactment
of depression relief measures, such as the Civilian Conservation Corps-Indian
Division (CCC-ID), and reversed unfair restrictions placed upon the Indians by
the Dawes Act of 1887.[1] The Dawes Act represented an attempt to assimilate
the Indians into the white man's culture by distributing reservation lands in
severalty. However, long before the 1920s, it became evident that this so-called
assimilation program had failed. All the Indians still living on reservations
remained miserably poor, while conditions for the South Dakota Sioux already
had passed the critical point. Not only had they suffered from the loss of part
of their land and much of their culture, but also from inadequate education and
poor health. Moreover, their lives were regimented by a seemingly indifferent
Bureau of Indian Affairs (BIA).

In 1923, after several Indian organizations and magazine articles condemned
the policies of the BIA, Secretary of the Interior Hubert Work instructed the
Board of Indian Commissioners to investigate the charges raised by the critics.[2]
When the findings of the board turned out to be nothing more than a "white-
wash" of the BIA, the Brookings Institute for Government Research launched
an extensive survey of economic and social conditions of all reservation Indians. The result of the survey, published as the Meriam Report, in effect, stated
that the Dawes Act had meant poverty for the Indians, and that giving them
allotments of land did not automatically make them farmers.[3] They needed
training in appropriate farming techniques. However, even if the South Dakota
tribes had possessed the necessary knowledge and machinery for dry-farming,
most of their reservation lands were totally unsuited for agriculture. On the

This essay originally appeared in *South Dakota History* 8 (Fall 1978): 340–56.

Pine Ridge reservation, the average Indian possessed no more tools than a hoe and rake and occasionally a walking plow to work the few acres of cultivable soil. Under such conditions, he had practically no alternative but to rent his land to a white rancher or farmer.[4]

The task of invoking radical new measures to solve the problems of the Indians fell to John Collier. Appointed by President Franklin D. Roosevelt in 1933 to head the Indian Bureau, Collier hoped to correct past wrongs inflicted upon one of the nation's longest suppressed minorities with a single comprehensive law. The result was the Wheeler-Howard or Indian Reorganization Act (IRA) of 1934, which exemplified Collier's philosophy and that of the New Deal. It abandoned the allotment system that had dominated federal Indian policy since 1887 and provided a $10-million "revolving fund" to assist Indian corporations in economic development.[5]

The Indian Reorganization Act granted the tribes limited home rule by allowing them to adopt their own constitutions and bylaws. This action curbed federal power over them but fell short of granting an autonomous form of government since it carried with it the stipulation that all constitutions must be approved by the secretary of the interior. Ramon Roubideaux, a Brulé Sioux and an attorney in South Dakota, viewed the extension of home rule to the Indians as a hoax because "self-government by permission is no self-government at all."[6] Indeed, the paternalistic attitude of the Indian Bureau had long since submerged much of the Indians' initiative and ambition.

Commissioner Collier also hoped to reform the entire program of Indian education, but the Wheeler-Howard Act only established a scholarship fund for higher learning. Additional legislation became necessary before he could carry out the desired changes and eliminate Indian boarding schools, develop day schools near the reservations, and encourage Indian children to attend public schools. The Johnson-O'Malley Act of 1934 authorized the secretary of the interior to enter into contracts with states for the improvement of Indian education and welfare. The federal government in turn made payments to school districts where Indian children lived on reservations and attended public day schools. Because Indian lands held in trust were nontaxable for educational purposes, the schools thereby used the funds in lieu of tax revenue. At the same time the federal government could help establish curriculum standards.[7] The act was hailed by most authorities as a step forward, while others saw it as the same old acculturation process of President Grant's Peace Policy.

Catholic missionaries in South Dakota especially reacted negatively to Collier's support of day schools in place of boarding schools. Much of the controversy involved a treaty between the United States and the Sioux Indians whereby

Catholic educational institutions had acquired 80 percent of the total government grant for religious education. When the treaty lapsed, the government planned to withdraw support from the Catholic Indian mission schools—except for physical maintenance. The savings would be used for the care of Indian children attending other parochial schools in all parts of the country. Catholic missionaries vehemently attacked Collier's program on the grounds that it would endanger the status of mission schools. However, the real reason for the attacks was fear of increased aid to Protestant establishments.[8]

Missionaries also became extremely antagonistic over the "radical new commissioner's" insistence that interference with the Indians' religious life or ceremonial expression would not be tolerated. Segregating the Indians from white society and encouraging old tribal traditions would undermine all missionary efforts to Christianize them. The missionaries had reason to be concerned over the Sioux returning to their native religions. The so-called pagan cults of the Ghost Dance and the Sun Dance directly conflicted with Christian teachings, as did the more popular Peyote cult or Native American Church.[9] Once relieved of government restrictions, these ceremonies would again be practiced actively on the reservations.

Even with the revived interest in their culture, education, and government, the basic fact remained that many Indians were starving because they lacked the means to support themselves. The "checkerboard" pattern of allotted land resulting from division by inheritance and leasing to whites deterred any attempt at proper land use. The Meriam Report had revealed that the average yearly per capita income of those residents of South Dakota reservations in 1926 was only $166.[10] This had not changed by the early 1930s, but in fact, the ravages of drought and depression had further complicated the situation. Therefore, when direct relief from federal and state agencies proved insufficient, special work-relief projects were started and continued until the outbreak of World War II.

To remedy worsening conditions, Congress created the Civilian Conservation Corps in March 1933 to relieve "the acute conditions of widespread distress and unemployment . . . and to provide for the restoration of the country's depleted natural resources.[11] It divided the corps among several bureaus in the Departments of War, Agriculture, Labor, and Interior—with Robert Fechner as the overall director. The act did not mention the Indians, but Collier and J. P. Kinney, director of Forestry, quickly made known to President Roosevelt the urgent need for conservation measures on the reservations. They insisted that special conditions warranted an independent program under the direction of the Office of Indian Affairs.[12] After careful consideration, Roosevelt authorized the Indian Emergency Conservation Work (IECW), which allowed reservation Indians to direct their own work in separate camps. Not only would Indians do all the labor, but tribal councils would help select the projects. To assist in technical matters, the bureau established six district offices in the Dakotas, Wyoming, Montana, and Nebraska under the jurisdiction of the Billings, Montana, district. Although given virtually independent action on the reservations, the Indian program had to meet most of the regular CCC regulations and when disagreements arose, the white CCC rules prevailed.[13]

Roosevelt placed the new program on a separate basis primarily because of objections by the Indians to quasi-military camps on their lands.[14] Thus, corps officials exempted workers in the reservation camps from the customary army conditioning period and at the same time gave preference to Indians for supervisory positions and a meager subsistence allowance for providing clothing and shelter. Because most of the supervisory jobs required technical skills or knowledge that the majority of the Sioux did not possess, whites filled these administrative positions. Later, a few Indians completed leadership training courses sponsored by the CCC-ID and advanced to project managers.

The regular CCC practice of employing 200 men in a camp for six months proved impractical on the sparsely settled reservations where there was little need for such a large labor force for an extended period of time. Roosevelt authorized the Indians to be mobilized into work units of forty to fifty men. Corps officials then established three principal types of domiciles: the permanent boarding camp for single men; the home camp for those desiring to live at home; and the family camp for projects of short duration where the entire household could reside temporarily in tents.[15] The family camps were popular with the Sioux and at the same time cost the federal government less than permanent units.

However, sanitation conditions in the twenty family units on the Rosebud reservation in 1937 were deplorable. There were no sewer or water systems, and open garbage pits were commonplace. Two agency doctors and four field nurses served the area but were unavailable to perform services for the CCC-ID camps. To combat these adverse conditions, workers resided in camps for one season only, and whenever possible they took advantage of living at home. At times this became extremely difficult. For example, at Pine Ridge a work crew even had to carry a two-week food supply with them because of the rough terrain and roads.[16]

Regardless of the conditions and type of work camps, the CCC-ID had more applicants than it could possibly accommodate. To allow the maximum number of Indians on the payroll, officials would stagger employment of CCC-

This view shows a CCC-ID temporary family camp at Crow Creek.
Sanitation conditions in the camps were deplorable, and workers
resided in these tents for one season only.
Roger Bromert, Weatherford, OK

ID enrollees and allowed them to work on neighboring reservations. In both situations a committee appointed by the tribal council selected the enrollees from among the men over eighteen years of age who were free from communicable diseases and able to perform ordinary labor. The basic wage was $30.00 a month, or $1.50 per day—plus a 60-cent subsidy for those living at home—for twenty workdays a month. Enrollees also received from $1.00 to $2.00 per day for use of their own teams of horses. Some eventually advanced to assistant foreman at $135.00 per month and a few to group foreman at $167.00. Administration officials held back a portion of each enrollee's paycheck until the winter months when little or no work was available.[17]

The CCC-ID was the first emergency legislation from which the Sioux benefited directly. Heretofore, CCC-ID funds could only be used for the necessities of life, but large-scale projects could now be undertaken to protect forest, range, and farm lands. Work began on several reservations by the summer of 1933, following the approval of the district office at Billings. Considerable confusion surrounded the first camp at Pine Ridge where seventy-six men lived in the rodeo building for several weeks with little to do except general clean-up work in the absence of construction tools, transportation, and equipment.[18]

The geography of South Dakota required special consideration for administrative officials. The Pine Ridge, Rosebud, Standing Rock, Cheyenne River, and Lower Brule reservations are located west of the ninety-eighth meridian in the Great Plains region. Grama and buffalo grasses and insufficient rainfall made the area unsuitable for large-scale agriculture. These conditions, accompanied by severe drought, forced the CCC-ID to concentrate on water development and irrigation projects to control erosion and overgrazing. The Standing Rock reservation, straddling the border between North and South Dakota, and the Cheyenne River reservation had sufficient timber for various forestation projects. Trees were too scarce on the other reservations to be of much value.[19]

The Crow Creek, Yankton, and Sisseton Sioux reservations are located east of the Missouri River, where the soil is richer and the yearly rainfall exceeds twenty inches. Here the enrollees carried out useful projects such as the construction of fences, roads, and telephone lines. At Sisseton and Yankton the Indians also revitalized several old springs and constructed a dam to impound water for a small irrigation project.[20] Regardless of the location, the CCC-ID's primary aim always was to increase the value of Indian resources even as the number of projects declined on the various reservations.

Inexperience and poor planning plagued the CCC-ID during its early years. Engineers in charge of projects were forced to use appropriated funds before expiration dates, since surplus money had to be redistributed to other districts. At first, few Indians knew how to operate the crude equipment necessary for road and dam construction, and as a consequence hundreds of small earth dams had to be rebuilt. By 1936, the Indians generally had gained sufficient confidence and experience to undertake more elaborate projects. Heavier and more sophisticated machinery replaced horse-drawn scrapers, and concrete spillways became a regular addition to the larger dams constructed on the Red Earth and Cheyenne rivers.[21]

Such structures marked a change in the original purpose of the CCC-ID in that the maximum amount of money should go into payrolls, not expensive equipment.[22] Building these larger projects necessitated the use of heavy equipment and skilled workers. Again, many of the Sioux were inexperienced in operating earth movers, dump trucks, cranes, and large cement mixers, so non-Indians filled some of the positions. With the stress on speed and efficiency, supervisors allotted little time for training new enrollees. The dependency on machinery increased the amount of work accomplished but had an unfavorable effect on Indian employment.

Several factors combined to cause the emphasis on the increased size of projects. Engineers in the district office could easily and accurately analyze the production cost of dam building. The immense area of the Billings district required concentration on projects that could be supervised and planned from a central office. Moreover, in 1936 when the CCC-ID began working with the Irrigation Division in developing irrigation facilities for subsistence gardens, the Billings office immediately drew up plans for several large reservoirs on the South Dakota reservations.[23]

Tom C. White, district coordinator, revitalized the character of the Billings district by constantly requesting new and expanded production roles. After Washington accepted most of his proposals, White would then seek permission to hire skilled whites to operate the machinery rather than train Indians for such duties. His policy was to keep enrollees in unskilled labor, so that the equipment would not be damaged or production delayed. This thoughtlessness for the welfare of the enrollees carried over into the education program, which lagged far behind other areas in off-duty activities. Any encouragement in vocational and educational training of CCC-ID enrollees came from reservation officials, not the Billings headquarters.[24]

Under White's insistence several small irrigated gardens, from two to fifteen acres each, were constructed on every South Dakota reservation by the end of 1936. The Irrigation Division assisted in the site selection, designed the irrigation system, and furnished the pumping equipment while Interior

A CCC-ID construction crew works to build a dam at Pine Ridge.

Roger Bromert, Weatherford, OK

Department officials selected the location on the basis of land ownership, soil quality, the number of families within a certain radius, and the quantity of water supply. No serious problems were encountered except an occasional legal question over water rights. The CCC-ID, with its existing organization for construction work, performed earth-moving operations and supervised the building. Responsibility for the gardens—usually small pumping projects along the Missouri River—fell to the reservation superintendents. The Sioux normally operated the gardens on a family basis except in a few instances where they participated in community enterprises with the produce being shared equally by everybody. All gardens yielded more than enough vegetables for personal consumption, thus allowing a surplus for marketing on the reservations.[25]

In addition to furnishing water for irrigation, the small storage dams provided a dependable water supply for both domestic and stock use, as well as improving the health and sanitation conditions for many reservation residents. Even though the subsistence gardens were financially successful and contributed to the economic rehabilitation of the Sioux, the plan did not meet White's expectations because, in complying with CCC-ID regulations, too much work had to be performed by hand labor![26]

The CCC-ID also cooperated directly with the Relief and Rehabilitation Program to provide facilities and opportunities for destitute Indians. Together these agencies strove to expand the economy of the Sioux people by developing truck-garden farms for food production and livestock industries for cash needs. The federal government selected the participants for the enterprises, with landless Indians receiving preferences, who would then come under direct supervision of the reservation superintendent.[27]

The Enrollee Program provided for the Indians' training, recreation, and welfare and was an integral part of the CCC-ID. Its major objective was to make Indian men more employable while presenting useful information applicable to everyday living. Because many of the enrollees could not read or write English, the program experienced more difficulty operating among the Sioux than with any other group in the country. The nature of the CCC-ID camps, coupled with the high turnover in employees, made it difficult to devise practicable training classes. Moreover, attitudes of area officials, like G. B. Arthur, the supervisor of project training at Pine Ridge, set the tone for the program's importance. "Work is the basis of CCC and is the all important thing. I am never going to allow anybody to take time out of our working day for training."[28] Given these problems and the fact that most enrollees who lived at home did not devote their off-duty time to education, on-the-job training became the principal method of instruction on the South Dakota reservations.

Despite White's insistence that production activities must dominate the CCC-ID camps, educational programs did much to boost the welfare and morale of the Indians. Corps officials provided a realistic concept of education that corresponded to the interests and needs of the enrollees and the reservations. The scope of the training was wider than the local conservation program itself. Many project leaders, truck drivers, and machine operators held first-aid certificates, and officials in the Extension Department sponsored educational discussion groups and weekend leadership workshops with supervisors, farm extension agents, physicians, and various government employees serving as classroom instructors. The Sioux received training in farm maintenance, carpentry, tractor operation and repair, Red Cross safety, and a variety of other fields. General adult education lagged behind more practical forms of instruction, but by the end of the 1930s officials at Pine Ridge and Cheyenne River had used CCC-ID funds to equip a truck with a traveling library.[29]

To assist the enrollees in their educational and recreational endeavors, camp administrators immediately purchased a movie projector. Educational movies on health, safety, gardening, and rodent control as well as films on CCC-ID activities were shown on a weekly basis. Entertaining movies, a novel experience for the Sioux, were viewed with mixed reactions. While watching a film about Yellowstone National Park, a number of people in the audience did not believe there were such things as geysers. Only after careful explanation and a reshowing of the film did the Cheyenne River officers convince the Indians that there were natural hot springs that intermittently ejected a column of water and steam.[30]

With the welfare of the enrollees as one of the main objectives of camp administrators, leisure time received considerable attention. The Indians enjoyed a variety of athletic games—from baseball to "ice snakes"—but native songs and dances like the "Omaha," the "Grass," and the "Rabbit" were most popular.[31] The relaxed nature of the camps allowed the Sioux considerable flexibility and freedom. A typical day in an Indian CCC camp began with the 6:00 a.m. reveille and ended with "lights out" at 9:30 p.m. Curfew violators received no disciplinary action if they were ready for work the following morning. Enrollees spent weekends with families or friends, depending upon the distance from camps and the availability of transportation. Some camps on the South Dakota reservations provided busses on weekends. In general, life in the Indian CCC camps was informally regulated.[32]

In 1937, Congress refused to make the CCC a permanent agency but did extend it for three more years. This supplementary legislation indirectly affected the Indian program by granting ten hours a week for general and vocational

Although education was not a primary goal of the CCC-ID,
enrollees on the Standing Rock Reservation participated
in a fire-prevention class in 1937.
Roger Bromert, Weatherford, OK

training. Reaction from the production-minded Billings district took the form of a series of feeble excuses explaining why more education would be impractical on the huge Sioux reservations, so their program remained relatively unchanged. One official at Pine Ridge complained that the CCC-ID employed too many men over forty who were uninterested in education; therefore, no time would be allowed for training during the working day.[33] Even with the reluctance of Billings officials to encourage enrollee instruction, the Sioux realized some positive benefits. Training activities brought a fuller understanding of the bureau's intentions and helped remove some of the Indians' suspicions. Far more important was the fact that the more ambitious and talented Indians took advantage of the opportunity to improve themselves.

Roosevelt's determination to economize in the late 1930s cut sharply into the CCC-ID appropriations. In compliance with the president's directive, Fechner, director of the corps, notified his organization that it must employ one enrollee for every $930 received in CCC-ID funds.[34] This forced the Billings district, which usually hired one man for every $1,500 received, to spend less money for supervisors and expensive machinery necessary for the elaborate projects. In order to execute the new policy, Billings officials abandoned projects that could not be completed with hand labor and negotiated cooperative agreements with other bureau agencies.

With World War II approaching, the CCC-ID became increasingly involved in war production activities. Government officials used the corps' existing facilities to teach various national defense courses, while opportunities opened up for enrollees in the private sector of the economy. Indians obtained employment as carpenters, truck drivers, mechanics, and welders—an impossibility during the Depression years. After Congress completely cut the 1942 CCC-ID budget, it was only a matter of time before field officers halted production and laid off the enrollees and supervisory personnel.[35]

In the midst of the activities to support the war effort, the Indian CCC came under harsh criticism from the Rosebud Tribal Council who charged that the uncertainty of the work benefited few Indians and that the dams served only the large cattlemen who leased the land. These attacks were largely unfounded because the CCC-ID provided the Indians with a substantial portion of their income during the depression, and without the dams nobody would rent the grazing land. Probably the most legitimate complaints were against the supervisory personnel's excessive spending for machinery to construct large "show projects" that required skilled non-Indian labor. Likewise, officials used funds for cars and home improvements while most Indians lived in tents. Granted some of the criticisms were valid, but the overall accomplishments of the Indian CCC made most of them unjustified.[36]

The council's proposal to redraft the CCC-ID came too late, for the program ended on 10 July 1942. In closing its operation the Billings office encountered many frustrations. Much of the equipment, which was to be transferred to the War and Navy departments or the Civil Aeronautics Administration, was scattered throughout the reservations and could not be accounted for. If these agencies rejected the property, it remained in the custody of the Indian Service. This all involved a tremendous amount of paperwork and when finally completed, Pine Ridge alone transferred over $75,000 worth of equipment to the Army and Navy departments and retained $53,709 for itself.[37]

The CCC-ID left the Sioux after nine years of conservation and rehabilitation. Although there were diverse opinions over the effectiveness of the corps, it undoubtedly was one of the most popular and productive Indian programs of the decade. In South Dakota the CCC-ID employed 8,405 Indians and spent over $4.5 million on the Rosebud, Standing Rock, and Pine Ridge reservations alone. At Standing Rock in 1940, 97 percent of the population was still dependent on some form of relief, and nearly one half of the money received came from the CCC-ID.[38]

Certainly, the Indian CCC was neither designed as an end in itself, nor did it propose to solve all the enrollees' problems. The wages were insufficient for those desiring a working capital to become self-supporting, and most reservations lacked the necessary land base to support the population. Their lands were suited solely for grazing, but even that became extremely difficult because of fragmentation by allotments. Some Indians who planted gardens began using their CCC-ID earnings to purchase vegetables and thus neglected their crops. In such situations the program was virtually ineffective.

Despite some shortcomings the CCC-ID kept many poverty-stricken Indians from starving and supplied hundreds of enrollees with skills and proper work habits necessary for off-reservation jobs. That the corps gave the Sioux confidence and a new outlook on life became evident by the great exodus of Indian men from the reservation to military service and private industries. Moreover, it helped reverse the downward drift of the Sioux and gave them something to cling to during the desperate years of the 1930s.

NOTES

1. The official name for the agency was the Indian Emergency Conservation Work (IECW), but it was popularly referred to as the Civilian Conservation Corps-Indian Division (CCC-ID) and will be written as such in this article.

2. *New York Times*, 26 May 1933, 2. President Grant established the Board of Indian Commissioners in 1869 to make yearly reports to the secretary of the Interior. Franklin Roosevelt abolished this ten-member advisory board in 1933.

3. Randolph C. Downes, "A Crusade for Indian Reform, 1922–1934," *Mississippi Valley Historical Review* 32 (Dec. 1945): 336–42; Michael T. Smith, "The Wheeler-Howard Act of 1934: The Indian New Deal," *Journal of the West* 10 (July 1971): 522; Richard N. Ellis, ed., *The Western American Indian* (Lincoln: University of Nebraska Press, 1972), 144–45; Herbert S. Schell, *History of South Dakota*, rev. ed. (Lincoln: University of Nebraska Press, 1968), 337.

4. Schell, *History of South Dakota*, 336–37; Smith, "The Wheeler-Howard Act of 1934," 522.

5. 48 Stat 576.

6. Ramon Roubideaux, quoted in Joseph H. Cash and Herbert T. Hoover, eds., *To Be an Indian: An Oral History* (New York: Holt, Rinehart and Winston, 1971), 132.

7. Ella C. Lebow, "Transition of Indian Education from Federal to State Schools on the Rosebud Indian Reservation, Rosebud, South Dakota, 1942–1955" (master's thesis, University of South Dakota, 1958), 37; Evelyn C. Adams, *American Indian Education* (Morningside Heights, NY: Kings Crown Press, 1946), 78; 48 Stat 596.

8. *Catholic Sioux Herald* (Marty, SD), 15 July 1933, 7; Kenneth Roy Philp, "John Collier and the American Indian, 1920–1945," (PhD diss., Michigan State University, 1968), 149–50. See also Jeffrey L. Viken, "Quick Bear v. Leupp: Amalgamation of Church and State on the Rosebud," *South Dakota Historical Collections* 38 (1976): 4–72, for an in-depth legal study of the use of federal and tribal funds for the support of sectarian schools.

9. James L. Satterlee and Vernon D. Malan, "History and Acculturation of the Dakota Indians," Rural Sociology Department, Agricultural Experiment Station Bulletin no. 126 (Brookings: South Dakota State University, 1970), 62–63; G. E. E. Lindquist, "The Government's New Indian Policy," *The Missionary Review of the World* 57 (Apr. 1934): 182–84; "The Indian Problem Today," ibid. (June 1934): 261–62; Flora Warren Seymour, "Federal Favor for Fetishism," ibid. 58 (Sept. 1935): 397–400; Elaine Goodale Eastman, "Does Uncle Sam Foster Paganism?" *Christian Century* 51 (8 Aug. 1934): 1016; Cash and Hoover, *To Be an Indian*, 158.

10. Oliver La Farge, ed., *The Changing Indian* (Norman: University of Oklahoma Press, 1942), 74; Lewis Meriam et al., *The Problem of Indian Administration* (Baltimore: Johns Hopkins Press, 1928), 449–50.

11. 48 Stat 17.

12. "Final Report of E.C.W. and C.C.C. Indian Division," 2, File 32114-44, General Service, 344, Civilian Conservation Corps-Indian Division, Record Group (RG) 75, National Archives (NA), Washington, DC (hereafter cited as Final Report); J. P. Kinney, *Indian Forest and Range: A History of the Administration and Conservation of the Redman's Heritage* (Washington, DC: Forestry Enterprises, 1950), 275–76.

13. *New York Times*, 1 May 1933, 9, 27 Aug. 1933, 12; "Standing Rock Council Active in

CCC-ID," *Indians at Work* (Oct. 1940): 34; Donald Lee Parman, "The Indian CCC" (PhD diss., University of Oklahoma, 1967), 32–33.

14. U.S. Department of the Interior, Office of Indian Affairs, *Annual Report of the Commissioner of Indian Affairs to the Secretary of the Interior, 1933* (Washington, DC: Government Printing Office, 1933), 69.

15. Ibid., 69–70; Arthur Lawrence Bach, "Administration of Indian Resources in the U.S., 1933–1941" (PhD diss., State University of Iowa, 1942), 169–70; "C.C.C. Activities for Indians," *Monthly Labor Review* 40 (July 1939): 94–95; *Report of the Commissioner of Indian Affairs, 1933*, 70.

16. O. H. Schmocker, Supervisor, CCC-ID, to C. R. Whitlock, Superintendent Rosebud, 4 Dec. 1940, File 54193-38, Enrollee Program, 346, CCC-ID, RG 75, NA; "Narrative Reports," File 11854-33, Pine Ridge, 344, CCC-ID, RG 75, NA; U.S. Department of Interior, Office of Indian Affairs, *Indians at Work* (Washington, DC: Government Printing Office, 15 Nov. 1934), 46.

17. R. Mitchell, Superintendent of IECW, to John Collier, 16 Mar. 1934, File 16854-33, Pine Ridge, Vol. 1, 344, CCC-ID, RG 75, NA (hereafter cited as PR, CCC-ID); Charles Price Harper, *The Administration of the Civilian Conservation Corps* (Clarksburg, WV: Clarksburg Publishing Company, 1939), 72–73.

18. R. Mitchell to John Collier, 16 Mar. 1934, PR, CCC-ID.

19. Walter Prescott Webb, *The Great Plains* (New York: Grosset & Dunlap, 1931), 31; R. Mitchell to John Collier, 16 Mar. 1934, PR, CCC-ID.

20. *Catholic Sioux Herald*, 15 Nov. 1934, 4; Roy W. Meyer, *History of the Santee Sioux: United States Indian Policy on Trial* (Lincoln: University of Nebraska, 1967), 329–30.

21. Parman, "The Indian CCC," 104–05; Harvey W. Morris, "Emergency Conservation Work at Cheyenne River Reservation, South Dakota," *Indians at Work* (1 Aug. 1936), 32.

22. *Report of the Commissioner of Indian Affairs, 1933*, 71.

23. Tom White, Productions Coordinating Officer, to John Collier, "Progress Report," 12 July 1937, File 57439-36, Subsistence Gardens, RG 75, NA (hereafter cited as Subsistence Gardens); Parman, "The Indian CCC," 106.

24. Parman, "The Indian CCC," 106–08.

25. Tom White to John Collier, "Progress Report," 12 July 1937, Subsistence Gardens.

26. Ibid.

27. "Project Reports," File 76071-P-1a, Rehabilitation and Relief, RG 75, NA.

28. G. B. Arthur, Supervisor of Project Training Pine Ridge, quoted in W. O. Roberts, Superintendent Pine Ridge, to Tom White, 11 July 1940, File 59039, General Services, 344, CCC-ID, RG 75, NA.

29. Robert M. Patterson, Supervisor IECW Education, to all districts, 4 June 1936, File 58839, General Services, 344, CCC-ID, RG 75, NA.; Parman, "The Indian CCC," 171;

"Progress Report," no file number, Enrollee Program, Box 108, Pine Ridge, 346, CCC-ID, RG 75, NA.

30. "Progress Report," no file number, Enrollee Program, Box 118, Cheyenne River, CCC-ID, RG 75, NA.

31. Martha Jane Buchner, "Shinny and 'Snakes' on Rosebud," *Indians at Work* (1 Aug. 1936): 30–31. Ice Snakes, played at community gatherings, is one of the oldest contest games known to the Sioux. The snakes, made of carefully selected beef rib bones and balanced with feather tails, were thrown on either ice or smooth ground. The art of the game lay in making the snakes and in throwing them long distances.

32. Louis C. Schroeder, "Indian Conservation Camps," *Recreation* 28 (Aug. 1934): 249–52.

33. 50 Stat 383; John A. Salmond, *The Civilian Conservation Corps, 1933–42: A New Deal Case Study* (Durham, NC: Duke University Press, 1967), 26; W. O. Roberts to Tom White, 11 July 1940, File 59039, General Services, 344, CCC-ID, RG 75, NA (hereafter cited as General Services).

34. W. O. Roberts to Tom White, 11 July 1940, General Services; Parman, "The Indian CCC," 216.

35. Final Report, 1.

36. Rosebud Tribal Council to Robert Fechner, 16 Apr. 1941, File 50871-36, Rosebud, 220, CCC-ID, RG 75, NA.

37. Final Report, 76.

38. Ibid., 23–24: "Rehabilitation Reports," no file number, Box 122, Standing Rock, RG 75, NA; "CCC-ID Work Program, Statistical Data," 10 Apr. 1941, File 50871-36, Rosebud, 220, CCC-ID, RG 75, NA.

LAURA WOODWORTH-NEY

THE DIARIES OF A DAY-SCHOOL TEACHER

DAILY REALITIES ON THE PINE RIDGE INDIAN RESERVATION

1932–1942

· · ·

On 12 October 1932, Marion Billbrough received a Western Union telegram from Charles J. Rhoads, United States commissioner of Indian affairs, offering her an elementary teaching position at Day School Number Five on the Pine Ridge Indian Reservation in western South Dakota. If she decided to accept the position, which paid $1,680 per year, she was to report immediately to the railroad station in Rushville, Nebraska, and then hire transportation for the ride to Oglala, South Dakota. Two days later, Billbrough received a letter from the United States Department of the Interior confirming her appointment, "subject to taking the oath of office," to the position of elementary school teacher "classification grade 7 . . . in the Indian Field Service." Billbrough, who at the age of thirty-six had recently acquired her teaching certification from Washington State College at Pullman, Washington, was pleased to hear of the position. Unintimidated by the isolation of the Pine Ridge reservation, she quickly activated her "indefinite" contract by signing the Interior Department acceptance forms on 18 October 1932.[1]

Upon arriving on the reservation, Billbrough began a record of her experiences that would encompass the years 1932 to 1942. Her diaries and scrapbooks reveal much about an educational system that was then focusing on the day school as an important tool. Government officials and Indian policy reformers had long viewed education as crucial to the assimilation of American Indians into white society. In 1900, Elaine Goodale Eastman, an early champion of day schools and a director of schools on the Pine Ridge reservation, spoke for many of her contemporaries when she stated that education could provide Indian people a way "out of the tribal bond; out of Indian narrowness and clannishness; out into the broad life of the Nation."[2] For decades, however, most government educators had believed that Indian children could be assimilated most rapidly if they were removed from the "negative" influences

This essay originally appeared in *South Dakota History* 24 (Fall/Winter 1994): 194–211.

of their homes to boarding schools either on or off the reservation. While day schools existed, they functioned largely as an alternative for families living in remote areas and for those unwilling or unable to send their children to public or boarding schools. By the time Marion Billbrough began her career in the Indian Service, that philosophy had changed. In 1928, an Institute for Government Research study known as the Meriam Report concluded that children taught at government day schools not only received a better education but also carried what they learned home, influencing other family members. The Meriam team recommended that off-reservation schools be used only for grades six through twelve because day schools were best suited for transferring "ideas of cleanliness, better homekeeping, [and] better standards of living . . . almost immediately [to] the home and community."[3]

As she worked to implement these concepts at Pine Ridge, Marion Billbrough encountered an educational system that was often long on ideals and short on resources. The success of day-school teachers on the Pine Ridge reservation was limited by an acute lack of goods and services, barriers of culture and language, and the physical and psychological isolation that came with living in a remote location. Such conditions often forced the day-school teacher to assume many unofficial roles that diverted his or her energies from the classroom. In addition to instructing children, Billbrough dispensed medical care, directed recreational activities, and served as an invaluable link between her students' families and the off-reservation world. The kinship ties formed when she married George Dreamer, a member of the Oglala Sioux Tribe, further enabled her to address the educational, material, and social needs of the Indian community in which she lived.

Billbrough married George Dreamer on 13 October 1935. While the only reference to the wedding in her personal papers is a government "status change" form, their union appears to have been solid. Billbrough took George Dreamer's family name, and two of his daughters from a previous marriage, Geraldine and Jarline, lived with the couple at the school. In the perception of her Sioux neighbors, the teacher's marriage transformed her from an outsider to a community member with ties to the reservation.[4] Following their wedding, George Dreamer worked for the Pine Ridge Agency in a part-time capacity. Marion Dreamer controlled the family's domestic finances, and her teaching position provided the bulk of their income. In fact, the Indian Office attempted to eliminate George Dreamer's position because of his wife's relatively high-paying job. "Its a shame when he is so anxious to work," Dreamer recorded in her diary a year after their marriage. "He is always so proud when he brings his paycheck home. He always gives it to me and we go to town and pay the bills."

George Dreamer spent much of his spare time working in the home and help-ing his wife in the school, a testament to the unique division of roles the couple practiced.[5]

Even with her husband's help, the physical challenges of life on the Pine Ridge reservation sometimes made the execution of Dreamer's official teach-ing duties difficult. Day School Number Five, also known as the Lone Man Day School, was located five miles from Oglala, the nearest population center. Dreamer and her family occupied a three-room apartment in the school build-ing, which had no plumbing. She noted that the school's well, where many people from the surrounding area obtained their water, attracted rattlesnakes that "liked to coil up under the spout on warm evenings." Behind the school building stood a barn, garage, and commissary, and "below the hill" were sev-eral large vegetable gardens that Dreamer tended.[6] From 1939 to 1942, she also taught at Grass Creek Day School near Manderson. Frontier-like conditions often prevailed at both locations; Dreamer once recorded a summer high tem-perature of 107 degrees and a winter low of 44 degrees below zero. For the duration of her stay at Grass Creek, the school needed a new heating plant.

Both day schools served their immediate areas, with Number Five receiving its students from the White Clay Creek drainage area and Grass Creek drawing children from Manderson. Most students apparently walked five miles or less to attend school. Enrollment stood at approximately twenty to thirty, but daily attendance figures varied greatly.[7] Dreamer's students ranged in age from five to sixteen years, and she taught them a variety of basic subjects, including read-ing and American history. Moral lessons also found a place in her classroom. In one scrapbook photograph taken in February 1939, Dreamer is pictured pre-siding over a class of twenty-seven at Grass Creek Day School. Behind her, the Ten Commandments are clearly delineated on the chalkboard. Her students also celebrated all of the American holidays. Halloween, for example, found the children carving pumpkins and fashioning masks out of brown paper.[8]

Dreamer's students were poor, as were many residents of the Pine Ridge reservation, which, in addition to suffering under the Great Depression, had few resources for capital development and a land base poorly suited to agricul-ture. The reservation's scattered population, rough terrain, and poorly main-tained roads made communication and travel both expensive and difficult. Dreamer found that the lack of transportation often denied reservation resi-dents the supplies, medical services, and printed communication that non-Indians took for granted. Because she had access to government vehicles, the teacher met many requests to run errands and help in personal emergencies. Families desperate to obtain groceries and other supplies frequently asked

As evidenced by the Ten Commandments chalked on the
blackboard behind Marion Dreamer, moral lessons supplemented
the basic subjects she taught in the Grass Creek classroom.
Manuscripts, Archives and Special Collections,
Washington State University Libraries, Pullman

Dreamer for assistance. "Mrs. Dreamer," wrote one man, "I wonder if we can buy Flour and Baking Powder or Yeast from the school. We are out of all Groceries but on account of the weather we cannot go to the store for it."[9] Lizzie Kills Enemy wrote, "If you going to Oglala Tomorrow, why please could you buy me 6 box of cracker, & 1 bb tea, and the rest I want close-pins." In the same message, George Kills Enemy asked Dreamer to pick up his mail in Manderson: "I'm expecting two Packages but I have no way of going to town. I hurt myself but soon as I'm better I will bring in the 50 cents worth of wood."[10] George Dreamer often drove members of the community to town in response to the pleas directed toward his wife, including one from a man who wondered if "Geo could take I and my old lady into Chadron this morning she has been suffering with her teeth for two weeks."[11]

Marion Dreamer received numerous other requests for medical aid, prompting her to provide not only transportation but also first-aid supplies and advice for many of her students and their families. One parent sought "some kind of stuff for my ear I have ear ach for three days."[12] Another inquired about "some powder for my baby."[13] One mother, probably referring to a case of impetigo, asked for some salve. "Levi has a sore on his mouth," she wrote, "and its getting all over his face so please send me some by Jonas if you can spare it."[14] Instructions from mothers concerning the dispensing of medicine to their children further illustrate the medical duties of the day-school instructor: "Please see that Bernice takes this medicine every two hours. She has a very bad cough."[15] Another mother wrote: "Please, don't give Irene any cod liver oil, she said it made her sick when ever she's think about it. I guess she dislike it."[16]

Dreamer accepted her unofficial role as a nurse, observing the health of her students carefully and intervening when she deemed it necessary. An April 1937 diary entry reveals her concern about one family whose children had been ill for some time. Dreamer noted that because one of the girls often "gives out by noon," she had been sending them home after lunch. "We [Marion and George Dreamer] went over to the house last Wed night to see the mother about them. She said she would take them to the hospital," Dreamer wrote. "Friday they went in but the children said the doctor was not there. At that time the little girl who had been in the hospital last week was running around with out any shoes." The family was "in desperate circumstances," Dreamer reported. "Two beds for nine of them with hardly any bedding. . . . To-day Irene is just as tired out as Mary Rose. She has sit around the school house all day."[17] Another April 1937 passage reveals the degree to which Dreamer monitored the health of her students: "All the children except Katherine Kindle are in school again. Her sister told me yesterday that she was sick and did not seem to get any better. She has been sick for three weeks. George took her to the hospital to-day and the doctor kept her there."[18]

Day-school absenteeism was one symptom of the desperate health conditions on the Pine Ridge reservation. General poverty, undernourishment, and wretched sanitary conditions contributed to a high incidence of infant mortality and an alarming frequency of communicable disease. In 1928, the Meriam Report had called the United States government's preventive work in combating tuberculosis and trachoma "weak" and had added that the "same word must be applied to the efforts toward preventing infant mortality and the diseases of children."[19] In nearly one-third of the eighteen states studied, the percentage of Indian children who died before the age of three was "double or more than double" that of the general population.[20] Trachoma, a highly contagious eye disease that could lead to blindness, affected many school-age children on the reservation. Doctors periodically conducted examinations at school, usually sending those who needed further treatment to the hospital. However, at one school, Dreamer related, the visiting physician "laid the children on a table, held the eyelids back and scraped them with a sharp knife."[21]

Despite Dreamer's admission on 9 April 1937 that "the Doctor came today and gave the children a pretty good examination. The best I've seen since I came to Pine Ridge," her diary entries suggest that Pine Ridge residents had experienced little improvement in health conditions in the years since the Meriam study. Within one four-day period in 1937, she recorded three deaths, two of infants. On 4 March, Dreamer wrote: "Mrs. He Dog died, Geo took Willie to Pine Ridge to get things for the feast. The Little Brings Him Back baby died too. Geo began digging the He Dog grave." Her account of another infant death on 8 March is sorrowful in its simplicity: "Geo went to McKinley Slow Bears to take his little baby to the cemetery. It is about a month old and died last night. It was burried in the Catholic Cemetry at Oglala. They took it in the back of the car."[22]

Family illness and death took its toll on classroom attendance. On 9 March 1937, two of the Slow Bear girls were excused from school to take care of their younger brother while their father was at the cemetery. Mrs. Slow Bear did not witness the burial of her baby, Dreamer recorded, because "she had to take another sick child (Rose Mary) in to the hospital."[23] Corine Stands, another of Dreamer's young female students, continually missed school because of recurring bouts of tuberculosis. Eventually, the onset of the late stages of the disease caused all of the school-age members of her family to miss class. On 2 December 1936, Dreamer recorded a visit from one of the girl's relatives, who relayed that "Corine was very bad" and "hardly pulled through the night." She died the next day.[24]

Acutely aware of the poverty and physical deprivation her schoolchildren suffered, Dreamer was often forced to meet their bodily needs. The problem of inadequate clothing was a constant hindrance to her administration of the day school. On a snowy day in December 1936, Dreamer observed "a child playing out doors with his shoes fastened with wire And no stockings. . . . His mother and father are dead. He lives with his uncle."[25] A lack of winter clothing prompted one mother to ask the teacher to "please excuse Alvina" because "I just couldn't find her last year's overshoes and so she won't be in school today."[26]

Dreamer received numerous requests for assistance in providing clothing for children. One woman asked whether the school could provide a pair of shoelaces for her daughter, while another adult "respectfully" inquired "whether John's shoes could be repaired at the Boarding school shoe shop."[27] The clothing problem eventually grew to such proportions that the day school instituted a clothes-making program in which a number of parents also participated. Dreamer took a leading role in the project, which, while needed, drew time away from academic pursuits. "We are helping the girls make their own dresses," she wrote in the fall of 1936. "My children cut theirs out and baste them together. There are twenty-two to be made. The older girls help with the hand work and machine work. I do a lot of the Machine work nights after supper. One mother offered to help and two of them came for patterns."[28]

The clothes-making effort was not without controversy, and Dreamer met some opposition while coordinating the program. Many families resented the assumption that they could not provide adequate clothing for their children, while others objected to the quality of the clothes provided. The comments of Mrs. Pretty Bird typified their objections: "I see Ollie underskirts is little tight and very short. . . . Ethel is not growing small, shes growing big that some of her dresses are to small. I have to do something to them so she could use them. If the parents have to buy the clothes, they have to be made so they can be worth buying. Otherwise they have to leave it alone and its best to go without it. I am telling you this to guide us."[29]

Other parents, however, welcomed the clothing program and expressed relief at its institution. Mrs. Effie T. Bulls thanked Dreamer "very much for the little clothes" and insisted that "we were very glad to get them." A Mrs. Gillespie wrote, "Billy is so worried about his clothes he wishes for me to write you a note and see if you could send them by George." Samuel Stands thanked

Dreamer for the stockings and shoelaces provided for his daughter Corine with the Lakota phrase "Nitakola miyo."[30]

In addition to clothing assistance, the day school provided morning snacks and a hot lunch—for some children, the day's only meal. According to Dreamer, twelve thousand of the twenty-six thousand seven hundred dollars appropriated to operate the Pine Ridge day schools in 1937 went for food.[31] A seventeen-year-old girl who had attended a Pine Ridge day school during the 1940s recalled, "The only good meal I had was in school, so I would never miss a day."[32] One mother's note to Dreamer stated, "Levi is going to school today but if its blowing or starts to please excuse him as he isn't very strong like the others we are hard up on grub and I want him in school today."[33] Dreamer remarked in her own memoirs that "children were sent to school very young so as to have them fed."[34] A particularly descriptive diary entry dated 27 April 1937 reveals Dreamer's concern for her hungry students: "Mary Rose and Irene came through all the rain with no overshoes on. They walk about two and a half miles. Mary Rose was crying. Their clothing was wet. I think they came to get a good meal." Dreamer immediately gave the girls some milk to drink "as I know that all they have is some flour, salt, baking powder, at home." She continued: "Irene just sits in her seat. George is not working to-day so he talked to her. She said her head ached. He asked her what they had for breakfast and she said bread and milk. I shall see Mr. Cummings about the family and find out what rashions they are working for."[35]

Dreamer's determination to confront Peter Cummings, the Pine Ridge Agency farmer, with the family's problem suggests a willingness to act as a liaison between the Oglala Sioux and the reservation administration.[36] The Indian Office dominated the economic life of the reservation as its main employer and consumer of goods and services. It also administered the reservation "relief" system, distributing the semi-monthly rations that consisted primarily of flour, sugar, and beans. In acting as an unofficial middleman, Dreamer facilitated Indian contact with the federal government, a task that could be accomplished only through the reservation's superintendent, who also had the power to distribute and withhold resources.[37]

Dreamer also helped to alleviate her students' economic distress by hiring them to execute minor jobs around the school grounds. One woman inquired about a job for herself, writing, "I would like to know if you have any work for me to do. I would like to work as I am very hard up and need work, and if you haven't any work for me to do I wonder if you care to have one of the boys work for you."[38] Another woman sent a note "by Franklin that Bernice and Neville are not coming because of the snow. . . . Mrs. Dreamer I wish you'd give the two older ones some work to do there at school so they can get over shoes. Thats if they're not high price."[39]

In addition to hiring students for odd jobs, Marion and George Dreamer offered them pay for produce. One correspondent wrote, "Isaac wanted to give you a melon today I am sending you two if you want just one its alright . . . you can give him what you think its worth." On occasion, the Dreamers also made the spoils of George's hunting excursions available for sale to community members.[40]

In one diary passage, Dreamer criticized a father for not providing for his family, thus revealing her own background in a patriarchical belief system. "He just will not work," she wrote, even though "Pete Cummings says that he can work [at the agency farm] for rations." Dreamer helped to ease the family's burden by providing work at the schoolhouse for two of the children, whose earnings went toward clothing.[41] In a scrapbook passage she later revealed that the children's mother "came and cleaned house for me once a week. We were always bothered with [her] borrowing food. . . . Many years later in a letter to me she said, 'How did you stand our borrowing and bothering so much?' Well, she had so many children and so little to feed them."[42]

Dreamer also helped her neighbors to meet their intellectual as well as physical needs. By providing access to magazines, newspapers, and books, she relieved some of the literary isolation of the community. May Gillespie asked Dreamer to "spare me the next household magazine when you are through with it if you please." In 1940, an anonymous correspondent wondered if she would lend him a Bible for "the old testament storieses. I will return it soon."[43] Another anonymous petitioner commented, "I'll like to know if you could let me have or borrow a couple of 'life' books or magazine's," adding with a touch of humor, "Maybe I won't destroy them like the [others] do."[44] The reading material Dreamer provided was especially valued during the colorless years of the Great Depression. In 1936, she wrote: "Am sending all of my magazines and papers either to some of the dam sights or to some of the homes. Some of the people ask for papers. Especially those people working on the dams as they have no amusement in the evenings except playing cards."[45]

In helping to meet the social, as well as physical and intellectual, needs of her students and their families, Dreamer filled the role of community builder. Under her direction, Day School Number Five emerged as a social gathering place, an embodiment of community spirit for the isolated locale. "There is a lot of talk about having an organized play program here in the Community with the school grounds as the meeting place," she noted in April 1937. "They are all pepped up about it and spend a lot of time in the school room talking about it. . . . There are forty young men that are not married in this community. There are seven young girls and many young children of school age. There has not been a wedding in two years. These young people live with their parents and there is nothing to keep them out of mischief. They need some place to play." Dreamer's role in the "play program" went beyond the mere expression of concern as she actively promoted the project to other reservation administrators.[46] Her school also became the site of meetings for the Young Men's Christian Association (YMCA), an active religious and social organization on the Pine Ridge. Fifty-two people attended one gathering. "They conducted a religious meeting first," Dreamer reported, "a singing meeting next, a play time next, and a lunch and then a business meeting. They left at eleven o'clock."[47]

Dreamer's constant presence at the school attests to the depth of her students' social needs and the lengths to which she went to fill those needs. "I work in the school room every night," she noted in the fall of 1936. "From two to three people come in and talk."[48] One diary entry for October 1936 reflects her lighthearted interaction with students during after-school hours: "Several of the children have been in [to the school] in the evening. Some of them came to get me to help them kill a skunk one night. We had a very exciting time. My house still smells of skunk."[49] Several months later, she wrote, "Every night there are several boys here playing basket ball until dark."[50] Baseball also became a unifying activity for reservation youth, and Dreamer reported that on one spring evening several boys "came to the school house to talk about having a base ball team in this community. They thought they could have two teams."[51]

Even on weekends, Dreamer spent time at school and made herself available to the people of her district. "The children from the Boarding School come in every week end to tell me about what is going on at school," she wrote in November 1936.[52] Late one Sunday several months later, Dreamer described the diverse activities that had taken place around the school that day: "The only people [left] around are Pough Young Man and Charlie Holy Pipe. Charlie read books and Pough worked on his time report for the farm chapter. All day long the people came about their children being sick or for basket balls. The last one came about nine o'clock for cod liver oil."[53]

Dreamer filled a social role among the adults as well, personally visiting parents to discuss the progress of their children and forming friendships and close community ties in the process. She also used the school as a site for social activities that included adults, such as the Halloween party she and George Dreamer hosted in 1936 and the community party they held in November.[54] On 22 December, she wrote, "two of the Indian people helped decorate the

In addition to educating children, Office of Indian Affairs day
schools served as centers for many social activities. Feasting on
watermelons from the school garden, community members celebrated
the first day of school at Day School Number Five in September 1934.
Manuscripts, Archives and Special Collections,
Washington State University Libraries, Pullman

Children model the masks they made for Halloween, one of the
many American holidays observed with parties and
treats at Day School Number Five.
Manuscripts, Archives and Special Collections,
Washington State University Libraries, Pullman

school room for Xmas," and on 23 December, "we had the school program" and "a feast for the people afterward. The office sent out the candy, oranges, and apples" for the entire community.[55]

Despite Dreamer's untiring work as a cultural liaison, her diary entries suggest an ambivalence toward the ideology of the Indian Service, which used the day schools to promote American cultural superiority and the assimilation of American Indians. While Dreamer's general view of the Sioux people was often stereotypical, her relationships with individuals expressed cultural acceptance and interaction. Historian Peggy Pascoe has found that Protestant missionary women on Indian reservations "forged cross-cultural bonds" more frequently and "with more genuine affection" than their own notions of Victorian moral superiority would seem to allow.[56] Similarly, Dreamer interacted culturally to a much greater degree than her overall view of American Indians would imply.

The diary entries that illustrate Dreamer's ethnocentric views employ language such as "these people" or "the Indians" in reference to the Sioux. For example, on 14 October 1936, Dreamer discussed in a positive manner two individuals involved in the clothes-making project at Day School Number Five. However, she went on to make the generally derogatory statement that the program would "make these lazy people work."[57] Dreamer also rationalized criticisms aimed at her and her husband with statements of racial intolerance. In the caption beneath a scrapbook photograph of George Dreamer's registered Hereford calves, Marion Dreamer wrote that the agency had received complaints that the cattle were kept on school land. "The office said it was all right as long as we were buying food for them," she explained. "In the spring, we had to pay pasture for them. Indians always complain if some other Indian has something better than he has. If you have money the relatives come and live with you until its gone."[58]

Dreamer's relationships with individuals stand in sharp contrast to these stereotypical views and indicate that she appreciated and participated in Sioux cultural customs. On 1 January 1937, Dreamer wrote that she had received "two small pair moccasins" and explained that "it is a custom among the Indians to give gifts at New Years time."[59] In return, she presented her students with gifts that she might have given to her non-Indian friends. "A friend of my mothers has a hat shop," Dreamer wrote in November of 1936. "She sent new hats for all of the little girls in my room. She also sent several hats for older people. These I sent over to the church womans club."[60] The generosity of Dreamer's mother was met with an extension of cultural gifts in return. At least one student expressed her pleasure at receiving a hat by bringing in a sample of beadwork for Dreamer to send home.[61]

Dreamer also purchased Sioux cultural objects for herself and encouraged the use of such items in the classroom. In 1937 she recorded, "Bought some bead work and a bow and arrows from Mr. Running Eagle. Mr. Eagle Hawk brought me some Indian things to use in the school room."[62] The November 1936 diary entry indicating that "Mrs. No Fat made a teepee for the school room" provided other examples of the extent to which Dreamer interacted with the Sioux community. The teacher noted at the same time that she had "sent quilt pieces to the Indian womans Church club" and that "several times this month some of the Indians have been in to dinner."[63]

An article Dreamer prepared for the *Journal of Health and Physical Education* further illustrated her active interest in Oglala culture. The essay, entitled "Recreation among the Sioux Indians," chronicled the survival of traditional games in the contemporary classroom. The game of "Bear," a traditional juvenile pastime, was originally played with a cactus attached to the end of a long stick; the object was to avoid being hit with the cactus by the child who had been designated "bear." According to Dreamer, her students substituted a "home made ball" for the original cactus, and the "teacher playing Bear with the children finds himself Bear all the time."[64] Dreamer also described the Sun Dance and indicated her agreement with Indian Commissioner John Collier's attempt to revitalize native culture on Indian reservations by removing restrictions on many traditional activities. "In some of the old regalias," Dreamer wrote, "the Indian danced partly naked," an activity that many whites frowned upon. In response, "the Indian bought the white man's union suit, colored it any color that pleased him and put it on under his regalia." Dreamer supported "the new order of things," which eliminated this "stupid regulation" and allowed one "to enjoy the beauty of the Indian dance by observing the muscular movements that accompany all such dances."[65] Dreamer concluded by expressing dismay over the decline of traditional American Indian culture. "Because the white man has belittled the things that were Indian," she contended, "he has caused the younger people to be ashamed of the old Indian culture" even though "modern civilization can learn a lot of good from the old Indians' way of living." In Dreamer's view, the greatest challenge for teachers in Indian schools was to make "both the Indian children and white people proud of the old Indian culture."[66]

Nothing attests more strongly to the development of Dreamer's intercultural respect than does her relationship with her husband. Although she never mentioned the intimacies of their private life in her diaries, she often referred to their shared activities. The couple hunted, vacationed, and took long walks together. On 20 September 1936, in a typical diary entry, Dreamer described a pleasant Sunday drive: "Went over to Chadron [Nebraska] and back home over the Black Tail Valley. We found the roads near Chadron pretty well washed out. We took our lunch and ate under some trees. We stopped at some dam after we reached the reservation and Geo got one duck."[67]

Most suggestive of the affection the two shared are the poems George Dreamer wrote for his wife after she resigned her teaching position in 1942 and moved temporarily to Shepherd, Michigan. Apart for four months while George Dreamer finalized details at their home on the Pine Ridge, the couple communicated primarily through letters. George Dreamer admitted in one letter that "I get along nicely during the day but when evening comes [I] begin to feel loneliness especially when its dark." In an accompanying poem, he wrote: "When Evening shadow falls/ . . . I begin to twiddle with my fingers/ And my heart seems to leave me/ to go on its way to you."[68] The text of a watercolor Christmas card George Dreamer made for his wife further illustrates the strength the pair found in each other: "Then let us smile/ when skies are grey/ And laugh at stormy weather/ And sing life's lonesome times away/ So worry/ and the dreariest day/ Will find an end together." Marion Dreamer later penciled on the back of the card, "My husband made this. He made all of my Xmas cards and did my note paper."[69]

The Dreamers had left Pine Ridge out of a frustration with the Indian Office bureaucracy and its effects on reservation life. George Dreamer had tried for years to obtain a "fee in patent" for two of his reservation land allotments, which would have given him complete control of the holdings. In all, he held interests in four allotments: his own and portions of those inherited from his mother, Rosa No Fat; his first wife, Lydia Little Spotted Horse; and his stepfather, Adam Red Shirt. Two of the allotments were located on the western side of the reservation where the Dreamers lived, but George's inherited interest in them was too meager to support a family. Dreamer leased out his other allotments, situated on the reservation's eastern border, but he received little in rent. He intended to acquire a fee patent for the eastern allotments so that he could sell the land and invest the money in livestock or machinery to use at his place of residence. Dreamer's plans were stymied, however, by legislation meant to protect American Indians.[70]

Under the Dawes Severalty Act of 1887, the land parcels issued to tribal members were to be held in trust by the United States government for twenty-five years, a stipulation intended to protect Indian lands from speculation. At the end of the trust period, the government would issue a fee patent, allowing the allottee to keep or dispose of the land as he or she saw fit. Modifications to the Dawes Act, such as the Burke Act of 1906, however, resulted in the early issuance of many fee patents with the inevitable result of immensely diminished tribal landholdings nationwide. The Indian Reorganization Act of 1934 reversed this trend by prohibiting further allotment and restricting the issuance of fee patents, thus creating a bureaucratic obstacle for George Dreamer.[71]

As early as 1936, Marion Dreamer revealed the couple's disillusionment with reservation life: "We are trying to locate a place in Idaho near Salmon. If we can get what we want we will leave in April." In the same entry, she disclosed what she believed to be the source of their problems. "If you vote for Roosevelt this fall," she asserted, "you can hope to live under just such conditions as the people here do. Its the way the government controls people. When things go over to Government control in this country we are leaving for Canada. Geo talks about it all of the time."[72] Dreamer's willingness to leave her job during the Great Depression attests to the level of frustration she must have experienced with the reservation bureaucracy.

Despite their problems, the Dreamers did not leave the Pine Ridge reservation until 1942, when they moved to Custer, South Dakota. Marion Dreamer's manuscript collection provides little information about either her husband or her life from 1944 to 1966, when she joined the Volunteers In Service To America (VISTA) program. During her six years with VISTA, she worked in Tempe, Arizona; Wolf Point, Montana; Sparta, Wisconsin; Marsing, Idaho; Nemo, South Dakota; and Waimea Kauai, Hawaii. After leaving VISTA in 1972, Dreamer traveled in Europe and worked for the Job Corps in Nemo, South Dakota. An extensive file of warm "thank you" letters from Job Corps participants attests to her contributions to that program. In 1977, Dreamer retired and moved to De Witt, Michigan.[73]

The diaries and scrapbooks of Marion Billbrough Dreamer reveal a life devoted to teaching under diverse and sometimes difficult conditions. Illness, a scarcity of goods and services, and the acute physical and emotional isolation inherent in living on the reservation often interrupted Dreamer's educational and administrative duties. Her unofficial roles as provider, nurse, and social director added to the complexity of the day school teacher's position. In return, however, Dreamer's personal interaction with reservation residents expanded her own perceptions of both the Oglala Sioux and her duties as a teacher among them. The record she left offers insight into the conditions non-Indian educators in government schools faced and the changes these conditions produced in the teachers' own cultural perceptions.

1. Rhoads to Billbrough (telegram), 12 Oct. 1932; J. Atwood Maulding to Billbrough, 14 Oct. 1932; and U.S. Department of the Interior, Office of Indian Affairs, Pine Ridge Agency, Acceptance Form 1-325 for Temporary Employment for Emergency Work in the Field, 18 Oct. 1932, all in Cage 69, File 1, Marion Billbrough Dreamer Papers, Manuscripts, Archives, and Special Collections, Holland Library, Washington State University, Pullman, WA. Marion Billbrough Dreamer donated her personal papers to Washington State University, where she also received a BS in zoology in 1944. The Dreamer Papers comprise approximately thirty-five items, most of which are diaries, scrapbooks, and letters. The collection spans sixty years, from the 1920s, when Dreamer taught on the Crow Indian Reservation in Montana, to the 1980s, when she retired to De Witt, Michigan. Quotations taken from materials in the Dreamer Papers remain in their original form, although punctuation has been added if its absence hindered understanding.

2. Elaine Goodale Eastman, quoted in Tom Holm, "Racial Stereotypes and Government Policies Regarding the Education of Native Americans, 1879–1920," in *Multicultural Education and the American Indian*, University of California, Contemporary American Indian Issues Series, no. 2 (Los Angeles, 1979), 18.

3. Lewis Meriam et al., *The Problem of Indian Administration*, Institute for Government Research, Studies in Administration (Baltimore: Johns Hopkins Press, 1928), 34–35, 411–12. See also Francis Paul Prucha, *The Great Father: The United States Government and the American Indians*, 2 vols. (Lincoln: University of Nebraska Press, 1984), 2:815, 821, 838; Francis Paul Prucha, *Indian Policy in the United States: Historical Essays* (Lincoln: University of Nebraska Press, 1981), 43–45. Urging extensive revision of governmental health, education, and economic programs on Indian reservations, the Meriam Report ushered in a new era of self-determination for American Indians and guided government policy until the early 1950s.

4. U.S. Department of the Interior, Office of Indian Affairs, Pine Ridge Agency, Status Change Form 1-612, 22 Oct. 1935, and 1937–1942 Scrapbook, 7, both in File 1, Dreamer Papers.

5. Dreamer, 1936 Diary, 3 Oct., File 1, Dreamer Papers. See also the entries for 5, 15, and 17 Oct.

6. Scrapbook, 1933–1937, 1, ibid.

7. Grass Creek Day School Quarterly Report, 30 June 1941, 1937–1942 File, Educational Decimal Files, General Records, Pine Ridge Agency, George C. Wells to Dreamer, 14 May 1941, Education Records Series, Pine Ridge Agency, and Day School Number Five Quarterly Report, 18 June 1942, Education Records Series, Pine Ridge Agency, all in Records of the Bureau of Indian Affairs, Record Group 75, Federal Archives and Records Center, Kansas City, MO; Dreamer, 1937 Diary, 27 Apr., File 1, Dreamer Papers.

8. Dreamer, Grass Creek Scrapbook, Feb. 1939, 28, File 1, Dreamer Papers, and Scrapbook, 1933–1937, Oct. 1934, 11.

9. J. Holy Rock to Dreamer, n.d., Scrapbook of Memos, 1932–1942, File 1, Dreamer Papers.

10. Lizzie Kills Enemy and George Kills Enemy to Dreamer, n.d., ibid.

11. George Kills Enemy to Marion Dreamer, n.d., ibid.

12. Lucy Stands to Dreamer, n.d., ibid.

13. Anonymous to Dreamer, n.d., ibid.

14. Annie Stands to Dreamer, n.d., ibid.

15. Mrs. Sunclaw to Dreamer, n.d., ibid.

16. Rose Slow Bear to Dreamer, n.d., ibid.

17. Dreamer, 1937 Diary, 26 Apr.

18. Ibid., 7 Apr.

19. Meriam, *Problem of Indian Administration*, 10.

20. Ibid., 199.

21. Dreamer, Grass Creek Scrapbook, Jan. 1941, 38. After 1937, sulfa drugs proved effective in fighting the disease. Prucha, *Great Father*, 2:863.

22. Dreamer, 1937 Diary, 4, 8 Mar., 9 Apr.

23. Ibid., 9 Mar.

24. Dreamer, 1936 Diary, 2, 4 Dec.

25. Ibid., 3 Dec.

26. Mrs. Fannie B. S. Life to Dreamer, n.d., Scrapbook of Memos.

27. Charles B. Yellow to Dreamer, 10 May 1937, ibid.

28. Dreamer, 1936 Diary, Oct. summary.

29. Mrs. Pretty Bird to Dreamer, n.d., Scrapbook of Memos.

30. Mrs. Effie T. Bulls to Dreamer, n.d., Mrs. Gillespie to Dreamer, n.d., and Samuel Stands to Dreamer, n.d., all ibid.

31. Dreamer, 1936 Diary, 2 Dec.

32. Murray L. Wax, Rosalie H. Wax, and Robert V. Dumont, Jr., *Formal Education in an American Indian Community* (N.p.: Society for the Study of Social Problems, 1964), 62.

33. Annie Stands to Dreamer, 19 Feb., Scrapbook of Memos.

34. Dreamer, Scrapbook, 1933–1937, 1.

35. Dreamer, 1937 Diary, 27 Apr.

36. The agency farmer, or "boss farmer," was appointed by the reservation agent to instruct individual Indians about farming their allotted lands. After 1900, agency farmers gradually acquired more supervisory responsibilities, becoming in effect "sub-agents" for the more isolated areas of the reservation. Meriam, *Problem of Indian Administration*, 14–15, 540–41.

37. Wax, Wax, and Dumont, *Formal Education*, 18; Martha Powers, *Oglala Women: Myth, Ritual, and Reality* (Chicago: University of Chicago Press, 1986), 32.

38. Annie Stands to Dreamer, 15 June 1936, Scrapbook of Memos.

39. Mrs. Sits Poor to Dreamer, 6 Jan. 1942, ibid.

40. Anonymous to Dreamer, n.d., Scrapbook of Memos. See also Peter Stands to Dreamer, n.d., ibid.

41. Dreamer, 1937 Diary, 27 Apr.

42. Dreamer, Scrapbook, 1933–1937, 26.

43. Mrs. May Gillespie to Dreamer, n.d., and Anonymous to Dreamer, 1 Nov. 1940, both ibid.

44. Anonymous to Dreamer, 25 Mar. 1941, ibid.

45. Dreamer, 1936 Diary, Oct. summary. The "dam sites" Dreamer refers to were part of the Oglala dam project, an Indian New Deal relief effort administered by the Office of Indian Affairs and the Civilian Conservation Corps-Indian Division. See Roger Bromert, "The Sioux and the Indian-CCC," *South Dakota History* 8 (Fall 1978): 340–56; and Prucha, *Great Father,* 2:945–48.

46. Dreamer, 1937 Diary, 10 Apr.

47. Dreamer, 1936 Diary, 15 Oct.

48. Ibid., Nov. summary.

49. Ibid., Oct. summary.

50. Dreamer, 1937 Diary, 6 Apr.

51. Ibid., 13 Apr.

52. Dreamer, 1936 Diary, Nov. summary.

53. Dreamer, 1937 Diary, 25 Apr.

54. Dreamer, 1936 Diary, Oct., Nov. summaries.

55. Ibid., 22, 23 Dec.

56. Peggy Pascoe, *Relations of Rescue: The Search for Female Moral Authority in the American West, 1874–1939* (New York: Oxford University Press, 1990), xxi.

57. Dreamer, 1936 Diary, 14 Oct.

58. Dreamer, Grass Creek Scrapbook, 1940, 23.

59. Dreamer, 1937 Diary, 1 Jan.

60. Dreamer, 1936 Diary, Nov. summary.

61. Anonymous to Dreamer, n.d., Scrapbook of Memos.

62. Dreamer, 1937 Diary, 5 Jan. Dreamer left many of the artifacts she collected while living on the Pine Ridge reservation to the South Dakota State Historical Society (SDSHS), Pierre, SD.

63. Dreamer, 1936 Diary, Nov. summary.

64. Dreamer, "Recreation among the Sioux Indians" (typed manuscript), n.d., 3, File 1, Dreamer Papers.

65. Ibid., 8.

66. Ibid., 11.

67. Dreamer, 1936 Diary, 20 Sept.

68. George Dreamer, "Evening" (poem), n.d., File 1, Dreamer Papers.

69. George Dreamer, Christmas card, n.d., ibid.

70. C. H. Powers to George Dreamer, 20 Sept. 1949, Marion Dreamer to Washington State University, n.d., E. W. Jermark to George Dreamer, 9 Feb. 1928, George Dreamer to Lease Department of Pine Ridge Reservation, 30 Dec. 1944, and George Dreamer to Francis Case, 27 Jan. 1947, all in File 2, Dreamer Papers. The tendency of allotments to become fragmented through inheritance, as happened with the Spotted Horse and Red Shirt lands, plagued the allotment program throughout its duration. If an allotted tribal member died intestate, the lands were divided equally among heirs. Prucha, *Great Father*, 2:873–74.

71. Prucha, *Great Father*, 2:872–79, 881, 895–96, 962; 48 Stat 984.

72. Dreamer, 1936 Diary, 9 Oct.

73. George Dreamer to Lease Department of Pine Ridge Reservation, 30 Dec. 1944; Marion Dreamer, VISTA Diary, 1, File 3, Dreamer to Washington State University, 2 Apr. 1979, File 2, Dreamer, Marsing Job Corps Scrapbook, File 4, and James O. Blakenship to Dreamer, 1 Oct. 1976, File 4, all in Dreamer Papers; David Hartley to Dreamer, 25 Jan. 1977, 73.24, Dreamer Collection, SDSHS.

3

HEALTH
ON THE
RESERVATION

JAMES R. WALKER'S CAMPAIGN
AGAINST TUBERCULOSIS ON THE PINE RIDGE
INDIAN RESERVATION

. . .

In 1896, James R. Walker, a forty-seven-year-old Indian Service physician, left his post at the Carlisle Indian Industrial School in Pennsylvania for the Pine Ridge Indian Reservation. Located in southwest South Dakota, the Pine Ridge was one of the country's largest Indian reservations, covering approximately three million acres, an area about one-half the size of Rhode Island. Five thousand full-blood Lakota, or western Sioux, Indians lived at isolated locations scattered across the semiarid terrain.[1] When Walker arrived, the sprawling reservation had twenty-nine government day schools and a boarding facility for more than two hundred children that was connected to a two-ward hospital run by the Indian Service. Episcopal, Presbyterian, and Catholic missionaries also worked with the reservation population.[2]

It was here among the Lakotas, most of whom belonged to the Oglala subtribe, that Walker began the efforts to combat tuberculosis that would bring him into prominence during the early twentieth century. Moreover, the knowledge he gained as he worked with traditional medicine men drew the attention of anthropologists Franz Boas and Clark Wissler, who sought to preserve knowledge of traditional American Indian cultures. They recruited Walker as a field operative to collect artifacts and document rituals, an avocation the Indian Service physician focused on throughout his retirement, contributing valuable knowledge to the field of anthropology.[3]

Walker's initial interest in medicine grew out of his experiences in the Civil War. He had enlisted at the age of fourteen in Company D of the Illinois Cavalry Volunteers on 29 January 1864. After five months in the army, Walker contracted dysentery, an ailment that eventually became chronic. At some point in his nineteen months of military service, he was assigned to the United States Sanitary Commission, which worked under the direction of famed landscape architect Fredrick Law Olmsted to improve cleanliness in field hospitals. Fol-

This essay originally appeared in *South Dakota History* 34 (Summer 2004): 109–26.

lowing the war's end in April 1865, Walker was mustered out at Pine Bluff, Arkansas, on 31 August.[4]

Still a teenager, Walker returned home and completed his public-school education. He then entered the Northwestern University School of Medicine in Chicago, where, according to family lore, he struggled financially, surviving on crackers and cheese. Walker took a heavy class load, studying late into the evening and sleeping little. Hard work had its rewards, however, and Walker graduated with a medical degree in the shortest time possible. In 1874, one year after completing his studies, the young doctor returned to his hometown of Richview, Illinois, and in rapid succession joined a practice with a local established physician, married, and began raising a family. In 1876, his ambition and determination earned him a place as a delegate to the International Medical Association convention.[5] Meanwhile, as the twenty-seven-year-old physician's medical career was on the rise, his own health began to decline. The demanding hours of the Richview practice further taxed an already weak constitution and forced Walker to seek treatment for his chronic dysentery.[6]

Medical pundits of the 1870s advocated plenty of fresh air, outdoor activity, and moderate exposure to cold as the keys to health. By the late nineteenth century, thousands of health seekers visited the northern states, Walker among them. Following this fad, he traveled to northern Minnesota but found few employment opportunities in the sparsely populated backwoods region. Fortunately, Walker learned of an opening for an Indian Service doctor on the White Earth Indian Reservation. In December 1878, he took the post and moved his family north to Leech Lake, Minnesota. What was to be little more than a chance to build his strength in the north country's fresh air turned out to be a fateful career decision.[7]

As the years passed, Walker went on to serve with the Indian Service in Washington State and then at the Carlisle Indian School before being transferred to the Pine Ridge reservation on 15 July 1896 for an assignment that would prove both demanding and rewarding. In his capacity as the Pine Ridge reservation physician, Walker received twelve hundred dollars annually and was responsible for tending to the medical needs of people spread thinly over a vast amount of territory. Lakotas who needed care often lived in the backcountry, requiring doctors to travel several days on horseback to administer medical treatment.[8]

As an Indian Service employee, Walker followed the United States government policy of "Americanization" aimed at assimilating the Indians. Historian Francis Paul Prucha explains that agency personnel and others who were permitted to live on the reservation were considered instruments for carrying out the government program of "civilizing" American Indians. According to Prucha, agency physicians were front-line soldiers in the campaign to replace the Indians' cultural patterns with those of European-American civilization. In fact, Commissioner of Indian Affairs Hiram Price remarked in 1884 that no one had a better opportunity to change the Indians than did the agency doctor. His successor, Commissioner John D. C. Atkins, not only advised doctors to educate the Indians in the proper treatment of the sick, but also to "use every effort to overcome the influence of the native medicine men."[9]

Walker's early years at Pine Ridge were primarily devoted to eliminating tuberculosis, which was widespread among tribal members. During the decade Walker actively campaigned against the disease, the rate of tuberculosis deaths among the general population of the United States was less than two per thousand, in contrast to Pine Ridge, where the number averaged eighteen deaths per thousand. The malady, which primarily attacks the lungs but may also affect other organs, is caused by *Mycobacterium tuberculosis*, a rod-shaped bacterium transmitted through the bacteria-carrying droplets expelled when an infected person coughs or sneezes. In the mid-1940s, after the development of a treatment with the drug streptomycin, the disease was nearly eradicated. Nevertheless, even today, half of all untreated tuberculosis cases are fatal, and the infection contributes considerably to illness and death around the world.[10]

In 1897, Walker's request to the Indian Service for an assistant physician was granted, allowing him to concentrate on treating the reservation's tuberculosis cases. In his 1899 report to the commissioner of Indian affairs, Walker wrote, "The prevailing disease among the Ogalalla Sioux Indians is tuberculosis, almost one-half of whom appear to be affected by it. The larger percentage is among the children. . . . At times there are more calls than the two physicians now at this agency can attend to."[11]

While Walker adhered to governmental guidelines in his dealings with the Indians, he also appears to have had considerable freedom in ministering to their health. In particular, Walker recognized that in order to treat his patients successfully he would have to gain the cooperation of the local medicine men.[12] "I was determined to know the Indian from the Indian point of view," he later recalled in a newspaper interview.[13] Understanding that many Oglala Lakotas still looked to traditional healing practices rather than western medicine, Walker began to study the medicine men's methods in order to devise strategies for doing away with their influence. He reported building friendships with the elders by "praising the good they did, supplying them with simple remedies and instructing them in their uses. But, privately, I charged them with their trickery and persuaded them to abandon such methods."[14] Unknown to Walker's colleagues was the fact that he was also secretly studying with a number of Oglala shamans including Little Wound, American Horse, and Lone Star. Walker was particularly interested in the medicine men's success in using psychological methods and "the power of suggestion" to lower fevers and relieve pain. He later disclosed, "I practiced some of their methods, sometimes with success."[15]

An article published in *Charities and the Common: A Weekly Journal of Philanthropy and Social Advance*, provides insight into Walker's methods for treating tuberculosis.[16] According to the physician, the Indians believed the disease was "caused by a worm eating away the lung[,] and medicine men supported this belief by the pretence of removing a worm from the chest and exhibiting it to the patient and his friends. Publicly, I agreed with the medicine men that tuberculosis is caused by something that destroys the lung, but privately I convicted them of their trick with the worm, promising them that if the sputa of the consumptive were brought to me I would show them the things which cause the disease." In several instances, Walker "stained and mounted the specimen in the presence of the medicine men to whom in some cases I succeeded in showing the bacilli. Such processes were repeated until I was able to establish confidence in my understanding of the disease."[17]

This technique, combined with a regimen of cleanliness, good food, and fresh air, proved successful. Between 1896 and 1903, the annual number of new tuberculosis cases diminished by 49 percent and the number of deaths fell by 44 percent. Walker attributed the decline to better medical supervision of his patients and the use of health-care practices he had learned while working for the Sanitary Commission during the Civil War. Unfortunately, after losing his medical assistant in 1903, he was unable to supervise the reservation population as closely as he had. This turn of events dismayed Walker, because without constant vigilance, the Lakotas reverted to their old ways of caring for the sick and were careless with infected materials. Some of the doctor's patients believed his absence meant that he had lost interest in their welfare. Over the next three years, the number of new tuberculosis cases increased by 30 percent annually, and the number of deaths rose by 62 percent each year. Hoping to check this rapid rise, Walker used it to show the Lakotas the importance of following his instructions. The lesson, though costly in human suffering, persuaded some individuals to heed Walker's advice.[18]

Concerned but undaunted, Walker started a campaign in 1906 to promote his discoveries about tuberculosis treatment and establish a sanitarium on the Pine Ridge reservation.[19] In January, he wrote to Commissioner of Indian Af-

James R. Walker is pictured here around the time
his methods for treating tuberculosis were
achieving their greatest success.
The Pine Ridge Reservation: A Pictorial Description
(N.p.: Ralph H. Ross, MD, 1909)

fairs Francis E. Leupp to request support for his plan. Leupp, who had been appointed by President Theodore Roosevelt in 1905, represented a philosophical shift from his predecessors. Whereas earlier officials entrusted with the welfare of native peoples had believed that Indian characteristics needed to be destroyed, Leupp "exhibited tolerance for Indian religion, sympathized with native customs and dress, and encouraged traditional arts and crafts."[20] His response to Walker's proposal was positive but reserved. "I am impressed favorable [sic] with your plan to combat the spread of this disease," the commissioner wrote, "and agree with you that an institution for tubercular patients should accommodate every case of the kind among the Indians. Under the present conditions, however, it would be impossible to prepare a sanitarium which would take in all such cases."[21]

Walker's medical work did not go unnoticed or unappreciated, however. Members of Congress, too, were concerned about the high death rate among American Indians on reservations. On 7 March 1906, the House Committee on Indian Affairs met to discuss the problem of tuberculosis and lauded "the long service of Doctor Walker at Pine Ridge and his interest in this subject [which] have enabled him to prepare tables unavailable at other reservations."[22] Especially revealing were Walker's statistics on death rates among the Pine Ridge Lakotas from 1896 to 1906. Over the ten-year period, 903 full-blood Oglalas and 70 mixed-blood individuals had died of tuberculosis out of a population of 5,000.[23] According to these figures, one-fifth of the tribe had succumbed to the disease. Tuberculosis mortality among the general American population during this decade was substantially less.

The meeting of the House committee ended with Congressman Charles H. Burke of South Dakota calling for prompt action to "check this disease among the Indians of the country." Burke proposed that the commissioner of Indian affairs investigate the subject further and report his findings to the next session of Congress.[24] Before the congressional session ended, lawmakers took even more decisive action, authorizing the commissioner to "investigate and report to Congress upon the desirability of establishing a sanitarium for the treatment of such Indians as are afflicted with tuberculosis, and to report upon a location and the cost thereof."[25] This request by Congress was timely for Walker, who had already envisioned a sanitarium at Pine Ridge. The Indian Service requested that Walker visit sanitariums off the reservation and gather information on the best way to treat the Oglalas.[26]

In May 1906, Walker pressed his case for establishing a sanitarium at Pine Ridge in a presentation before the National Association for the Study and Prevention of Tuberculosis in Washington, DC. His paper, "Tuberculosis among the Oglala Sioux Indians," was also published in the *American Journal of Medical Science* and the *Southern Workman*.[27] The report noted that American Indians were not inherently more susceptible to tuberculosis than whites but that the higher incidence of the disease among Indians was due to poor living conditions. Unlike many of the other communicable diseases that ravaged the Lakotas, Walker claimed, tuberculosis had existed among the Indians prior to white contact, but the number of cases had likely been substantially fewer.[28]

Walker argued that the Lakotas' traditional nomadic lifestyle had resulted in less contact with contaminates. Confining the Indians to permanent log dwellings with earthen floors meant that infected persons had a greater chance of contaminating their surroundings and, therefore, their families. In the past, sick individuals had expectorated into the campfire of the tipi, where the bacteria were destroyed, but in reservation housing, they spit onto the dirt floor. Dust from the floor then carried the pathogens into the air to infect any occupants or visitors to the poorly ventilated shacks. Ironically, the attempt of the Indian Service to improve living conditions with permanent housing contributed to the spread of disease among the Indians.[29] Walker concluded his report by pointing out his success in removing infected patients from government housing and into tipis or tents. He also lamented the loss of his assistant and the inability of one person to tend to the needs of patients spread over a territory "the size of the state of Connecticut."[30]

In September 1906, Walker answered a request from the commissioner of Indian affairs for information on tuberculosis with a nine-page letter. It was "practically impossible," Walker noted, to supervise the Lakotas in their homes. The only practical way to suppress the disease, he contended, "is by placing every case of tuberculosis in a sanitarium, and keeping it there untill [sic] it has been terminated." To strengthen his argument, Walker asserted that "tuberculosis Indians are a constant source of danger to the white people, especially of the staes [sic] in which reservations are located" and that "the welfare of the citizens of the Dakotas demands that the United States shall institute and carry out measures to prevent the spread of infection of tuberculosis Indians." This facet of Walker's argument probably carried little weight, since relatively few non-Indians inhabited the area around the Pine Ridge Reservation. Walker went on to explain the health benefits of housing patients in tents and point out the cost savings over conventional wards or dormitories. Essentially, Walker's plan was a tent camp with a number of buildings for administration. The report concluded with a detailed description of the water and soil-type needs for a future sanitarium site at Pine Ridge.[31]

Twenty-three days later, Charles F. Larrabee, acting commissioner of Indian

With their dirt floors and poor ventilation, permanent housing
contributed to the spread of tuberculosis on the reservation.
Aleš Hrdlička, *Tuberculosis among Certain Indian Tribes of the United States*,
Smithsonian Institution, Bureau of American Ethnology, Bulletin no. 42
(Washington, DC: Government Printing Office, 1908)

affairs, responded by recommending that the site Walker had selected be considered for development. On 13 November 1907, in a letter that reflected congressional pressure to develop sanitarium sites, Leupp reiterated his support for the project but asked Walker to consider using only one or two sections of Indian land instead of the four sections Walker had requested.[32] A 2 December letter, signed by Walker, Pine Ridge Indian Agent John Brennan, and Special Allotting Agent Charles H. Bates, made the final recommendation of a tract of land suitable for the sanitarium with property adjacent for agricultural purposes and pasturage. On 13 December 1907, Acting Commissioner Larrabee acknowledged receipt of the letter.[33]

Six months later, Walker wrote his superior, John Brennan, regarding the difficulties he foresaw in establishing a camp at Pine Ridge, including the problem of getting patients to enter the facility and remain there. "A sufficient number of these would enter a sanatory camp to make a good beginning," Walker noted, "but it would probably require the exercise of police authority to keep them in camp untill [sic] they should be removed from it." He went on to outline his plans for sanitation and proper diet. Reflecting tuberculosis treatment methods current at the time, Walker emphasized that an abundance of food was key to a cure. "It is of more importance to have a competent cook," he wrote, "than it is to have medical supplies, nurses, or even the physicians. . . . To establish a camp for tuberculosis patients without . . . a competent cook, would repeat a costly experiment that has often been made without success."[34]

On 18 July 1908, Walker elaborated his plan to Commissioner Leupp in great detail. To treat the 539 cases of tuberculosis then current at Pine Ridge, he recommended beginning the camp in an economical manner, with one tent for every two patients, a furnished kitchen and dining room, furnished laundry, warehouse, outhouses, barn, employee housing, and fencing. The tents, twelve by fourteen feet, were to be furnished with a single bed, chair, drinking cup, washbasin, cuspidor, and chamber pot for each of the two occupants. A camp stove, water bucket, pitcher, slop pail, washstand, and lantern were also to be included.[35]

Walker proposed staffing the camp with a physician in charge, a cook, a laborer, a laundress, a nurse, and a matron. The laborer was to have police powers. The fresh food so important for treating the ill was to come from beef cattle, milk cows, and chickens. Arable land would be tended by a farmer supplied with a work team, harness, wagon, agricultural implements, and seed. The cost of setting up the sanatory camp was estimated at between three thousand and thirty thousand dollars "depending on the quality and completeness of the plant." Excluding staff salaries, Walker assumed operating expenses for fifty patients would cost ninety dollars per month if food was purchased, or fifty dollars if food was produced on site.[36]

Leupp responded by sending Walker a copy of blueprints for a tuberculosis camp at the Salem School in Oregon. Walker replied in a four-page letter that argued against constructing wooden buildings like those used in Oregon. Adamant about the benefits of tents over permanent housing, Walker reiterated the importance of ventilation and sunlight, not to mention the cost savings and ability to disinfect. He also brought up Lakota fears and traditions. The Indians, Walker explained, would refuse to live in a permanent building where a person had died. If a patient passed away in a tent, it could be disinfected and moved to another site. Walker ended his letter to Leupp stating, "To plan a sanatory camp so it will be best adapted for the purpose of it [sic] establishment it is necessary to know what these purposes are; that is, whether it is intended to admit to the camp tuberculosis cases of any type, or only pulmonary tuberculous patients, or only curable cases of pulmonary tuberculosis. The arrangement and conduct of the camp should differ accordingly to the class of cases admitted to it."[37]

Although the prospect of building the Pine Ridge camp looked favorable initially, the Indian Service ultimately denied Walker's sanitarium plan for a number of reasons. First, officials elected to adopt a regional approach to treating the disease, eventually building the Sioux Sanitarium in Rapid City, an institution that continues to operate today. According to Michael E. Teller, author of *The Tuberculosis Movement: A Public Health Campaign in the Progressive Era*, the main focus prior to 1908 had been on treating the disease in the home, sanitarium, and camp. A new move by medical professionals, and one supported by papers presented at the Sixth International Congress on Tuberculosis, emphasized the need to isolate dangerously advanced cases to hospitals such as the Sioux Sanitarium.[38] Thus, a reaction grew up against programs similar to Walker's endeavor. Even Commissioner Leupp, who recognized the difficulties involved in removing American Indians from their families and homes, noted that tuberculosis and other infectious diseases must be "handled from the point of view of the safety of society rather than the comfort or pleasure of the individual."[39]

Second, many of Walker's peers viewed his methods as impractical. In October 1908, physician Aleš Hrdlička presented his own study on American Indians to the Sixth International Congress on Tuberculosis. Hrdlička's work, conducted under the auspices of the Office of Indian Affairs and the Smithsonian Institution, confirmed a number of Walker's ideas on the cause and spread of

Tents such as this one offered good ventilation and could be disinfected,
making them Walker's choice for housing tubercular patients.
Aleš Hrdlička, *Tuberculosis among Certain Indian Tribes of the United States*,
Smithsonian Institution, Bureau of American Ethnology, Bulletin no. 42
(Washington, DC: Government Printing Office, 1908)

the disease but disputed aspects of his treatment plan. The report examined five tribes, including the Oglalas in South Dakota.[40] Hrdlička acknowledged the problems inherent in log dwellings, where contaminated dust from dirt floors floated through the air and bedding, blankets, and clothes were filthy. He further noted the ill effects of the Indians' poor diet and irregular eating habits. Even so, Hrdlička disparaged the tents in which some Indians lived during the summer, finding them "oppressively hot" during the day, cold at night, and affording "but poor protection during a severe rain or hail storm, as the writer personally experienced" on a visit to the reservation. This opinion on tent housing did not help Walker's camp project.[41]

Another factor contributing to the rejection of Walker's plan was limited government funds. In 1908, the Indian Service began an official federal Indian health program by creating the post of chief medical supervisor. The first supervisor, physician Joseph A. Murphy, began to institute reforms, among them improved sanitation on the reservations, but his program suffered from lack of staff and money. In fact, the first congressional appropriations specifically earmarked for Indian health care did not begin until 1911 and then amounted to only forty thousand dollars.[42]

The final factor that doomed Walker's plan was his own study and practice of traditional Oglala ways, activities that did not go unnoticed by the reservation staff and missionaries. "Good men connected with missionary work among the Oglala," Walker wrote, "complained that I encouraged the people in heatheish [sic] customs." Eventually, a United States inspector, Colonel James McLaughlin, was sent to investigate the charges. Following a report to the secretary of the interior, Walker received notice that he was not violating any current policy of the Office of Indian Affairs regarding the civilizing of the Indians.[43] Although he was not officially reprimanded, Walker's unconventional behavior undoubtedly affected prospects for the implementation of his project.

In the years that followed, Walker intensified his anthropological study of the Oglala Lakota shaman tradition under the tutelage of Clark Wissler, curator of ethnology for the American Museum of Natural History in New York City. At the same time, he remained a devoted Indian Service physician. Writing in November 1913, Walker told Wissler that even though important Lakota ceremonies such as the Sun Dance remained largely unexplored, "my official work has been increased very much, so that I have had little leisure to do work for you."[44] On 5 May 1914, Walker, then sixty-five-years of age, retired after thirty-six years of government service. He relocated to a ranch in Fort Lupton, Colorado, and gave up medical practice but maintained contact with his colleagues in the study of anthropology. In 1916, he invited his friend Wissler to visit. "I have not much of a place," Walker wrote. "Only a shack, four acres of land, some bees and hens. But I can give you a place to sleep, something to eat, and *acres of good air*. . . . You see I live high, about a mile high, where the air is rare and the women vote."[45]

Walker's correspondence with Wissler following his retirement exhibits the former physician's dedication, concern for accuracy, and occasional frustration in translating Oglala rituals, myths, and ceremonies but reveals no open remorse about his unrealized sanitarium plans. "I have been fully occupied with my new vocation," he affirmed in one letter to Wissler.[46] In 1918, due to failing health, Walker moved to Wheat Ridge, Colorado, to live closer to his daughter and granddaughter. In an interview conducted that year by a reporter for the *Rocky Mountain News*, Walker mentioned his efforts among the Lakotas to combat tuberculosis, which he called "the disease that is sweeping them away." Although most of the interview was devoted to Walker's anthropological studies, he remarked with pride that "at one time I had 7,000 of them under my observation. And, because of my study of tuberculosis conditions, it was under consideration that I go to France to help combat the disease which has grown their [*sic*] from trench life."[47] The study of Oglala traditions continued to dominate Walker's last days. He died at the age of seventy-seven in Denver's Mercy Hospital on 11 December 1926.[48]

It is not surprising that anthropological work dominated Walker's last days. No doubt he lamented the shift in focus that prompted the United States government to consolidate treatment of the region's ailing American Indians at the Sioux Sanitarium in Rapid City. Even more profound must have been the feelings he harbored for the Indian lives that might have been saved. Nevertheless, Walker's dedicated work in combating tuberculosis on the Pine Ridge reservation earned him the respect of the Oglala elders whose trust he needed to cultivate in conducting the anthropological studies for which he is best known today.

NOTES

1. William P. Philpott, *A Guide to the Dr. James R. Walker Collection* (Denver: Colorado Historical Society, 1989), 6. Walker noted in a 1906 article that the Pine Ridge population also included 1,816 persons of mixed blood. Walker, "Tuberculosis among the Oglala Sioux Indians," *American Journal of the Medical Sciences* 132 (Oct. 1906): 600.

2. *The Pine Ridge Reservation: A Pictorial Description* (N.p.: Ralph H. Ross, M.D., 1909), n.p.,

Folder 12, James R. Walker, M.D., Collection, Colorado Historical Society, Denver; James R. Walker, *Lakota Belief and Ritual*, ed. Raymond J. DeMallie and Elaine A. Jahner (Lincoln: University of Nebraska Press, 1980), 7.

3. Franz Boas (1858–1942) founded the relativistic, culture-centered school of anthropology that dominated the twentieth century. A specialist in North American Indian cultures and languages, Boas mentored a number of scientists who developed the field further, including Clark Wissler, Ruth Benedict, Margaret Mead, and Edward Sapir. For Walker's anthropological work, see James R. Walker, *Lakota Belief and Ritual*; Walker, *Lakota Society*, ed. Raymond J. DeMallie (Lincoln: University of Nebraska Press, 1982); and James R. Walker, *Lakota Myth*, ed. Elaine A. Jahner (Lincoln: University of Nebraska Press, 1983).

4. Declaration for Original Invalid Pension, 1896, Folder 58:1, and "Oldest Member of Red Cross Is Denver Visitor" (unidentified newspaper clipping), 1924, Folder 38:1, Walker Collection; "Medicine in the Civil War," http://www.cl.utoledo.edu/canaday/quackery/quack8.html (accessed 28 July 2004). Recognized as one of America's leading landscape architects, Olmsted designed grounds for the country's Gilded Age elite, Central Park in Manhattan, Prospect Park in Brooklyn, and the 1893 World's Columbian Exposition in Chicago. Richard B. Morris, ed., *Encyclopedia of American History* (New York: Harper & Row, 1976), 762.

5. Maude Walker Wensley, "Shamans' Secrets" (typescript), 1–2, Folder 326, Walker Collection. The rise of the new middle class in the late 1800s and early 1900s led many individuals into the fields of medicine, law, economics, and social work. Over two hundred professional associations were formed during this era, including the International Medical Association and the American Medical Association, which were organized in response to the proliferation of quacks and nostrums during the mid-nineteenth century. See Robert H. Weibe, *The Search for Order, 1877–1920* (New York: Hill & Wang, 1967); and Burton J. Bledstein, *The Culture of Professionalism: The Middle Class and the Development of Higher Education in America* (New York: W. W. Norton & Co., 1976). See also Paul Starr's definitive work on the history of medicine in the United States, *The Social Transformation of American Medicine* (New York: Basic Books, 1982).

6. Wensley, "Shaman's Secrets," 1–2.

7. Michael E. Teller, *The Tuberculosis Movement: A Public Health Campaign in the Progressive Era* (New York: Greenwood Press, 1988), 9–11; Wensley, "Shamans' Secrets," 2–3.

8. Maurice Frink, "Pine Ridge Medicine Man: Dr. James R. Walker and the Oglala Dakotas," typescript, Folder 305:1, Walker Collection. For an excellent overview of agency physicians and their role in tuberculosis treatment, see David S. Jones, *Rationalizing Epidemics: Meanings and Uses of American Indian Mortality since 1600* (Cambridge, MA: Harvard University Press, 2004).

9. Prucha, *The Great Father: The United States Government and the American Indians*, 2 vols. (Lincoln: University of Nebraska Press, 1984), 2:645–46.

10. Richard E. Chaisson, M.D., "Tuberculosis," http://hopkins-id.edu/diseases/tb/tb_epi

.html; "Trudeau Institute History: Looking for the Cure," http://www.trudeauinstitute.org/info/history/history.htm (accessed 28 July 2004).

11. U.S. Department of the Interior, Office of Indian Affairs, *Annual Reports of the Department of the Interior for the Fiscal Year Ended June 30, 1899*, pt. 1, Indian Affairs, 336–37.

12. Walker, *Lakota Belief and Ritual*, 10–12.

13. *Rocky Mountain News*, 3 Nov. 1918.

14. James R. Walker, "Tuberculosis and the Indian," *Charities and the Common: A Weekly Journal of Philanthropy and Social Advance*, n.d., n.p., Folder 42:1, Walker Collection.

15. James R. Walker, "The Sun Dance and Other Ceremonies of the Oglala Division of the Teton Sioux," *Anthropological Papers of the American Museum of Natural History* 16, no. 2 (1917): 3.

16. Published by the Charity Organization Society of New York City between 1905 and 1909, *Charities and the Common* embraced early developments in Progressive thinking, dealing with issues such as child labor, housing, and the settlement movement.

17. Walker, "Tuberculosis and the Indian."

18. Ibid.; Walker, *Lakota Belief and Ritual*, 11; *Cong. Rec.*, 59th Cong., 1st sess., 1906, 40, pt. 4: 3553–54; Aleš Hrdlička, *Tuberculosis among Certain Indian Tribes of the United States*, Smithsonian Institution, Bureau of American Ethnology, Bulletin no. 42 (Washington, DC: Government Printing Office, 1908), 5.

19. In his dedication and persistence, Walker exhibited all the characteristics of the professional ideal of the early 1900s as defined by Burton Bledstein: "Self-reliant, independent, ambitious, and mentally organized[,] he structured a life and a career around noble aims and purposes, including the ideal of moral obligation" (Bledstein, *The Culture of Professionalism*, 91–92).

20. Robert M. Kvasnicka and Herman J. Viola, eds., *The Commissioners of Indian Affairs, 1824–1977* (Lincoln: University of Nebraska Press, 1979), 231.

21. Leupp to Walker, 24 Feb. 1906, Folder 2:7, Walker Collection.

22. *Cong. Rec.*, 59th Cong., 1st sess., 1906, 40, pt. 4:3553–54. In addition to winning recognition for his fight against tuberculosis, Walker earned a medal from President Theodore Roosevelt in 1906 for his efforts to control the spread of a smallpox epidemic on the White Earth reservation in Minnesota during winter of 1882–1883. *Rocky Mountain News*, 13 Nov. 1918. An unidentified newspaper clipping from 1924 entitled "Oldest Member of Red Cross Is Denver Visitor" (Folder 38:1, Walker Collection) erroneously indicated that Walker received the medal in 1908 for his tuberculosis work.

23. *Cong. Rec.*, 59th Cong., 1st sess., 1906, 3553–54.

24. Ibid.

25. Charles J. Kappler, comp. and ed., *Indian Affairs: Laws and Treaties* (Washington, DC: Government Printing Office, 1913), 3:195.

26. Walker to Leupp, 4 Sept. 1906, Folder 207:1, Walker Collection.

27. Walker, *Lakota Belief and Ritual*, 12. Formed in June 1904, the National Association for

the Study and Prevention of Tuberculosis promoted the scientific study of the disease and its social and economical impacts, as well as the concept that tuberculosis was preventable and curable. Teller, *Tuberculosis Movement*, 30–31.

28. Walker, "Tuberculosis among the Oglala Sioux Indians," 600–601. Because data were lacking, Walker was unable to make specific comparisons between tuberculosis and other indigenous diseases.

29. Ibid., 601–04.

30. Ibid., 604–05.

31. Walker to Leupp, 4 Sept. 1906.

32. Larrabee to Walker, 27 Sept. 1906, Folder 2:10, and Leupp to Walker, 13 Nov. 1907, Folder 3:2, both Walker Collection. Why it took Leupp more than a year to respond to Walker is unknown.

33. Brennan, Bates, and Walker to Leupp, 2 Dec. 1907, Folder 3:3, and Larrabee to Walker, 13 Dec. 1907, Folder 3:4, both ibid.

34. Walker to Brennan, 4 May 1908, Folder 3:6, ibid.

35. Walker to Leupp, 18 July 1908, Folder 207:2, ibid.

36. Ibid.

37. Walker to Leupp, 12 Sept. 1908, Folder 3:7, Walker Collection.

38. Teller, *Tuberculosis Movement*, 85.

39. Francis E. Leupp, *The Indian and His Problem* (New York: Charles Scribner's Sons, 1910), 355–56.

40. Hrdlička, *Tuberculosis among Certain Indian Tribes*, iii.

41. Ibid., 12–13.

42. Jon F. Rice, Jr., "Health Conditions of Native Americans in the Twentieth Century," *Indian Historian* 10 (Fall 1977): 15.

43. James R. Walker, Preface to "Legends of the Oglala" (unpublished manuscript), Folder 84:1, Walker Collection.

44. Walker to Wissler, 5 Nov. 1913, Wissler Archive, Division of Anthropology Archives, American Museum of Natural History, New York, NY.

45. Walker to Wissler, 25 Feb. 1916, ibid.

46. Walker to Wissler, 8 Aug. 1915, ibid.

47. *Rocky Mountain News*, 13 Nov. 1918. No records have been found to confirm Walker's statement about taking his methods to France.

48. Philpott, *Guide to the Dr. James R. Walker Collection*, 12.

SCOTT RINEY

POWER AND POWERLESSNESS

THE PEOPLE OF THE CANTON ASYLUM FOR INSANE INDIANS

. . .

On the evening of 14 September 1930, Leda Williamson, an inmate at the Asylum for Insane Indians in Canton, South Dakota, refused to move from the asylum's dining room to her room in the women's ward. Attendant Ada DeCory asked her husband Benjamin, who also worked in the asylum, to assist in moving Williamson. According to Williamson, Benjamin DeCory knocked her down and kicked her several times before picking her up and shoving her against a bench, breaking it. He then threatened to kill her. Inmates Ida Roubideaux, Stella Fast Horse, and Lillian Chavez all corroborated Williamson's story, although Fast Horse stated that she feared retaliation from Ada DeCory. Examining Williamson the following day, nurse Lorena L. Sinning found that she suffered from a swollen elbow and shoulder injuries.[1]

The attack on Leda Williamson raises both interpretive and methodological issues. David J. Rothman, author of *Conscience and Convenience: The Asylum and Its Alternatives in Progressive America*, notes that violence against and among inmates was a fact of life at state hospitals for the insane in the early twentieth century. To varying degrees, Canton Asylum evidenced the same causative factors Rothman found, such as an "air of hopelessness . . . difficult patients, short-handed and badly trained staff, overcrowded wards, and ineffective treatments."[2] At the same time, several aspects of the attack on Leda Williamson distinguish it from the abuse of inmates that Rothman detailed. Canton Asylum, which operated from 1903 to 1934, was not a state institution but rather the only dedicated psychiatric facility of the Bureau of Indian Affairs (BIA). Leda Williamson's alleged attacker, Benjamin DeCory, was himself an American Indian, as was his wife. Both had been employed at the Rapid City Indian School, also a BIA institution, where Benjamin DeCory worked as an automobile mechanic and driver and Ada DeCory as a small boys' matron. DeCory's actions toward Williamson suggest that the power relationship between attendants and inmates could be stronger than any ties of shared race or background.[3]

This essay originally appeared in *South Dakota History* 27 (Spring/Summer 1997): 41–64.

Culture, class, and especially the nature of the institution shape the story as well. Individual inmate records from an insane asylum are medical records and are protected as such. Too few records from the Canton Asylum survive to make statistical study possible, and respect for inmate privacy forbids any other use. Social history places a high value on information derived from diaries, letters, and other forms of personal narrative; yet, few such records exist from an institution that neither encouraged literary habits nor considered inmate materials worth preserving. American Indian voices do not emerge from Canton Asylum. For example, one study of the institution, Diane T. Putney's "The Canton Asylum for Insane Indians, 1902–1934," published in 1984 in *South Dakota History*, followed the contours of the available evidence, creating an institutional history that focused on the white actors who produced most of the documentation. Putney ably described inmate care but focused primarily on the ways in which changing societal expectations affected both the BIA and the institution.[4]

To bring the inmate voices forth and give them status as actors in the institution's history, a different approach seems necessary. The most applicable interpretive frameworks are those Erving Goffman suggested in his classic work, *Asylums: Essays on the Social Situation of Mental Patients and Other Inmates*, based on his field work at Saint Elizabeths Hospital in Washington, DC. For its inmates, the Canton Asylum for Insane Indians resembled Goffman's model of the "total institution," one that in its all-encompassing character effectively isolated them from the outside world, challenging their autonomy and their identities as both American Indians and human beings.[5]

A small facility, poorly equipped, the Asylum for Insane Indians was situated just east of the town of Canton, South Dakota. Lawns and small trees surrounded the institution, built on a low rise and set back from the highway. The main building, which faced south, was a two-story brick structure set on a stone foundation, with short hallways connecting its two wings to the central portion. It comprised the only structure for housing inmates and asylum employees, who also lived at the facility and dined in the same room with their charges.[6] Completion of the two-story hospital building in 1917 with a separate dining room for employees reportedly made asylum workers "very much more contented."[7] Although the brick-and-concrete structure was smaller than the main building, its layout was similar and it faced the other building fifty yards to the east. Despite its name, the hospital had no medical facilities beyond a drug room on the first floor and a simple operating room with two wash bowls and a slop sink, none of which were for the patients' daily use, on the second.

After 1917, Canton Asylum's hospital building (right) provided housing
while the main building (left) served administrative functions.
The grounds lacked walls, but the institution's distance from
Indian reservations effectively isolated inmates.
State Archives Collection, South Dakota State Historical Society

Each floor had beds for twenty-one patients, all of whom shared one bath and toilet. The hospital building served primarily as housing, with administrative functions concentrated in the main building.[8]

Much like the "total institution" environment of Saint Elizabeths in Goffman's study, Canton Asylum separated its inmates from the outside world, especially their homes and families. No walls surrounded the asylum, but its placement near a white community in southeastern South Dakota effectively isolated South Dakota inmates from state Indian reservations. Many inmates were from reservations hundreds or thousands of miles away. Dr. Harry R. Hummer, asylum superintendent from 1908 until the institution's closing in 1934, filed census reports with the BIA in 1910, 1911, 1921, and 1924. The data they contain reveal an inmate population that was tribally and geographically diverse and evenly divided between men and women. Between 1910 and 1924, the number of inmates housed at the asylum in any given year grew from 61 to 97. By 1924, Canton Asylum had housed a cumulative total of 306 inmates from eighteen states and fifty-three different tribes.[9]

While inmates came from as far away as California and North Carolina, most were from the Northern Great Plains and Upper Midwest. Lakotas and Dakotas (grouped together as "Sioux" in census records) by far made up the largest group, having contributed 68 people to the total inmate population by 1924. The asylum's Chippewa and Menominee inmates (cumulative totals of 40 and 20, respectively) formed the next largest segment. Despite the institution's distance from the American Southwest, 17 Navajos and 12 Papagos had been committed there.[10]

Distance deterred escape attempts, and since most of those who did flee headed toward home, their movements were predictable to law officers. Authorities captured Tommie Hawk, for example, in or near Rushville, Nebraska, just outside South Dakota's Pine Ridge Indian Reservation, and returned him to Canton Asylum, where he died in 1929. A bid for freedom by Luke Stands by Him ended in the Tripp County jail in Winner, South Dakota, twenty miles east of the Rosebud Indian Reservation.[11] A successful, if unusual escape occurred in 1909, when a boy tired of waiting for his release date "released" himself. The boy's father had promised to take him home in June. When June passed and the father failed to appear, the boy "took matters into his own hands and left without permission," authorities reported. Apprehended at Faulkton, South Dakota, he was allowed to go home "on account of his very comfortable mental condition."[12] While few escapes were actually attempted from 1903 to 1933, eleven of the seventeen on record were successful.[13]

More important, distance combined with asylum policy to deter family visits. Relatives sometimes sent money to inmates for the purchase of clothes, candy, and gifts, but few traveled to the facility. While inspecting Canton Asylum before its closure in 1933, Dr. Samuel Silk of Saint Elizabeths Hospital in Washington, DC, recorded only three family visits over a three-week period. Superintendent Hummer, in fact, discouraged such encounters, theorizing that the presence of relatives delayed or prevented recovery. Relatives often pleaded to have their family members released, but Hummer would not allow home paroles on even a trial basis. In this way, Canton Asylum went beyond maintaining strict control over inmates' lives to engage in a program Goffman identified as a "curtailment of self." In denying inmates roles outside the institution, such as that of family member, asylum officials deprived them of a source of individual autonomy.[14]

The commitment process, which legally consigned individuals to Canton Asylum, was itself a denial of autonomy. Few inmates, if any, entered the institution of their own volition. In fact, the process of detachment from family and community often began with reservation superintendents confining their wards in agency jails while seeking commitments.[15] Haphazard at best, the process provided Indians no real legal safeguards. When asked in 1933 to advise Secretary of the Interior Harold L. Ickes about the legal issues surrounding commitments to Canton Asylum, Nathan R. Margold, the department's acting solicitor, responded that the BIA's Washington offices had no documents relating to the inmates' commitments.

The initiative in commitment cases lay with reservation superintendents, who requested and received BIA authorization to seek a commitment and an accompanying adjudication of insanity from the state courts. The states, Margold pointed out, had no jurisdiction over the federal government's Indian wards, but the assent of state courts was obtained "to avoid any charge of deprivation of liberty without due process of law." Margold could discover nothing about the terms of the commitments, but he speculated that state courts simply "committed" Indians "to the custody of the Secretary [of the Interior]."[16]

The lack of more extensive legal safeguards led to abuses. Emma Amyotte, an American Indian enrolled at a United States agency, suffered a stroke in 1923 while living in Canada. She received treatment for the stroke at a hospital for the insane in Ponoka, Alberta, where, after a recovery period, she was judged to be in good physical and mental health. At the request of the Canadian government, the United States commissioner of immigration in Montreal tried to return Amyotte to her agency. Somehow she landed at Canton Asylum, where Dr. Hummer confined her, entirely without the benefit of court proceedings. Even though he had been informed shortly after her admission that Canadian officials had specifically advised against her commitment to any institution, Hummer kept Amyotte at Canton Asylum for the next ten years.[17]

The long duration of Amyotte's confinement proved to be typical. Responding in 1927 to a query from the Institute for Government Research (compilers of the Meriam Report, a survey of the BIA that led to reform in the administration of Indian affairs), Dr. Hummer provided a breakdown of the inmate population by length of confinement. Canton's inmates were overwhelmingly long-term residents: of the ninety-two men and women then confined, sixty-five had been at the asylum for five years or more. Anecdotal evidence suggests that some inmates spent even more time there. When Dr. Silk traveled to Canton Asylum at the time of its closing in 1933, he found one inmate who had been confined for twenty-four years.[18]

Such long-term confinement was possible and all the more reprehensible because of the relative youth of Canton Asylum's inmate population. In 1924, a little more than half of the inmates were under thirty years of age, with the vast majority in their twenties. Fifteen inmates were aged twenty or less, including four who were under ten years old. Only nine inmates were sixty or older. Asylums housing non-Indians tended to become dumping grounds for the aged senile in the early twentieth century. The Canton institution clearly did not fit that pattern, suggesting something unique about the Asylum for Insane Indians.[19]

A partial explanation for the youth of its inmate population lay in the asylum's use as a penal institution. During congressional deliberation over the bill establishing the facility, Sac and Fox Agent Horace M. Rebok wrote that regulations "should most vigilantly guard against the incarceration of unfortunate Indians whose friends may attempt to get rid of them for personal reasons."[20] Agent Rebok would have done well to advise checks on the authority of reservation superintendents, too, for in 1933, Dr. Silk found that only twenty-five to thirty of the ninety inmates at Canton actually belonged in a mental hospital. Some twenty to twenty-five were mentally deficient, but without psychoses; they could be cared for in an institution for the feebleminded. Another fifteen to twenty were "epileptic, defective, and mildly psychotic (mostly senile)"; these individuals were "quiet, well behaved, and could live on a reservation or with relatives under very nominal supervision." Rounding out the asylum's population were twenty or so inmates in no way defective or impaired who "could make an adjustment in any community, let alone on a reservation."[21] Canton Asylum, Dr. Silk noted, housed a large number of young people "sent to that institution because of some difficulty at a school or agency—a fight with a white man, or a fight with a husband or wife. Almost from the first day of their admission to the asylum their behavior has been normal in every way; they have performed useful work on the farm, in the dairy, kitchens, dining rooms, sewing room, etc., with only nominal supervision or without any at all."[22]

Contained in Silk's observations was a fact he shied away from stating explicitly: BIA reservation and school superintendents buttressed their authority by sending sane Indians to Canton Asylum. Dr. Hummer was an excellent jailer. Because he had judged these inmates to be mentally deficient (on no criteria that Dr. Silk could discern), he would not release them without first sterilizing them. Since he had no way to perform sterilizations, Dr. Hummer simply refused to set inmates free. Commitment to Canton Asylum was effectively terminal. Of the estimated ten discharges per year, nine occurred through the death of the inmate. Some of those who died at the asylum were buried at their agencies, others in a cemetery on the asylum grounds.[23]

The full impact of confinement to Canton Asylum and the magnitude of the injustice perpetrated there can be understood from an examination of the inmates' activities. As Ellen Dwyer notes in *Homes for the Mad: Life inside Two Nineteenth-Century Asylums*, asylum superintendents believed simple manual labor to be therapeutic for inmates and of practical value to institutions. This view dovetailed neatly with BIA expectations that Canton Asylum, like many other state and federal institutions of the period, be as self-supporting as possible.[24] In 1910, Dr. Hummer reported that of the sixty-one inmates then confined, approximately twenty-five worked, "either attended or unattended," in the laundry, the kitchen, the asylum's farm, or the wards. Of these inmates, "practically every one . . . is a willing worker." In fact, inmates were often overworked. "In several instances with both males and females," Hummer wrote, "I have been compelled to exercise a certain amount of supervision of this work, especially in the wards, to see that the inmate was not imposed upon by the employee." Other observers expressed concern for the safety of those inmates who had to herd cattle on the highway right-of-way when the asylum's pasturage proved insufficient.[25]

Even though inmates may have been exploited, the work offered relief from another feature of asylum existence—boredom. The degree of freedom permitted Canton Asylum inmates varied with the seasons and appears to have decreased over the years. In 1910, asylum staff allowed more than half the inmates to wander about the asylum lawns. In good weather, they went fishing and trapping nearby on the Big Sioux River. While on a 1929 inspection tour to investigate conditions at the asylum, Dr. Silk reported that staff took some of the men to work on the asylum farm in the summer, but fall and winter found them back indoors where, like the other inmates of both sexes, they had little to do but sit and smoke. The asylum had no lounge areas, and inmates spent their days in the wards — surely a dismal prospect for all but the most deteriorated individuals. Despite the fact that many of the inmates were able to read and write, asylum staff made little attempt to educate them.[26] Though often idle, Canton Asylum inmates were at least well fed, although institutional fare, not traditional tribal foods, made up their diet. During his 1929 inspection, Dr. Silk observed them lunching on "fresh pork, boiled potatoes, gravy, spinach, bread, oleomargarine, milk, and tea." Dinner consisted of "peas, potatoes, apple sauce, cinnamon buns, bread, milk, and tea."[27]

Most asylum employees probably had little knowledge of the inmates' various tribal cultures and histories, which must have played a role in interpersonal dynamics within the wards and might have been used to promote inmate well-being. No reference is made in asylum records to tribal backgrounds aside from population summaries prepared for the BIA. Evidence suggests that Dr. Hummer attempted to force inmates into purely clinical models of behavior, and then more for administrative than therapeutic purposes. A recurring concern for the staff was the care of epileptic inmates. Particularly worried about the disruptive effect of their seizures on other inmates, Dr. Hummer made a practice of putting one of the more capable inmates from each dormitory in charge of assisting the one in distress.[28] This practice of involving Indian inmates in the care of their fellows apparently bore some fruit, for when Dr. Silk made the rounds of the wards at night, he found the inmates to be quiet and "much less difficult to manage when compared to a similar group of the white race."[29] Nor did attendants report feeling threatened by their charges, even when making night rounds.[30]

Disease may well have taken a toll on the inmates' ability or willingness to resist their overseers, for standards of physical care at the asylum were dismally low. Despite the fact that some inmates' mental and physical deterioration was due to syphilis, Dr. Hummer made no use of the diagnostic Wassermann tests or the Salvarsan cure. The causes and prevention of tuberculosis, which had killed fifty-two of Canton Asylum's inmates by 1924, were common knowledge by the 1920s, yet Hummer conducted no sputum tests and failed to isolate those with active coughs. Nor were dishes sterilized. Inmates had no toothbrushes and received no dental care of any sort. Dr. Silk judged the standards of medical attention and custodial care to be even lower than that of a typical prison. The existence of Canton Asylum might have been justified had it given the mentally ill better care than they could receive in reservation guardhouses or the homes of friends and relatives, but the surviving evidence from the institution surely calls that capability into question.[31]

Conditions at Canton Asylum affected not only inmates but staff as well. In his work at Saint Elizabeths, Erving Goffman found staff torn between institutional and humane interests; the functioning of the institution demanded efficiencies in the handling of patients that conflicted with the humane standards of care the institution had been created to provide.[32] At Canton Asylum, the deficiencies in humane standards for patients combined with the nature of the work and poor conditions for employees exacerbated the contradiction. Attendants at the asylum worked long hours at demanding jobs, under circumstances that would not encourage them to see the inmates as anything but burdens. The male night watchman, for example, made rounds of the asylum grounds in all weather, attended to fires in all boilers and heaters, and spent "any spare time in the wards." Dr. Hummer admitted that during the winter, a lengthy season in eastern South Dakota, "spare time" did not exist.[33]

Attendants lived in quarters at the asylum and were required to remain on the grounds except on their days off: one afternoon a week, every other Sunday, legal holidays, and thirty vacation days a year. Excluding legal holidays and vacations, their twelve-hour shifts meant an average work week of seventy-two hours. Because the asylum normally operated with only eight attendants, four male and four female, few workers were available to take up the slack when others took time off, particularly because regulations did not allow attendants to care for inmates of the opposite sex. The fact that only one female and one male attendant worked at night meant that a day attendant had to work an eighteen-hour shift if a night attendant was absent. A seventy-two-hour week thus became a seventy-eight-hour week. Frequent turnover among the employees and delays in hiring replacements made the problems of excessive workload worse.[34] Under conditions such as these, Goffman noted in a similar case, "We may expect staff to feel they are suffering special hardships."[35]

Workers' fatigue only compounded more basic problems. Racism played a role in some of the white attendants' perceptions of inmates. When one attendant asked Vernon E. Ball, a laborer at the institution, what kind of inmate new arrival Mark Hart was, Ball's reply was simply, "an Indian." Nurse Frances L. Caldwell interpreted the comment as flippant and reported the exchange. To Ball, if not to Caldwell, the fact of Hart's race, not the nature of his affliction, was salient.[36]

However they were inclined to view American Indians, the asylum's nurses and ward attendants found themselves in a situation for which few had been prepared. Most had no experience in institutional work, much less actual training in the operation of psychiatric wards. Newly hired employees were sometimes put in the wards with no instructions or information about the inmates. Under such circumstances, attendants might well become frustrated with or frightened by their charges. Such feelings, particularly when race entered the picture, made employees more likely to objectify the inmates than to perceive their underlying humanity.[37]

In his 1929 inspection of Canton Asylum, Dr. Silk found several attendants who themselves needed care. One night attendant, a "strong, healthy young woman, good natured," possessed "mental equipment . . . not above that of a moron." While she could help on the wards if supervised, Dr. Silk did not think she was fit to look after half the inmate population by herself, as her duties required.[38] One "nervous, irritable, and disgruntled" elderly attendant displayed symptoms of Parkinson's disease. Although her temperament could partly be explained by the eighteen-hour shifts she sometimes worked, her health clearly did not permit her to tend two full wards adequately.[39]

In the difficulties that such overworked, sometimes impaired attendants faced in fulfilling basic institutional tasks can be found the origins of the sort of frustrations taken out on Leda Williamson. Even those staff members trained in psychiatric work could be overwhelmed by the volume and difficulty of their work. The asylum's first trained nurse, who arrived in 1927, came under the scrutiny of Meriam Report contributor Dr. H. R. Edwards. He described her as "very capable but bewildered at the responsibilities thrust upon her," despite prior experience at Saint Elizabeths. How her untrained and inexperienced predecessors coped with their work is a mystery.[40]

Problems with workload extended to the superintendent who, in theory, should have had the support of another physician acting as assistant superintendent. Such an arrangement was instituted in August 1909, when Dr. L. M. Hardin transferred to Canton from the reservation at Leech Lake, Minnesota. Three months later, however, Hardin left the asylum for private practice. The institution's annual report listed the position for many years thereafter, but it was never filled, leaving Dr. Hummer the only medical doctor at the asylum.[41]

Superintendent Hummer had served his internship at Saint Elizabeths Hospital in Washington, DC, but since his 1908 posting to Canton, far from any sizable medical community, he had been effectively cut off from his profession. The duties of his position also confined him to a largely administrative role. Instead of supervising the care and treatment of inmates — he visited the wards at no regular time and rarely examined inmates — Dr. Hummer found himself preoccupied with clerical duties.[42] An inspector found the superintendent "spending most of his time taking care of his commissaries, preparing property reports and vouchering, and answering correspondence with his own typewriter."[43] The weight of the administrative workload left Dr. Hummer in no position to intervene in staff-inmate relationships.

In his research at Saint Elizabeths, Goffman noted that staff and inmates were divided into clearly defined groups, with each one "tend[ing] to conceive of the other in terms of narrow, hostile stereotypes" engendered by their respective roles in the institution. In Goffman's terms, the two became pitted against each other because the asylum had to make inmates pliable to the demands of the institution and amenable to processing as groups. Only people humiliated at some fundamental level, he observed, could be forced to relinquish the basic freedoms of movement and activity that adults on the outside take for granted. At Canton Asylum, staff undertraining and overwork compounded the institutional bias for efficiency. Inmates suffered a program of mortification, or defacement of the self, that Goffman identifies as a characteristic of total institutions.[44]

Defacement of the self entered every aspect of an inmate's life, from dress to hygiene to freedom of movement. At Canton Asylum, inmates might be left barefoot or clothed only in an open-backed shirt or in overalls with no underwear. The asylum's rooms and dormitories were bare, devoid of everything but iron beds and uncovered chamber pots. (In Dr. Hummer's view, decorations and furniture would only serve as weapons for combative inmates—an administrative decision of the sort that Goffman dismissed as a rationalization for inmate mortification.) Unless they used either a bed or the floor, inmates had nowhere to sit. Dirt and soot picked up from the floors by the inmates' bare feet and the hard water used in the laundry turned their sheets black. Although the wards had windows, attendants rarely opened them, especially in the main building where steel padlocked guards on the inner window frames made them exceedingly difficult to open.[45]

Inmates in the main building had two sinks, two unenclosed toilets, a slop sink, and a water fountain per floor, while sanitary facilities in the hospital building consisted only of a single toilet, wash basin, and bathtub per floor. When attendants locked the inmates in their rooms at night or after meals (so that the attendants could eat), the inmates' only recourse was to use uncovered chamber pots.[46] Sickened by the stench, Dr. Silk in his 1929 evaluation described the situation as "intolerable," particularly in the dormitories where eight inmates with eight chamber pots might be confined overnight with windows tightly shut. "Without desiring to be hypercritical," Silk wrote, "one could refer to the institution as a place of padlocks and chamber pots."[47]

Even though the main building at Canton Asylum had many windows,
attendants kept them tightly locked. Most inmates were confined to bare
rooms and were rarely allowed out for recreation on the grounds.
State Archives Collection, South Dakota State Historical Society

The basis for Dr. Silk's reference to padlocks could be found in the staff's heavy reliance on restraints and locked doors. At night, attendants confined female inmates behind ordinary locked doors and male inmates behind padlocked doors. Except in emergencies, inmates did not leave their rooms at night. In fact, some rarely got out during the day. Dr. Silk found one inmate who had spent three of his six years at the asylum locked in his room. Let out for an hour or so at a time, he might be taken for a walk outdoors or allowed to scrub the floor. He had been confined, supposedly, because of a tendency to fight, but Silk found him good-natured, neat, and clean. Although diagnosed as an epileptic, the man had had no seizures while at Canton Asylum. Dr. Silk also noticed a half-naked paraplegic girl sleeping on a mattress on the bathroom floor, where she had been locked overnight so that she would not disturb the other inmates in her eight-bed dormitory.[48]

Restricting inmates' movement was particularly invasive when it involved the use of restraining devices like the camisole (straitjacket), a garment with closed sleeves that could be tied to immobilize the inmate's hands and arms. Canton Asylum's ward attendants also had at their disposal ten pairs of metal wristlets with which to restrain troublesome inmates by locking them to their bed frames. Dr. Silk commented only on the physical effects of the use of wristlets, calling for an end to the practice because it rendered the restrained person nearly helpless in case of fire or attack by other inmates. At times, the wristlet keys had disappeared, forcing attendants to resort to hacksaws to free inmates from their beds.[49]

The Canton Asylum also had a pair of shackles, on loan from the local sheriff, which had been used to fasten an inmate's ankle to an exposed water pipe. The standard foot-long chain could be extended to six feet if attendants decided to allow the inmate to do more than just sit next to the pipe. Dr. Silk encountered one epileptic girl, "ordinarily . . . quiet and child-like," who was frequently restrained in this way after her seizures, when she tended to become disoriented and throw things. Since her chain was attached next to a hot-water pipe, he considered it a miracle that she had not been seriously burned.[50]

Inmates were sometimes restrained for long periods of time. In 1929, Dr. Silk reported that attendants had kept two inmates fastened to their beds with wristlets for several months. Workers also routinely placed an "idiot boy" in a camisole so that he would not tear his clothes. When let out of the locked room where he was usually confined, the young man "objected strenuously" to being returned; left alone, he simply walked to the window, where he stood looking out, making no disturbance. Dr. Silk considered the routine use of restraints unusual and badly out of step with then-current practices. A Canton

Asylum employee with experience in the Wisconsin and Connecticut state hospitals expressed similar sentiments.[51]

Attendants also had extraordinary latitude in the use of restraints, reinforcing their position of dominance in the wards. "In no well regulated institution for mental cases," Dr. Silk wrote, "would application of any form of restraint to patients be allowed unless specifically ordered so by a physician." Yet at Canton Asylum, attendants had only to go to the office of the financial clerk, who kept the devices in his vault. While they were expected to note all unusual occurrences in the asylum's general report book, attendants did not have to justify their use of restraints.[52]

In this context, the attack on Leda Williamson occurred. Poorly trained or untrained attendants, overworked and undersupervised, confronted inmates in an environment where the program of defacement of self worked all too well. The disorder, filth, and ever-present padlocks and chains combined with the indignities of mental illness to degrade inmates in the eyes of attendants. As Gerald Grob notes in *The Mad among Us: A History of the Care of America's Mentally Ill,* "few staff members could maintain any degree of enthusiasm or demonstrate consistently high morale" when confronted with the bizarre behavior and deteriorated physical condition of many inmates.[53] Under such circumstances, even employees who shared common heritage might be tempted to vent their frustrations on particularly "troublesome" inmates.

Such may have been the case with Benjamin DeCory, for only a month after the incident with Williamson that Roubideaux, Fast Horse, and Chavez witnessed, the attendant once again treated the same patient roughly. When Williamson would not sit down at once after Ada DeCory brought her into the dining room, Benjamin DeCory "rushed over & sat her (Leda) down in the chair with considerable force. This caused Leda to become very noisy and unmanageable." Nurse Elsie Behrman reported the incident, protesting to Dr. Hummer that Benjamin DeCory "should not help discipline the female inmates unless asked to do so by the female attendant or nurse or else in a case of sudden violence."[54] The individual prone to sudden violence, it would seem, was Benjamin DeCory.

Nor could Ada DeCory be considered blameless. On 2 April 1931, Dr. Hummer left a note in her file recording his discovery of multiple abrasions on the lower extremities of inmate Kittie Spicer. The nurse on duty reported that inmate Edith Shroder had seen DeCory put creosol, a derivative of creosote, in Spicer's bath. When confronted, DeCory "denied using anything but 'government soap'" on the unfortunate inmate. Because no asylum personnel witnessed the act, Ada DeCory received no immediate punishment. Not long after, however, she and her husband were transferred to Jicarilla Sanitarium, another BIA institution, in New Mexico.[55]

A similar incident occurred when a Nurse Kershner, a white asylum employee, misused an even more toxic chemical. Asked to apply a prescribed amount of mercury to the scalp of an elderly Chippewa woman as a delousing treatment, Kershner applied so much that ward attendants Agnes Foreman and Anna Endicott had to scrape it away from the woman's pillowcase with a knife. Both women reprimanded the nurse and were told in return that "there would be no more bugs on this woman's head." The pillowcase, potential evidence against Kershner, disappeared when the ward attendants took the inmates for exercise. Kershner resigned and fled the institution the following day. The elderly woman remained ill with mercury poisoning for two weeks.[56]

The worst recorded incidents of inmate abuse involved white laborer Vernon E. Ball. On 27 November 1930, Ball received a written reprimand from Dr. Hummer for visiting a female inmate in the evening, an action that violated asylum rules. In June 1931, attendant Nellie Hill filed a series of complaints after she saw Ball standing beneath the window of a different female inmate, talking to the woman and gesturing toward the basement. This same inmate was reported missing on 12 July 1931. Ball returned the woman on 27 July, claiming to have found her in Sioux City, Iowa. The inmate told attendant Gertie Boom a different story. Ball, she said, had taken her from the asylum in his car and had slept in the same bed with her at his home and in a tourist camp.[57]

Dr. Hummer took the incident seriously and sought prosecution, although much of the evidence against Ball was either circumstantial or inadmissible since the alleged victim, as a mentally incompetent person, could not testify. Hummer also noted in a letter to the commissioner of Indian affairs that most of the female employees at Canton Asylum were "intensely afraid of Mr. Ball."[58] Although Special Agent Werner Hanni of the United States Department of Justice opened a file on the matter as a possible violation of the White Slave Traffic Act, there is no record of legal action. Hummer soon fired Ball, however, for exposing himself to the same inmate in view of nurses Lorena Sinning and H. Winchell. The inmate, perhaps identifying with her assailant, asked to be allowed to go with Ball when he was dismissed. Ball's wife, who also worked at the asylum, was let go as well.[59]

While these incidents sound horrendous today, much of what went on at the Canton Asylum for Insane Indians was, for the time, unexceptional. State hospitals of the early twentieth century were not known for either humane or effective treatment of the insane. Yet certain aspects of life at Canton Asylum stand out as particularly harsh. Underfunded and backward in its practices, the asylum submitted inmates to a defacement of self that was severe even for the time. Through poor sanitation and absence of medical treatment, lack of respect for inmates' modesty and personal appearance, the misuse of restraining devices, and the complete isolation of inmates from their families and tribal cultures, Canton Asylum quite thoroughly abused its inmates.

Not surprisingly, the BIA shut down Canton Asylum in 1934, early in the incumbency of Commissioner of Indian Affairs John Collier, architect of the movement for self-determination and cultural revitalization known as the Indian New Deal. Although unique among BIA institutions, the Canton facility was outdated in both its physical plant and operating philosophy. "By the 1930s," Diane Putney writes, "mental institutions were expected to do more than fulfill a community's economic needs and provide decent care for the insane. Asylums had to successfully diagnose, treat, improve, and cure patients."[60] Such expectations were clearly beyond the capabilities of Canton Asylum, where even "decent care for the insane" was lacking. In its role as a warehouse for Indian inmates, sane or not, the asylum practiced the techniques described by Erving Goffman to a frightening degree. In the "total institution" that was Canton Asylum, Benjamin DeCory was staff and Leda Williamson simply a bothersome inmate.

NOTES

1. Lorena L. Sinning to Harry R. Hummer, 15 Sept. 1930, Ada DeCory personnel file, Box 6, Program Mission Correspondence Files, 1914–1934, Canton Indian Asylum (PMCF-CIA), Records of the Bureau of Indian Affairs, Record Group 75 (RG 75), Federal Archives and Records Center, Kansas City, Mo. (FARC-KC).

2. Rothman, *Conscience and Convenience: The Asylum and Its Alternatives in Progressive America* (Boston: Little, Brown & Co., 1980), 360.

3. Description of Records, Canton Asylum for Insane Indians, RG 75, FARC-KC; Annual Calendar, 1927–1928, U.S. Indian Boarding School, Rapid City, SD, Box 9, School Annuals File, and Graduate Programs, School Paper File, Superintendent's Subject Correspondence Files, both in Rapid City Indian School Collection, RG 75, FARC-KC.

4. Putney, "The Canton Asylum for Insane Indians, 1902–1934," *South Dakota History* 14 (Spring 1984): 1–30.

5. Erving Goffman, *Asylums: Essays on the Social Situation of Mental Patients and Other Inmates* (Chicago: Aldine Publishing, 1961). Goffman's study, though dated, offers valuable firsthand observations of life in a large institution before the reforms that swept psychiatry in the 1960s and 1970s.

6. Samuel A. Silk, "Survey of Asylum for Insane Indians, Canton, S. D., March 20–26,

1929" (hereafter cited as Silk Report, 1929), Acc. No. H83.1, 3–4, 37–38, State Archives, South Dakota State Historical Society (SDSHS), Pierre, SD; U.S. Department of the Interior, Bureau of Indian Affairs, *Canton Asylum Annual Report* (1911), 8–9, RG 75, National Archives Microfilm Publication M1011, Reel 7.

7. *Canton Asylum Annual Report* (1917), 2, M1011, Reel 8.

8. Silk Report, 1929, 3–4, 7; Lewis Meriam et al., *The Problem of Indian Administration*, Institute for Government Research, Studies in Administration (Baltimore: Johns Hopkins Press, 1928), 305–06.

9. U.S. Department of the Interior, Bureau of Indian Affairs, Canton Asylum, 1921, 1924, *Indian Census Rolls, 1885–1940*, RG 75, National Archives Microfilm Publication M595, Reel 15.

10. Ibid.

11. E. W. Jermark to H. R. Hummer, 12 Dec. 1927, and McKean to H. R. Hummer, 19 Nov. 1929, both in Telegrams-Duplicate & Incoming File, DC 143, Box 5, PMCF-CIA.

12. *Canton Asylum Annual Report* (1910), 5, M1011, Reel 7.

13. *Canton Asylum Annual Reports* (1903–1933), M1011, Reels 7–8.

14. Correspondence on money for inmates in Various Superintendents File, DC 006, Box 3, PMCF-CIA; Samuel A. Silk, "Asylum for Insane Indians, Canton, S.D., September–1933" (hereafter cited as Silk Report, 1933), Acc. No. H83.1, 7, 13–14, State Archives, SDSHS; Goffman, *Asylums*, 14–15.

15. Silk Report, 1929, 37.

16. Acting Solicitor, Department of the Interior, to Secretary of the Interior, 21 Aug. 1933, Acc. No. H83.1, State Archives, SDSHS. (Margold is listed as solicitor in *Congressional Directory*, 73d Cong., 1st sess., June 1933, 318.) Among non-Indians, family members most often initiated commitments. The part American Indian families played in persuading superintendents to begin commitment proceedings is unclear; still, the role of the superintendents was exceptional. Richard W. Fox, *So Far Disordered in Mind: Insanity in California, 1870–1930* (Berkeley: University of California Press, 1978), 83–86; Gerald N. Grob, *Mental Illness and American Society, 1875–1940* (Princeton, NJ: Princeton University Press, 1983), 9–10.

17. Silk Report, 1933, 10. Information about Amyotte's mental condition comes from the Silk Report and not from the institution's inmate files, which are not released to researchers.

18. Hummer to Herbert R. Edwards, 11 July 1927, DC 005, Box 2, PMCF-CIA; Silk Report, 1933, 5.

19. Canton Asylum, 1924, *Indian Census Rolls*, M595, Reel 15; Grob, *Mental Illness and American Society*, 180–87.

20. Senate Committee on Indian Affairs, *Asylum for Insane Indians*, 55th Cong., 2d sess., 1898, S. Rep. 567, 7.

21. Silk Report, 1933, 15.

22. Ibid., 9.

23. Ibid., 7–9, 13–15; Hummer to CIA, 21 Sept. 1926, Box 1, Letters Received, 1916–1930, PMCF-CIA. Between 1907 and 1940, doctors in South Dakota sterilized some 577 people, primarily those they judged to be feebleminded. In his determination to hold inmates, Dr. Hummer turned away an average of twenty new commitments per year. Grob, *Mental Illness and American Society*, 174; Silk Report, 1933, 13.

24. Dwyer, *Homes for the Mad: Life inside Two Nineteenth-Century Asylums* (New Brunswick, NJ: Rutgers University Press, 1987), 14–17; Meriam, *Problem of Indian Administration*, 306–07.

25. *Canton Asylum Annual Report* (1910), 3–4. Although Grob has argued that inmate labor in mental hospitals had only a minor effect on institutional finances, Canton's inmates did, in fact, perform much of the manual labor necessary to the asylum's operation. Such labor was unlikely to show up in budgets or on balance sheets, however vital it may have been. Grob, *Mental Illness and American Society*, 23–24.

26. *Canton Asylum Annual Report* (1910), 3–4, 12, (1911), 18; Silk Report, 1929, 42–43.

27. Silk Report, 1929, 22.

28. Hummer to CIA, 9 May 1927, Hummer to CIA, 19 Oct. 1928, and Hummer to M. C. Guthrie, 5 Nov. 1927, all in DC 004, Box 2, PMCF-CIA; Silk Report, 1929, 45–46.

29. Silk Report, 1929, 64.

30. Ibid., 74–75, 78.

31. Ibid., 31–33, 42, 94–95; Silk Report, 1933, 11–12; Canton Asylum, 1924, *Indian Census Rolls*, M595, Reel 15; Meriam, *Problem of Indian Administration*, 307.

32. Goffman, *Asylums*, 74–78.

33. Hummer to CIA, 9 May 1927, DC 004, Box 2, PMCF-CIA.

34. Silk Report, 1929, 36–38. These hours were consistent with those worked by employees of state hospitals for the insane. Rothman, *Conscience and Convenience*, 353–54.

35. Goffman, *Asylums*, 7n.3.

36. Caldwell to Hummer, 18 July 1931, Vernon E. Ball personnel file, Box 6, PMCF-CIA.

37. Silk Report, 1929, 31.

38. Ibid., 74.

39. Ibid., 38. See 65–92 for additional personnel profiles.

40. Meriam, *Problem of Indian Administration*, 307.

41. *Canton Asylum Annual Report* (1910), 1.

42. Silk Report, 1929, 27–28, 43–44.

43. Unnamed inspector to CIA Cato Sells, 11 June 1917, M1011, Reel 8.

44. Goffman, *Asylums*, 7, 18–35.

45. Silk Report, 1929, 6, 14–17; Goffman, *Asylums*, 20–21, 43–47; Hummer to CIA, 19 Oct. 1928, DC 004, Box 2, PMCF-CIA; Meriam, *Problem of Indian Administration*, 305.

46. Meriam, *Problem of Indian Administration*, 306; Silk Report, 1929, 6, 14, 23.

47. Silk Report, 1929, 17, 22.

48. Ibid., 17–18, 24–25.

49. Ibid., 61–62.

50. Ibid., 62–63.

51. Ibid., 14, 62, 85.

52. Ibid., 29–30; quotation on 64.

53. Grob, *The Mad among Us: A History of the Care of America's Mentally Ill* (New York: Free Press, 1994), 127.

54. Behrman to Hummer, 13 Oct. 1930, Ada DeCory personnel file.

55. H. R. Hummer, Note, 2 Apr. 1931, Ada DeCory personnel file. See also Lorena L. Sinning to Hummer, 15 Sept. 1930, ibid.

56. Unnamed inspector to CIA Cato Sells, 11 June 1917.

57. Hummer to Ball, 27 Nov. 1930, Hill to Hummer, 9 June 1931, Frances L. Caldwell to Hummer, 10 June 1931, Hummer to CIA, 28 July 1931, and unsigned note (probably Caldwell) to Hummer, 6 Aug. 1931, all in Vernon E. Ball personnel file.

58. Hummer to CIA, 6 Aug. 1931, ibid.

59. Sinning to Hummer, 23 Aug. 1931, Winchell to Hummer, 23 Aug. 1931, Hummer to CIA, 24 Aug. 1931, and Hanni to Hummer, 8 Feb. 1932, all ibid.

60. Putney, "Canton Asylum for Insane Indians," 30.

4

CHANGES IN
GOVERNMENT
POLICY

RICHMOND L. CLOW

TRIBAL POPULATIONS IN TRANSITION

SIOUX RESERVATIONS AND FEDERAL POLICY, 1934-1965

. . .

The third quarter of South Dakota's first century of statehood was a difficult transition era for the state's tribal population. As poverty stalked Sioux communities, federal programs were inaugurated that emphasized dissimilar economic schemes to alleviate distress, ranging from reservation resource development to the relocating of unemployed tribesmen. Contrary to federal plans, the situation on Sioux reservations did not improve from 1934 to 1965, but, instead, living conditions and economic opportunities declined. Departing from its procedures in previous policy decisions, however, the federal government did not act alone during this time period. Tribal leaders participated in policy discussions, presenting ideas to Congress that were, in part, incorporated into the era's evolving reservation programs. Generally, Sioux leaders opposed any increase in federal authority, but, at the same time, they also opposed any termination or reduction in federal assistance or the removal of tribal land from trust status. Reconciliation between these two paradoxical positions was difficult and constantly tested tribal leaders and their leadership skills.

By the mid-twentieth century, few concerns were as important to both policy makers and tribal leaders as the fortune and future of reservation economies. South Dakota Sioux leaders recognized that improved reservation economic conditions were tied to improved living standards, which, in turn, were essential to eliminating the tribesmen's federal dependency. Since Sioux living standards were higher in the first three decades of the twentieth century (1900–1930) than in the following three decades (1930-1960), any program from 1930 to 1960 encountered difficulties. Many reservation residents described the earlier years as good because individual families were able to build small cattle herds from early government-issue stock. For example, ten thousand cattle on the Pine Ridge reservation in 1885 had increased to forty thousand by 1912. In 1917, Red Shirt Table residents on Pine Ridge stocked their own range land

This essay originally appeared in South Dakota History 19 (Fall 1989): 363–91.

and derived their livelihood from cattle. World War I increased beef prices, and federal authorities encouraged Sioux cattlemen to sell their animals to capitalize on high wartime prices.[1] Increasing wheat prices accompanied higher beef prices. As a result, Red Shirt Table landowners leased their now-empty range to white farmers who paid them a one-year lease at a price equal to "one-half the value of the land" during the last years of the war, enabling the tribesmen to maintain an income from their lands without working them.[2]

As a whole, South Dakota agriculture prospered during and briefly after the war, then declined. During these years, 1915 through 1920, a pattern of agricultural underdevelopment was established that eventually impoverished the Sioux. While reservation residents participated in the local farm economy as suppliers and laborers, they largely became agrarian capitalists dependent upon outside farm operators to lease or purchase their lands. Many operators eventually defaulted on both their leases and land purchases when the state's agricultural economy dropped following the war, thus depriving many Sioux of any revenue. In addition, improved agricultural mechanization decreased manual labor requirements on local farms and reduced this important tribal employment source.[3]

The Sioux dependence on lease rents and land sales (both sources of unearned income) for subsistence in the 1920s was often greater than their dependence on wages (earned income). Yankton Sioux reservation per-capita individual income in 1926 was $149, of which $72 was unearned and $77 was earned income. The reserve's small land base and proximity to white communities enabled the tribesmen to find some wage work. In contrast, the more isolated western Sioux reservation populations depended more on land-lease and land-sale income. The Standing Rock reserve, for example, possessed more acreage available for either lease or sale in 1926, resulting in a per-capita income of $167, of which $112 was unearned income and only $55 was earned income. These statistics also reflected the lower number of wage opportunities available to Standing Rock residents.[4]

This reliance upon unearned income in the 1920s constituted an economic pattern that was ill-suited for long-term stable growth, and it contributed to reservation underdevelopment. To offset this negative economic trend on the nation's reservations, the Office of Indian Affairs inaugurated a "Five Year Program" to stimulate the economy on the Blackfeet reservation in 1921. This program stressed intense farming and ranch development for five years and was soon introduced on several Sioux reservations. Commissioner of Indian Affairs Charles Burke (a South Dakotan) supported the Indian Service's Five Year

Program, which was directed toward improving individual families' economic rehabilitation. The cash loans provided to develop family resources supplemented individual income during the mid-to-late 1920s, when reservation unearned and earned incomes dropped.[5]

The end of the Five Year Program coincided with an increasing number of farm operators who defaulted on tribal land leases and sales. In addition, Sioux citizens who possessed fee-patented land began to default on their real estate taxes and mortgages and, as they lost their homes, moved to relatives' homes. As a result, Sioux income levels and earning potential on the reservation declined after 1926. This loss of income and resources forced many Sioux to rely for their survival on relief, which included direct help from the Indian Service and county assistance, when possible, for the Sioux citizen. The Pine Ridge residents were eating their horses during the winter of 1926–1927, illustrating their destitute condition.[6]

While the state's reservations were economically distressed in the 1920s, the tribesmen's poverty intensified following Wall Street's 1929 crash. Unlike the majority of the South Dakota population, reservation residents did not participate in the economic recovery that followed the 1930s Depression. Historically underdeveloped, the Sioux reserves participated only marginally in the region's agricultural economy when times were good.[7]

Prior to 1929, only 530 individual Sioux living on the Lower Brule, Crow Creek, Pine Ridge, Rosebud, Standing Rock, and Yankton reservations (which had a combined population of about thirteen thousand) received direct relief. By 1933, 1,953 individual Sioux received aid on those same five reservations, and that increase reflected the growing reservation poverty. After the 1929 stock market crash, the American Red Cross provided direct aid to Pine Ridge Sioux. Also hit hard was the Yankton reservation, where the annual per-capita income dropped to $1.28 by 1933, representing a 98 percent plunge since 1926. All Sioux reservation incomes dropped from 1926 to 1933, except for Pine Ridge, where annual income rose from $50.00 to $79.94. Increased direct-relief (and in-kind) payments accounted for this slight rise. In general, the Sioux were more dependent upon direct relief for their survival by 1933 than they were after World War I.[8]

Against this background of expanding reservation poverty, President Franklin D. Roosevelt appointed John Collier in 1933 to the office of commissioner of Indian affairs. The commissioner soon put forth a New Deal for the American Indian, stressing that tribal self-rule would create economically self-sufficient communities and end reservation dependency upon federal sources or outside lessees. Before that could happen, Collier believed that tribes had to reorganize their existing political and economic systems and create tribal corporations to manage tribal assets.[9]

Collier authored the Indian Reorganization Act (IRA) of 1934 to implement his program. Congress added extensive amendments and revisions, but Collier continued to support the IRA because it contained the core of his original ideas for reform. The final IRA legislation repealed the allotment laws and contained provisions for land consolidation, but it was unlike any previous federal program in that tribes voted either to participate or not participate in the self-governing aspects of the law. If tribal members voted to participate, they then either approved or rejected a new constitution. After the constitution was accepted, one-third of the tribe's members could petition for a charter of tribal incorporation, which the tribe had either to accept or reject by majority vote. The charter illustrated Collier's emphasis upon tribal economic development and, once ratified, allowed a tribe to manage its own resources.[10]

South Dakota reservation populations acknowledged the importance of improving reservation conditions, but tribal support was divided for Collier's agenda. During Senate hearings on the proposed legislation, Rosebud reservation delegate Sam La Point defended Collier's concept of land consolidation and tribal management of reservation resources. La Point claimed that the commissioner's government reorganization scheme would increase tribal self-rule, returning initiative to the Sioux, something that had been missing. Though La Point was from Rosebud, his observations applied to all the state's reservations as he noted that in the existing system, "We have become a people dependent on somebody else to do something for us all the time."[11]

Following congressional passage of the IRA, Indian Service officials urged Sioux residents on each reservation to accept the new legislation. Next, the Office of Indian Affairs encouraged tribal endorsement of the new constitutions and pushed for tribal sanction of economic charters. Sioux IRA opponents charged Office of Indian Affairs personnel—who assumed a high profile during reservation elections—with pressuring tribal work-relief participants to campaign for the IRA by threatening them with loss of their jobs. Reservation dissidents claimed that Office of Indian Affairs officials promised almost unlimited funds to tribes accepting the IRA and accused both agency and tribal supporters of discriminating against IRA opponents in loan and credit schemes.[12] Despite Office of Indian Affairs persuasion and destitute tribal populations who had need of the promised loans, reservation Sioux did not overwhelmingly support the IRA.

While a major objective of the IRA was reservation economic revitalization, only five of the state's nine reservations adopted the law, making them eligible for its loan provisions. The low percentage of IRA constitution adoption and an even lower acceptance of charters illustrated the tribesmen's initial distrust of the New Deal program and their increasing disapproval of Collier's program once implemented. Crow Creek, Yankton, Sisseton, and Standing Rock residents rejected the IRA; Cheyenne River, Lower Brule, Flandreau, Pine Ridge, and Rosebud accepted the IRA and adopted new constitutions. Of these five, only Rosebud, Flandreau, and Lower Brule approved tribal economic charters.[13]

Political factions within the tribe that had specific focuses, such as treaty and claims organizations, now opposed Collier's New Deal, suspecting that the new tribal governments might threaten the rights and influence of the older, pre-IRA groups. The voluntary, inter-reservation Black Hills Treaty Council was the most important claims organization. Loosely organized for decades, the council worked to settle the Sioux Indians' longstanding Black Hills claim against the United States. Being a descendant of a signatory band present at the Fort Laramie Treaty of 1868 was the only requirement for membership. The (Pine Ridge) Wounded Knee survivors association was another claims group composed of survivors of the 1890 Wounded Knee massacre who sought compensation for loss of life and property. The Yankton reservation business and claims committee also functioned as the reservation government, handling both tribal business and Yankton Pipestone quarry claims.

The members of these tribal claims organizations were philosophically conservative, but they were well versed in the principles of sovereignty. Past Sioux and United States treaty relations gave the claims groups both their strength and their security. Members argued that treaties established tribal relations with the United States and that these treaties defined federal obligations to the Sioux and stressed Sioux rights. Treaty and claims groups denounced the IRA, foreseeing their own loss of power within the community. Under the New Deal program, if adopted, the new political governments had the potential to assume the exclusive tribal claim function by usurping the right to employ counsel.[14] Since unsettled Sioux claims existed against the United States and were central to these groups' existence, members decried the New Deal on the grounds that the IRA would deny the Sioux "rights which are guaranteed to us by previous treaties." In addition, claims members prudently and conservatively argued that old business should be settled before moving on to something new. Many asked, "Why should not these things be settled, to give us what is already due us before asking us to engage in a new organization?"[15]

The tribal factions, the ongoing depression, and the harsh drought severely tested Collier's New Deal program in Sioux country. While the IRA was directed toward greater tribal self-rule and the rebuilding of reservation economies, when neither occurred, even the Sioux who supported the IRA often joined the claims and treaty groups, increasing tribal opposition to the Indian New Deal. As Collier's promises of greater self-rule and increased property evaporated, claims groups argued that greater economic potential existed in obtaining compensation from the United States for past wrongs than in supporting the IRA. There appeared to be truth to their claim. The Sioux Nation's Black Hills case was pending in the United States Court of Claims, and several bills had been introduced in Congress to compensate 1890 Wounded Knee survivors.[16] As a result, the Black Hills Treaty Council, with sixteen hundred members residing on the western reservations, became more vocal. Eugene Little of Rosebud revealed the sentiments of the organization, remarking that the reservation residents would "be fed and clothed and be prosperous" if Sioux governments operated according to treaty stipulations.[17]

Collier himself was partially responsible for Sioux opposition to the New Deal. Promises he made to tribal leaders concerning reservation self-rule and economic development remained unfulfilled. For example, IRA constitutions preserved the Department of the Interior's role in tribal affairs, continuing the tribal wardship status. Collier acknowledged this problem in 1940, claiming that "Congress was pretty conservative and did not go nearly as far in the self-government direction," and, as a result, the IRA "did not go nearly as far as the bill [he had proposed] in this way." On the other hand, Collier defended secretarial approval clauses in the IRA constitutions because federal supervision would prevent the tribes from making "a grave mistake."[18]

Those tribesmen who opposed the IRA claimed that tribal acceptance of the act simply changed the Indian from an involuntary ward to a voluntary ward because tribally approved IRA constitutions authorized the secretary of the interior to review and approve tribal-council-approved ordinances relating to specific topics.[19] Secretarial review maintained wardship, contrary to Commissioner Collier's promise of self-rule, making this broken pledge to the Sioux even more bitter. Since the commissioner had been the leading crusader against the Office of Indian Affairs and its paternalistic regulations in the 1920s, Sioux leaders now criticized him remorselessly for preserving the autocratic office. Cheyenne River resident J. E. High Hawk expressed the Sioux opponents' sentiment when he said: "Mr. Collier used to advocate for the Indians and kick the Indian Bureau also, but when he was given a job and placed there as Commissioner of Indian Affairs, why he never tried to do anything for the Indians."[20] The Sioux had taken Collier's first statements at face value, and as a consequence, they personally blamed Collier for failing to fulfill his promises.

Sioux disillusionment with Collier also heightened their scrutiny of the reservation operations of the Office of Indian Affairs. Many tribesmen accused Indian affairs personnel on the reservation of doing nothing to reduce Sioux suffering. Sioux people expressed their frustration with the field office for assigning two "Indian days" a week. Under this system, agency personnel set aside two days each week for tribal members to walk into the agency and transact business, and they reserved the other work days to conduct federal duties but would receive tribesmen by appointment. The Sioux interpreted this restrictive work schedule as both discriminatory and detrimental to their ability to conduct business. It forced tribal people to wait long periods in the outer office for meetings, providing them ample time to observe agency personnel quickly receiving white visitors. The tribesmen also complained that Office of Indian Affairs employees often failed to pay landowners their lease money immediately but were quick to lease tribal lands and to collect rent moneys. Since many Sioux could handle their own lease money, some tribal leaders argued that no justification existed to keep the Office of Indian Affairs on the reservation. Trips to county and state office buildings and courts, which kept much more liberal hours, led Sisseton resident Sampson Renville to declare, "Naturally we feel, therefore, that the county officials and employees are more sympathetic towards us than our own agency itself."[21] As this statement suggests, by the 1940s, some South Dakota Sioux believed that local government was more receptive to tribal welfare and social needs, and that perception gave impetus to the tribesmen's support for diminishing the reservation responsibilities of the Office of Indian Affairs when questions pertaining to termination began to emerge.

New Deal tribal program officer D'Arcy McNickle claimed that economic development was the main purpose of the IRA, but that, too, failed in Sioux country. Sisseton resident Simon J. Kirk proclaimed that Sioux living standards were modest in 1910 but declined after the Indian New Deal. He, like many, wanted to return to 1910 standards of reservation living, fearing that the future would bring greater despair.[22] Collier acknowledged the existence of the Sioux reservation's deep economic problems, confessing, "The situation of the Sioux Tribes is a desperate situation." Fractionalized heirship lands and lack of credit demonstrated the failure of past federal programs to develop reservation resources as secure employment bases for tribal populations. Collier even conceded that the "Indian Reorganization Act may have come too late in the case of the Sioux."[23]

Given the historical underdevelopment of Sioux reservations, the downward spiral of economic activity hit the tribes particularly hard. The state's reservation residents had participated in South Dakota's 1920s farm economy primarily as land leasers, land sellers, and seasonal workers. In the 1930s, economic depression and drought crippled the state's farming industry and destroyed the seasonal job market as well as the demand for land, causing the Sioux even greater economic distress than their non-Indian neighbors. South Dakota Representative Francis Case articulated the results of this chain reaction in 1938, noting that 85 percent of the state's farmers were on relief and the same conditions "made it doubly difficult for the Indian."[24]

Sioux tribesmen hoped the Indian Reorganization Act's economic component would improve reservation conditions, but continual funding delays and declining reservation conditions turned hope into disillusionment. Sioux on Pine Ridge had, for several years, eaten their horses to survive, and subsequently, by 1937, they had horses neither to eat for survival nor to carry firewood for winter fuel. Instead, the people carried firewood on their backs, and the heavy winter snows of 1936–1937, accompanied by a killing flu, caused many reservation deaths. The Sioux, unlike their white neighbors, did not blame former President Herbert Hoover for their plight in the 1930s, but instead blamed President Roosevelt's administration. Spotted Owl from Pine Ridge and a member of the Black Hills Treaty Council claimed: "We were getting along first rate until the Democrats got in and then we do not get along so good. Ever since the Democrats were in power, the Indians did not die from sickness so much as from hunger." Rosebud resident Walter Bull Man specifically blamed the IRA itself, claiming that the act "has had the effect of making me eat my own horses" and that the solution rested in "shooting" the corporate charters and IRA.[25]

Change also accompanied the hardship associated with the drought and Depression. New Deal work relief projects employed reservation residents, and for many Sioux, it was the first time they had ever worked for wages. Officially, the Indian Emergency Conservation Work (IECW), also commonly known as the Civilian Conservation Corps-Indian Division (CCC-ID), provided work programs to reservation residents. Together, all the federal relief projects raised Rosebud reservation's annual per-capita income to $150.50 by 1939, and 95 percent of the Rosebud Sioux population received some form of federal relief during 1939 and 1940. Pine Ridge's yearly per-capita income reached $120.00 in 1942, revealing the tribesmen's growing dependency on, and the importance of wage income to, reservation workers. In that year, Pine Ridge per-capita

Disillusioned with the Indian New Deal, some Sioux criticized the
policies and day-to-day operations of the Office of Indian Affairs.
Shown here is the agency office at Pine Ridge in 1956.
State Archives Collection, South Dakota State Historical Society

incomes were divided between 60 percent earned income and 40 percent unearned income, figures that were representative for other reservations.[26]

Anthropologist Gordon Macgregor observed in 1946, "Labor then must be regarded as one of the great resources of the reservation." He warned that terminating any reservation work program would reverse the small gains of the past because these wage-dependent people were "living in a strictly rural area, where opportunities for industrial and agricultural wage work are normally very limited or irregular, [and therefore] a satisfactory permanent economic adjustment based on wage work becomes problematical."[27]

Macgregor made his bleak assessment after World War II had interrupted the New Deal reservation resource planning and development. Coinciding with the loss of New Deal programs, South Dakota farming and ranching also changed. During the war years, the state's farms became larger with fewer operators. A changing local farm economy prohibited a large number of tribesmen from ever becoming independent operators competing for a share of the local agricultural economy. Technology changed farming and ranching practices forever, requiring fewer people to use more land. The expense of the new technology made it economically impossible for reservation residents to begin farm or ranch operations. As a result, the average white operation in western South Dakota in 1940 was 40 percent larger than that of a nearby Indian farm and was worth twice as much. The trend toward fewer, but larger, farming operations simply prohibited the Sioux from using their small, fractionalized lands to develop larger competitive and efficient farming or ranching operations. Average farm income also revealed the economic gap between the state's tribal and non-tribal populations. In 1940, the Pine Ridge mean family income was about $458, while the average gross value of products produced on neighboring white farms ranged from $837 to $1,063, and tribal farm sizes were one-half as large as white operations.[28]

Stimulating industrial production, America's entrance into World War II ended the nation's economic depression as businesses hired large numbers of wage laborers. This type of wartime prosperity did not come to South Dakota's reservations, where the economic depression continued throughout the 1940s. Reservation distress remained hidden from public view as the nation focused all its resources on the war effort. Only the returning wet cycle brought some help, enabling reservation residents to plant subsistence gardens and find seasonal agricultural work in local potato and sugar beet fields, but most tribal families still continued to receive some form of relief.[29]

Congress abolished the Civilian Conservation Corps in the summer of 1942, ending the government's most extensive New Deal reservation work program.

The loss of this direct work relief program and several indirect relief programs forced the tribesmen to find alternative aid. Military service provided many reservation Sioux with assistance because servicemen often participated in the dependency grant program, in which money from an individual's service pay was sent to the man's family. Particularly during World War II, the armed services provided indirect relief to the reservation communities, replacing defunct New Deal work relief programs.[30]

World War II industrial employment opportunities continued to elude reservation populations. In the spring of 1942, 75 percent of the employable Rosebud work force wanted off-reservation work; only 20 percent of these found employment, while the other 80 percent did not find positions simply because they did not have the financial ability to travel to distant military-industrial jobs. The small number who left reservations often found employment nearby, for example, at the Black Hills Ordnance Depot in Igloo, South Dakota. Most off-reservation relocatees found gang work as unskilled laborers, but a small number of Sioux obtained positions as skilled painters, carpenters, plumbers, mechanics, and heavy-equipment operators.[31]

Since only a small percentage of the state's tribal population obtained off-reservation war employment, most remained on the reservation (except those in the military) and continued to receive either direct or indirect reservation relief. The federal government also changed reservation ration issues during the war when the Office of Indian Affairs ceased direct reservation rations to most of South Dakota's Sioux population and provided relief through purchase orders issued to local merchants. In addition, congressional passage of the Social Security Act of 1935 and the creation of the Social Security Administration changed other aspects of reservation relief programs. The Social Security Administration assumed control of specific welfare and social programs as early as 1941 on Cheyenne River reservation and shortly thereafter on the remaining Sioux reservations. By war's end, the agency administered direct aid to the state's reservations through state assistance programs, including old-age assistance, aid to dependent children, and aid to needy blind.[32]

At about this time, several Sioux tribal governments also initiated small reservation relief programs. The Lower Brule relief committee obtained funds from the tribal cattle enterprise to aid destitute tribesmen who were unable to obtain assistance from other sources. The demise of the tribal cattle enterprise in the early 1950s ended the program.[33] The importance of the tribal assistance committees and the new Social Security programs cannot be underestimated. These new welfare programs not only supported tribal members but also created tribal dependency on state and federal agencies that were outside the Office of Indian Affairs. For example, Clarence Gray Eagle from Standing Rock received eighteen dollars a month in 1944 to live, as did many reservation elderly, even though he did "not know where it comes from." He added, "That is all I have to live on."[34] Gray Eagle's subsistence level represented the usual, not the unusual, wartime Sioux reservation standard of living.

Shifting part of the reservation assistance programs from the Office of Indian Affairs to the state programs redirected Sioux dependency toward the state of South Dakota. This trend continued after the war, and, as a result, state leaders demanded a greater role in tribal affairs in order to force rules compliance, especially when tribal appropriations from the state increased. By 1955, South Dakota was expending $135,279 a month on tribal welfare.[35] This rapidly increasing figure sparked controversy between state reservation populations and state authorities. Tribal lands were tax exempt and beyond state control; yet, tribesmen were eligible for state services supported by state tax revenues. This early welfare issue was a prelude to future state-tribal jurisdiction conflicts in South Dakota.

During World War II, the tribesmen adjusted to state assistance programs, reflecting, in part, their wish to reduce the Office of Indian Affairs reservation presence in order to increase tribal governance on the reservations. Sioux leaders understood that greater self-rule was possible only with corresponding reduction in federal control. Despite tribal criticism that the IRA did not provide greater self-rule, an enduring legacy of the Collier era had been his encouragement of tribal participation in federal policy decisions. Congressional hearings provided the vehicle for tribal input, enabling tribesmen to participate in policy decisions. The United States Senate investigations initiated in 1928 at John Collier's instigation represent a significant example of tribal input. The Senate Committee on Indian Affairs concluded their investigation in 1943 after fifteen years of hearings. Senators heard reservation leaders across the nation reiterate common concerns: (1) settle past tribal claims against the United States; (2) improve reservation health, welfare, and employment opportunities; (3) reduce the reservation responsibilities of the Office of Indian Affairs.[36]

In 1944, the House Committee on Indian Affairs initiated further study of the nation's reservations, and before the hearings commenced, committee members sent a questionnaire to reservations asking tribal leaders to list reservation problems, to declare the need to vote again on the IRA, to update tribal claims against the United States, and to articulate the tribe's opinion of the Indian Service and what activities could be eliminated, among other things.[37] Sioux responses to the House committee questions were predictable.

Collectively, poor housing, inadequate land base, inferior schools, high unemployment, absence of credit, and racial prejudice plagued the state's reservations. Despite their criticisms of the IRA, some of the IRA reservations favored retaining the law in order to give the governments and the tribal courts time to succeed. Standing Rock reservation requested the abolishment of the reservation court to save tribal funds. More important, the Sioux wanted to curtail Indian Service programs through staff reductions. Pine Ridge leaders specifically requested the elimination of the Office of Indian Affairs "arts and crafts, anthropology, organizers, regional offices, social service, road department, forestry, and grazing."[38]

Yankton Sioux Claims Committee secretary Clarence E. Forman articulated Sioux sentiments toward the Indian Service when he told the investigating committee: "Keep Indian Service employees out of our life's pathway and we will go forward. Take down the bars obstructing our social advancement." On the other hand, Forman, like other Sioux, demanded that the government maintain trust restrictions on allotments. He added, "Give to us and our Indian soldiers who are sacrificing their all on the battlefields what our Americans and allies are fighting for, freedom and equal justice to all."[39] The state's tribal populations seemed to believe that reduction of Indian Service programs would enable more dollars to reach reservation residents while at the same time decreasing government paternalism. The tribesmen's advocacy of the continued tax exemption of trust lands from local assessments illustrated their desire to perpetuate the reservation's political autonomy from the state and thereby prohibit South Dakota from encroaching on the reservations as federal authority decreased.

During House committee hearings, tribal leaders from reservations close to urban areas, such as Sisseton, Flandreau, and Yankton, ranked the improvement of educational conditions to increase the tribesmen's wage work opportunities as their first priority. Their reliance upon land reserves was nearly impossible since their lands were highly fractionalized, making it difficult either to farm or lease remaining lands efficiently. On the other hand, while the larger, isolated western reservation populations supported better education, their top concern was the obtaining of credit to build reservation stock operations, utilize local land resources, and create tribal self-sufficiency programs.

After hearing tribal testimony, the committee recommended extending IRA loan provisions to non-IRA tribes, thus eliminating discriminatory Indian Service credit regulations. In addition, the committee advocated settling tribal land claims, consolidating fractionalized heirship lands, and teaching the Indian to live outside the reservation boundaries. The House committee concluded, "The improvement of Indian homes and the development of a stable and secure economic base for the Indian family is fundamental to the final solution of the Indian problem and ranks second only to education."[40] Both Sioux leaders and members of the House committee agreed on the fundamental reservation problems and the tentative direction for future solutions.

Despite economic hardships and poor living conditions, Sioux leaders stressed the importance of greater tribal autonomy and informed members of the House that the reservations' future depended upon either modifying or eliminating federal supervision over tribal affairs. Lower Brule resident Harvey Big Eagle gave voice to this Sioux attitude toward the Office of Indian Affairs when he stated that the "Indian Bureau . . . does not do anything that spells salvation for the Indians," especially, he added, when 69 percent of the agency's budget "goes for the salaries of the Indian Service people and 31 percent goes for conferences, cars, gas."[41] Standing Rock resident Guy W. Jones voiced an even stronger statement: "I have no finances to back me but I am just as well off as any white man. So I urge you to abolish the Indian Bureau."

Many criticized the Indian Service for spending $32 million when Sioux poverty and distress were so high. Joseph Eagle, also from Standing Rock, added that the Sioux received nothing from that appropriation, and therefore, "we want to abrogate the Indian Bureau, . . . but we also want our land."[42] The Sioux favored partial termination of federal control, but they wanted to maintain the trust status of their lands since many Sioux could not pay the property taxes and still make a living. Tax exemption also preserved their political sovereignty and provided them with the freedom to make responsible decisions that affected their scarce resources. Sioux leaders clearly wanted the Indian Service's responsibilities either reduced or eliminated; based on tribal testimony nationwide, Congress acted but moved beyond tribal wishes.

Members of the House Committee evaluated these tribal comments and concluded that "the Indian witnesses appearing before our committee were on the whole, well informed, reasonable, practical, and persistent."[43] After hearing the tribes' request for "partial" termination of the Office of Indian Affairs, Congress began reducing the Indian Service's responsibilities, thereby inaugurating the termination era. Reducing the Indian Service's role was essential if tribes were to gain greater control over their own affairs, but termination of federal paternalism also increased their risks of failure. Scholarship has not yet evaluated tribal input into Congress' termination decisions but, instead, has generally blamed an irresponsible Congress for permitting "Indian affairs [to slip] into obscurity during the war, [as] Congress began recklessly entertaining a rash of minor bills and major legislation to terminate Indian services."[44]

After the institution of the Indian Reorganization Act,
tribes sought greater autonomy in a variety of areas, including education.
In this 1941 photograph, a delegation from the Rosebud reservation
meets with officials of the Education Division of the Office of
Indian Affairs in Washington, DC.
Lakota Archives and Research Center,
Sinte Gleska University, Mission, SD

This interpretation reduces the tribes to the passive role of receiving policy when, in fact, they were active participants in congressional policy decisions, just like other constituents. The difference between Congress' termination legislation and the Sioux desire for elimination of federal paternalism was one of degree. In the early 1950s, Congress went further toward removing wardship status than Sioux leaders and other Indian tribes wished and recommended eliminating the trust status of land, ending tribal government, and abrogating treaty rights. At that juncture, the Sioux opposed termination, but at the same time that situation created an unresolvable dilemma affecting tribal self-rule. Greater autonomy was possible only with a corresponding reduction of federal paternalism, which the Sioux ultimately protected. Risks accompanied any change, and the Sioux tribesmen's conservative posture enabled them to blame Congress and rely on "the Indian Bureau as a combination foster-father, Santa Claus, and scapegoat."[45] Fearing termination, Sioux leaders scrutinized congressional legislation to determine if that was the legislation's objective even though they clamored for greater self-rule. Their fear of termination was offset only by their fear of increased federal control over reservation affairs, and that irreconcilable dilemma would restrict both tribal and congressional decisions in the future.[46]

The possibility of Congress terminating any South Dakota reservation was remote. In 1947, the Bureau of Indian Affairs ranked tribes according to their abilities to manage their own affairs. Of all South Dakota reservation populations, only the Cheyenne River Sioux were judged to possess the resources and skills necessary to manage their own affairs within the next ten years. The remaining Sioux reservations in South Dakota, according to the Bureau of Indian Affairs, would not be capable of managing their own affairs for an indefinite time.[47]

The Bureau of Indian Affairs, Aberdeen Area Office, reevaluated the state's reservations in 1954 and reported that the residents of the Sisseton and Yankton reservations were ready for federal withdrawal in five years because of the populations' high education level and the tribesmen's inability to use fractionalized heirship lands. Their futures, the office concluded, lay in off-reservation employment.[48] Yet, in 1953, the Sisseton Sioux themselves did not want the Bureau of Indian Affairs removed from the reservation; a standard reply was "our people are not ready for it."[49] Writing in 1949, anthropologist John Embree compared this tribal reluctance to end the dependent paternalistic relation with the federal government to the Japanese-American experience during World War II at War Relocation Authority camps. Despite a dislike of their wardens, the internees feared release, for "wardship insured security—freedom might be dangerous."[50]

In an ironic twist to this dilemma, Congress indirectly compelled tribes to forget their hesitancy and to assume greater sovereignty when the lawmakers reduced federal tribal appropriations after World War II, forcing tribes to replace lost monies with tribally generated revenues. The reduction of federal funds in 1947 decreased Pine Ridge reservation services, especially in the area of law and order. Revenue reductions forced the Pine Ridge tribal council to enact a lease tax (Res. No. 34–49) in 1949 to create tribal taxes to fund necessary services. Individuals leasing farming and grazing land were required to pay a yearly tax of three cents per acre for grazing land and fifteen cents per acre for farming land. Nontribal lessees challenged the tribe's action in court, but their suit failed because the court held that the Pine Ridge tribe possessed all the inherent attributes of sovereignty "excepting where restrictions have been placed" by Congress.[51] Despite the Pine Ridge lease tax, which was important in defining the boundaries of tribal sovereignty, the tribe still depended, for the most part, on outside land users to support reservation services. Reservation economic development continued to languish behind the local economy.

After World War II, reservation economic improvement emerged as an essential but elusive component of any contemplated federal withdrawal. From 1934 to 1950, Congress emphasized first reservation resource development and then worker relocation, but neither concept worked successfully. Reservation unemployment increased after the war when returning veterans and workers forced the state's reservations into deeper poverty. By 1956, approximately 60 percent of Pine Ridge reservation residents were landless, had no opportunities to obtain credit, and were thus eliminated from using reservation resources. In addition, the tribe was equally poor, having a net worth of $121 per person. Increased state relief to tribal populations and wage work were now crucial to reservations without other resources. In 1955, 42 percent of all Standing Rock income came from wages, 23 percent of the reservation income derived from welfare payments, 22 percent of the individual income was lease money, and 13 percent came from individual agricultural operations. Sisseton Tribal Chairman Melvin Robertson described his reservation's postwar cycle of dependency as one in which most of the reservation's population received public assistance for seven months a year and found seasonal work for the remaining five months.[52]

The escalating poverty after World War II illustrated the hopelessness of reallocating reservation resources among reservation residents. Sioux veterans, without military dependency grants, returned to reservations, adding to the reservation's postwar poverty. The Bureau of Indian Affairs created a relocation program to counter this economic dilemma in 1949, and Congress accelerated the program in 1953. Moving rural reservation Sioux to urban jobs offered a short-term solution to a deep-seated problem since reservation resources would never provide adequate local employment opportunities for growing tribal populations. The Sioux partially supported relocation because urban centers offered employment opportunities that were absent on the reservations. Twelve families from a group of 107 families at Bullhead on the Standing Rock reservation wanted to relocate. Despite their willingness, few Sioux left the reservations, and those who did often returned, further aggravating reservation unemployment. In 1956, 10 percent of the Pine Ridge work force of two to three thousand individuals found full-time employment on the reservation. Roughly 50 percent, or about fifteen hundred workers, found seasonal farm labor in Colorado, Nebraska, and Wyoming.[53]

The Bureau of Indian Affairs relocation program eventually sent Sioux to several out-of-state cities, especially Chicago, Dallas, and Oakland. Rapid City received most of the in-state relocatees. Most men who went to Rapid City in the late 1940s and early 1950s possessed construction skills that provided them with seasonal employment. These workers also brought their dependents to Rapid City, forcing city officials to confront problems associated with seasonal unemployment and housing shortages. The local Catholic church attempted to respond to the need through the Mother Butler Center in north Rapid City, aiding the new refugees from the state's reservations to find adequate housing, training, and year-round jobs. The needs of this in-state Sioux migration put a greater financial stress on both local and state welfare programs. Numerous off-reservation critics voiced their complaints, claiming that tribal people paid minimum state taxes, and the situation heightened hostility between Sioux and non-Sioux citizens of South Dakota. By and large, Sioux relocation was a calamitous reallocation of both reservation resources and problems. The tribesman's urban employment was generally sporadic, and local agencies did not possess resources to deal with the growing urban populations. In addition, the social transition was often difficult. Veterans, who had spent time off the reservation, adjusted most easily, but their spouses, who had never left the reservation, often quickly returned to their rural homes. When relocation was achieved, it frequently extended problems, including underdevelopment, from the reservation to the cities.[54]

An alternative was to bring industry to the reservation. By 1955, Commissioner of Indian Affairs Glenn Emmons pushed reservation industrial development as a substitute to relocation. Congress also supported this concept but preferred to tie economic development nationwide into one rehabilitation package. In that way, Congress classified and included reservations as a region of rural poverty like any other depressed rural area, sidestepping individual reservation redevelopment bills. A national industrial and rural-area redevelopment bill passed Congress in 1954, but President Dwight D. Eisenhower vetoed the legislation. Illinois Senator Paul Douglas had added grant amendments that were contrary to Eisenhower's conservative monetary views, even though the president had verbally supported the redevelopment concept.[55]

South Dakota Sioux also supported area redevelopment because the concept offered the hope of decreasing tribal relocation, with its associated problems, and increasing both reservation wage opportunities and tribal authority. Pine Ridge leader William Fire Thunder supported area redevelopment since only a small number of educated reservation residents had successfully relocated. He also observed that "cattle raising and farming cannot support us and we know that relocation will not solve our problem for a long time," but area redevelopment would create "new employment opportunities on and near our reservation [and] will help us solve our problem. That is why we have been in full favor of the program of the commissioner to try to attract industry to reservations."[56]

Since industrial cooperation was also in the state's best interests, nontribal groups worked with several reservation leaders on economic rehabilitation, and local communities provided tribes with limited assistance. Sisseton tribal chairman Melvin Robertson cooperated with the Sisseton Chamber of Commerce in 1956, encouraging business to relocate to that reservation, but without success.[57] Sisseton was an area of intense long-term poverty, making it difficult to entice any industry to relocate on the reservation. The Sioux understood the negative effects of reservation conditions on industry's willingness to develop reservation ventures. Pine Ridge leader Henry Black Elk, Jr., summarized their predicament, "Our basic problem is poverty."[58]

Reservation poverty escalated throughout the 1950s while Congress and the president struggled to develop a national program. Finally, the general economic rehabilitation legislation became law in 1961, coinciding with the beginning of the nation's emerging War on Poverty. An area redevelopment act provided government loans to private industry for either plant relocation to depressed areas or improvement of plants already located within depressed areas. In addition, the law furnished federal assistance to a depressed area's local government to assist its agencies with additional relief services.[59] This program was of limited value to reservations because it attempted only to relieve the effects of poverty, such as unemployment; it did not seek to end reservation poverty by destroying causes associated with historical underdevelopment. Besides, the legislation emphasized industrial development and did not assist South Dakota's regional agricultural economy, which the reservations marginally served. Finally, the legislation neither encouraged industry to seek reservation business locations nor advocated local economic planning.

Congress corrected some shortfalls of the area redevelopment legislation, particularly by stressing greater community involvement, economic development, and participation, when it created the Office of Economic Opportunity (OEO) in 1964. Under the guidance of the first director, R. Sargent Shriver, OEO issued grants to local communities that had designed their own antipoverty programs. Sioux reservation leaders closely followed the OEO legislation and supported the law's concept. The Pine Ridge Tribal Council requested federal antipoverty assistance in 1963, the same year that Henry Kranz, a member of President John F. Kennedy's poverty study group, visited the reservation. Because widespread rural poverty was synonymous with reservation life, specific tribal OEO programs such as Indian Community Action Program (ICAP) and the Indian Branch of the Special Field Programs were created. Project Head Start and Legal Services remain OEO legacies.[60]

Unlike past economic development programs administered by the Bureau of Indian Affairs, OEO required tribal participation and stressed improving both reservation educational opportunities and living conditions. Tribal organizations created Neighborhood Youth Corps (NYC), recognizing growing reservation juvenile problems, but the OEO programs largely bypassed adult issues. Job training for permanent employment and long-term reservation economic development, both essential to ending chronic underdevelopment, were not included in the range of OEO programs. Despite OEO shortcomings, this non-Bureau of Indian Affairs program stressed tribal self-determination and instilled confidence among the state's reservation populations, a confidence necessary to overcome past federal constraints associated with tribal assumption of greater self-rule.

The need to exercise more tribal self-rule was only one of many new demands the state's reservation populations encountered from 1934 to 1965. Increased tribal governance, based on federal assistance, placed multi-million-dollar figures in tribal council budgets by the mid-1960s and partially realigned reservation dependency away from the Bureau of Indian Affairs and toward other federal agencies. In short, the tribesmen gained greater participation in the decisions affecting reservations but did not gain materially greater tribal sovereignty. Though reservation political autonomy remained diluted, tribal

Improvements in housing were one outgrowth of the
economic development programs of the 1960s. In this scene at
Rosebud, a new house is being built next to an older home.
State Archives Collection,
South Dakota State Historical Society

exertion of sovereignty changed tribal-state relations, laying the foundation for inevitable jurisdiction conflicts with the state in the years to come.[61]

In this time of transition and flux on the reservations, residents witnessed an urban migration that reallocated tribal populations and problems (and conflicts), the addition of wage employment in tribal economies, increased state services, and continued government intervention in tribal life. Declining ranching and farming opportunities, increasing unemployment, and a declining standard of living were also conspicuous elements of South Dakota's reservation experience. Life on the reservations primarily changed for the worse as the various programs established to diminish Sioux country's historical underdevelopment failed.

NOTES

1. Ruth Hill Useem, "The Aftermath of Defeat: A Study of Acculturation among the Rosebud Sioux of South Dakota" (PhD diss., University of Wisconsin, 1947), 156; Gordon Macgregor, *Warriors without Weapons: A Study of the Society and Personality Development of the Pine Ridge Sioux* (Chicago: University of Chicago Press, 1946), 38–40. Useem noted that individuals who were one-half or more Sioux believed they lived better at the turn of the century under the "Old Deal" than in the years after 1930 under the New Deal.

2. William O. Roberts, "Successful Agriculture within the Reservation Framework," *Applied Anthropology* 2 (Apr.–June 1943): 38.

3. Herbert S. Schell, *History of South Dakota*, 2d ed. (Lincoln: University of Nebraska Press, 1968), 351–52; Macgregor, *Warriors without Weapons*, 38–41.

4. Lewis Meriam et al., *The Problem of Indian Administration, Institute for Government Research, Studies in Administration* (Baltimore: Johns Hopkins Press, 1928), 451–56.

5. Roberts, "Successful Agriculture," 38; Francis Paul Prucha, *The Great Father: The United States Government and the American Indians*, 2 vols. (Lincoln: University of Nebraska Press, 1984), 2:887.

6. Meriam, *Problem of Indian Administration*, 447.

7. Roberts, "Successful Agriculture," 38–39.

8. South Dakota, State Planning Board and Works Progress Administration, *Indians of South Dakota*, 1937, 45–46; Meriam, *Problem of Indian Administration*, 452.

9. Senate Committee on Indian Affairs, *To Grant to Indians Living under Federal Tutelage the Freedom to Organize for Purposes of Local Self-Government and Economic Enterprise: Hearing before the Committee on Indian Affairs on S. 2755*, 73d Cong., 2d sess., 1934, pt. 1, 16–21. For a concise analysis of Collier's program, see "Tribal Self-Government and the Indian Reorganization Act of 1934," *Michigan Law Review* 70 (Apr. 1972): 955–86. The Indian Reorganization Act of 1934 comprised the core of Collier's tribal rehabilitation program.

10. Graham D. Taylor, *The New Deal and American Indian Tribalism: The Administration of the Indian Reorganization Act, 1934–45* (Lincoln: University of Nebraska Press, 1980), 20–29.

11. *To Grant to Indians Living under Federal Tutelage the Freedom to Organize*, pt. 2, 225.

12. Senate, *Repeal of the So-Called Wheeler-Howard Act*, 76th Cong., 1st sess., 1939, S. Rep. 1047, serial 10295, 1–3.

13. *Report with Respect to the House Resolution Authorizing the Committee on Interior and Insular Affairs to Conduct an Investigation of the Bureau of Indian Affairs*, 82d Cong., 2d sess., 1952, H. Rep. 2503, serial 11582, 51.

14. Section 16 of the act provided for tribal employment of counsel. See "Tribal Self-Government," 965.

15. House Committee on Indian Affairs, *Conditions on Sioux Reservations: Hearings before the Committee on Indian Affairs on H. R. 5753*, 75th Cong., 1st sess., 1937, 7.

16. The Black Hills claim, Sioux Tribe of Indians v. United States, had been filed in the United States Court of Claims on 7 May 1923, and claim organizers were waiting for a favorable decision. The court examined United States offsetting claims, and when final decision came in 1944, the court ruled against the Sioux. The progress of bills to compensate Wounded Knee survivors can be followed in House, *Sioux Indians, Wounded Knee Massacre: Hearings before the Subcommittee on Indian Affairs on HR 2535*, 75th Cong., 3d sess., 1938. A similar piece of legislation was introduced before the 74th Congress (HR 11778), but neither bill became law.

17. *Conditions on Sioux Reservations*, 11.

18. House, *Wheeler-Howard Act—Exempt Certain Indians: Hearings before the Committee on Indian Affairs, on S 2103*, 76th Cong., 3d sess., 1940, 65–66. While Commissioner Collier philosophically supported tribal self-rule, practical considerations ultimately governed his final decisions. For example, in the end scarce tribal resources would continue to be governed by federal administrators to minimize any chance for error. Government control, though, ultimately contributed to continuing underdevelopment, both social and economical, of the reservations.

19. *Repeal of the So-Called Wheeler-Howard Act*, 3.

20. House, *Investigate Indian Affairs: Hearings before a Subcommittee of the Committee on Indian Affairs, Pursuant to HR 166*, 78th Cong., 2d sess., 1944, pt. 3, 153.

21. Ibid., 90.

22. Taylor, *New Deal and American Indian Tribalism*, 176n.3; *Investigate Indian Affairs*, pt. 3, 85.

23. *Wheeler-Howard Act—Exempt Certain Indians*, 53.

24. *Conditions on Sioux Reservations*, 6.

25. Ibid., 6–7, 10–12; quotations on 10, 17.

26. John Useem, Gordon Macgregor, and Ruth Hill Useem, "Wartime Employment and Cultural Adjustments of the Rosebud Sioux," *Applied Anthropology* 2 (Jan.–Mar. 1943): 1–2;

Roger Bromert, "The Sioux and the Indian-CCC," *South Dakota History* 8 (Fall 1978): 340n; Macgregor, *Warriors without Weapons*, 49.

27. Macgregor, *Warriors without Weapons*, 50.

28. Useem, Macgregor, and Useem, "Wartime Employment," 1–2; Macgregor, *Warriors without Weapons*, 49–50.

29. Useem, Macgregor, and Useem, "Wartime Employment," 1–3.

30. *Present Relations of the Federal Government to the American Indian*, 85th Cong., 2d sess., 1958, House Committee Print no. 38, 127.

31. Useem, Macgregor, and Useem, "Wartime Employment," 3–4.

32. Macgregor, *Warriors without Weapons*, 51n.10; *Present Relations of the Federal Government to the American Indian*, 125.

33. *Present Relations of the Federal Government to the American Indian*, 127.

34. *Investigate Indian Affairs*, pt. 3, 139.

35. *Present Relations of the Federal Government to the American Indian*, 80.

36. S. Lyman Tyler, *A History of Indian Affairs* (Washington, DC: Government Printing Office, 1973), 139–40.

37. *Investigate Indian Affairs*, pt. 3, 4–5; Tyler, *History of Indian Affairs*, 141–42.

38. *Investigate Indian Affairs*, pt. 3, 38, 85–87, 121, 148, 171–72, 175–78, 199–201, 221–22; quotation on 222.

39. Ibid., 199–201.

40. Ibid., pt. 4, 342.

41. Ibid., pt. 3, 167.

42. Ibid., 139, 140.

43. Ibid., pt. 4, 347.

44. Donald L. Fixico, *Termination and Relocation: Federal Indian Policy, 1945–1960* (Albuquerque: University of New Mexico Press, 1986), 21.

45. *Report with Respect to the House Resolution Authorizing the Committee on Interior and Insular Affairs to Conduct an Investigation of the Bureau of Indian Affairs*, 83d Cong., 2d sess., 1954, H. Rep. 2680, serial 11747, 78 (hereafter cited as H. Rep. 2680).

46. Mamie L. Mizen, *Federal Facilities for Indians: Tribal Relations with the Federal Government* (Washington, DC: Government Printing Office, 1967), ix–x.

47. Tyler, *History of Indian Affairs*, 163–64.

48. H. Rep. 2680, 23.

49. Ibid., 406.

50. Embree, "The Indian Bureau and Self-Government," *Human Organization* 8 (Spring 1949): 12.

51. Iron Crow v. Ogallala Sioux Tribe of the Pine Ridge Reservation, South Dakota, 129 F. Supp. 15; Iron Crow v. Oglala Sioux Tribe of the Pine Ridge Reservation, South Dakota,

231 F. 2d 89; Barta v. Oglala Sioux Tribe of Pine Ridge Reservation of South Dakota, 259 F. 2d 553.

52. *Area Redevelopment: Hearings before the Subcommittee on Labor of the Committee on Labor and Public Welfare on S 2663*, 84th Cong., 2d sess., 1956, pt. 2, 892–95, 938–39; Fixico, *Termination and Relocation*, 8–9; *Sioux Indian Tribes, North and South Dakota: Hearings before the Subcommittee on Indian Affairs of the Committee on Interior and Insular Affairs, Pursuant to HR 30*, 84th Cong., 1st sess., 1955, 78; H. Rep. 2680, 109; U.S. Department of the Interior, Bureau of Indian Affairs, *Cultural and Economic Status of the Sioux People, 1955, Standing Rock Reservation, North and South Dakota, Missouri River Basin Investigations Project*, Report no. 151, (Billings, MT, 1957), 44.

53. *Sioux Indian Tribes, North and South Dakota*, 7–9; *Area Redevelopment*, pt. 2, 900–902.

54. Ibid., 45–47, 118. For more on social adjustment problems of relocation, see Fixico, *Termination and Relocation*, 190–92.

55. *Area Redevelopment Act: Hearings before a Subcommittee of the Committee on Banking and Currency on S 268, S 722, and S 1064*, 86th Cong., 1st sess., 1959, 3; Larry W. Burt, *Tribalism in Crisis: Federal Indian Policy, 1953–1961* (Albuquerque: University of New Mexico Press, 1982), 70–72; Sherman Adams, *Firsthand Report: The Story of the Eisenhower Administration* (New York: Harper & Bros., 1961), 362.

56. *Area Redevelopment*, pt. 2, 902–03.

57. Ibid., 938–39.

58. *Sioux Indian Tribes, North and South Dakota*, 96.

59. Alan B. Batchelder, *The Economics of Poverty* (New York: John Wiley & Sons, 1966), 144–45.

60. Mizen, *Federal Facilities for Indians*, 25–26; Sar A. Levitan and Barbara Hetrick, *Big Brother's Indian Programs—with Reservations* (New York: McGraw-Hill Book Co., 1971), 90–91.

61. For more on jurisdiction, see Richmond L. Clow, "State Jurisdiction on Sioux Reservations: Indian and Non-Indian Responses, 1952–1964," *South Dakota History* 11 (Summer 1981): 171–84.

STEVEN C. SCHULTE

REMOVING THE YOKE OF GOVERNMENT

E. Y. BERRY AND THE ORIGINS OF INDIAN

TERMINATION POLICY

. . .

Scholars acknowledge the distinctiveness of the West as a region and of western politics in general. Grouped together, the western states constitute, in one observer's words, "a geographical reality, and a culturally distinct region as well."[1] Beginning with the earliest settlement of the West, both settlers and politicians have viewed the Indian presence as an obstacle to European-American standards of progress. Historically, the states and their dominant white populations have resented what they perceive as the "locking up" of valuable islands of land and resources by American Indians. Western politicians have traditionally been caught in a dilemma that forces them to choose which side to champion, the Indian or the non-Indian.[2] This study, focusing on South Dakota Congressman E. Y. Berry, offers insights into the relationship between western conservative politicians and American Indians during the termination era, 1945–1970.

During the twentieth century, the attitudes of white citizens of western states have continued to reflect, in many instances, the early, frontier prejudice toward American Indians. Many westerners have desired Indian lands and the timber, minerals, farming, and grazing resources they contain. A close connection exists between western resentment of the federal landlord and attempts to undermine Indian landownership. In times of federal neglect, for instance, tribal lands have been coveted by white ranchers, real estate developers, and energy companies who view the reservations as some of the last, exploitable frontier regions. This state of mind most influenced federal Indian policy during the business-boom times of the 1920s and 1950s.[3]

Historians have yet to reach a consensus regarding the role of Congressman E. Y. Berry in the 1950s Indian policy known as "termination," which involved the withdrawal of federal protection and services from Indian tribes. His career has not received the emphasis it deserves. Utah Republican Senator Arthur V.

This essay originally appeared in *South Dakota History* 14 (Spring 1984): 48–67.

Watkins, in most estimations, dominated the formulation of the "withdrawal," or termination, policy. Berry, however, exhibited an equal amount of interest and enthusiasm for termination questions by laboring contentedly, usually away from the public limelight, to accomplish these goals throughout his twenty-year congressional career. Western politicians such as Berry and Watkins have usually chosen to satisfy the demands of white constituents in issues involving Indians and non-Indians.[4] During the termination era, such issues included legislation to lessen, minimize, or remove restrictions on the leasing and purchase of Indian lands. From 1945 to 1970, 133 separate bills were introduced in Congress, mostly by western politicians, to permit the transfer of land from Indian to non-Indian ownership. In addition, about one hundred tribes and rancherias were severed from federal protection.[5] Typically, this legislation announced that it would "free" the individual Indian or tribe from the "paternalistic" and "dictatorial" care of the Bureau of Indian Affairs (BIA). Such rhetoric offered these bills a thin disguise for what many critics claimed were their true intentions—to relieve Indians of land.[6]

While promotion of white economic interests and development was undoubtedly important in Berry's advocacy of termination, other factors must be examined to arrive at a balanced assessment of his intent as a champion of such legislation. Berry's background before coming to Congress offers revealing insights into his philosophical justifications for Indian policy. Unfortunately, scholars have tended to overlook the importance of termination politicians' backgrounds and possible economic motivations by concentrating on the actual formulation of the policy.[7] While this approach is important and fruitful, it is time to move beyond discussions of when or why the termination issue evolved, to an analysis of its proponents' motivations.

Berry and other terminationists held a conservative, laissez-faire, pro-business orientation that colored their views of Indian policy. Many had been staunch opponents of New Deal programs in general and of the Indian New Deal program in particular. Ellis Yarnell Berry had spent most of his adult life on the Standing Rock Indian Reservation in the town of McLaughlin, South Dakota. Born in western Iowa in 1902, he moved to a ranch near Philip, South Dakota, when he was fourteen years old. Philip is located between the Cheyenne River and Pine Ridge Indian reservations, and it served as a frequent camping site for Sioux traveling between the two reservations during Berry's early life. After graduating from the University of South Dakota's law school in 1927, Berry began practicing law in McLaughlin. Almost immediately, he became deeply involved in local and state Republican politics, serving as county judge, state senator, state's attorney, and finally, after 1950, United States con-

Congressman E. Y. Berry sought to eliminate Sioux dependence on
the federal government by increasing job opportunities.
Special Collections, E. Y. Berry Library,
Black Hills State University, Spearfish, SD

gressman. Berry also carved out a career as a newspaper editor and publisher, owning two publications in small towns on the Standing Rock reservation. As a result, Berry became intimately acquainted with Indians and formed definite opinions about the direction of federal Indian policy.[8]

Berry firmly believed that until the advent of the 1934 Indian Reorganization Act (IRA), which was the "centerpiece" of the Indian New Deal, the Sioux Indians were on their way toward the desirable goal of complete assimilation.[9] The IRA, also known as the Wheeler-Howard Act, ended the disastrous allotment policy that had severely reduced the total American Indian land base. It provided measures to restore and consolidate reservation land holdings and created a revolving credit fund to promote Indian economic development. The IRA also offered mechanisms for chartering and reorganizing tribal governments. To Berry and other western conservatives, the IRA and Commissioner of Indian Affairs John Collier's Indian New Deal fostered a retrogressive dependency on the federal government while wasting the taxpayers' money.[10] In Berry's words, Collier "was a socialist . . . a pure unadulterated socialist."[11] Berry formed this assessment, in part, because of Collier's stance toward Indian heirship lands. Collier tried to prevent the further dividing and subdividing of Indian lands into small and often useless parcels by purchasing such areas for tribal, not individual, control. Berry argued that this practice encouraged an archaic dependency on old tribal communal customs. Furthermore, it was contrary to the American and particularly western, rugged individualism in which he so strongly believed.[12]

Berry's attempts to "liberate," or terminate, the Indians from the federal trust relationship, which had thus been reaffirmed by the IRA, can be ascribed, at least to some extent, to his idealization of Sioux life before the Indian New Deal. Indeed, during the 1950s, Berry desired to "turn back the clock" to the 1920s when individualism and business ethics reigned supreme and Republicans ran the country. "The Indian people were so much better off then than they are today," Berry recalled. "There was no law and order problem. The Indian was growing in respect and prestige in the community."[13] According to Berry, Indians caught the same business fever that infected their white counterparts during the pre-1929 years. When compared with the post-New Deal era, Indians of the 1920s had an abundance of "freedom" to control, lease, or sell their allotted land. Each Indian handled, with a minimum of government interference, the disposition of his own property. To Berry, leasing provided an excellent Indian training school in practical American business enterprise. If the Indian needed money, an advance on the next year's lease payment could be arranged. As Berry viewed it, leasing was a simple and uplifting process through which "the Indian was learning to handle his own affairs, take care of his own land, send his children to school, and teach them the value of individual enterprise."[14]

Yet, the 1920s were not the "golden years" that Berry alleges. One historian has called the era from 1900 to 1930 the time of the "Great Indian Depression."[15] In 1887, the General Allotment Act (Dawes Act), hailed by contemporaries as the "Indian Emancipation Act," had been implemented in an attempt to transform the Indians into yeoman farmers. The law had provided for the allotment of reservation land to individual Indians, with title to be held by the United States for twenty-five years. After a reservation had been allotted, any surplus land was opened to general settlement. The Allotment Act allowed land-hungry settlers to acquire over ninety million acres of Indian land by 1930. Later amendments to the bill significantly reduced restrictions upon the leasing and sale of land from individual Indians to whites, providing the individual freedom that Berry had observed in the 1920s. But, even though the agency superintendents had to give final approval to all leasing arrangements and the secretary of the interior had to approve all land sales, this system led to massive alienation of Indian property. In short, much of the white-leased land eventually passed from Indian to white ownership. The Indian New Deal, despite its many shortcomings, reversed this trend toward massive Indian land alienation and changed the emphasis of federal Indian policy from forced assimilation to a belief in cultural pluralism.

Berry and other conservative politicians, however, saw the IRA's protective legislative mechanisms as attempts to place tribesmen into reservation "concentration camps on doles and relief," thereby preventing them from fully integrating into "the rest of society and [being] given the same chance that all Americans have."[16] Thus, the Indian New Deal, to Berry and others, was nothing more than a liberal scheme to force the unwilling Indian "back to the blanket."[17] By encouraging tribal revitalization and enterprise, the IRA attempted to keep the Indians as living "museum pieces." "It made Indians out of them," Berry concluded somewhat ironically, "and they lost all hope."[18]

Berry also believed that the New Deal community programs served as a laboratory to "test out communist ideas."[19] He was not alone in this opinion, for both conservative politicians and Indian critics linked the IRA with communism. The American Indian Federation (AIF), a group of right-wing, pro-assimilation, Christian fundamentalist Indians became the most vigorous opponent of Collier's programs, waging a ten-year war against "communism, Collier, and the New Deal." The AIF and like groups often appeared before congressional committees at the behest of conservative politicians during the 1930s and 1940s to discredit the Indian New Deal. As one federation member wrote, Commissioner John Collier was "distinctly un-American in both thought and action . . . a menace to the ideals of a free America."[20]

Berry's unapologetically conservative vision of America and his philosophy of Indian affairs[21] received a more sympathetic hearing in the post-World War II era. While it can be argued that the Indian New Deal had been under attack and on the defensive in Congress since as early as 1937,[22] it was in postwar America that an attitude of widespread disillusionment with utopias of both the Left and Right occurred. American society had become more integrated and homogeneous than at any time in its history.[23] Many western lawmakers began to call into question the American Indians' special status.

Berry, Republican Congressman Karl Mundt of South Dakota, and other termination advocates believed that the Indian suffered from the dead hand of the federal government. In 1943, Mundt had chaired a thorough investigation into the operation of the IRA. The committee concluded that the IRA had "rebounded to the distinct advantage of the Indian on some reservations" but, in general, remained an obstacle to individual Indian progress.[24] Berry came to Congress in 1951 with a similar conclusion about the state of Indian affairs. He believed he could best satisfy his "desire to do something for the Indian people" by attempting to remove the burdensome collar of the federal government from their necks.[25]

In 1952, the Republicans gained control of Congress for only the second time in two decades. Soon, Berry, Senator Arthur V. Watkins, and other western conservatives seized upon this chance to implement their philosophy of Indian affairs. Wyoming Republican Congressman William Henry Harrison fired the "first shot" in the western conservatives' "twentieth century Indian war" by introducing House Concurrent Resolution 108 in June 1953.[26] The resolution unequivocally repudiated the goals of the IRA while expressing a desire to phase out the BIA, end the Indians' wardship status, and make American Indians subject to the same rights and laws as other Americans. In an unprecedented move, Berry, the head of the House Indian Affairs Subcommittee, and Watkins, who chaired the Senate Indian Subcommittee, decided to hold joint hearings on the question of terminating the federal trust status of an agreed upon list of tribes.[27]

Berry and Watkins had previously agreed that the potential rewards of holding joint hearings far outweighed any political drawbacks.[28] They believed that the savings of the taxpayers' money, "plus the fact that we didn't have to bring witnesses into two different hearings," justified this unorthodox policy-making procedure. As Berry later recalled, the decision to hold joint hearings "worked out very successfully," although "that was the only time that they [the congressional Indian subcommittees] have done that."[29] At the start of the termination hearings, Watkins explained that identical bills would be introduced in both the House and Senate. "We have not gone into the legalities of it [the joint hearings]," Watkins stated, "but the evidence will be considered by both Houses and the Committees of both Houses."[30] Joint hearings, on any subject, are an uncommon procedure in Congress. In this instance, they permitted rapid action and allowed western conservatives to force undesirable and hastily conceived termination legislation upon tribes. The affected tribes, in every case, were ill prepared to cope with freedom from federal supervision. Furthermore, the preponderance of evidence indicates that the tribes concerned had rarely been consulted about the decisions to terminate their federal trust status.[31]

The termination hearings, involving several large tribes and dozens of smaller bands, took place at whirlwind speed. Those opposed to the legislative goals of the joint subcommittee had little opportunity to marshal an adequate defense during the hearings. Beginning on 15 February 1954, the joint subcommittee concluded its business two months later on 19 April. Despite the importance of this legislation, the hearings drew but scant attention from most other subcommittee members. Only Senator Watkins and Congressman Berry made any effort to attend all the hearings. Clearly, they were the moving forces behind the termination legislation.[32] By August 1954, Berry and Watkins had made an effective start toward implementing their uniquely western philosophy of Indian affairs. Several dozen tribes, groups, bands, communities, and rancherias had been stripped of federal services and protection. Terminated tribes included the Klamath of Oregon, the Menominees of Wisconsin, the Ottawa, Wyandot, and Peoria tribes of Oklahoma, and the Paiute tribe of Utah.[33]

Berry demonstrated his satisfaction with Congress' work in a newsletter to Indian constituents in which he summarized the accomplishments of the termination legislation. Calling it the "greatest privilege of my life" to serve as chairman of the House Indian Affairs Subcommittee, Berry pointed out that Congress had passed bills authorizing Indians "to take over the management of their own affairs" on more than a dozen reservations. Now these Indians could "run their own businesses, manage their own lives, and . . . free themselves from the domination of the Indian Bureau." Berry believed Congress had made an impressive start toward reinstituting the old Indian policy of benign neglect and individualism, the policy he had first encountered on the Standing Rock reservation before 1930. Through termination, Berry could work to reimplement the programs that he thought had placed his Sioux neighbors on the road to assimilation and full American citizenship during the 1920s.[34]

In the aftermath of this legislation, many of the terminated Indian groups became strife-torn and poverty-ridden because of an inability to make the transition to the freedom and individualism envisioned by Berry and Watkins. The most tragic and publicized case involved the Menominee tribe of Wisconsin, which managed, after a long legislative battle, to reverse the federal termination mandate in 1973 and return to its former protected reservation trust status. Other terminated tribes have not been as fortunate.[35]

The 1954 termination hearings represented the most spectacular and undisguised demonstration of Berry's philosophy of Indian affairs. By the late 1950s, advocates of direct termination had been placed on the defensive and had to defend their program against congressional liberals.[36] Nevertheless, the concept of termination persisted in Indian programs advocated by Berry and other western conservatives. Berry, however, may have sensed that public exuberance for termination was not well received beyond white communities adjacent to Indian lands. His respect for the Indian vote also mitigated his public stand on termination. Berry made a determined effort every two years to court and capture Indian ballots. Despite the advice of some that the Sioux "never voted Republican," he always solicited their vote.[37] Typically, before election day, Berry would give a feast on the various Sioux reservations. One person recalled that the Berry campaign on the Standing Rock reservation fed the Indians upstairs in a school on election day and sent them downstairs to the polls.[38] Berry also sent personalized brochures and letters to Sioux constituents, signing them Mahto Cuwiyuska, or "Bear Ribs," his adopted Sioux name.

Berry usually fared well on the northern reservations, Standing Rock and Cheyenne River. On the larger southern reservations, Pine Ridge and Rosebud, Berry always had difficulty getting votes. The Sioux on the southern reservations, beginning in the late 1950s, became highly politicized and concerned for their tribal rights. As a result, they probably feared Berry's advocacy of "individual rights . . . individual freedom, and the need for the individual to have control over the property he owns" as a threat to tribal sovereignty.[39] Berry's long residence on the Standing Rock no doubt contributed to his better showing on the northern reservations.

Only rarely after 1955 did Berry, an able politician, publicly advocate the abolition of the BIA. With over thirty thousand Sioux Indians living in his district, his political sense undoubtedly dictated a safer course. Nevertheless, Berry continued to promote termination philosophies and programs to constituents who held similar views. In 1966, Berry offered a vigorous defense of Menomi-

Congressman Berry, whose adopted Sioux name was "Bear Ribs,"
poses with Benjamin American Horse and his granddaughter.
Special Collections, E. Y. Berry Library,
Black Hills State University, Spearfish, SD

nee Indian termination from the floor of the House, arguing that federal law-makers had made no mistake by assisting "an individual in gaining his individual rights, his individual freedom, and the authority of him as an individual to own and control property."[40]

Berry also continued to lambaste the BIA and government paternalism before Congress. A particularly effective method of presenting such views was to bring highly assimilated Indians before congressional committees where they would attack New Deal philosophies and Indian Bureau restrictions on individual Indians. Berry, in 1961, called his friend and political supporter Edison Ward, a mixed-blood Sioux and successful rancher, pilot, and entrepreneur, to come before Senator Sam Ervin's Subcommittee on the Constitutional Rights of the American Indian. Ward attacked the "dictatorial" policies of the BIA, which, in his opinion, restricted the individual Indian's initiative.[41] Ward's views identically reflected Berry's philosophy of Indian affairs, but they had more impact coming from Ward, a Sioux Indian.

Berry's tactical change toward Indian policy is best symbolized by his advocacy of programs that would eventually eliminate the need for the BIA—but at a future time. He pursued programs that promoted rapid reservation industrialization in combination with increased educational efforts. This plan, he believed, would force the Indians into the American mainstream. Berry labeled his industrial program "Operation Bootstrap—Indian Style," a direct imitation of the program used to industrialize Puerto Rico following World War II. During a 1958 House Interior Committee tour of Puerto Rico and after long discussions with its governor, Luis Muñoz Marín, Berry decided that the Puerto Rican Operation Bootstrap could be tailored to meet the needs of American Indians. First introduced into Congress in 1959, Operation Bootstrap—Indian Style would have encouraged industry to locate on Indian reservations by exempting it from corporate, state, federal, and property taxes for ten years. It also offered government aid in conducting on-the-job training for Indian employees. Because of the isolated location of most reservations, tax incentives were believed necessary to induce industry to relocate. Such assistance would have offset additional transportation costs necessitated by locating far from major population and market areas.[42]

Berry premised Operation Bootstrap, or "Operation Moccasin" as he liked to call it, upon the same individualistic beliefs that he had applied to his analysis of the Sioux community before 1930. Operation Moccasin would enable the Indian to "lift himself up by his own bootstraps, if given the freedom of opportunity."[43] Berry estimated in 1959 that 80 percent of the nation's Indians had no opportunity to find work. In his opinion, most of those dependent on the BIA for aid "would gladly swap a Government relief check for a weekly paycheck."[44] For twelve years, Berry fought an uncooperative Congress that refused to pass his plan, with either negative reports from the Interior Department or Democrat-dominated congressional committees impairing Operation Bootstrap's legislative progress. Berry had another explanation for the project's perennial lack of congressional success as well: "They [the Indian Bureau] didn't want some . . . congressman getting a bill through that would put them out of a job."[45]

Operation Bootstrap—Indian Style represented Berry's most creative response to what he believed was a bankrupt federal Indian policy. "For one hundred years the Indian Department had no program other than to make farmers and ranchers out of the Indians," Berry proclaimed. While a certain percentage of the population, Indian or non-Indian, could adapt to agricultural pursuits (Berry estimated about 20 percent), "nothing," he claimed, "has been done for the other eighty percent."[46] Operation Moccasin, Berry believed, was but a partial solution toward finding employment for the nation's neglected Indian population. Relocation to urban areas, an integral component of the termination program of the 1950s, offered another solution to the problem posed by the nonfarming Indian population. Jobs and work opportunities must be made off the reservation, Berry maintained, for those willing to leave. "I think probably the greatest step forward [for the Indian people] in the past fifty years is the new program for relocation," Berry wrote in 1956.[47]

In the mid-1950s, Berry also argued once again that the individual Indian "must be permitted to sell and dispose of his land." Like the pre-New Deal Indian allotment policy, this process would serve as a practical educational tool to teach the Indian the methods of American business. It would also "give him that economic boost and . . . break the property ties that keep him on the reservation."[48] Thus, reservation industry, relocation, and freedom to dispose of property represented three complementary approaches to termination advocated by Berry and other western conservatives. This three-part program rested on the same individualistic shibboleths that had been used to justify outright termination. Nonetheless, these methods were especially effective because they did not resemble or overtly imply a unilateral abandonment of treaty and trust obligations that outright severance of federal relations did.[49]

Berry had thus modified his basic approach toward what he referred to as the "Indian problem." Following the termination hearings of 1954, he began to champion Indian programs more subtle in scope. Outside of his congressional support of Operation Moccasin, Berry primarily labored behind the scenes to attain his philosophical goals in Indian affairs. While his public face rarely showed a fervent interest in termination, his private actions attempted to mold South Dakota's Indian relations to his own conceptions. Several examples demonstrate this approach.

In 1959, the chairman of the Rosebud Sioux Tribe, Robert Burnette, created a tremendous controversy throughout South Dakota by publicly charging the state's white population with prejudice and discrimination toward American Indians. Burnette's frightening allegations, submitted to the House Indian Affairs Subcommittee, caught the imagination of the national press. Burnette argued that "discrimination is not speculative [in South Dakota], it exists now as it has since prior to statehood."[50] Burnette's list of alleged Indian civil rights violations included the chaining of Indian prisoners in county jails, general police brutality, and blatant discrimination in state courts. Burnette supplied documents to the subcommittee in support of his charges and also presented his evidence to South Dakota governor Ralph Herseth, who acknowledged, according to Burnette, that many of his white constituents were pressing him to counter the adverse publicity given the state by Burnette's activities.[51]

Congressman Berry moved quickly to minimize the damage caused by Burnette's allegations. Until this time, Burnette and Berry had maintained a strained but cordial friendship.[52] Now, working away from public view, Berry encouraged both Indian friends and white supporters to "tell the truth" to the national media about Burnette's stories. In explaining Burnette's "wild statements," Berry suggested that the Indian leader "got carried away by some of these do-gooders here in Washington . . . but he seems to let them influence him unduly."[53] Specifically, Berry blamed Burnette's "corruption" upon the leaders of the National Association for the Advancement of Colored People and the National Congress of American Indians.[54] Berry also submitted rebuttals of the allegations into the *Congressional Record*, reading a letter from the Todd County Taxpayers' League, Inc., an association of white citizens from a county adjoining Burnette's home Rosebud reservation. The league denounced Burnette and lauded the generally good race relations in South Dakota.[55]

A final demonstration of Berry's quiet, background support of his white constituents' views centered around what has been called the "state jurisdiction controversy." It has been a credo of Republican party faith, as well as of most western conservatives, that state government is a far more efficient governing mechanism than the more distant and less accountable federal bureaucracy. From 1952 to 1964, South Dakota's politicians sought to implement Public Law 280 (83d Congress), which gave states the opportunity to assume civil and criminal jurisdiction over Indian reservations provided they took legislative action to amend their state constitutions or statutes. The law, however, did not provide for obtaining tribal consent, which became a serious issue with Indian leaders in both South Dakota and the nation. In March 1963, the South Dakota State Legislature approved House Bill 791, extending state jurisdiction over the Indian reservations.[56]

Though the bill was described by Rosebud Sioux Tribal Chairman Cato Valandra as "the Wounded Knee of 1963," South Dakota Governor Archie Gubbrud signed House Bill 791 into law. It was scheduled to go into effect on 1 July 1963. Sioux Indian leaders feared that state jurisdiction would lead not only to discriminatory law enforcement but also to eventual taxation of tribal lands to pay for law enforcement. The next logical step would be confiscation of Indian lands when the owners could not afford to pay taxes and the resale of the lands to whites. Valandra, Burnette, and other Sioux leaders thus portrayed the state jurisdiction bill as a land-grab scheme. In desperation, the Sioux tribes turned to the state's referendum procedure. After the tribes gathered the requisite fourteen thousand signatures on petitions, the state scheduled a referendum vote on the state jurisdiction question for the general election of November 1964.[57]

Though managing to steer away from the intense public controversy surrounding this issue, Congressman Berry provided background impetus for proponents of state jurisdiction. As early as 1952, Berry had favored state jurisdiction, but only if the federal government would underwrite the cost of the law enforcement program. "I want to see the Indian Department go out of business," Berry had stated, "but not at the expense of the state."[58] By 1954, Berry had formulated a firm position on the jurisdiction issue. "The law itself," he said, "should be the same for all citizens regardless of whether they are white or red, and regardless of whether they are full-bloods or mixed-bloods."[59]

The South Dakota campaign for state jurisdiction accelerated in the early 1960s, with Berry prodding the state administration toward that goal. He argued that the state would take over jurisdiction on reservations "whenever the State Legislature musters enough courage to pass a law definitely and directly accepting jurisdiction."[60] From 1961 to 1963, Berry worked with State Senator James Ramey, who became the moving force behind the jurisdiction bill. Berry offered to help the campaign in any way possible, often suggesting word changes in legislation drafts to make the proposed bill more constitutionally acceptable. After the bill's passage in early 1963, Berry continued to work with state officials, helping to prepare them for the responsibility of state jurisdiction. He also tried to secure federal appropriations to assist in funding the state's law enforcement efforts on the reservations. Merton Glover, the president of the South Dakota Stockgrowers' Association and a white rancher who lived on the Pine Ridge reservation, encouraged Berry's participation by asking him to use his influence to smooth the transition to state control.[61]

In pledging his full cooperation to Glover, Berry did not foresee the determined and growing Sioux opposition to the measure. What Berry and other proponents feared was a congressional repeal of Public Law 280, but Berry, writing to stockman Glover, did not see that as a real possibility either, since Democrat James Haley of Florida, the chairman of the House Indian Affairs Subcommittee, was "as conservative as you or I."[62] Berry was surprised, therefore, when the Indians mobilized, hired a publicity firm, and defeated the referred bill. Berry later claimed that "outsiders" had misguided the tribes into fighting the jurisdiction legislation.[63]

While his approach to Indian policy in later years may have differed from outright termination, Berry's goals always remained the same—to get the federal government out of the Indian business. Indeed, Berry continued to argue that government interference in the life of the individual Indian, beginning during the New Deal years, constituted the greatest impediment to Indian progress. As he succinctly remarked, "There is no Indian problem that could not be solved by the return of this country to the principles of individual rights and a return to the original concept of property rights."[64]

Never wavering in his philosophy and basic prescription for solving the Indian problem, Berry nevertheless held a great respect for the Indian peoples in his congressional district. He remained convinced that his ideas represented the only path to progress for the Sioux and, by implication, for all American Indians. Calling Berry an "Indian hater"[65] is far too simplistic a label for a man who maintained a sincere, lifelong desire to help the American Indian. Berry's perspective was conditioned by over thirty years of residence on an Indian reservation and by his day-to-day interaction with both Indian peoples and the bureaucracy of the Indian Office. His career provides an instructive example of the limitations of many western politicians' response to the problems of American Indians. All too often, Berry and other western conservatives were held captive by an inability to move intellectually beyond their own backgrounds—to overcome the modified strains of frontier prejudice and ethnocentric belief in the superiority of Anglo-Saxon values that characterized their approach to Indian affairs.

NOTES

1. Lynton R. Hayes, *Energy, Economic Growth, and Regionalism in the West* (Albuquerque: University of New Mexico Press, 1980), 53.

2. See Thomas C. Donnelly, ed., *Rocky Mountain Politics* (Albuquerque: University of New

Mexico Press, 1940), for an early and general discussion of the nature of western politics. For a more recent view, see Hayes, *Energy, Economic Growth, and Regionalism.*

3. Arrell M. Gibson, *The American Indian: Prehistory to the Present.* (Lexington, MA: D. C. Heath & Co., 1980), 517–21. Gibson states: "The twentieth century brought Indians no respite from private and public exploitation and abuse. Greedy non-Indians continued to prey upon allotments and tribal resources" (517).

4. To date, there are no studies that analyze the motivations of termination proponents. Most textbook treatments of termination mention Watkins as the main force behind termination, though Berry is often cited as termination's House proponent. Vine Deloria, Jr., in *Custer Died for Your Sins* (New York: Avon Books, 1969), assigns Watkins and Berry equal responsibility for devising and implementing termination. Most studies, however, cast Berry's role as subordinate to that of Watkins. Kenneth R. Philp ("Termination: A Legacy of the Indian New Deal," *Western Historical Quarterly* 14 [Apr. 1983]: 168–80) argued that termination gained credibility because of the collapse of New Deal Indian reform. This interpretation is solid, but it does not demonstrate why congressmen such as Berry, Watkins, and other western conservatives were attracted to termination as an Indian-policy panacea.

5. U.S. Commission on Civil Rights, *Indian Tribes: A Continuing Quest for Survival* (Washington, DC: Government Printing Office, 1981), 14, 22–23.

6. The clearest published example of terminationist rhetoric and arguments is Arthur V. Watkins, "Termination of Federal Supervision: Removal of Restrictions over Indian Property and Person," *Annals of the American Academy of Political and Social Science* 311 (May 1957).

7. Philp, "Termination: A Legacy," and Clayton R. Koppes, "From New Deal to Termination: Liberalism and Indian Policy, 1933–1953," *Pacific Historical Review* 46 (1977): 543–66, are outstanding examples of this genre in termination historiography.

8. E. Y. Berry, interview, Rapid City, SD, 14 July 1981; Gary Orfield, *A Study of the Termination Policy* (Denver: National Congress of American Indians, 1964), 2–4; David B. Miller, "The E. Y. Berry Papers: An Unexpected Resource for Students of Recent South Dakota History," *South Dakota History* 3 (Winter 1972): 34; Ruth Fairchild, interview, Philip, SD, 4 Aug. 1983. Berry owned and published the *McLaughlin Messenger* and the *Corson County News.*

9. Berry, interview, 14 July 1981.

10. Commission on Civil Rights, *Indian Tribes*, 22; Berry, interview, 14 July 1981. Until the late 1960s, scholars judged Collier's Indian New Deal to be an unqualified success. Recent scholars, however, have probed beneath its surface and found it lacking in several respects. For examples of the critical approach, see Lawrence C. Kelly, *The Navajo Indians and Federal Indian Policy* (Tucson: University of Arizona Press, 1968), which was the first critical evaluation of the Indian New Deal; Donald Parman, *The Navajos and the New Deal* (New Haven, CT: Yale University Press, 1976); Graham D. Taylor, *The New Deal and American Indian Tribalism: The Administration of the Indian Reorganization Act, 1934–45* (Lincoln: University of Nebraska

Press, 1980); and Laurence M. Hauptman, *The Iroquois and the New Deal* (Syracuse, NY: Syracuse University Press, 1981). Kenneth R. Philp's *John Collier's Crusade for Indian Reform, 1920–1954* (Tucson: University of Arizona Press, 1977) offers a more favorable and balanced evaluation of the Indian New Deal.

11. Berry, interview, 14 July 1981.

12. "Statement of E. Y. Berry, Prepared for the House Indian Affairs Subcommittee, February 2, 1963," Box 135, E. Y. Berry Papers, Black Hills State College, Spearfish, SD.

13. Ibid.

14. Ibid.

15. Herbert T. Hoover, "Yankton Sioux Experience in the 'Great Indian Depression,' 1900–1930," in *The American West: Essays in Honor of W. Eugene Hollon*, ed. Ronald Lora (Toledo, Ohio: University of Toledo, 1980), 53. Hoover quotes from an interview with a Sisseton Sioux who discussed the Indian depression idea. Another interview that suggests the poor conditions in the 1920s is published in Joseph H. Cash and Herbert T. Hoover, eds., *To Be an Indian: An Oral History* (New York: Holt, Rinehart, & Winston, 1971), 108–09. For a more optimistic appraisal of the pre-World War I era, see Frederick E. Hoxie, "From Prison to Homeland: The Cheyenne River Indian Reservation before WWI," *South Dakota History* 10 (Winter 1979): 1–24.

16. Berry, interview, 14 July 1981.

17. Berry to Mrs. Robert Meredith, 12 Jan. 1956, Box 192, Berry Papers.

18. Berry, interview, 14 July 1981.

19. Berry to Charles O. Jones, 8 July 1955, Box 192, Berry Papers.

20. Joseph Bruner to Alfred F. Beiter, 18 June 1935, Joseph C. O'Mahoney Papers, American Heritage Center, University of Wyoming, Laramie, WY. For the American Indian Federation, see Laurence Hauptman's *The Iroquois and the New Deal*, 46–54, in which he argues that the federation deserves reevaluation as a serious organization representative of an important segment of Indian opinion. See also Hazel W. Hertzberg, *The Search for an American Indian Identity: Modern Pan-Indian Movements* (Syracuse, NY: Syracuse University Press, 1971), 289.

21. As David B. Miller noted, "The forceful and unapologetic fashion in which Berry states his philosophy in many documents . . . leaves the impression that he is not reluctant to be labeled conservative and rural-oriented" (Miller, "E. Y. Berry Papers," 36).

22. Many authors so argue. For a sampling, see Deloria, *Custer Died for Your Sins*, 60–61, and Philp, *John Collier's Crusade for Indian Reform*, 187–213. Donald Parman's *Navajos and the New Deal* shows both tribal and congressional opposition to the Indian New Deal developing as early as 1935.

23. J. Rogers Hollingsworth, "Consensus and Continuity in Recent American Historical Writing," *South Atlantic Quarterly* 61 (Winter 1962): 40. Several studies develop the climate of anticommunism in this period and its effects on the dominant society's attitudes toward minority groups. See Alonzo Hamby, *Beyond the New Deal: Harry S. Truman and American Lib-*

eralism (New York: Columbia University Press, 1973); Eric F. Goldman, *The Crucial Decade and After, 1945–1960* (New York: Vintage Books, 1960); and Koppes, "From New Deal to Termination."

24. House Select Committee to Investigate Indian Affairs and Conditions, *An Investigation to Determine Whether the Changed Status of the Indian Requires a Revision of the Laws and Regulations Affecting the American Indian*, 78th Cong., 2d sess., 1943, H. Rep. 2091, 1–3.

25. Berry, interview, 14 July 1981.

26. The idea that termination is the twentieth century's answer to the old Indian wars is Vine Deloria's in *Custer Died for Your Sins*, 68.

27. The affected tribes were listed in House Concurrent Resolution 108 and included the Flatheads, Klamaths, Menominees, Potawatomis, Turtle Mountain Chippewas, and all groups within California, Florida, New York, and Texas. For a concise discussion of HCR 108 and its implications, see Larry W. Burt, *Tribalism in Crisis: Federal Indian Policy, 1953–1961* (Albuquerque: University of New Mexico Press, 1982), 22–23.

28. This statement reflects the author's conclusion after weighing the available evidence from the E. Y. Berry Papers and from conversations with Congressman Berry.

29. Berry, interview, 14 July 1981.

30. *Termination of Federal Supervision over Certain Tribes of Indians: Joint Hearings before the Subcommittees on Interior and Insular Affairs*, 83d Cong., 2d sess., pt. 1, 1.

31. Burt, *Tribalism in Crisis*, 29–33. Burt calls the decision to hold joint hearings "an unusual move to ensure prompt action" (29).

32. Ibid., pp. 139–40n.1; Orfield, *Study of the Termination Policy*, 4.

33. Gibson, *The American Indian*, 551.

34. E. Y. Berry to Indian Constituents, 9 Aug. 1954, Box 183, Berry Papers.

35. For the story of the Menominee experience, see Nicholas C. Peroff, *Menominee Drums: Tribal Termination and Restoration, 1954–1974* (Norman: University of Oklahoma Press, 1982). William A. Brophy and Sophie D. Aberle, comps., *The Indian, America's Unfinished Business: Report of the Commission on the Rights, Liberties, and Responsibilities of the American Indian* (Norman: University of Oklahoma Press, 1966), 192–207, contains many examples of some of the devastating effects of termination upon several tribes.

36. Burt, *Tribalism in Crisis*, 95–123, and Larry J. Hasse, "Termination and Assimilation: Federal Indian Policy, 1943 to 1961" (PhD diss., Washington State University, 1974), 263–303, describe the reassertion of liberal Indian policy-making initiative in the later 1950s.

37. Marvis T. Hogen, interview, Pierre, SD, 4 Aug. 1983. See also Cash and Hoover, eds., *To Be an Indian*, 173.

38. Dale Lewis, interview, Philip, SD, 5 Aug. 1983.

39. Berry to Indian Constituents, 15 Oct. 1962, Box 128, Berry Papers.

40. E. Y. Berry, Speech to Congress, 25 Aug. 1966, Box 135, Berry Papers.

41. Edison Ward, "Testimony before Senate Judiciary Subcommittee on the Constitutional

Rights of the American Indians," 30 Aug. 1961, Box 193, Berry Papers. Ward wrote both Berry's and Senator Francis Case's testimony before the same subcommittee.

42. Berry, interview, 14 July 1981; Berry to Galen Weaver, 5 Aug. 1954, Box 183, Berry Papers.

43. Berry, interview, 14 July 1981.

44. "Operation Bootstrap—Indian Style," *Congressional Quarterly Weekly Report*, 7 Aug. 1959, 1074, Box 205, Berry Papers.

45. Berry, interview, 14 July 1981.

46. "Statement of E. Y. Berry, Prepared for the House Indian Subcommittee, February 6, 1963," Box 135, Berry Papers.

47. Berry to Bernard D. Fagan, S.J., 21 July 1956, Box 192, Berry.

48. Ibid.

49. One of the better studies of the relocation program to date is Donald Lee Fixico, "Termination and Relocation: Federal Indian Policy in the 1950s" (PhD diss., University of Oklahoma, 1980).

50. Associated Press report, 22 Mar. 1959, Box 127, Berry Papers.

51. Robert Burnette, *The Tortured Americans* (Englewood Cliffs, NJ: Prentice-Hall, 1971), 63.

52. Berry and Burnette's friendship first became strained during the 1958 election campaign when Burnette campaigned against the incumbent congressman. To counteract Burnette's attack, Berry organized a "Sioux for Berry" club based in his hometown of McLaughlin. See Mrs. R. S. McLaughlin to Rosebud Sioux Tribe, Box 128, Berry Papers.

53. Berry to Abe Crawford, 2 Mar. 1959, Box 127, Berry Papers.

54. Berry to Mrs. E. P. Kositzsky, 24 Feb. 1959, Box 127, Berry Papers.

55. *Cong. Rec.*, 86th Cong., 1st sess., 1959, A3340-41. From 1959 on, Berry and Burnette clashed on many issues, including the discrimination issue.

56. Richmond L. Clow, "State Jurisdiction on Sioux Reservations: Indian and Non-Indian Responses, 1952–1964," *South Dakota History* 11 (Summer 1981): 175–79. Clow's article is the first published study of the South Dakota state jurisdiction controversy.

57. Ibid., 175–80; Cato Valandra, interview, Vermillion, SD, 29 July 1983.

58. Berry to Governor Sigurd Anderson, 31 May 1952, Box 168, Berry Papers.

59. Berry to Henry Cottier, 6 July 1954, Box 168, Berry Papers.

60. Berry to Lloyd E. Hole, 19 May 1960, Box 175, Berry Papers.

61. Berry to Senator James Ramey, Rep. Ellen Bliss, Merle Lofgren, 19 Jan. 1961, Box 175; Berry to Senator James Ramey, 11 Mar. 1963, Box 175; and Merton Glover to Berry, 29 Mar. 1963, Box 176, all in Berry Papers.

62. Berry to Merton Glover, 29 Apr. 1963, Box 176, Berry Papers.

63. E. Y. Berry, interview, Rapid City, SD, 12 July 1983. The defeat of the state jurisdiction bill in the November 1964 referendum is described in Clow, "State Jurisdiction on Sioux

Reservations," 179–84. The state legislator who advocated state jurisdiction, Senator James Ramey, had his life disrupted after the defeat. Ramey's reservation leases were canceled by the tribe as a result of his advocacy of state jurisdiction. He eventually moved away from the reservation and started a ranch in the northern Black Hills region. Fred Cozad, interview, Martin, SD, 5 July 1983.

64. "Statement of E. Y. Berry, Prepared for the House Indian Affairs Subcommittee, February 6, 1963," Box 135, Berry Papers.

65. This label was applied to Senator Watkins by one of Michael Lawson's Indian informants in his book *Dammed Indians: The Pick-Sloan Plan and the Missouri River Sioux, 1944–1980* (Norman: University of Oklahoma Press, 1982), 95. Through his close association with Watkins, Berry has also had the same label applied to him. Lawson points out that Berry "was influenced too much by local white ranchers to be objective about Indian problems and was too paternalistic toward the tribes when he did consider them" (95).

MICHAEL L. LAWSON

"WE LOST OUR WAY OF LIVING"

THE INUNDATION OF THE WHITE SWAN COMMUNITY

. . .

In 1952, the waters of the Missouri River rose behind the newly closed Fort Randall Dam, creating a huge reservoir later named Lake Francis Case and completely inundating White Swan, a traditional and self-sustaining community on the Yankton Indian Reservation. Other reservations in South Dakota had been or would be affected by the system of large dams that the United States Army Corps of Engineers constructed on the Missouri River between 1945 and 1966. Tribal communities such as Lower Brule, Fort Thompson, and Cheyenne Agency were moved to higher ground and reestablished. The White Swan community, however, was completely dissolved and its residents dispersed to whatever areas offered housing or land, including communities on other Sioux reservations. Those former residents of White Swan still living retain fond and vivid memories of their pre-dam homeland and recall the trauma of being forced to break connections with their environment, their neighbors, and their past. The Army Corps of Engineers seized their property by right of eminent domain, and the federal government generally failed to provide them with either fair compensation or support adequate to reestablish themselves in a similar environment. Many community members never fully recovered either emotionally or financially from the obliteration of White Swan.

The Fort Randall Dam is one of six large dams the Corps of Engineers built on the main stem of the Missouri as part of the Missouri River Basin Development Program. Authorized under the Flood Control Act of 1944, this program became known popularly as the Pick-Sloan Plan, so named after its primary engineers and promoters.[1] The Fort Randall project, constructed in southeastern South Dakota between 1945 and 1954, flooded 21,593 acres of Sioux land on the Yankton, Rosebud, Lower Brule, and Crow Creek reservations and dislocated approximately 151 Indian families.[2] Within the Yankton Sioux reservation, the dam inundated 2,851 acres of Indian trust land and required the

This essay originally appeared in *South Dakota History* 36 (Summer 2006): 135–71.

relocation and resettlement of at least twenty families, constituting approximately 8 percent of the resident tribal population.[3]

The primary purpose of the Pick-Sloan main-stem dams and reservoirs was to control flooding in the lower Missouri River Valley below Sioux City, Iowa. Navigation, hydropower, improved water supplies, and enhanced recreation were also important project purposes. The Corps of Engineers has estimated that the project's overall contribution to the national economy averages $1.9 billion annually. For the Yankton Sioux Tribe and other tribal entities along the Missouri, however, the human and economic costs have far outweighed any benefits received. The Pick-Sloan projects disproportionately affected Indian lands, destroying entire tribal communities and economies. In fact, the Pick-Sloan Plan caused more damage to Indian reservation lands and communities than any other public-works project in the nation's history. Whether or not its architects deliberately chose to impact Indian rather than non-Indian land and resources, as some tribal leaders charged, their projects ultimately affected twenty-three reservations. In total, the six massive dams constructed on the main stem of the Missouri inundated over five hundred fifty square miles of Indian land and displaced more than nine hundred Indian families.[4]

The Missouri River tribes heard little about the Pick-Sloan Plan while it was being proposed, even though legal precedents and, in some cases, treaty rights provided that tribal land could not be taken without a tribe's consent. In November 1943, Representative Francis H. Case of South Dakota urged Major General Thomas M. Robins, acting chief of the Army Corps of Engineers, to insert language in the proposed legislation to provide appropriate authority for acquiring Indian lands and paying just compensation to the affected tribes and tribal members. In Case's view, this compensation included reimbursement for relocation costs. General Robins assured the senator that his recommendations would be fully considered. In an effort to keep Indian officials informed of this exchange, Representative Case circulated the information to the commissioner of Indian affairs, the superintendents of all Indian agencies located along the Missouri, and the leaders of every tribe whose reservation lands might be impacted.[5] This action constituted the only known instance in which a government representative informed tribal councils of the possible adverse affects of the Pick-Sloan Plan prior to its enactment.

Despite Case's efforts, the portions of the Flood Control Act of 1944 that authorized the Pick-Sloan Plan did not contain any language regarding the protection of tribal interests. Although the Bureau of Indian Affairs (BIA) was fully aware of the potential impacts of the legislation, it made no effort either to keep tribal leaders informed or to object to the Corps of Engineers' proposals

Designed for flood control, navigation, hydropower, and other purposes,
the Missouri River dams flooded thousands of acres of land. This aerial view
from 1956 shows Lake Francis Case extending behind Fort Randall Dam.
State Archives Collection, South Dakota State Historical Society

while they were being debated in Congress in 1944. The Indian Bureau did not inform the tribes of the damages they would suffer in a comprehensive way until 1949. The legislation establishing the Pick-Sloan Plan also ignored the Indians' reserved water rights under the legal principle known as the Winters Doctrine.[6]

The location selected for the Fort Randall Dam was on the western boundary of the Yankton Indian Reservation and what had until 1904 been the eastern boundary of the Rosebud Indian Reservation. The actual dam site lay partly on Indian land within the Yankton reservation. The entire project area also straddled the border between Charles Mix and Gregory counties.[7] The dam took its name from the old military post that had once occupied the portion of the project site on the west bank of the Missouri. Brevet Brigadier General William S. Harney, a seasoned veteran of the Indian wars, established Fort Randall in 1856 to serve as one of the army's principal fortifications on the upper Missouri. Although the fort was rebuilt between 1870 and 1872, it became a skeleton post in 1884 after the army relinquished the adjoining military reservation. The fort and reserve were officially abandoned in 1892. All that remains today are the ruins of the post chapel, constructed by the garrison's enlisted men in 1875.[8]

The Corps of Engineers began subsurface exploration of the Fort Randall Dam site in November 1941 and continued this work through at least 1947. Initial surveys, foundation investigations, and engineering studies were conducted in 1945; surplus buildings were moved to the site in 1946; and construction of access roads and a townsite for construction workers and their families began in 1947. New access facilities included a six-mile-long road connecting with United States Highway 18 at Lake Andes, as well as a nearly seven-mile-long link with a main line of the Chicago, Milwaukee, St. Louis & Pacific Railroad, also near Lake Andes. These routes required rights-of-way across parcels of Indian land, for which the army filed condemnation suits in United States District Court under the right of eminent domain as early as 1946. Upon determining the exact location of the dam site, the Corps of Engineers discovered that a portion of the dam and a considerable part of the construction area would be located on Indian-owned land. The army quickly filed condemnation petitions and obtained declarations of taking for the needed rights-of-way and construction sites, giving the corps immediate possession of the land. This legal maneuvering was accomplished without the required consent of either the Yankton Sioux Tribe or its federal trustee, the secretary of the interior.[9]

The Army Corps of Engineers began conducting extensive surveys of the White Swan community, one of the four major settlement areas on the Yankton reservation, as early as 1945. The agency carried out this activity without the knowledge or consent of either BIA or tribal representatives. In February 1946, Robert J. Trier, the BIA district road engineer, advised the commissioner of Indian affairs that it appeared that the Fort Randall project would flood the entire White Swan community. This occasion may have been the first time anyone in the BIA became aware of the fact that White Swan would be inundated. The BIA then began minimal efforts to protect the interests of tribal members. In the meantime, the Corps of Engineers proceeded to condemn and gain immediate possession of thirty-one additional tracts of Yankton land. By April 1948, the task had been accomplished, and the corps began charging rent to tribal members who still wished to occupy the lands taken from them.[10] Staying on the land became impossible for most former owners because they had not yet received compensation for the condemned land. Moreover, the affected tribal members operated primarily within a subsistence economy in which cash was rarely used. Such circumstances also compelled families to move from their homes without the resources to cover either their moving expenses or to obtain housing or land elsewhere.

The original development of the White Swan settlement had been contemporaneous with the establishment of the military post at Fort Randall. The area was named for White Swan, or Magaska, a prominent Yankton Sioux chief. Catholic missionary Pierre Jean DeSmet described the chief's encampment in 1867 as situated three miles above Fort Randall. Reported as being "quite an old man" in 1882, White Swan then resided "2 1/2 miles up the river" from what became the White Swan settlement.[11] The White Swan area included Sun Rise Hill, White Swan Bottom, and White Swan Island, also known as Beebe Island, which gradually became attached to the bank of the Missouri River. Sun Rise Hill owed its name to another Yankton tribal member who lived at the top. A large Yankton Sioux settlement developed near Sun Rise Hill during the occupation of Fort Randall, whose soldiers frequently visited the community.[12]

White Swan featured a post office serving the Fort Randall area, as well as a stage stop on a line that followed the Missouri River north from Sioux City to Fort Pierre. Volunteer soldiers erected barracks and stables while stationed at the White Swan settlement temporarily in 1863. The community also had ferry service. Tribal members moved the Yankton Dance Hall to the White Swan area in 1881, where it served for many years as an important social and ceremonial gathering place. Two missionary churches also took root in the community. Saint Philips Church was established as an Episcopal mission in 1869 and later moved to a site north of White Swan. Roman Catholic missionaries established Saint Francis Church closer to the settlement and about a mile from the river

The White Swan community was named for White Swan,
or Magaska, a Yankton Sioux chief who lived in the area at the
time of Fort Randall's establishment.
State Archives Collection, South Dakota State Historical Society

bottomlands. Two government schools, Little Bird School and White Swan School No. 5, also served the community. At the beginning of World War II, a cannery operated near White Swan where community members processed peas, corn, and other vegetables. During the war, workers donated a percentage of the canned goods to the war effort.[13]

By the late 1940s, White Swan was a mixed community of Indian and non-Indian families who lived off the land and the abundant natural resources of the riverine environment. For the most part, they coexisted in harmony and cooperated in a number of economic and social activities. They maintained small farms and gardens and, in general, lived in a manner that more closely resembled a rural community of the late nineteenth century rather than the mid-twentieth century. Most families lived in small log cabins or unpainted frame houses, some with dirt floors. A few lived in tents year-round, while others did so for at least part of the year.[14] Sometimes in early summer, the bottomland residents would experience what they called a "June raise." If the Missouri appeared ready to overflow its banks and flood their homes, they would move to higher ground and live in tents until the water receded.[15]

None of the homes had electricity or indoor plumbing. Candles and kerosene lamps provided lighting, and the only toilet facilities were outhouses. A few families enjoyed the comparative luxury of having oil stoves, but most depended on wood from the bottomlands for their fuel. Driftwood collected from the banks of the Missouri was preferred because it seemed to burn better. Residents also gathered dead and down timber. When necessary, they cut and stacked green willow and cottonwood trees during the summer, allowing the wood to dry until winter. Beebe Island was a favorite source for timber, and families cooperated in gathering, cutting, and storing wood. Those who had horse-drawn wagons hauled timber from the bottoms and distributed it throughout the community.[16]

Water was hauled from the river in wooden barrels and distributed to most of the various small farms in a similar manner. Residents believed that the Missouri's rapid current and sands purified the water; none could recall anyone ever getting sick from drinking river water.[17] Those who used it also claimed that it made the best coffee because, as Louie Archambeau recalled, it never "turned black."[18] Some families were fortunate enough to have wells, while others lived close to creeks that provided for their water needs. Former resident Raymond Drapeau told of a creek so clear that its bottom, rocks, and fish were always visible. In winter, some individuals cut blocks of ice from the frozen creeks and river and hauled them home. Stored in cellars, covered with sawdust, the blocks kept food chilled during warm weather. Ice cut from frozen streams also helped preserve corpses in caskets because it was difficult to take them to a mortician for embalming.[19]

Only three or four White Swan families had motorized vehicles. Those with a car or truck gave rides to others, but most people got around on foot, on horseback, or in horse-drawn farm wagons. Tribal members commonly walked or rode horseback to and from Lake Andes, Marty, and other reservation settlements. Some children also rode horses to their one-room schoolhouses. One former student recalled that even though the horses were left untethered in the schoolyard all day, they never ran away.[20]

White Swan families raised horses, cows, hogs, chickens, and turkeys. Some let their livestock take shelter in the timbered bottomlands, while others maintained barns, hen houses, and other outbuildings. One family kept a herd of up to forty horses. Money from surplus milk and eggs sold in Lake Andes or Wagner paid for coffee, sugar, salt, spices, and other staples that could not be grown or harvested. People butchered their livestock as needed and stored the meat as best they could. Families planted and harvested corn, oats, hay, and alfalfa using antiquated horse-drawn machinery. In addition, they maintained large gardens in which they grew potatoes, carrots, peas, and even peanuts and watermelon. They supplemented what they raised with food obtained from the bottomlands.[21]

Hunting, trapping, and fishing provided both food and opportunities for recreation. As long as the activity took place within the reservation boundaries, there were no limits regarding the take or season and no need to obtain a license. Hunters bagged deer, ducks, rabbits, pheasants, geese, grouse, and prairie chickens in the bottomlands and on Beebe Island. In winter, they could cross the ice-covered Missouri to hunt in the western bottomlands. Some of the older men, including a non-Indian trapper who had a cabin on Beebe Island, made their living trapping beaver, muskrat, skunk, otter, and mink. They sold the pelts in town and ate the beaver and muskrat meat. At various times, they could also collect bounties on raccoons, coyotes, and even magpies.[22]

Fish were an abundant food source, and tribal members used pole lines, set lines, and nets to catch primarily catfish and northern pike. They also harvested fish left trapped on land after the river receded following a June raise. Community fish fries became common and popular social events, as one family might catch up to one hundred fish and then share the bounty with others. Fish not consumed immediately were dried and stored for later use. Former resident Ramona O'Connor recalled that as a schoolgirl she fished every day of the summer. Her father also used a willow cage to trap river turtles in order to gather the eggs.[23]

White Swan residents, like those in this 1935 photograph, lived simply, residing in log cabins, maintaining small farms, and hunting and gathering in the bottomlands along the Missouri River.
State Archives Collection, South Dakota State Historical Society

A generous supply of wild fruit, vegetables, herbs, and other useful plants grew in the bottomlands, particularly on Beebe Island. Tribal members from all over the reservation came to the White Swan area to gather these resources. Depending on the season, they could take their choice among strawberries, cherries, plums, buffalo berries, chokecherries, gooseberries, and crab apples. They could also gather mushrooms and wild turnips. Beebe Island became well known for its wild grapes. Blue and about the size of a pea, they were good for making wine. A non-Indian resident of the island, Jack Stack, was well known as a vintner who received visitors fond of sampling his product.[24] Members of the Bon Homme Hutterite Colony near Platte also came to the island to pick grapes from which they made "a wonderful wine," according to Jeff Archambeau.[25]

White Swan families canned, dried, or made jelly from the various wild fruits. They also gathered a variety of wild plants for medicinal use. The community still had a few traditional medicine people, or healers, who were knowledgeable about herbal cures but did not often divulge their secrets. Yet, even the average family knew about herbs, roots, or leaves that could help to remedy common ailments. Teas made from the leaves of various plants, for example, relieved colds and respiratory problems. Natural products from the bottomlands filled a variety of other purposes, as well. Scrapings from red willow bark, for example, were smoked like tobacco and used for both recreational and ceremonial purposes. Braided wild turnips decorated homes until they were eaten.[26]

White Swan community members led lives that were truly interconnected, both with the environment and one another. Families shared their time, energy, food, and resources, especially with the needy or indigent. When haying time came, people would volunteer to go from one farm to another to bring in the hay because not everyone had the needed equipment. They also assisted each other in cutting and storing wood. Families pooled their money or produce to hire a man with a buzz saw and then divided the wood among the group. When the community was snowed in during winter, someone with a box sled would go to town to pick up groceries and supplies for everyone.[27]

Because the community was close-knit, it exercised considerable control over individual behavior. The Episcopal and Catholic churches also served as positive focal points. Most families belonged to one or the other of the congregations, and worship services and church gatherings formed an important part of their routine. The Sioux, who had always valued visiting and sharing, incorporated non-Indians into these activities at White Swan. A community member could go to a farmhouse, walk right in, and be invited to sit down and eat.[28]

Local families attended each other's life events: the births, baptisms, christenings, marriages, funerals, and wakes. They would hold community-wide meetings to discuss issues and affairs and then feed everyone in attendance. Sometimes these meetings took place at the cannery, where they would show movies with the aid of a portable generator. At other times, the community held boxing matches for the youth so that they might channel their energy in a positive way. In winter, storytellers who went from farm to farm also provided entertainment. At each house they were honored and fed.[29]

Tribal members who grew up at White Swan in the late 1940s have fond memories of relatively simple pleasures. Wendell Flying Hawk recalls the great thrill of riding in his aunt's car to a grocery store in Lake Andes, where she introduced him to the wonderful taste of oyster crackers. Another remembers looking forward to the arrival of a peddler's cart. Jack Stack, the winemaker, was also a peddler of sorts who brought his cart of wares, including pots and pans and perfumed soaps, around to each household. Because her family seldom went into town, one young girl enjoyed trading some of the milk and eggs from her farm for her favorite trinkets.[30]

The loss of this way of life, as well as land and possessions, were not the only issues that concerned White Swan community members. Most distasteful to the Yanktons, who strongly believed that the dead should remain undisturbed, was the necessity of moving two cemeteries and a number of isolated burials. Beginning in 1948, 509 graves were ultimately relocated. Of this number, 428 graves were in the Saint Philips Episcopal Cemetery. These were moved, along with the church itself, to Lake Andes. The cemetery of the Saint Francis Catholic Church held 65 graves, 25 of which were moved to the Catholic cemetery at Marty, with the remainder reburied at various locations around the reservation. The church building was removed to Lake Andes. In accordance with Army Corps of Engineers regulations, the district engineer contracted with private firms to identify, relocate, and rebury these remains.[31]

A number of isolated and mostly unmarked Indian burials also existed within the taking area. White Swan tribal members knew of some of these graves, but others were beyond their memory or experience, perhaps because they predated the establishment of White Swan or even the Sioux occupation of that area. Because the Corps of Engineers did not maintain good communications with the Yanktons regarding its construction plans, the tribe did not become aware of the removal of even known isolated burials until workers accidentally excavated two of them and dumped the remains into the dam embankment. In July 1948, White Swan residents Rebecca Highrock and Jesse O'Connor informed John J. Backus, the BIA subagent at Yankton, of the incident, which involved the graves of O'Connor's brother and Highrock's aunt. Highrock also stated that the corps had placed a survey stake on the hill where her parents were buried. Fearing that they, too, might soon be disinterred, she asked that the remains be moved to the Catholic cemetery at Marty.[32]

The BIA informed the Corps of Engineers of this situation and enlisted two representatives from the White Swan community to assist Backus in identifying and marking other isolated burials. Sixteen of these graves were eventually located and the remains reburied elsewhere. The corps never fully completed the process of burial identification, however, and the fluctuating water levels of Lake Francis Case continue periodically to unearth skeletal remains, caskets, and funerary objects in the White Swan area. The problem of unmoved and/or unidentified burial plots in the White Swan area will likely persist well into the future.[33]

By March 1950, three years had passed since the Corps of Engineers had gained possession of Yankton lands through declarations of taking, but the defendants in the condemnation suits had yet to receive payment. The corps presented tribal members with the appraised value of the property, instructing them to accept or reject the figures. One family reportedly rejected the government's offer, but the outcome of that case is not known. Several tribal members later told the BIA they had no other option but to accept the appraisal values because they desperately needed money to relocate and believed any protest to be futile. Having functioned in a primarily subsistence economy, they probably had little way of knowing whether the price offered for their property was fair or equitable. To some individuals, the amount might have seemed substantial.[34]

Neither the Yankton Sioux Tribe nor its affected tribal members had the benefit of private counsel in these condemnation cases. Nor does it appear that they made personal appearances at the hearings conducted at the federal courthouse in Sioux Falls. While most tribal members could probably not afford an attorney, it is not clear from the existing record whether they were informed of their right to exercise that option. Instead, they were requested to sign forms granting power of attorney to the BIA and were represented in court by BIA attorney A. B. Melzner and the Rosebud Agency superintendent, C. R. Whitlock.[35] Paul Fickinger, director of the BIA's Billings Area Office, objected to this arrangement, pointing out to the commissioner of Indian affairs that tribal members suffered from a disadvantage because "there exists no statutory authority whereby they can be adequately represented in court inasmuch as the Department of Justice is representing the Corps of Engineers."[36] While the BIA might have authorized private counsel to represent tribal interests on a contingency basis, as permitted, for example, in cases before the Indian Claims Commission, no evidence has been found to indicate that the agency considered this option.

Overlooked during the three years the Yankton condemnation suits stood pending was the fact that the Army Corps of Engineers lacked the requisite legislative authority to condemn land held in trust in the name of the Yankton Sioux Tribe. In accordance with the Act of 3 March 1901, individually allotted trust lands could be condemned "for any public purpose under the laws of the state . . . where located" in much the same way as with non-Indian lands held by fee title.[37] The United States Supreme Court, however, held in the case of *Minnesota v. United States* in 1939 that such actions could only be brought before federal courts and that the United States must be joined as a party. In regard to the federal government's condemnation of tribally held trust land, the Court ruled in the 1941 case of *United States ex rel. Hualpai Indians v. Santa Fe Pacific* that congressional statute must specifically and unambiguously authorize the taking.[38]

Neither the Flood Control Act of 1944, which authorized the Pick-Sloan Plan, nor any subsequent legislation had specifically permitted the Corps of Engineers or the Bureau of Reclamation to condemn Sioux tribal land. The decision of the corps to do so in the case of the Yankton Sioux Tribe seems to have been based on a calculated risk that the move would succeed. Unfortunately for the Yanktons, time proved the military lawyers to be correct. The condemnation of Yankton Sioux tribal land went unchallenged, with the tribe apparently unaware of its legal rights regarding eminent domain and the district court magistrates failing to research the legal precedents thoroughly before entering final judgment.

None of the Yankton families impacted under the Fort Randall project received compensation for their relocation costs at the time of taking. The Corps of Engineers had no authority to cover these expenses until 1952, when Congress mandated that landowners affected by military eminent-domain takings be paid up to 25 percent of the appraised value of their property to cover moving costs.[39] This law proved beneficial to both tribal members and non-Indians affected by takings for later Pick-Sloan projects, but it was of no help to the Yankton Sioux because it did not apply retroactively.

The Corps of Engineers did allow tribal members to salvage improvements and timber on their land, but much confusion developed over how the process was to proceed. Many families believed that corps personnel would move their improvements, as it had in earlier takings at Fort Berthold in North Dakota. Others thought that any member of the tribe could salvage timber within the taking area. The salvage policy implemented in the case of the Yanktons, however, required property owners to move their own improvements and limited timber removal only to those tribal members being compelled to relocate.[40]

Moving homes and other improvements proved to be unaffordable in terms of both cost and time for many tribal members. Levi Archambeau, for example, lived with his wife and five children in the four-room house where he had been born on land within the taking area. Perhaps because he did not own the land but, rather, leased it from the tribe, the Army Corps of Engineers failed to serve him with a proper eviction notice.[41] In a letter to Senator Francis Case, Archambeau claimed that an official came to his house and advised him that if he did not move the structure by 9:00 o'clock the next morning, the corps would burn it down. "They came at 4' O' Clock in the evening," he wrote, "so it was burned."[42] The Levi Archambeau family was among five tribal families who received no payment from the condemnation proceedings because they did not own the land on which their homes sat. While the Archambeaus and another family residing on tribal land eventually received part of a supplemental reestablishment fund, the remaining three families received no compensation whatsoever because they resided on church land.[43]

Other families, though notified sufficiently, remained in a state of denial until the end. The Garrett Hopkins family, for example, waited too long to salvage their house and only managed to save the possessions they could fit into a car. By that time, the Corps of Engineers could no longer do anything but abandon the structure. The Hopkins family watched as the swirling waters separated the house from its foundation and floated it away. They moved to the Rosebud Indian Reservation temporarily to live with relatives and returned to Yankton two years later.[44]

Buying or even leasing land of the same quality as the river bottomlands that had been evacuated proved difficult.[45] The Rosebud Agency superintendent reported as early as April 1949 that development of the Fort Randall Dam had inflated land prices "so that on the Yankton Reservation there is a seller's market."[46] The BIA also noted in a 1952 memorandum that the non-Indian residents and officials of Charles Mix County would resist any attempt to purchase replacement fee land and bring it under federal trust status because of the decrease it would cause in local tax revenues.[47]

Those forced to relocate received little assistance in finding homes comparable to what they had left. The majority moved to Lake Andes or Marty. Many

moved into a Lake Andes motel that had gone bankrupt. Several leased or purchased one- or two-room tract houses that came to be called "the Lake Andes
shacks." Fourteen family members occupied one two-room house. Although
they eventually received some reestablishment funds, several tribal members
lived in this housing until they died. Others left only after a tornado destroyed
many of the homes in the early 1960s.[48]

The more fortunate families were able to move to other allotments in which
they held an interest or to purchase land elsewhere on the reservation. The
family of Robert and Mary Spotted Eagle, for example, moved five miles north
of White Swan to the original allotment of a grandfather. This land, however,
was prairie and lacked the resources of the bottomland environment. The
William O'Connor family was able to purchase a forty-acre allotment near
Lake Andes and move their house, but they lost an eighty-acre farm. One of
the daughters recalled that the most traumatic part of the move for her was
having to sell their horses. As a child, she was especially attached to one horse
and wonders to this day what became of it. The Levi Archambeaus moved to a
tribally owned tract near Lake Andes. Although they could still see the river, its
rich bottomlands were a long distance away. Farming the new tract failed to
sustain the family, and they were compelled to seek wage work to supplement
their income.[49]

Most of the new locations to which tribal members moved lacked the water
and timber resources of their former homes. Families previously engaged in
truck farming or the sale of wild fruit or firewood experienced a sudden drop in
income. Everyone faced higher living costs after the move because of the need
to purchase water and fuel and pay rent and utilities. Yankton families who
did not have to move experienced an economic impact, as well. Most of those
residing near the Missouri and its tributary streams depended on these sources
for their domestic water supply. Because no provision was made for proper
sewers at the construction settlement of Pickstown, the town discharged its
raw sewage directly into the river, making the water hazardous to use. In addition, the dam's disruption of the free-flowing Missouri increased the amount
of plankton, making the water taste bad.[50]

The loss of timber resources impacted an even greater proportion of Yankton tribal members. Almost half of the resident families on the Yankton Indian
Reservation had depended on wood from the taking area as a fuel source for
heating and cooking. Most collected driftwood along the river banks rather
than cutting standing timber. In the process of stabilizing the Missouri, the
Fort Randall Dam eliminated most of the flow of driftwood, and the standing
timber remaining on the reservation was too sparse or inaccessible to serve as

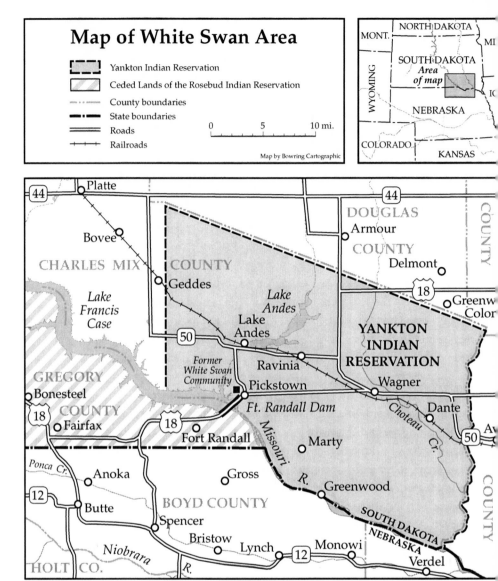

Map of White Swan Area

Yankton Indian Reservation

Ceded Lands of the Rosebud Indian Reservation

County boundaries

State boundaries

Roads

Railroads

0   5   10 mi.

Map by Bowring Cartographic

NORTH DAKOTA

MONT.

MI

SOUTH DAKOTA
Area
of map

WYOMING

NEBRASKA

IO

COLORADO

KANSAS

44

Platte

44

Bovee

DOUGLAS

Armour

CHARLES MIX

COUNTY

COUNTY

Delmont

Geddes

Lake
Francis
Case

Lake
Andes

18

Greenw
Color

Lake
Andes

YANKTON
INDIAN
RESERVATION

50

GREGORY

Former
White Swan
Community

Ravinia

Pickstown

Wagner

COUNTY

Ft. Randall Dam

Choteau Cr.

Dante

Bonesteel

18

50

A

Fairfax

18

Fort Randall

Marty

Ponca Cr.

Anoka

Gross

Greenwood

12

Butte

BOYD COUNTY

Missouri R.

SOUTH DAKOTA

Spencer

NEBRASKA

Bristow

Niobrara

Lynch

12

Monowi

Verdel

HOLT CO.

R.

The location of the former White Swan community can be seen near the
center of this map of the Yankton Indian Reservation and surrounding area.
The inundation of White Swan forced many residents to relocate to
communities such as Marty and Lake Andes.

Michael L. Lawson, Anandale, VA

a substitute source. Yet, not even the condemnation suits included any value for either the utilitarian or commercial use of timber. The BIA estimated the annual cost for replacement fuel sources in 1954 at fifteen thousand dollars, or $120 per family for the 125 families who had previously depended on driftwood or other timber from the White Swan area. Many families outside the taking area had also gathered wild fruit from the bottomlands, particularly from Beebe Island, and hunted game in the area. Again, the Yankton Sioux Tribe never received compensation specifically for these losses. The value of timber, wild-life habitat, and wild-fruit products was never included in any reestablishment compensation paid to the tribe or its members, largely because BIA appraisers considered it "impractical to attempt to reestablish these conditions."[51]

The BIA did attempt, however, to obtain greater compensation for the Yankton Sioux in other ways. In 1946, it organized the Missouri River Basin Investigations (MRBI) project within its regional office in Billings, Montana, to assess the damages to Indian land and resources resulting from all of the Pick-Sloan projects. Initially, the MRBI unit conducted extensive reservation surveys and appraisals to estimate replacement costs as well as social and economic damages resulting from inundation. Over time, MRBI staff also worked to help tribes gain equitable settlements and assisted with relocation and reconstruction activities.[52] When the MRBI found that its appraisals on the Yankton reservation arrived at much higher valuations than those of the Corps of Engineers, it proposed the idea of special legislation to compensate the Yankton Sioux. However, Major General Lewis A. Pick, the Missouri River Division engineer for the corps and architect of the plan for main-stem dams, wanted to avoid congressional involvement. Accordingly, he agreed to negotiate with the BIA and informed Acting Commissioner of Indian Affairs William Zimmerman, Jr., that he was "hopeful that the problem can be solved without additional legislation."[53]

Representatives of the Army Corps of Engineers and the BIA held four negotiation conferences between March and October 1948 but failed to reach a complete agreement. The BIA then proceeded to propose legislation appropriating a payment of eighty-five thousand dollars for Yankton tribal members who had been forced to relocate, in addition to the settlements they had received from the condemnation proceedings. On 19 June 1949, Senator Chandler Gurney of South Dakota introduced a bill in Congress incorporating the BIA proposals, but the measure failed to gain consideration during the course of the Eighty-first Congress.[54]

In 1951, the BIA drafted another legislative proposal to grant additional compensation for the Yankton Sioux. Rosebud Superintendent C. L. Graves and Aberdeen Area Director J. M. Cooper, who both held jurisdiction over the Yankton reservation, provided detailed justification for a supplementary settlement of $123,250. The commissioner of Indian affairs, however, authorized just $106,500, the amount included in a bill South Dakota Representative E. Y. Berry introduced on 19 June 1952. When the Eighty-second Congress failed to take up this legislation before it adjourned, Berry reintroduced his request for $106,500 in the Eighty-third Congress on 29 January 1953.[55]

Meanwhile, the MRBI staff continued to evaluate the social and economic impacts of the Fort Randall Dam on the Yankton Sioux. On 1 February 1954, MRBI Director Walter U. Fuhriman reported to the BIA Program Division in Washington, DC, that the initial MRBI damage estimates for the Yankton had been based on 1947 appraisal data, while the value of South Dakota agricultural lands had increased dramatically since that time. The index of farm real-estate values, he pointed out, gained 26 percent between 1947 and 1950. By November 1951, when the MRBI conducted appraisals on the Standing Rock, Cheyenne River, Crow Creek, and Lower Brule reservations, general farm values for those reservations had escalated to a level about 57 percent higher than those of the Yankton appraisal. Fuhriman estimated that when adjusted for inflation, the net additional appropriation the tribe needed for reestablishment and for timber, wildlife, and wild-product losses came to $245,600. This estimate did not include the commercial value of the timber or intangible damages.[56]

The amount of compensation the Eighty-third Congress debated when it took up the matter in 1954 was, thus, far below what the MRBI considered to be just. Even the MRBI estimates omitted other values, such as general reservation rehabilitation, that were then being considered as compensation for other Sioux tribes impacted by Pick-Sloan dam projects. Settlement legislation introduced in the Eighty-third Congress for the Cheyenne River Sioux, for instance, included payments of more than $6.8 million for "future tangible damages," such as lost grazing leases, timber, wildlife, wild fruit, and other resources, and more than $12.8 million for rehabilitation of the entire reservation.[57] Although Congress trimmed these requests considerably, the final legislation enacted on 3 September 1954 provided the Cheyenne River Sioux with $3.1 million in severance damages and $5.1 million for rehabilitation.[58]

The Department of Justice objected strongly to the amount of compensation proposed for the Yankton Sioux, even though the sum was paltry in comparison to the monies awarded other tribes. In a letter to the Senate Committee on Interior and Insular Affairs, Justice Department officials contended that the $106,500 represented an additional payment of 80 percent above the court's property settlement, in violation of the 1952 statute that limited compensation for relocation prompted by military projects to not more than 25 percent of the appraised property value. The department suggested that if the Indians were in such dire need of financial assistance they should seek separate legislation for rehabilitation and not tie their request to a property settlement. The Justice Department could not support enactment of the bill, the letter concluded, "because it would serve as an undesirable precedent with respect to the acquisition of property by the United States."[59] In the end, the Senate ignored the department's objections and kept the $106,500 intact in the bill it finally passed. President Dwight D. Eisenhower signed the legislation on 6 July 1954.[60]

Just before this measure won approval, ten Yankton tribal members who had lived in the White Swan community petitioned the secretary of the interior to appoint a referee to oversee distribution of the additional appropriation. Members of the O'Connor family led the petitioners, who complained that payments previously awarded through the United States District Court and placed under the jurisdiction of the Rosebud Indian Agency had been "doled out" in such a manner as to be of "little or no benefit." If the supplemental appropriation were handled in the same way, they predicted, "Indian families themselves will benefit but little." The group requested further that the funds be distributed "in proportion to the damages and loss sustained" by each family.[61]

The former White Swan residents hired L. E. Schreyer, an attorney in Lake Andes, to represent their interests, and it was Schreyer who forwarded their petition to the secretary.[62] In response, Commissioner of Indian Affairs Glenn L. Emmons informed Schreyer that the secretary of the interior held "complete responsibility for administering the fund" and that the BIA was not aware of "any need for the employment of an attorney by the individual Indians who may share in the relocation fund."[63] The BIA appointed no referee and subsequently proposed to distribute funds on a per-capita basis rather than in proportion to the loss sustained. What was worse, White Swan families had to wait for more than two years before any of them received funds, and then not all of those forced off the land gained compensation.

The distribution of the funds was stalled while the BIA scheduled the appropriation into its budget and the MRBI staff developed a long-delayed distribution plan. Twenty families who had been forced to relocate were originally designated to divide the money, but in January 1956 Solicitor J. Reuel Armstrong, chief legal officer for the Department of the Interior, set forth new eligibility criteria. In a formal opinion issued to the commissioner of Indian affairs, Armstrong established three prerequisites for entitlement in the distribution. In addition to being a member of the Yankton Sioux Tribe, the individual must have resided on the land taken for the project, and the land must have been either tribal or allotted trust land.[64]

The new criteria immediately eliminated five families previously considered eligible for a portion of the funds. The two families headed by brothers George O'Connor and Oliver O'Connor had resided on a twenty-acre tract at White Swan that was fee-patented church land. This acreage had originally been allotted in trust to a Yankton Sioux tribal member who deeded it to the Bureau of Catholic Indian Missions in 1917. The Catholic church permitted the O'Connor families to live on the land, but they had no ownership rights. The George Selwyn family found themselves in a similar situation. Selwyn, a minister at the Episcopal church, and his family resided in a church-provided house on former trust land that had been deeded to the church. The family of Luella Foreman Morgan also failed to meet the revised eligibility standards. Morgan was a tribal member, but she resided with her non-Indian husband on deeded land within the taking area. Although these families had suffered losses of homes and livelihoods just as their neighbors had, they never received compensation because they did not reside on tribal or allotted trust land.[65]

Tribal member Susan Rondell had reared her family in a two-story home on allotted trust land of which she was the sole owner. At the time this land was condemned, Rondell was a widow, approximately eighty years old, who moved about and stayed with various relatives. Upon receiving payment for her property, she moved a section of her house and remodeled it at her own expense, thereafter making it her home. She was denied additional compensation, however, because the BIA ruled that she had not been residing on her allotted land at the time of taking. In addition to these five cases, the families of two other tribal members were denied additional compensation. These families had not been forced to move, but they had lost land and resources as a result of right-of-way easements the Corps of Engineers obtained for constructing the access railroad from Lake Andes to Pickstown.[66]

In October 1955, Superintendent Guy Robertson of the Rosebud Indian Agency compiled a list of twenty-three other tribal families living in the White Swan area at the time of taking. Although not forced to relocate, they had been deprived of the natural resources of the bottomlands, which they depended on because of their proximity to the taking area. In regard to these families, Superintendent Robertson suggested to the Aberdeen Area BIA director that "it would probably be equitable to assume that they should receive at least one-third as much as any of [the families within the taking area] inasmuch as the law must have intended that all Yankton Sioux people who suffered this loss should be paid proportionately for what they lost." He concluded, "I believe that unless some arrangement is made to take this into consideration, that there will be repercussions that will be hard to withstand."[67]

The superintendent was correct in his predictions. The jealousy, resentment, and general hard feelings that the final BIA distribution plan provoked still resonate across the Yankton reservation. The families found eligible for supplemental compensation received far less than their counterparts on the other Sioux reservations. Yet, many who were denied compensation for their losses could not help feeling that the proportional share of the fifteen qualified families should have been even less. This situation resulted from the fact that no matter how the Department of the Interior tried to limit the number of people receiving compensation, the overall amount was inadequate to compensate them fairly.

By the time the funds were actually distributed to the eligible families in the fall of 1956, nine years had passed since most of the tracts were condemned. Six years had gone by since the families had been forced to move, and more than two years had elapsed since Congress had approved a supplemental appropriation for their reestablishment. Although the $106,500 appropriation was based on the BIA's compromise estimate of 1952, no adjustment was made for inflation. If the money had been appropriated and deposited in the United States Treasury soon after Congress approved the measure in 1954, families would at least have received the benefit of a small amount of interest while waiting for the BIA to develop and approve a distribution plan.

The BIA deposited each family's supplementary funds in Individual Indian Money (IIM) trust accounts, determining how the funds could be spent and closely monitoring every purchase. Amounts allotted to individual families ranged from $14,153 down to $500. Not a cent was expended without BIA supervision and approval. Once the actual purchasing began, officials discovered that farm machinery cost more than had been estimated. Consequently, the balance of the reestablishment fund, amounting to $6,153, went to purchase equipment for four qualified families.[68]

The fifteen eligible families from White Swan used their funds in a variety of ways. Eight purchased homes, three repaired existing homes, and eleven bought home furnishings. One family purchased a service station, four bought or repaired machinery, and two obtained farms. One bought a car, another a pickup truck, and another purchased a bull. The funds also paid for education, medical and dental care, and the development of wells. In addition, five older tribal members were permitted to draw small monthly stipends from the balance of their funds.[69]

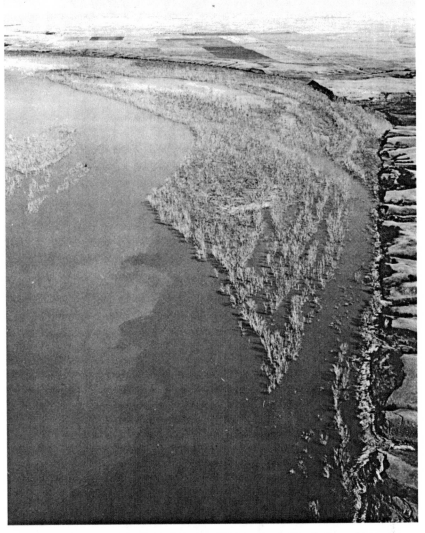

The waters rising behind Fort Randall Dam flooded the timber and
agricultural resources of the Missouri River bottomlands.
South Dakota Department of Game, Fish and Parks, Pierre

Significantly, nine families used their money to pay existing debts, representing the second-largest expenditure next to the purchase of homes. The amount was also 250 percent more than the BIA had programmed for debt payments. In addition, actual expenditures for food turned out to be 500 percent more than budgeted, and clothing was 300 percent more.[70] These figures reflected the difficulty most White Swan families faced in adjusting to a cash economy. Once they were no longer able to grow, barter, or sell as much of their own food products, indebtedness often became their only alternative.

The BIA concluded in 1957 that most of the families derived "considerable permanent benefit" from the reestablishment fund.[71] By contrast, the consensus among the Yankton Sioux is that the majority of families were considerably worse off after reestablishment than before relocation. They had to switch rapidly from subsistence to a cash economy. Families living in the bottomlands did not need to purchase many items. After relocation, however, many were forced for the first time to pay rent and bills for water and electricity or to buy stove wood or heating oil from non-Indians. Instead of using home cures derived from wild plants, they had to purchase over-the-counter medicine. They shopped for canned goods instead of canning their own and bought meat, dairy products, and eggs instead of producing their own. This situation created much hardship for those not readily able to find a way to generate income.[72]

Relocation disrupted the lifestyles of all the families and contributed to the dysfunction of some. Whereas White Swan tribal members had previously enjoyed the agricultural pursuits and private space of allotted lands, many were now crowded together in town, often without room for even a small garden. Although the families made an effort to continue visiting each other, they gradually lost the cohesiveness that had characterized their former community. They now lived scattered all over the reservation and even beyond its boundaries. Some were farther away from churches and schools. Slowly, they lost some of the spirituality and much of the connectedness they had known at White Swan.[73] "We lost more than our homes," observed former resident Louie Archambeau, in his sixties when interviewed in 1998. "We lost our way of living, a part of our culture. That is something we will never get back."[74]

With the White Swan area inundated, there was no other place like it to move on the reservation. Most of those who managed to obtain replacement land had less of it. They also had fewer livestock but faced greater costs for shelter, feed, and water.[75] The net result was a rapid decline in agriculture on the reservation. "There were a lot of Indian farmers back in those days," observed one former resident about the White Swan era. "Now there are hardly any."[76]

While hunting has continued to be good on the Yankton reservation, fishing and trapping are far less prevalent. A common reaction among many former White Swan residents to their forced relocation inland has been a gradual aversion to fishing or even eating fish. While these people once enjoyed free access to the fish and wildlife of the bottomlands, hunting, fishing, and trapping are now heavily regulated by the state of South Dakota within the Fort Randall taking area and by the tribe within the reservation. When one former White Swan resident tried to gather firewood near the reservoir, he was further informed that those resources now belonged to the Army Corps of Engineers.[77]

In 1960, the MRBI staff conducted a comparative study of six Indian reservations, including the Yankton reservation, that were impacted by the mainstem Missouri River dams. Their figures revealed that the average total damage payment received per family within the taking area at Yankton was $5,605, compared to an average payment per family of $16,680 on the other five reservations. The reservation with the next lowest per-family payment was Crow Creek at $10,363, while Fort Berthold families received the highest amount at $30,962. Had these funds been distributed on a per-capita basis to all families resident on the reservations, Yankton families would have received just $485, while families on the other five reservations would have gained an average of approximately $8,606. Again, Fort Berthold families would have garnered the most, a total of $24,184 each. This wide disparity reflects the fact that the Yankton Sioux Tribe was the only one of the six that did not receive rehabilitation funds over and above the amount individual families received as part of their property and relocation settlements.[78]

This development resulted from a combination of factors. The Corps of Engineers challenged any congressional settlement for the Yankton Sioux, and the Department of Justice specifically opposed rehabilitation funding as part of the tribe's Fort Randall settlement.[79] Congress generally paid less attention to the situation at Yankton than it did to the other five reservations, where damages were even greater.[80] During the late 1940s and 1950s, as well, the BIA became the target of severe budget cuts, and those who supported the so-called termination of the government's trust responsibility for and services to Indian tribes threatened to abolish the agency.[81]

A comparatively weak tribal government at the time further hurt the Yankton Sioux. The tribe had refused to organize or incorporate under the provisions of the Indian Reorganization Act of 1934, preferring instead to keep decision-making in the hands of a traditional but cumbersome general council consisting of all eligible tribal voting members.[82] Of the six tribes the MRBI compared in its 1960 study, the Yanktons were alone in not having developed an independent appraisal of the damages it sustained to use in negotiating a settlement. The Rosebud Sioux and the Santee Sioux of Nebraska, two tribes not included in the MRBI study, also failed to develop tribal appraisals and did not receive rehabilitation funds. These tribes, however, sustained fewer damages than did the Yankton Sioux. Some of these factors—the determination of the corps, the indifference of Congress, and the relatively weak advocacy of the BIA and tribal government—may also explain why the Yanktons were the only tribe compelled to suffer the complete dispersion of one of its communities.

None of the tribes impacted by the Pick-Sloan dams on the Missouri River considered their compensation to be adequate. All, in fact, determined their final settlements to be less than their actual damages. Beginning in the 1980s, several tribes approached Congress with requests for additional compensation. In particular, two North Dakota tribes—the Three Affiliated Tribes of Fort Berthold and the Standing Rock Sioux—sought further reparations.[83]

Congress eventually responded to these requests, enacting legislation in 1992 that authorized the establishment of development trust funds, or recovery funds, capitalized at $149.2 million for the Three Affiliated Tribes and $90.6 million for the Standing Rock Sioux Tribe.[84] This legislation acknowledged for the first time that the United States government had not adequately compensated tribes for the taking of land and resources for the Pick-Sloan projects. It also established the precedent that tribes were thus entitled to additional compensation. Following this precedent, Congress established similar recovery funds for the Crow Creek Sioux Tribe in 1996, the Lower Brule Sioux Tribe in 1997, and the Cheyenne River Sioux Tribe in 2000.[85]

In an effort to obtain additional compensation for themselves, as well, the Yankton Sioux Tribe in 1999 commissioned and submitted a report to Congress that attempted to justify the establishment of a $34-million recovery fund based on the precedent of previous tribal-recovery appropriations.[86] After considering the proposal over a three-year period, Congress elected in 2002 not to accept its level of compensation. Lawmakers did, however, authorize the appropriation of $23,023,743 to be placed in a development trust fund for the Yankton Sioux. This figure was based on the per-acre amount Congress granted in 1997 as additional compensation to the Lower Brule Sioux Tribe ($1,763 per acre) multiplied by 438 percent. The multiplier represented the average amount over and above property damages that five other Missouri River tribes received from Congress between 1947 and 1962 for reservation rehabilitation. The Yankton Sioux had not received funds for this purpose as part of their additional settlement package in 1954.[87]

More than a half-century after the residents of White Swan were forced to give up their homes and farms and struggle to find a new life elsewhere, the tribe to which they belonged finally received further compensation for the loss. The recovery fund, however, will not be distributed to the tribal members actually impacted or to their heirs. Rather, it will be used to fund tribal programs at the discretion of the Yankton Sioux Tribal Business and Claims Committee, as the tribal council is formally known. A grassroots movement is now afoot on the Yankton reservation to reestablish a new White Swan community along the Missouri River.[88] Yet, given the many pressing demands on tribal resources, it seems unlikely that White Swan will ever again be more than just a pleasant but fading memory.

NOTES

1. 58 Stat 827. The Pick-Sloan Plan represented a compromise between the separate water-resource programs developed by Colonel (later Major General) Lewis A. Pick of the Army Corps of Engineers and William G. Sloan of the Department of the Interior's Bureau of Reclamation. For more information, see Michael L. Lawson, *Dammed Indians: The Pick-Sloan Plan and the Missouri River Sioux, 1944–1980* (Norman: University of Oklahoma Press, 1994), ix–xxvi, 9–26.

2. U.S. Department of the Interior (DOI), Bureau of Indian Affairs (BIA), Missouri River Basin Investigations (MRBI) Project, *Damages to Indians of Five Reservations from Three Missouri River Reservoirs in North and South Dakota*, Report No. 138 (Billings, MT, 1954), 1, 18–19, 47, *Appraisal of Indian Property on the Fort Randall Reservoir Site within the Lower Brule and Crow Creek Indian Reservations, South Dakota*, Report No. 135 (Billings, MT, 1953), 1–7, *Problems of Indian Removal and Rehabilitation Growing Out of the Fort Randall Taking on Crow Creek and Lower Brule Reservations, South Dakota*, Report No. 136 (Billings, MT, 1953), 1–6, 17–20, and *Report of Ownership Status of Restricted, Allotted, and Tribal Indian Lands on the Crow Creek, Lower Brule, and Rosebud Reservations, South Dakota, Affected by Fort Randall Dam and Reservoir Project*, Report No. 83 (Billings, MT, 1949), 1–4; "Summary and Evaluation of Experiences of Six Indian Reservations Affected by Large Dam and Reservoir Projects on Missouri River," General Programs, Missouri Basin, 1960, MRBI, pt. 1-A, File 1766-074.1, 5–10, 44–45, Records of the Bureau of Indian Affairs, Record Group (RG) 75, Washington National Records Center (WNRC), Suitland, MD.

3. DOI, BIA, MRBI, *Distribution of Funds to Indian Families, Yankton Sioux Reservation, South Dakota*, 4th Supp. to Report No. 141 (Billings, MT, Mar. 1957), 2; *Separate Settlement Contracts, Sioux Indians, Lower Brule and Crow Creek Reservations for Lands Taken by Reason of Construction of the Fort Randall Dam*, S.Dak., 83d Cong., 2d sess., 1954, S. Rep. 1594, 2–3; "Summary of Memorandum undated to Ben Reifel, Area Director, Aberdeen, South Dakota, with respect to P.L. 478, 83rd Congress, as to Indian families participating in $106,500," ca. Oct. 1955, Yankton Indian Agency, Box 37, Yankton Sioux Special Tribal Records, 1958–1964, RG 75, National

Archives–Central Plains Region (NA-CPR), Kansas City, MO; DOI, BIA, MRBI, *Social and Economic Conditions of Resident Families on the Yankton Sioux Reservation, South Dakota*, Report No. 141 (Billings, MT, Jan. 1954), 1.

4. Michael L. Lawson, "Historical Analysis of the Impact of Missouri River Pick-Sloan Dam Projects on the Yankton and Santee Sioux Indian Tribes: Prepared for the Yankton Sioux Tribe, Marty, South Dakota, and the Santee Sioux Tribe, Santee Nebraska," Apr. 1999, Morgan, Angel & Associates Office, Washington, DC, 1–2; Michael L. Lawson, "Federal Water Projects and Indian Lands: The Pick-Sloan Plan, a Case Study," in *The Plains Indians of the Twentieth Century*, ed. Peter Iverson (Norman: University of Oklahoma Press, 1985), 171–72.

5. Case to Commissioner of Indian Affairs (CIA), 27 Nov. 1943, Rosebud Indian Agency, Box 588, File "General Correspondence Decimal 1930–1950," Folder 309, "Island and Swamp Lands," RG 75, NA-CPR.

6. The Winters Doctrine was propounded by the United States Supreme Court in 1907 in Winters v. United States. The Fort Belknap Indians of Montana brought suit against an upstream farmer, Henry Winter (erroneously entered as "Winters" on court documents), to enjoin him from interfering with the flow of the Milk River, a tributary of the Missouri, through their reservation. The court ruled that when the Indians gave up their rights to their former lands in exchange for the arid, unirrigated reservation lands, sufficient water was reserved from the Milk River to enable the tribe "to become a pastoral and civilized people." The court also held that the Indians' right to the water could not be diminished by any rights created under state law. Later decisions, such as Conrad Investment Company v. United States, further extended the Winters Doctrine, establishing that Indians have prior and superior rights to present and future beneficial uses of water. The Supreme Court reaffirmed these early decisions in the 1963 case of Arizona v. California, which granted five lower Colorado River tribes water sufficient to "irrigate the irrigable portions" of their reservations. See Winters v. U.S., 207 U.S. 564, 575–77 (1907); Conrad Investment Company v. U.S., 161 F. 829 (CA9, 1908); and Arizona v. California, 373 U.S. 546, 598–600 (1963).

7. DOI, BIA, MRBI, *Appraisal Report: Yankton Reservation Trust Lands, Fort Randall Project, South Dakota* (Billings, MT, 15 Dec. 1947), pt. 1, 1; U.S. War Department, Corps of Engineers, Office of the District Engineer, Omaha, NE, "Data for Contractors Meeting Pickstown, South Dakota," 15 Oct. 1947, 1, Corps of Engineers, Omaha District Office, Fort Randall 1946–1957, Box 1, Records of the Office of the Chief of Engineers, RG 77, NA-CPR.

8. Merrill J. Mattes, "Report on Historic Sites in the Fort Randall Reservoir Area, Missouri River, South Dakota," *South Dakota Historical Collections* 24 (1949): 482–86. For a history of Fort Randall, see Jerome A. Greene, *Fort Randall on the Missouri, 1856–1892* (Pierre: South Dakota State Historical Society Press, 2005).

9. "Data for Contractor's Meeting, Pickstown, South Dakota," 3–6; U.S. Department of the Army, Corps of Engineers, *Annual Report of the Chief of Engineers, U.S. Army, 1945*, pt. 1, vol. 2

(Washington, DC: Government Printing Office, 1946), 1, 385–90; U.S. Department of the Army, Corps of Engineers, *Annual Report of the Chief of Engineers, U.S. Army, 1946*, pt. 1, vol. 2 (Washington, DC: Government Printing Office, 1947), 1, 526–32; *Distribution of Funds to Indian Families, Yankton Sioux Reservation*, 2–3.

10. Robert J. Trier, District Road Engineer, BIA, to CIA, 25 Feb. 1946, Yankton Sioux Tribal Office Files, Marty, SD; "Brief in Justification of a Bill to Authorize the Appropriation of $85,000 for Benefit of Certain Yankton Sioux Families Whose Homes Are within the Taking Line of the Fort Randall Reservoir Site, 1948," Box A-1, Rosebud Agency, File 869, Yankton Flood Papers, RG 75, NA-CPR.

11. Mattes, "Report on Historic Sites," 488–89.

12. Ibid., 490.

13. Ibid., 489–90; Jeff Archambeau, interview, Wagner, SD, 24 Oct. 1998.

14. Edith Spotted Eagle Selwyn, interview, Wagner, SD, 24 Oct. 1998; Christine Medicine Horn, interview, Wagner, SD, 23 Oct. 1998; Louis Jesse Medicine Horn, Sr., interview, Wagner, SD, 24 Oct. 1998; Wendell O. Flying Hawk, interview, Wagner, SD, 23 Oct. 1998.

15. Louie Archambeau, interview, Wagner, SD, 23 Oct. 1998.

16. Flying Hawk, Selwyn, Louie Archambeau, and Jeff Archambeau, interviews; Vincent Cavender, interview, Wagner, SD, 23 Oct. 1998; Armand Hopkins and Kenneth R. Hopkins, interview, Wagner, SD, 23 Oct. 1998.

17. Armand Hopkins and Kenneth R. Hopkins, interview.

18. Louie Archambeau, interview.

19. Selwyn, interview; Raymond Drapeau, interview, Wagner, SD, 24 Oct. 1998; Armand Hopkins and Kenneth R. Hopkins, interview.

20. Drapeau, Louie Archambeau, and Louis Jesse Medicine Horn, Sr., interviews; Ramona O'Connor, interview, Wagner, SD, 23 Oct. 1998.

21. Selwyn, O'Connor, Armand Hopkins and Kenneth R. Hopkins, Louie Archambeau, and Jeff Archambeau, interviews; Anonymous (by request), interview, Wagner, SD, 24 Oct. 1998.

22. Flying Hawk, Cavender, Selwyn, O'Connor, Raymond Drapeau, Armand Hopkins and Kenneth R. Hopkins, Louie Archambeau, and Jeff Archambeau, interviews.

23. Flying Hawk, Selwyn, O'Connor, Louie Archambeau, and Armand Hopkins and Kenneth R. Hopkins, interviews.

24. Florence Drappeau, interview, Wagner, SD, 24 Oct. 1998; Armand Hopkins and Kenneth R. Hopkins, Jeff Archambeau, Anonymous, and Flying Hawk, interviews.

25. Jeff Archambeau, interview.

26. Selwyn, O'Connor, Louie Archambeau, Armand Hopkins and Kenneth R. Hopkins, and Drapeau, interviews.

27. Armand Hopkins and Kenneth R. Hopkins, Jeff Archambeau, interviews.

28. O'Connor, Cavender, and Jeff Archambeau, interviews.

29. Raymond Drapeau, Jeff Archambeau, and Selwyn, interviews; Faith Spotted Eagle, interview, Wagner, SD, 24 Oct. 1998.

30. Flying Hawk, O'Connor, interviews.

31. DOI, BIA, MRBI, *Removal of Indian Burials Located within and Adjacent to the Yankton Reservation from the Taking Area of Fort Randall Dam and Reservoir, South Dakota*, Report No. 75 (Billings, MT, 1949), 1–6; W. R. Goodall, Jr., Chief, Real Estate Division, Office of the Missouri Division Engineer, to C. R. Whitlock, Superintendent, Rosebud Agency, 24 June 1948, Rosebud Indian Agency, Box 588, General Correspondence Decimal 1930–1950, Folder 307.0 Cemeteries, RG 75, NA-CPR.

32. Backus to Whitlock, 17 June 1948, Rosebud Indian Agency, Box 588, General Correspondence Decimal 1930–1950, Folder 307.0 Cemeteries, RG 75, NA-CPR.

33. Backus to Allen G. Harper, Assistant Regional Director, BIA, Billings, Mont., 12 July 1948, ibid.; *Removal of Indian Burials Located within and Adjacent to the Yankton Reservation*, 1–6; Flying Hawk, Armand Hopkins and Kenneth R. Hopkins, O'Connor, and Spotted Eagle, interviews.

34. Paul L. Fickinger, Billings Area Director, BIA, to CIA, 23 Mar. 1950, Yankton Sioux Tribal Office Files; *Social and Economic Conditions of Resident Families*, 5; O'Connor, interview.

35. See, for example, U.S. v. 119.03 acres of land, et al., Civil No. 518 SD, Final Judgment No. 2 as to Tract No. A-5, 5 Apr. 1950, U.S. District Court, South Dakota, Records of the District Courts of the United States, RG 21, NA-CPR.

36. Fickinger to CIA, 23 Mar. 1950.

37. 31 Stat 1083.

38. United States ex rel. Hualpai Indians v. Santa Fe Pacific Railroad, 314 U.S. 339 (1941). For discussion of legal precedents regarding the condemnation of allotted and tribal land, see Rennard Strickland and Charles F. Wilkinson, eds., *Felix S. Cohen's Handbook of Federal Indian Law* (Charlottesville, VA: Michie Bobbs-Merrill, 1982), 521–22, 622.

39. 66 Stat 624.

40. *Social and Economic Conditions of Resident Families*, 5.

41. Ibid., 6; Jeff Archambeau, interview; "Summary of Memorandum undated to Ben Reifel."

42. Archambeau to Case, 10 Aug. 1956, CCF, Rosebud Agency (1948–1952), Box 170, Missouri River Basin, Fort Randall Project, Section I, General, Yankton Reservation, RG 75, National Archives, Washington, DC (NA-DC).

43. "Summary of Memorandum undated to Ben Reifel"; Guy Robertson, Superintendent, Rosebud Indian Agency, memorandum to Ben Reifel, Aberdeen Area Director, 10 Oct. 1955, 1–8, Yankton Indian Agency, Box 37, Yankton Sioux Special Tribal Records, 1958–1964, RG 75, NA-CPR.

44. Armand Hopkins and Kenneth R. Hopkins, interview; "Summary of Memorandum undated to Ben Reifel."

45. *Social and Economic Conditions of Resident Families*, 6.

46. C. R. Whitlock to CIA, 5 Apr. 1949, Yankton Indian Agency, Box 37, Yankton Sioux Special Tribal Records, 1958–1964, RG 75, NA-CPR.

47. "Memorandum of Information (To authorize an appropriation for the removal from the taking area of the Fort Randall Dam and Reservoir, Missouri River Division, and the reestablishment of the Indians of the Yankton Reservation)," ca. 1952, FRC Old Box 29696, Miscellaneous Correspondence and Reports, RG 75, National Archives-Rocky Mountain Region (NA-RMR), Denver, CO.

48. Flying Hawk, O'Connor, interviews; Yankton Reservation, South Dakota Individual Program for Use of Damage Payment Funds for the Ft. Randall Project-Peter Archambeau, CCF, Rosebud Agency (1948–1952), Box 170, Missouri River Basin, Fort Randall Project, Section I, General, Yankton Reservation, RG 75, NA-DC.

49. Selwyn, O'Connor, and Jeff Archambeau, interviews.

50. *Social and Economic Conditions of Resident Families*, 6.

51. Walter U. Fuhriman, Director, MRBI, to G. Warren Spaulding, Director, BIA Program Division, Washington, D.C., 1 Feb. 1954, FRC Old Box 29696, Miscellaneous Correspondence and Reports, RG 75, NA-RMR.

52. DOI, BIA, MRBI, *Annual Report, Fiscal Year 1948* (Billings, MT, 1948), 6–8; "Programs and Accomplishments of Interior Agencies Using Missouri River Transfer Funds," DOI Report, 7 Jan. 1958, Missouri Basin Project, 1955–58, File 50745-44-074, RG 75, NA-DC.

53. Pick to Zimmerman, 28 Feb. 1948, CCF, General Correspondence of the Commissioner of Indian Affairs, File 5491-48-308, RG 75, NA-DC.

54. "Brief in Justification of a Bill to Authorize the Appropriation of $85,000 for the Benefit of Certain Yankton Indian Families Whose Homes Are within the Taking Line of the Fort Randall Reservoir Site," ca. 1949, 3, 6–7, Yankton Indian Agency, Box 37, Yankton Sioux Special Tribal Records, 1958–1964, RG 75, NA-CPR; *Distribution of Funds to Indian Families*, 4; *Cong. Rec.* 81st Cong., 1st sess., 1949, 90: 8580.

55. Cooper to CIA, 27 Dec. 1951, Yankton Sioux Tribal Office Files; *A Bill to Authorize the Negotiation and Ratification of Separate Settlement Contracts with the Sioux Tribes of the Lower Brule and Crow Creek Reservations . . . and to Authorize an Appropriation for the Removal from the Taking Area of the Fort Randall Dam and Reservoir, Missouri River Development, and the Reestablishment of the Yankton Sioux Reservation in South Dakota*, 82d Cong., 2d sess., 1952, HR 8293; *A Bill to Authorize the Negotiation and Ratification of Separate Settlement Contracts with the Sioux Tribes of the Lower Brule and Crow Creek Reservations . . . and to Authorize an Appropriation for the Removal from the Taking Area of the Fort Randall Dam and Reservoir, Missouri River Development, and the Reestablishment of the Yankton Sioux Reservation in South Dakota*, 83d Cong., 1st sess., 1953, HR 2231.

56. Fuhriman to G. Warren Spaulding, Director, 1 Feb. 1954, FRC Old Box 29696, Miscellaneous Correspondence and Reports, RG 75, NA-RMR.

57. *Cong. Rec.*, 83d Cong., 1st sess., 1953, 99: 647.

58. 68 Stat 1191.

59. William P. Rogers, Deputy Attorney General, to Senator Hugh Butler, Chair, Senate Committee on Interior and Insular Affairs, 2 June 1954, in Senate Committee on Interior and Insular Affairs, *Separate Settlement Contracts, Sioux Indians, Lower Brule and Crow Creek Reservations for Lands Taken by Reason of Construction of the Fort Randall Dam, S. Dak.*, 83d Cong., 2d sess., 1954, S. Rpt. 1594, 4–5.

60. 68 Stat 452.

61. William O'Connor et al., "Petition to the Department of the Interior and the Department of Indian Affairs in the Matter of Award for Relocating Members of the Yankton Sioux Tribe," ca. 3 June 1954, Yankton Indian Agency, Box 37, Yankton Sioux Special Tribal Records, 1958–1964, RG 75, NA-CPR.

62. Schreyer to Hon. Douglas McKay, Secretary of the Interior, 3 June 1954, ibid.

63. Glenn L. Emmons, CIA, to Schreyer, 2 July 1954, ibid.

64. Armstrong, Memorandum to CIA, 5 Jan. 1956, ibid.; *Distribution of Funds to Indian Families*, 5.

65. "Summary of Memorandum undated to Ben Reifel"; L. P. Towle, Acting Aberdeen Area Director, to CIA, 27 Apr. 1956, Yankton Indian Agency, Box 37, Yankton Sioux Special Tribal Records, 1958–1964, RG 75, NA-CPR; Robertson to Reifel, 10 Oct. 1955, 2, 5.

66. Robertson to Reifel, 10 Oct. 1955, 5–6.

67. Ibid., 7.

68. Ibid., 6, 9–11

69. Ibid., 6, 8; Billy Bologna, Administrative Assistant, Yankton Sub-Agency, BIA, to Walter U. Fuhriman, Director, MRBI, 27 Nov. 1956, Rosebud Indian Agency, Yankton Flood Papers, Boxes A-1, 869, A-1, 870, RG 75, NA-CPR.

70. *Distribution of Funds to Indian Families*, 6, 8.

71. Ibid., 8.

72. Flying Hawk, Armand Hopkins and Kenneth R. Hopkins, Louie Archambeau, and Selwyn, interviews.

73. Flying Hawk, Armand Hopkins and Kenneth R. Hopkins, Selwyn, Cavender, and O'Connor, interviews.

74. Louie Archambeau, interview.

75. O'Connor, Louie Archambeau, Selwyn, and Jeff Archambeau, interviews.

76. Armand Hopkins and Kenneth R. Hopkins, interviews.

77. Jeff Archambeau, interview.

78. "Summary and Evaluation of Experiences of Six Indian Reservations Affected by Large Dam and Reservoir Projects on Missouri River," 15.

79. Pick to Zimmerman, 28 Feb. 1948; Rogers to Butler, 2 June 1954.

80. For example, in other cases Congress clearly established statutory guidelines that provided that it would legislate a settlement if the affected tribes were not successful in

negotiating a satisfactory agreement with the Corps of Engineers and BIA. See, for example, 64 Stat 1093.

81. Donald L. Fixico, *Termination and Relocation: Federal Indian Policy, 1945–1960* (Albuquerque: University of New Mexico Press, 1986), 35–36, 59–60, 168–69.

82. Herbert T. Hoover and Leonard R. Bruguier, *The Yankton Sioux*, Indians of North America Series (New York: Chelsea House Publishers, 1988), 63–64; Herbert S. Schell, *History of South Dakota*, 4th ed., rev. John E. Miller (Pierre: South Dakota State Historical Society Press, 2004), 314.

83. U.S. DOI, BIA, *Final Report of the Garrison Unit Joint Tribal Advisory Committee* (Washington, DC, 26 May 1986), 1–10.

84. 106 Stat 4731–32. The Three Affiliated Tribes lost 175,716 acres of land to the Garrison Dam project. The Standing Rock Sioux Tribe lost approximately 56,000 acres to the Oahe Dam project.

85. The Crow Creek Sioux Tribe Infrastructure Development Trust Act of 1996 (110 Stat 3026–28) established a $27.5-million recovery fund for the Crow Creek Sioux Tribe of South Dakota, while the Lower Brule Sioux Tribe benefited from a $39.9-million recovery fund created by the Lower Brule Sioux Tribe Development Trust Fund Act of 1997 (111 Stat 2563–67). The Crow Creek and Lower Brule tribes lost 15,693 and 22,296 acres of land, respectively, to the Fort Randall and Big Bend Dam projects. The Cheyenne River Sioux Tribe Equitable Compensation Act of 2000 (114 Stat 2365–68) appropriated $290,722,958 plus interest for the establishment of a recovery trust fund for the Cheyenne River Sioux. This amount represents the largest settlement ever awarded to an Indian tribe impacted by a Pick-Sloan project.

86. See Lawson, "Historical Analysis of the Impact of Missouri River Pick-Sloan Dam Projects."

87. 116 Stat 2838–43; Lawson, "Historical Analysis of the Impact of Missouri River Pick-Sloan Dam Projects," 82–84.

88. O'Connor, interview.

5

CONFRONTATION
AND
RADICAL ACTION

SPONTANEOUS COMBUSTION

PRELUDE TO WOUNDED KNEE 1973

. . .

On 27 February 1973, a group of Lakota Sioux residents of the Pine Ridge Indian Reservation and members of the American Indian Movement (AIM) took over the reservation town of Wounded Knee, South Dakota. Tribal officials, aided by various arms of the United States government, immediately laid siege to the occupiers. The resulting seventy-one-day stand-off witnessed countless fire fights, the deaths of two activists, the paralyzing of one United States marshal, a frenzy of national media coverage, a multitude of arrests, and the virtual destruction of Wounded Knee.[1] One common misconception about the event, known as Wounded Knee 1973, is the idea that the Indian occupation was a well-orchestrated, premeditated effort to court the national media, disrupt tribal proceedings, and play on the heartstrings of American citizens. For example, Francis Paul Prucha, in his highly respected and comprehensive two-volume analysis of federal Indian policy, *The Great Father*, describes it as an "engineered" action at a site "consciously chosen as a symbol" because of the 1890 massacre there of Big Foot's Minneconjou Sioux band by the United States Army's Seventh Cavalry.[2] Even though a degree of planning was involved and the site clearly chosen for its impact, the occupation of Wounded Knee was largely a spontaneous event. The Indians who took over the town of Wounded Knee on the night of 27 February conceived their plan of action, including the site of its execution, mere hours before it came to fruition.

Two controversies in the year leading up to Wounded Knee 1973 helped to raise political consciousness and exacerbate antagonisms on the Pine Ridge reservation, contributing to an environment ripe for a spontaneous mass protest. The first was the violent death of Raymond Yellow Thunder, a fifty-one-year-old Oglala Lakota from Pine Ridge. On 12 February 1972, a group of white people forcibly abducted and beat Yellow Thunder in Gordon, Nebraska, a border town just south of the reservation. He died from his wounds several

This essay originally appeared in *South Dakota History* 29 (Fall 1999): 229–44.

days later. Despite the brutal, racist nature of the crime, the perpetrators, who had picked their victim because he was American Indian, were charged with false imprisonment and manslaughter rather than murder. Nebraska authorities were less than forthcoming concerning the details of Yellow Thunder's death, and his body was returned to the reservation in a sealed coffin, fueling rumors, later disproved, that he had been tortured and mutilated. At the family's behest, AIM initiated a series of protests in Gordon that garnered national media attention, forced Nebraska officials to address the treatment of Indians in the state, and raised political consciousness on Pine Ridge.[3]

That spring, a second event fed the unrest when Richard ("Dick") Wilson defeated incumbent Gerald One Feather in a bitterly contested election for the tribal chairmanship of Pine Ridge. In the months that followed, One Feather's defeated constituency grew increasingly alienated from the new administration, accusing it of nepotism, patronage, graft, and corruption. Although no hard-and-fast rules characterized the two men's constituencies, One Feather's largely rural franchise was more likely to be fluent in the Lakota language, adhere to Lakota religion, and show concern for issues like treaty rights. The Wilsonites, who tended to live in the reservation towns, were more apt to be Christian English-speakers who adhered to middle-class American values.[4] The initial antagonism between Wilson and his political opposition only worsened with time. Wilson assembled a private army, which nicknamed itself the "GOON [Guardians of the Oglala Nation] Squad" and conducted a campaign of terror against its opponents. To counter Wilson's policies and tactics, the ousted faction turned for help to AIM, whose growing involvement in reservation politics added fuel to the fire.[5]

From its roots as an urban Indian activist group in Minneapolis in 1968, AIM had quickly branched out to advocate Indian causes across the United States. Noting the success of the 1963 civil rights March on Washington, DC, AIM leaders discussed a similar march when they gathered for the Sun Dance in the summer of 1972 on the Rosebud Indian Reservation property of Leonard Crow Dog, the group's spiritual adviser. Activists such as Dennis Banks, former Rosebud tribal chairman Robert Burnette, and other AIM members participated in the planning. AIM coordinated with other activist groups in scheduling three caravans to leave from Seattle, San Francisco, and Los Angeles in October. Stopping to pick up followers at reservations along the way, they hoped to arrive in the capital during the last week of the 1972 presidential race between Richard Nixon and George McGovern. If the race was close, the leaders reasoned, they might be able to obtain concessions from the eventual winner regarding a list of twenty demands concerning treaty rights and sovereignty that Assiniboine activist Hank Adams had drafted.[6]

On 25 October, the caravans converged on Minneapolis. There, AIM leaders Russell Means, Dennis Banks, Vernon Bellecourt, and Clyde Bellecourt contacted the regional office of the Bureau of Indian Affairs (BIA) to request funding and housing assistance for the marchers in Washington.[7] When the caravan, now over one thousand members strong, arrived on 2 November, they found their reserved quarters in an unheated, rat-infested church basement. The following day, seeking a remedy, the Indians waited in the auditorium of the BIA building until 5:00 p.m., when officials ordered them to leave. The already-tense situation came to a head, and a full-scale riot erupted in which the Indians took over the building, destroying much of its contents.[8]

Although AIM had a penchant for courting the press and the takeover could not have been better scripted for that purpose, most accounts agree that the action was spontaneous. "Nobody, not even the AIM leaders, had planned to takeover the building," Leonard Crow Dog later observed. "It just happened because the government broke its word to provide accommodations."[9] Mary Brave Bird, a caravan member from the Rosebud Indian Reservation who eventually married Crow Dog, corroborated his account. "It was a typical spontaneous Indian happening," she wrote in a memoir. "Nobody had ordered us to do it. We were not very amenable to orders anyhow."[10] In his autobiography, Russell Means concurred, stating, "Spontaneously and with no thought of consequences, we took control."[11] Surrounded by policemen who periodically threatened to storm the doors, the building remained occupied until 9 November, two days after Nixon's victory over McGovern. In return for their leaving the premises, the government promised to consider the Indians' "Twenty Points," guaranteed participants partial amnesty from prosecution, and provided $66,650 in expense money for their trip home.[12]

The occupation of the BIA building represented a higher level of political involvement for AIM. While the organization had previously dealt with municipal or state governments, its efforts were now being taken seriously by officials in Washington, DC. The federal government likewise set a precedent by threatening to resort to armed intervention in dealing with AIM and its allies.

Both of these factors played a role in the next incident involving AIM in South Dakota. On 21 January 1973, twenty-two-year-old Wesley Bad Heart Bull was stabbed to death in a bar in Buffalo Gap, South Dakota, by Darld Schmitz, a white gas-station operator. Both men possessed violent histories, and their fatal encounter was a spillover from a fight Bad Heart Bull was involved in.

Officials charged Schmitz with involuntary manslaughter and released him on a five-thousand-dollar bond. Sarah Bad Heart Bull, the dead man's mother, appealed to AIM for help in securing justice. Russell Means responded with a call for an AIM caravan to travel to the county courthouse in Custer, South Dakota, on 6 February to demand that murder charges be leveled against Schmitz.[13]

While Means boasted that he expected one thousand protesters, the weather kept the crowd down. Snowfall punctuated the cold winter evening, and about two hundred Indians showed up. A number of government officials had prepared to meet with the group, including the state's attorneys for Custer and Fall River Counties, two agents from the state's Division of Criminal Investigation, and the Custer County sheriff. Only five Indian representatives were allowed inside the courthouse, despite the fact that it was a public building and that press and television crews had been given access. Russell Means, Dennis Banks, Leonard Crow Dog, and a Choctaw named Dave Hill entered the building, joining Bob High Eagle, who was already present. Meanwhile, state and local law officers watched the door to deny further admittance and stood in reserve to control the crowd, if necessary.[14]

After the delegation failed in its attempt to have the charges against Schmitz raised to murder, Means and Hill went outside to rouse their supporters, who had taken shelter in their vehicles. When troopers at the courthouse door refused to allow Hill back inside, Means grabbed the collar of an officer and threw him to the ground so that Hill could slip past. Meanwhile, Sarah Bad Heart Bull entered a verbal confrontation with a trooper, who attacked the woman with his club. A full-scale riot ensued.[15]

Law enforcement officials used smoke bombs, tear gas, and fire hoses on the crowd. Indians took gasoline from a nearby service station to make Molotov cocktails. In addition to vandalizing stores, the enraged protesters wrought substantial destruction on the town's infrastructure in the two-and-one-half-hour fight. When it was over, the chamber of commerce building had been burned down, the courthouse damaged by fire, and two police cars destroyed. The *Washington Post* reported thirty-seven people arrested on charges of rioting and arson.[16] Both sides blamed each other for the eruption. A reporter for the *New York Times* noted the spontaneous nature of the skirmish, writing, "No one here seems sure how the violence began. . . . The police were prepared for the demonstration, which had been announced days ago, but apparently they had not expected violence."[17]

Back on the Pine Ridge reservation, antagonism between AIM and tribal chairman Dick Wilson had steadily worsened, beginning with an announce-

Dick Wilson (right), controversial president of the Oglala Sioux Tribal Council,
stands near a marble monument during the 1973 AIM occupation of Wounded Knee.
Western History Collection, Denver Public Library (image no. X-31926)

ment by Means that he planned to run for the tribal chairmanship in the 1974 election. Following the Trail of Broken Treaties event in November 1972, Wilson had abrogated the Pine Ridge constitution by unilaterally suspending the tribal vice-president for participating in AIM activities, and his GOON Squad beat up, shot at, and burned the homes of political opponents. Later in November, the tribal chairman funneled a sixty-two-thousand-dollar BIA grant for an auxiliary police force to his GOON Squad under the guise of protecting the reservation from the kind of destruction AIM had wrought in the nation's capital. In response to the alleged abuses, the chairman's adversaries brought him up on impeachment charges.[18]

The eve of Wilson's impeachment hearing on 14 February 1973 found more than one hundred United States deputy marshals stationed in the town of Pine Ridge. Complementing this force was the Federal Bureau of Investigation (FBI), which conducted ongoing surveillance of AIM. As the federal government's elite information-gathering organization, the bureau used covert infiltrations and COINTELPRO (a counterintelligence program directed against dissidents) to net countless pieces of inside information.[19] When Pine Ridge reservation superintendent Stanley D. Lyman questioned Reese Kash, chief of the security division of United States marshals, about the reliability of some information, Marshal Kash reportedly replied, "Well, I can't tell you that it is from wiretapping because that is illegal. Let me just say it is from a very reliable source." Lyman commented, "Naturally this made me wonder how the FBI and U.S. Marshall Service manage to get some of the information they get. They, of course, would not reveal this, but they must have wiretaps and they must have undercover people because otherwise there would be no way of knowing some of the things they know."[20]

In addition to fears of a confrontation at Wilson's impeachment proceedings, agents expressed concern about possible violence on the one-year anniversary of AIM's demonstrations in Gordon, Nebraska, over the murder of Raymond Yellow Thunder. The February 1972 protest had succeeded in drawing attention to both AIM and the Yellow Thunder case, but nothing transpired on the anniversary of the event.[21] Despite the use of infiltrators and other intelligence-gathering methods, the FBI's inability to ascertain the what, where, or when of the Wounded Knee takeover reflected the impromptu nature of the action.

Trying to anticipate AIM's next move, the FBI also kept tabs on a fluctuating number of AIM members (never more than one hundred) staying at the Mother Butler Indian Center in Rapid City, South Dakota. A 14 February FBI teletype advised: "These Indians may possibly be going to Pine Ridge, SD Indian Reservation and, if so, they may attempt to take over the Bureau of Indian Affairs

(BIA) office there." Agents, however, were not sure if Pine Ridge would be the destination. "It is also possible that the group may be going to [an]other area instead; notably, Tucson, Arizona, or Hot Springs, SD."[22] In response to this communication, the government stationed eighty United States marshals, twenty-eight BIA law enforcement officers from outside reservations, seventeen local BIA officers, fifteen deputized BIA employees, and one FBI agent on the Pine Ridge reservation in February 1973. Locales as far off as Chicago and Dallas were also checked for possible AIM activity.[23]

In the meantime, Wilson postponed his 14 February impeachment hearing for one week on the pretext of poor traveling conditions. On 16 February, agents reported that Wilson expected no violence at the rescheduled hearing, just an oral confrontation. In the first in a series of escalations and deescalations, Marshal Kash stipulated that forty marshals could leave the reservation on 17 February, while the remaining forty would wear civilian clothes and stay until the twenty-third.[24]

On 17 February, the FBI reported that all was quiet at the Mother Butler Center but that Russell Means and Vernon Bellecourt had scheduled television appearances on KRSP-Rapid City for the twentieth.[25] Clyde Bellecourt had also requested that AIM chapters "converge on Rapid City, South Dakota, immediately."[26] Bureau of Indian Affairs officials speculated that AIM hoped to create an "incident" preceding Wilson's impeachment hearing.[27] The FBI, however, stated authoritatively on the same day that AIM had "not made plans to enter Pine Ridge Indian Reservation."[28] On 18 February, the BIA police at Pine Ridge concurred with that assessment, stating that AIM probably would not show up for the Wilson hearing on 22 February.[29]

Two days before the rescheduled proceedings, however, Joseph Trimbach, special agent in charge of the FBI's Minneapolis office, prognosticated that AIM would stage a violent confrontation at the site of the hearing, the BIA building in Pine Ridge. AIM members reportedly planned to kidnap the reservation superintendent, "arrest" law enforcement officials, and declare the reservation a sovereign state. Trimbach issued a plan of action that called for a force of eighty marshals, augmented by forty-five BIA officers and twenty-five South Dakota patrolmen who had been deputized as United States marshals.[30] In his diary for 22 February, Pine Ridge superintendent Stanley Lyman wrote, "I spoke to U.S. Marshall Reese Kash, who told me that AIM was definitely coming today."[31]

Not only was Kash's prediction off by five days, but federal authorities still mistakenly assumed that an attack would center in Pine Ridge, where on 22 February, the hearing went on as scheduled, although the location was changed from the BIA building to more spacious quarters in Billy Mills Hall nearby. When, in a surprise move, Wilson chose to waive a twenty-day waiting period and face trial the next day, the opposition protested on the grounds that they needed time to prepare their case. Wilson prevailed, however, in what turned out to be a masterful stroke.

At the end of the first day, Superintendent Lyman wrote that AIM had not yet appeared in town, supporting "everyone's conjecture that AIM is waiting for a call from Pine Ridge."[32] At the trial on the twenty-third, the council dismissed the impeachment charges by a vote of fourteen-to-zero with one abstention. The session had ended after Lyman left with Dick Little and Birgil Kills Straight, two Wilson opponents, so that the superintendent could copy some important documents for the men. Unaware of the purpose of their exit, the remainder of the council's anti-Wilsonites misconstrued the departure as an act of protest and left the meeting. Lyman and his companions were completely unaware of the ramifications of their absence until they returned to find that Wilson had taken a vote and adjourned the meeting.[33]

An AIM celebration anticipated for the night of the twenty-third "failed to materialize," according to FBI records. By the twenty-fourth, federal officials again believed the threat of a confrontation had passed, sending home half of the visiting BIA police and scheduling half of the marshals to depart on the twenty-fifth. FBI agents from outside divisions were set to be released the following day. Two American Indian agents working undercover were likewise ordered to return to their respective offices. Just three days before the takeover of Wounded Knee, the bureau decided to stop pursuing possible conspiracy charges against AIM, citing "no indication" that an armed caravan was on its way to Pine Ridge.[34]

The peace did not last long. On the twenty-fifth, the Rapid City Journal reported that AIM members, including Clyde and Vernon Bellecourt, had vacated the Mother Butler Center and begun moving toward Pine Ridge. All marshals who had been released the previous day were returned to active duty. FBI surveillance of AIM revealed no concrete plan of action, nor any intent to go to Wounded Knee. The bureau did receive a tip that AIM was storing weapons at Calico Hall, the impromptu headquarters of Wilson's opponents, located five miles north of the town of Pine Ridge. Marshals searched the facility but found nothing.[35]

Business on the reservation came to a standstill on 26 February as people paid their respects at the funeral of Ben Black Elk, son of the famous Oglala Lakota holy man. That same day, law enforcement officials observed ten cars of AIM members from the Mother Butler Center heading toward the reservation. After the funeral, about one hundred fifty traditional Lakotas and anti-Wilsonites assembled at Calico Hall to air grievances and plot a course of action.[36] Among the group was Mary Crow Dog, who described the gathering as "peaceful," recalling a scene in which "kids were playing Frisbee" and "elders were drinking coffee out of paper cups." Although some of the group would participate in the Wounded Knee takeover the following day, she later wrote: "To tell the truth, I had not joined the caravan with the notion that I would perform what some people later called 'that great symbolic act.' I did not even know that we would wind up at Wounded Knee. Nobody did."[37]

The meeting at Calico Hall continued on to the twenty-seventh, and it was then, on the actual day the siege began, that the decision to go to Wounded Knee was made. The hours of discussion had elevated the crowd's desire to act. "I think everybody who was there felt the same way—an excitement that was choking our throats," observed Brave Bird. "But there was still no definite plan for what to do [emphasis added]."[38] Then, in the late afternoon, several traditional Lakota elder chiefs and medicine men, including Frank Fools Crow and Pete Catches, met privately in the basement. Upon returning upstairs, they invited a select contingent to meet with them. Dennis Banks, Russell Means, and several men and women belonging to the Oglala Sioux Civil Rights Organization (OSCRO), a local group opposed to Wilson, accompanied the elders across the street to the Holy Rosary Catholic Church. There, just a matter of hours before the siege actually began, the group decided to go to Wounded Knee. The majority of people at Calico Hall remained ignorant of the plan right up until its execution. Concerns about informants and panicking the crowd led to an announcement that the group, which now numbered almost three hundred, would caravan to a larger meeting space in the town of Porcupine. The towns of Pine Ridge and Wounded Knee were on the way.[39]

As the larger group was organized, two carloads of AIM's most ardent and capable warriors, men who had participated in events such as the Custer riot and the BIA building takeover in Washington, went ahead to secure firearms and ammunition from the trading post at the town of Wounded Knee.[40] Their actions, in part, have led some scholars to view the takeover incorrectly as a well-orchestrated plan. For example, Rolland Dewing in his book Wounded Knee: The Meaning and Significance of the Second Incident quotes a Rapid City Journal article that described the hit on the trading post as "a commando raid in the most accurate sense, well organized and lightning fast, and executed in almost total darkness."[41]

Federal authorities had been expecting a confrontation at the BIA building in Pine Ridge for weeks. United States marshals manned three sandbagged

Once they had decided on a plan of action, AIM protesters headed for the Wounded Knee trading post to secure arms and ammunition. Western History Collection, Denver Public Library (image no. Z-110)

command posts on the roof of the building, which the opposition dubbed "Fort Wilson." Inside the building, an armed command post, complete with communications center, sniper rifles, gas masks, and grenades, had been set up in the south wing.[42] Despite their elaborate preparations, government and tribal officials were nonetheless surprised when the final showdown came. "We drove right through Pine Ridge, the whole caravan of fifty-four cars crammed with people," Leonard Crow Dog recalled. "We roared right by them. We saw them standing on the roof of the tribal council [BIA] building. It was all lit up. We saw Wilson standing there, open-mouthed. We passed some goons on the road. They were bug-eyed. They didn't catch on. It didn't occur to any of them where we were headed. We got to the Knee after nightfall."[43] Mary Crow Dog corroborated her husband's account. "I counted some fifty cars full of people. We went right through [the town of] Pine Ridge. The half-bloods and goons, the marshals and the government snipers on their rooftop, were watching us, expecting us to stop and start a confrontation, but our caravan drove right by them, leaving them wondering."[44]

Bedlam followed the caravan's arrival. Much to the chagrin of the leaders, who were impotent to prevent it, caravan members eagerly looted the small town's trading post and museum.[45] The rampant disorganization of the occupiers reflected the unplanned nature of the event and paralleled the confusion that had plagued the government in its attempt to anticipate the action. As Stanley Lyman observed, "It took place not on February 22 or 23, as we had thought it would, but on February 27."[46]

The line of cars that had made their way through the town of Pine Ridge arrived in Wounded Knee at about eight o'clock in the evening. As the Indians proceeded to take over the hamlet, the FBI and United States marshals set up roadblocks on the four routes leading in, sealing off the area. The occupation of Wounded Knee would prove to be a protracted event. In contrast to its abrupt beginning, its conclusion would not come about until 8 May 1973, after more than two months of extensive negotiations. In fact, the takeover of Wounded Knee was only the first and most widely covered episode in a conflict that would persist until after the defeat of the Wilson administration in 1976.[47]

NOTES

1. Rolland Dewing covers the occupation in depth in *Wounded Knee: The Meaning and Significance of the Second Incident* (New York: Irvington Publishers, 1985).

2. Prucha, *The Great Father: The United States Government and the American Indians*, 2 vols. (Lincoln: University of Nebraska Press, 1984), 2:1119.

3. *Voices from Wounded Knee, 1973, in the Words of the Participants* (Rooseveltown, NY: Akwesasne

Notes, 1974), 13; Dewing, Wounded Knee, 54–61; Gordon Journal, 23 Feb., 1, 7 Mar. 1972; Omaha World Herald, 27 Feb. 1972; Paul Chaat Smith and Robert Allen Warrior, Like a Hurricane: The Indian Movement from Alcatraz to Wounded Knee (New York: New Press, 1996), 112–20.

4. Choice of housing reflected the differences between the two groups. In 1962, Pine Ridge became the first reservation to acquire federal cluster housing in towns. Wilsonites tended to embrace the contemporary, urban-style dwellings as symbols of progress, while proponents of traditional Lakota values often stayed in isolated homes that lacked indoor plumbing and electricity and were situated on family allotments. Dowell Harry Smith, "Old Cars and Social Productions among the Teton Lakota" (PhD diss., University of Northern Colorado, 1973), 221, 225–28.

5. Dewing, Wounded Knee, 70–71; Voices from Wounded Knee, 14–19; Vine Deloria, Jr., Behind the Trail of Broken Treaties: An Indian Declaration of Independence (New York: Dell Publishing Co., 1974), 70; Stanley David Lyman, Wounded Knee 1973: A Personal Account (Lincoln: University of Nebraska Press, 1991), xix; Smith and Warrior, Like a Hurricane, 191; Ward Churchill and Jim Vander Wall, Agents of Repression: The FBI's Secret Wars against the Black Panther Party and the American Indian Movement (Boston: South End Press, 1988), 136.

6. Smith and Warrior, Like a Hurricane, 114; Deloria, Behind the Trail of Broken Treaties, 46–47; Russell Means with Marvin J. Wolf, Where White Men Fear to Tread: The Autobiography of Russell Means (New York: St. Martin's Press, 1995), 223–30; Dewing, Wounded Knee, 64; "The 20-Points Position Paper," Legislative Review 2 (Nov. 1972): 57–64.

7. Teletype, Special Agent in Charge (SAC) Minneapolis to Acting Director of FBI (ADFBI), 24 Oct. 1973, Doc. 25, in The FBI Files on the American Indian Movement and Wounded Knee, ed. Rolland Dewing, microfilm ed. (Frederick, MD: University Publications of America, 1986), File 105–142483, Vol. 1, Reel 1, Frames 46–47 (hereafter cited as FBI Files).

8. Leonard Crow Dog and Richard Erdoes, Crow Dog: Four Generations of Sioux Medicine Men (New York: HarperCollins, 1995), 172–73; Means, Where White Men Fear to Tread, 230–31.

9. Crow Dog, Crow Dog, 173.

10. Mary Crow Dog and Richard Erdoes, Lakota Woman (New York: Grove Weidenfeld, 1990), 86.

11. Means, Where White Men Fear to Tread, 231.

12. Ibid., 235; Crow Dog, Crow Dog, 173–75.

13. Peter Matthiessen, In the Spirit of Crazy Horse (New York: Viking Press, 1983), 62; Dewing, Wounded Knee, 75–80; Omaha World Herald, 1 Feb. 1973; Means, Where White Men Fear to Tread, 243.

14. Teletype, ADFBI to SACs Albuquerque, et al., 5 Feb. 1973, Doc. 397, and teletype, SAC Minneapolis to ADFBI, SACs Denver, Omaha, 7 Feb. 1973, Doc. 400, both in FBI Files, File 105-203686, Sec. 6, Reel 3, Frames 57–58, 762–68; Means, Where White Men Fear to Tread, 243–44; Crow Dog, Crow Dog, 183; Dewing, Wounded Knee, 82.

15. Crow Dog and Erdoes, *Lakota Woman*, 118–19; Means, *Where White Men Fear to Tread*, 244–45; Smith and Warrior, *Like a Hurricane*, 184.

16. Crow Dog, *Crow Dog*, 183–84; Crow Dog and Erdoes, *Lakota Woman*, 119–21; Means, *Where White Men Fear to Tread*, 245–46; *Washington Post*, 8 Feb. 1973.

17. *New York Times*, 8 Feb. 1973.

18. *Voices from Wounded Knee*, 14–16; Means, *Where White Men Fear to Tread*, 236–37; Churchill and Vander Wall, *Agents of Repression*, 236; *Omaha World Herald*, 1 Feb. 1973.

19. Churchill and Vander Wall, *Agents of Repression*, 139; Means, *Where White Men Fear to Tread*, 250–51; Lyman, *Wounded Knee 1973*, xvi.

20. Lyman, *Wounded Knee 1973*, 5. Informant Douglas Durham, for example, entered Wounded Knee on the side of the besieged with press credentials from *Pax Today*, a leftist Des Moines newspaper. He eventually became Dennis Banks's personal bodyguard and pilot, feeding the FBI information all along. Matthiessen, *In the Spirit of Crazy Horse*, 86–87, 108–115.

21. *Voices from Wounded Knee*, 13; Teletype, SAC Minneapolis to ADFBI, 12 Feb. 1973, Doc. 416, *FBI Files*, File 105–203686, Sec. 7, Reel 4, Frames 21–23; *Gordon Journal*, 7 Mar. 1972; *Omaha World Herald*, 27 Feb. 1972.

22. Teletype, SAC Minneapolis to ADFBI, 14 Feb. 1973, Doc. 412, *FBI Files*, File 105–203686, Sec. 7, Reel 4, Frames 7–8.

23. Teletype, SAC Minneapolis to ADFBI, 14 Feb. 1973, Doc. 413, Airtel, SAC Dallas to ADFBI, 14 Feb. 1973, Doc. 420, and Teletype, SAC Chicago to ADFBI, SACs Buffalo, Minneapolis, 14 Feb. 1973, Doc. 421, all in *FBI Files*, File 105–203686, Sec. 7, Reel 4, Frames 9–14, 31–34.

24. Teletype, SAC Minneapolis to ADFBI, 16 Feb. 1973, Doc. 423, ibid., File 105–203686, Sec. 7, Reel 4, Frames 37–39.

25. Teletype, SAC Minneapolis to ADFBI, 17 Feb. 1973, Doc. 425, ibid., File 105–203686, Sec. 7, Reel 4, Frames 41–49.

26. Quoted in teletype, SAC Minneapolis to ADFBI, SACs Albuquerque, et al., 17 Feb. 1973, Doc. 426, ibid., File 105–203686, Sec. 7, Reel 4, Frames 50–51.

27. Teletype, SAC Minneapolis to ADFBI, 17 Feb. 1973, Doc. 428, ibid., File 105–203686, Sec. 7, Reel 4, Frames 53–56.

28. Teletype, SAC Minneapolis to ADFBI, 17 Feb. 1973, Doc. 430, ibid., File 105–203686, Sec. 7, Reel 4, Frames 59–61.

29. Teletype, SAC Minneapolis to ADFBI, 17 Feb. 1973, Doc. 428, and ADFBI to SAC Minneapolis, 18 Feb. 1973, Doc. 431, both ibid., File 105–203686, Sec. 7, Reel 4, Frames 62–65.

30. Teletype, SAC Minneapolis to ADFBI, 20 Feb. 1973, Doc. 442, ibid., File 105–203686, Sec. 7, Reel 4, Frames 95–98.

31. Lyman, *Wounded Knee 1973*, 5.

32. Ibid., 7.

33. Ibid., 5–12.

34. Teletype, SAC Minneapolis to ADFBI, 24 Feb. 1973, Doc. 452, *FBI Files*, File 105-203686, Sec. 7, Reel 4, Frames 124–28.

35. Teletype, SAC Minneapolis to ADFBI, 25 Feb. 1973, Doc. 456, ibid., File 105-203686, Sec. 7, Reel 4, Frames 138–41; *Rapid City Journal*, 25 Feb. 1973.

36. Teletype, SAC Minneapolis to ADFBI, 26 Feb. 1973, Doc. 468, *FBI Files*, File 105-230686, Sec. 7, Reel 4, Frames 182–85.

37. Crow Dog and Erdoes, *Lakota Woman*, 122–23.

38. Ibid., 123.

39. *Voices from Wounded Knee*, 31–32; Crow Dog, *Crow Dog*, 187–88; Crow Dog and Erdoes, *Lakota Woman*, 122–24; Vine Deloria, Jr., *God Is Red* (New York: Grosset & Dunlap, 1973), 257; Means, *Where White Men Fear to Tread*, 252–53, 257.

40. Means, *Where White Men Fear to Tread*, 257.

41. Dewing, *Wounded Knee*, 100.

42. Lyman, *Wounded Knee 1973*, 4–5; Crow Dog, *Lakota Woman*, 122.

43. Crow Dog, *Crow Dog*, 188.

44. Crow Dog and Erdoes, *Lakota Woman*, 125.

45. Crow Dog, *Crow Dog*, 189; Crow Dog and Erdoes, *Lakota Woman*, 128–130; ADFBI to SACs Minneapolis, Oklahoma City, 28 Feb. 1973, Doc. 461, *FBI Files*, File 105-203686, Sec. 7, Reel 4, Frame 152; Means, *Where White Men Fear to Tread*, 258.

46. Lyman, *Wounded Knee 1973*, 17.

47. ADFBI to SACs Minneapolis, Oklahoma City, 28 Feb. 1973, Doc. 461, *FBI Files*, File 105-203686, Sec. 7, Reel 4, Frame 152; Smith and Warrior, *Like a Hurricane*, 263–65; Matthiessen, *In the Spirit of Crazy Horse*, 419–20.

JOSHUA GARRETT-DAVIS

THE RED POWER MOVEMENT AND THE YANKTON SIOUX INDUSTRIES PORK-PROCESSING PLANT TAKEOVERS OF 1975

. . .

In 1975, racial tensions between whites and American Indians in South Dakota, as in many other parts of the country, stood at a high point. Following the takeover of California's Alcatraz Island by Indian activists in 1969, the so-called Red Power movement had gained momentum across the United States. The militant style of Red Power activism, most famously illustrated by the American Indian Movement (AIM), held a match up to a tinderbox of cultural, economic, and historical conditions in and around Indian Country. A pair of flare-ups ignited on the Yankton Indian Reservation in south-central South Dakota in the spring of 1975. In March and again in May, small groups of Yankton Sioux tribal members forcibly occupied the tribally-owned, white-managed Yankton Sioux Industries pork-processing plant in the small reservation town of Wagner. Both takeovers were products of their era, coming in the wake of the well-publicized occupations of the Bureau of Indian Affairs building in Washington, DC, in 1972 and the town of Wounded Knee on the Pine Ridge Indian Reservation in southwestern South Dakota in 1973. The first takeover, accomplished by AIM members in March, was more organized and orderly than the second; it represented a forceful, yet carefully contemplated act of last resort for a group of people who found themselves powerless. A handful of young men, some of them still teenagers and some of them intoxicated, staged the second takeover and the associated burglary of a local hardware store. It was a destructive and ill-planned action. Neither takeover accomplished its ostensible goal of improving the pork plant's success in providing sustainable economic development for the reservation. Both, however, reflected and contributed to a larger accomplishment of the Red Power movement: the bold renunciation of the powerlessness that had hung over Indian Country for more than a century.[1]

This essay originally appeared in *South Dakota History* 36 (Summer 2006): 172–207.

The second action at the Yankton pork plant is perhaps better remembered because of the dramatic response of local, state, and federal law enforcement officials, which was reminiscent of the earlier, nationally publicized occupations. In the wee hours of 2 May 1975, four or five young Yankton Sioux men broke into the Coast to Coast hardware store on Main Street in Wagner, South Dakota. In doing so, they set off a frantic and tense day in South Dakota history. The men had allegedly planned the burglary along with four other individuals at a local house earlier that night. Everyone in the group was between the ages of eighteen and twenty-one. The burglars broke through the front door of the store, smashed a glass display case, and stole a number of guns and boxes of ammunition. One of the young men, James Weddell, had hitchhiked from Sioux Falls to Wagner with the intention of planning an armed political action for that night. Mark Winckler accompanied Weddell, who also asked Michael Honomichl, brothers Godwin and Michael Weston, and Donald Cournoyer, Jesse Costello, and others to come along. Weddell later recalled that his cohorts had been partying and likely would not have joined in had they been sober.[2] Whether any of the young men were sober when the night began is not entirely clear.

Around 2:30 or 3:00 a.m., Dethmar ("Dutch") Huebbling was at his job as a clean-up man at the Yankton Sioux Industries pork-processing plant, a recently established economic-development venture of the Yankton Sioux Tribe. Huebbling was nearing the end of his long shift, which had begun at four o'clock the previous afternoon. He noticed a commotion outside the north door of the plant. "I had just come in with an armful of laundry in the back room," he testified later, "and I seen someone banging on there, and I said, 'What the hell is going on there?' And it wasn't very damn long until I found out what was going on."[3] Eight or nine young American Indian men then broke through the glass next to the door and entered the building armed with their own guns and weapons stolen from Coast to Coast.[4]

The sixty-two-year-old Huebbling hurried to the women's locker room where his twenty-year-old coworker Kenneth Wynia, the only other employee present, was cleaning. Making some assumptions about the young men, Huebbling told Wynia that AIM had just broken into the plant for the second time in two months. Soon the two white employees were hostages in the women's locker room, tied up at gunpoint.[5] When asked in court if he had had "an opportunity to be very close to some of these weapons" and could identify them, Huebbling responded, "I was hit with one."[6]

Three hours later, between 5:30 and 6:00 a.m., the intruders set Huebbling and Wynia free. The employees called plant manager Melvin Rosenthal's house, but word of the takeover had already gotten out, and the manager and the police were separately on their way. One of the armed intruders met Rosenthal at the door and dismissed him from the property. The occupiers then shot at and hit Rosenthal's car.[7]

Sometime before authorities started to arrive, one or two of the occupiers may have left the plant. When the first police officers came on the scene around seven o'clock in the morning, only seven young men remained inside: Weddell, Winckler, Honomichl, the Weston brothers, Cournoyer, and Costello. The gathering police, sheriff, and highway patrol personnel sealed the area on all sides. As state troopers and state Division of Criminal Investigation (DCI) agents sped into Wagner, first from neighboring counties and then from across South Dakota, they gradually mounted a force of over one hundred.[8]

On the checkerboard of Indian and non-Indian property that makes up the Yankton reservation, the pork plant stood on Indian, or tribal, land. Since the 1831 *Cherokee Nation v. Georgia* decision by the United States Supreme Court, American Indian tribes had been legally defined as "domestic, dependent nations." This unique legal status meant that tribal lands within South Dakota were not subject to South Dakota state laws. The prosecution of serious crimes committed on tribal land, such as the takeover of the Wagner pork plant, fell under federal jurisdiction as defined by the Major Crimes Act of 1885. On the Yankton Sioux reservation, where Indian and non-Indian properties closely intermingled, the balancing of tribal, state, and federal authority was complicated.[9]

In any case, the state of South Dakota lacked the legal power to send its own special weapons and tactics (SWAT) team inside to fetch the young rebels and would have to wait for the federal government to act. The state agencies could, however, stop well-armed militants, especially high-profile AIM activists, from entering the plant with weapons or explosives. At similar incidents throughout the state in the two years following the occupation of Wounded Knee, such "quarantines" had kept weapons from getting in and, in the opinion of then-superintendent of the State Highway Patrol Dennis Eisnach, had prevented bloodshed. The highway patrol immediately notified the Federal Bureau of Investigation (FBI), which agreed to send a SWAT team from Minneapolis, Minnesota.[10] Meanwhile, the town of Wagner waited in fear.

From inside the plant, the occupiers fired approximately twenty-five to thirty rounds of ammunition toward the waiting authorities outside.[11] This action proved counterproductive to their half-hearted request to meet with members of the Yankton Sioux Tribal Council, which officially controlled a 51 percent interest in the facility. The council convened an emergency meeting and, like the highway patrol, requested federal intervention. "Negotiations cannot be conducted under these conditions," the council concluded, "and we find it necessary to ask for assistance from special forces of the United States government to intervene and take necessary action to remove those individuals illegally occupying tribal property."[12] Similarly, Loren Farmer, the Bureau of Indian Affairs (BIA) superintendent for the Yankton reservation, observed, "There are no negotiations. There is nothing to negotiate."[13]

The occupants probably had little to negotiate except the terms for their getting out. By morning, certainly, the effects of the alcohol had worn off (only one beer bottle was later found in the plant),[14] and while they might not have admitted it, they were likely fearful of the large presence of law-enforcement agents surrounding them. At some point during the day, they penned a vague manifesto on a piece of Yankton Sioux Industries stationery. It read, in part: "Cruel, foul and greedy people are thriving on our blood, asking more than we can give. Respect is something that cannot be seen, our people are mighty although we have come to pass." These young men already showed a politics of desperation and fatalism; their only demands were futile ones: "This is what the people would like to see—Loren Farmer and Melvin Rosenthal out of everything that has to do with the Yankton Sioux Nation."[15] To them, Farmer represented the bureaucratic tyranny of the BIA and the federal government in general over American Indian life, while Rosenthal symbolized the ongoing exploitation of Yankton people by whites. Whether their demands spoke for all Yanktons is doubtful, but many people likely sympathized with the occupiers' desperation and frustration over the American public's neglect of their problems. Donald Cournoyer, one of the seven, later remembered feeling an urgent need to take some kind of action to draw attention to their situation.[16]

The "Pork Plant Seven" or "Yankton Seven," as they later came to be known, did not call the media to make a statement. Either they never thought to do so, or law-enforcement officers had cut the phone line. In fact, telephone use was restricted for the whole town. The seven-person takeover and the one-hundred-strong police reaction had sent Wagner into a panic. Local officials dismissed all students just after school began that morning.[17] Around 1:00 p.m., the mayor and city council declared a state of emergency and imposed a twenty-four-hour curfew. All businesses closed, except for one café to serve the highway patrolmen, and persons who left their houses could be punished with thirty days in jail and a one-hundred-dollar fine. Residents evacuated the Wagner Indian Housing development, located about one-half mile from the pork plant. Reporters were rumored to be locked in a house and denied telephone access to call in their stories. One newspaper article the next day used tumbleweed-drama imagery in describing the streets of Wagner as looking like "the 'shoot out at high noon' scene in a Western movie."[18]

Many Wagner residents recall this "state of emergency" as an imposition of martial law. Alan Pirner, who sat on the city council at the time but was not present for its emergency meeting that day, remembered: "It started when the Attorney General, who was Bill Janklow at that time, came and then he declared martial law. There was no traffic going on in the streets. . . . It was real different, you know, you always heard about it in other places, but never in a little town like Wagner." Pirner concluded, "I didn't know South Dakota had that many highway patrol."[19]

William J. Janklow had defeated the incumbent state attorney general just six months earlier, rolling to an overwhelming victory on a law-and-order, anti-AIM platform and on his successful prosecution (as assistant attorney general) of AIM members the year before. The takeovers of the Wagner pork plant were among the first militant-related incidents of his term. Although the attorney general's responsibility in law enforcement was limited to prosecution (state law enforcement officers, except county sheriffs, fell under Governor Richard F. Kneip's authority), Janklow traveled to Wagner to direct the police force personally. Once there, he criticized the bureaucracy of the federal government for delaying a resolution to the crisis.[20]

As darkness descended around 8:50 p.m., about eighteen hours after the break-in, an officer reported seeing someone crossing a corn field west of the plant. In order to flush this individual out of the dark acreage and prevent others from exiting or entering the plant before federal authorities arrived, the highway patrol decided to use tear gas.[21] As reported in an FBI document, a highway patrolman "apparently [acting] on his own, shot tear gas onto [the] roof of the building which entered the plant via the air ducts."[22] Soon the gas inside the plant became intolerable. Four of the young men inside walked out the west door and then reentered the building. About a minute later, all seven came out. A BIA policeman who had just arrived from the Lower Brule Indian Reservation used his bullhorn to order them to raise their hands and walk toward the plant's south gate. They hesitated but, seeing no other way out, obeyed.[23]

Law-enforcement officers took the seven to nearby Lake Andes to await arraignment. As reported in FBI records, Minneapolis-based agents (about forty of them, according to a newspaper account) were traveling to Wagner in a chartered DC-3 and learned of the surrender during a refueling stop at Mitchell. The Minneapolis personnel arrived at Wagner around 9:30 p.m., too late for them to make the arrests.[24] "Janklow was told," said the FBI report, "that we had gone to considerable expense and inconvenience to assemble and transport a large number of FBI personnel to Wagner, South Dakota, and if the South Dakota authorities were going to act on their own they should have advised us so the need to charter a DC-3 airplane could have been avoided." According to the report, Janklow responded that the tear-gassing of the building had not been intended but was "one of those things that will happen."[25] Publicly, however, Janklow claimed credit for directing the tear-gas attack, which was reported in the press as a purposeful "barrage" rather than an accident. "It's always the state that has to do the federal government's work," Janklow told reporters. "They've got to start taking the bull by the horns."[26]

As the interplay between law enforcement agencies indicated, the situation on the reservation was complicated, and the Yankton Sioux Tribe's unhappiness with reservation conditions was longstanding. From their first contact with white explorers and settlers, the Yanktons had been among the most accommodating Sioux tribes. They made several treaties with the United States government during the first half of the nineteenth century, ceding millions of acres in present-day Minnesota and Iowa. Finally, tribal leaders—some of them possibly coerced—signed the Treaty of Washington, DC, also known as the Treaty of 1858, which opened most of what is now eastern South Dakota to white homesteaders. This treaty, brokered by white entrepreneurs with ambitions in real estate, helped to set the stage for the tense relationship the tribe would have with the incoming settlers.[27]

The Treaty of 1858 also served to divide the tribe between those who wished to accommodate the whites and those who wanted to maintain traditional ways of life. The fact that many tribal leaders and members opposed the treaty, which, in addition to ceding land also provided funding to instill in the Yanktons "habits of industry" and "practical knowledge of agriculture and the mechanic arts," presaged the conflicts between "progressives" and "traditionals" that would follow the tribe through the twentieth century.[28]

In 1887, the United States Congress passed the General Allotment, or Dawes, Act. This new policy, intended to turn American Indians into farmers, gave each Indian head of household one quarter-section (160 acres) of land. The government then declared any leftover lands "surplus" and open for sale to non-Indians. These policies diminished the Yankton Sioux Tribe's landholdings from 430,405 acres following the Treaty of 1858 to 96,000 acres by 1916. Around the turn of the twentieth century, a flood of white settlers, many of them Czech and other European immigrants, homesteaded on the surplus land, creating the checkerboard of tribal and non-tribal ownership that later proved confusing in matters of jurisdiction.[29]

Federal Indian policy in the twentieth century swung back and forth between supporting tribal self-government (or "self-determination"), and pushing American Indians to assimilate and tribes to disband. In the 1930s, the "Indian New Deal" encouraged tribes to adopt constitutions to govern themselves. By the 1950s, the federal government had begun a program to relocate American Indian people from rural reservations to large cities like Minneapolis and Oakland, California, with the ultimate goal of terminating many tribes as legal entities. The growing communities of urban Indians, in turn, became seedbeds for the activism that would flourish over the next two decades. In the mid-1960s, President Lyndon Johnson's "War on Poverty," with its federal aid for local economic-development projects, became the government's preferred solution to the so-called Indian problem in America.[30]

As early as 1968, Yankton Tribal Chairman Percy Archambeau made his vision for the tribe clear. He stated that an unnamed company had chosen a site to set up a new industry on the Yankton reservation. In his view, it represented the private enterprise system and gave the tribe a chance to work to surmount the problems that plagued the reservation.[31] It appeared, indeed, that conditions on the reservation had hit rock bottom, and Archambeau optimistically forged ahead to make things materially better for his tribe. In the 1970s, only about one-third of the American Indian population of Charles Mix County worked full-time, and half fell below the federal poverty level.[32] Archambeau believed that jobs for tribal members would help to solve the problems on the reservation.[33] Many local whites respected and encouraged Archambeau's work ethic. Local businessman Alan Pirner recalled him as "one hell of a man" who did "a lot for the Yankton Sioux Tribe." The Wagner City Council, on which Pirner served, avidly supported Archambeau's economic-development efforts.[34]

Percy Archambeau's optimism reflected that of the federal policy makers at the time. Between 1965 and 1970, federal financing of economic-development projects for American Indians nationwide doubled from $57.6 million to $117.7 million. In March 1971, the Yankton Sioux Tribe received $34,737 in federal grants and local matching funds to plan and implement an economic-development program on the reservation. Archambeau and other Yankton leaders had already settled on meat processing as an industry in which tribal members could readily acquire skills that would transfer to meat-packing plants off the reservation in nearby Yankton or Sioux Falls. The tribe's Business and Claims Committee in 1969 had located a white investor to direct and manage a plant—Melvin Rosenthal from the First Street meat-processing corporation in Fort Worth, Texas. Rosenthal, whose family had been in the meat business for three generations, agreed to move to Wagner to run the operation.[35]

Yankton tribal chairman Percy Archambeau envisioned businesses
and industries on the reservation that would provide tribal members
with jobs and help them rise above poverty.
Photograph by Milo Dailey, *Yankton Daily Press & Dakotan*

In June 1971, the federal government, through the Small Business Administration, responded to the tribe's economic-development plan with four hundred thousand dollars in loans. Six months later, the tribe received federal grants totaling over five hundred thousand dollars for an "industrial park" where the meat-packing plant would be located. The City of Wagner donated sewage facilities for the plant. Despite construction delays, the project continued to win tens of thousands of dollars more in grants from various agencies over the next two years. In June 1973, Yankton Sioux Industries, Incorporated, hosted the formal dedication of the industrial park located just south of Wagner. Its twenty-two-thousand-square-foot packing plant was nearly completed and scheduled to open within a few months.[36]

Both whites and Indians in Wagner expected that Melvin Rosenthal and his sons would gradually turn over control of the plant to tribal members who worked their way up to management positions. The tribe retained a minimum controlling interest of 51 percent in the enterprise in order for Yankton Sioux Industries to qualify for federal benefits as a socially and economically disadvantaged small business. According to the contract terms, the Rosenthals would run the plant for ten years, until 1983, to recover their investment plus interest and a profit, at which point the tribe could buy them out for $110,000 plus the value of the three most profitable years of operation. When the company incorporated in 1972, its board of directors was composed of four white members: Melvin Rosenthal and his two sons, Joel and Stephen, and Don Juffer, a local banker in Wagner. The next year, Yankton Sioux Industries added Percy Archambeau to the board.[37]

At the beginning of 1974, the vast investment of time, energy, and grant money finally accomplished its goal. The city of Wagner had hard-surfaced the gravel road south from Main Street as a veritable red carpet to the new pork-processing plant.[38] In early February 1974, the facility, billed in the local newspaper as the "only meat processing plant located on an Indian Reservation in South Dakota," started production with eleven workers. Joel Rosenthal predicted that this number would soon rise to seventy-five.[39] The plant would not slaughter hogs but would receive chilled pork from outside companies, which it would then bone and process into ham and bacon. Yankton Sioux Industries planned to market its product under the label "Smoke Signal" to chain stores, industrial caterers, and government institutions. The front page of the *Wagner Post* for 7 February 1974 pictured the new employees in matching smocks, looking like an industrious operating-room team as they worked at a table boning pork.[40] When the United States Department of Agriculture officially certified the plant a few weeks later, an area supervisor from Fargo, North Dakota, assured the community, "This is a mainstream industry which is bound to succeed."[41]

While local leaders worked to establish a viable industry on the Yankton reservation, another movement was gaining momentum across Indian Country. Buoyed by the civil rights victories of the 1960s and, in part, by the same flood of federal money that built the Yankton Sioux Industries pork plant, American Indian political activism emerged as a new force on the nation's horizon.[42] In 1969, eighty-nine American Indian activists living in the San Francisco Bay area landed on Alcatraz Island, which the government had recently abandoned as a prison. Their symbolic reclaiming of the territory in the name of "Indians of All Tribes" instituted the period of militant Indian activism broadly called the Red Power movement. As Red Power spread from urban Indian activists back to the rural reservations from which many of them had relocated in the 1950s and early 1960s, a number of similar incidents followed. These events culminated in South Dakota in 1973 with a riot by AIM members outside the Custer County Courthouse during a hearing in the case of an Indian man killed by a white man in a bar fight in Buffalo Gap, and, of course, with the seventy-one-day AIM takeover of Wounded Knee on the Pine Ridge reservation.[43]

Red Power activism and the resurgence of American Indian culture appeared on the Yankton Sioux reservation virtually coincidental with the pork-processing plant. Just a week and a half before Wounded Knee, the Yankton Sioux chapter of AIM held its first public meeting in Lake Andes. Soon after, Yankton AIM members took a number of grievances to tribal and BIA officials. They complained of abuse of power and funds by the tribal council, police brutality on the part of tribal law enforcement, and an apathetic tribal school board.[44] Greg Zephier, a founding director of the Yankton AIM chapter, also spoke of a climate of silent resentment in and around Wagner. "Why should an Indian be looked down upon when they enter a restaurant or public place?" he asked.[45] Still, Zephier and his father, Fred Zephier, also an AIM member, assured the *Wagner Post* there would be no "Custer" or "Wounded Knee" on the Yankton reservation.[46]

Whites across the state had responded to events like the Custer courthouse riot and the Wounded Knee takeover with confusion and fear. By and large, the press characterized AIM as a small gang of roving malcontents intent on stirring up trouble in an already troubled Indian population. The names Russell Means, Dennis Banks, Clyde Bellecourt, Vernon Bellecourt, Leonard Crow Dog, and others appeared again and again. Some of these spokesmen participated in nearly every occupation and protest around the United States in the early 1970s. According to a typical editorial in the *Sioux Falls Argus-Leader*, white South Dako-

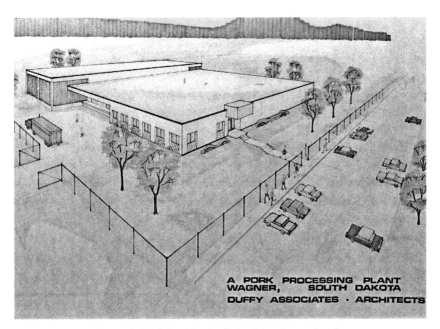

A PORK PROCESSING PLANT
WAGNER, SOUTH DAKOTA
DUFFY ASSOCIATES · ARCHITECTS

Financed with federal funds, the Yankton Sioux Industries
pork-processing plant was designed as a modern facility that would
produce meat products to be marketed under the "Smoke Signals" label.
State Archives Collection, South Dakota State Historical Society

tans resented being labeled racist "by AIM leaders who don't even represent most of our Indian friends." The editorial went on to state that AIM-related incidents, in fact, created racism where previously there was none.[47]

While AIM certainly did not soften race relations in South Dakota, its appeal to American Indians in the state lay in the long and painful history that such editorials ignored. One white woman whose husband was a Methodist minister in Wagner, where he had supported Indian activism, explained years later: "Today in our church bulletin there was a little thing about Martin Luther King [Jr.]. He wrote this letter from jail saying that what bothered him most was middle class people who would just never stand up. They were probably on the right side, . . . but they never got up and actually stood up for anybody. I think that's kind of the way it was in Wagner."[48] Non-Indians around the Yankton Sioux reservation witnessed the enduring poverty of their Indian neighbors, as well as the decades of government intervention, and came to resent or pity the tribe. One white attorney in Wagner expressed a typical complaint, stating that tribal members failed to take care of their homes, which had been provided for them at government expense. Whites in Charles Mix County, however, also benefited from Indian-related government spending. For example, the federal government paid for 80 percent of the cost of a new school in Wagner in 1972, thanks to the Yankton population in the district.[49]

Even so, when a local AIM chapter organized on the reservation, the action may have seemed unnecessary and ungrateful to non-Indians. Many viewed the tribe as benefiting richly from government generosity with the development of the Yankton Sioux Industries pork plant. An anonymous submission to the *Wagner Post* just after Greg Zephier and Fred Zephier held the first AIM meeting in Lake Andes exposed a usually unspoken side to the views of some whites in the region. This letter, thinly disguised as a joke, was published under the title "Another Movement Forms." It began, "Calling on all members of the tribes of Slovaks, Cvechs [sic], and Moravians, commonly known as Bohemians." (Many of the whites of Charles Mix County had immigrated to South Dakota from Czechoslovakia around the turn of the twentieth century.) The author purported to belong to a fictitious organization bearing the moniker "the Bohemian Movement, or simply B.M." In a parody of Indian activists' cultural and political demands, the writer stressed his group's intent to "Outlaw Bohemian jokes" and "Petition the Great White Father in Washington for AID to teach our young people the ancient and honorable crafts of making home brew, kolaches, sauerkraut, etc. as practiced by our ancestors."[50]

The letter further laid out as "secondary objectives" a list of demands directed pointedly at what many deemed to be American Indian perquisites:

A. Remove all property from the tax rolls.

B. Free housing.

C. Free medical care.

D. Take our children off the streets and put them back in the alleys and pool rooms.

E. Anything else that a good strong B.M. can get for nothing.

The satire concluded with a crude innuendo, "We feel that if all Bohemians get behind this movement and push hard the B.M. will get bigger from day to day!"[51] Although many whites in Wagner must have felt sympathy for their Indian neighbors, a dark resentment must also have been common enough for such an expression to be deemed publishable in the local newspaper.

Despite such attitudes on the part of some in the community, the Yankton Sioux Industries plant opened in February 1974, and the operation ran like clockwork under Melvin Rosenthal's watchful eye. Bells marked the beginning and end of each shift. One former white employee recalled that bathroom visits were limited to break times, also signaled by ringing bells. A tribal member who worked at the plant described the Rosenthals as no-nonsense, business-focused managers. They also apparently believed in the ideal of equal opportunity. According to Owen Ray Wipf, the Rosenthals' attorney in Wagner, they chose not to ask for nationality on their application form even though they had received over a million dollars in federal grants and loans specifically to provide jobs to Indian workers. Overall, they ran a tight ship, personally monitoring the staff, which soon increased to about forty-five.[52]

Yankton Indian culture did not square with the capitalistic rhythms of the Rosenthals' factory. From the start, those involved in the project had had to ignore the skepticism of local whites who expressed doubt that Indians would adapt to the white workaday world.[53] According to Wipf, when the plant first started operations, the Rosenthals hired a workforce made up of approximately 60 or 70 percent American Indians. He concluded resignedly, however, that what is commonly known as "Indian Time," or the practice of arriving at work two or three hours late or skipping days, interfered with the efficient operation of the plant. The term "Indian Time" was not simply a pejorative expression invented to degrade American Indian culture, although it has been used as such. In part, as historian Herbert T. Hoover has noted, the tendency of the Yankton employees to miss work or appointments reflected their strong sense of obligation to family and friends, an obligation that filled houses with long-term guests, emptied already scant bank accounts, and took precedence over the demands of outsiders. Traditional Yanktons often took time to travel long distances to other reservations for powwows, giveaways, and other cultural and religious events.[54]

Rural poverty and long distances also caused problems. The Rosenthals sometimes excused employees for not calling in sick if they lived in the country without a telephone (as late as 1980, about half of reservation families did not have telephone service). At other times, however, the managers appeared overly harsh to employees who had to survive on scant resources. Tribal member Sam Weddell recalled that the Rosenthals showed little tolerance when workers' ten-or twenty-year-old cars broke down on what, for many, was a long commute to Wagner. The family member sent to rescue the broken-down driver might also miss an appointment; another old car might break down on the way to a powwow or the wake of a relative on a distant reservation, meaning days spent away from home and work. Poverty and cultural obligations often overrode punctuality on the Yankton reservation, as on many other Indian reservations.[55]

Also conspiring against the success of many Indian people in a mechanized environment was a lack of job experience. Before the pork plant opened, the eight-hour workday was essentially nonexistent on the reservation. Tribal member Steve Cournoyer, Jr., who long endeavored to create job opportunities for the Yankton people, acknowledged the difficulties inherent in employing those who had never had a job. (Cournoyer himself had his identity as an Indian questioned for his adoption of the white workday schedule.) Most Yanktons' lives revolved around cycles other than work: cultural calendars, family, welfare schedules, or, in some cases, alcoholism. Some anthropologists and historians who have studied the Sioux place these cycles on a continuum between the ancient seasonal pace of the buffalo hunt and its so-called opposite, the mechanical lockstep of an industry such as the pork plant. Other observers have explained the phenomenon in similar but blunter terms. Cournoyer called it a lack of the work ethic; Wipf called it a lack of responsibility.[56]

Working at the Yankton Sioux Industries plant required not just a "work ethic" and "responsibility," but rigor, stamina, and patience. New employees spent their first few months standing at a table checking ham cans for rust and scrubbing out rust spots with vegetable oil. Once established as reliable, employees were promoted to the refrigerated back room, where they helped to cut up between one-hundred-thousand and one-hundred-fifty-thousand pounds of cold pork every day. These workers were frequently cold, and their bodies tired from standing for eight hours at a time, or from ten to twelve hours in the event of a special shipment. Older employees, especially, suffered repetitive-motion injuries from making the same cut hundreds of times per shift. The layers of clothing worn under their smocks interfered with their wielding of long knives. Fat fibers slickened the floors, and hog fat turning sour in the drains emitted foul gasses that gave people headaches. The gas became severe enough only a handful of times for managers and inspectors to remedy the problem, but it added continuing unpleasantness to the disorienting monotony of the work.[57]

The meat-packing industry today has the highest injury rate of any industry in the United States, especially since its consolidation in the 1960s, when large corporations subsumed small companies like the Rosenthals' family enterprise in Fort Worth. While the Wagner processing plant moved at a slower pace than the ultramodern plants in today's American West, it was still dangerous. A white former employee noted that injuries were relatively uncommon and that nobody lost limbs or suffered life-threatening injuries. He himself, however, had his hand crushed by a slightly faulty machine. Part of the Rosenthals' investment in the pork plant was a fleet of World War II-era mixers, grinders, and other machines from their business in Texas. In addition to the dangers the sticky grinders posed, employees also suffered gashes as they repeatedly drew their knives toward themselves in the meat-cutting process. About once a week somebody needed stitches.[58] The fear of injury contributed to the unfamiliar environment of the plant, especially for Yankton employees.

Richard Leasure, a tribal member who worked at the pork plant some time after the takeovers, recalled the mood of individuals on the lines as solemn, noting that workers endured the cold conditions simply for the paycheck and spent most of the day wanting to go home. Todd Morrow, a white worker, was more philosophical, stating that for the place and time the plant offered good-paying jobs for unskilled laborers. Some whites, like Morrow, went in knowing what to expect. For Yanktons who had grown up with different realities, however, the packing industry was not a warm introduction to a new way of life. Even Steve Cournoyer, Jr., who had stood next to Melvin Rosenthal and held up a ham for the news camera at the plant opening, became disillusioned when Yankton Sioux Industries failed to evolve into a desirable place to work. Cournoyer, whose wife had worked at the plant for a time, noted that the management seemed to discourage employees from gaining experience and developing company loyalty. In particular, he complained of sporadic work hours. Depending on the supply of unprocessed pork, workers might put in a full day or be dismissed after a few hours on the line and be told to come back later. In the meantime, they would go into town and sit in the bars.[59]

Sam Weddell, who opposed Cournoyer politically but also promoted economic development for his tribe, agreed, stating that some people could not get forty hours of work per week and received more money by staying on welfare. Although some American Indian people—including two of Weddell's uncles—succeeded in working at the plant, many more became disenchanted with it.[60] Some Indian people blamed the Rosenthal family's Jewish ethnicity for their business style and the cultural conflict at the pork plant. But this reaction appeared to be primarily a vocabulary for lashing out at the outsider bosses, rather than a deep-seated anti-Semitism. Melvin Rosenthal himself did not consider anti-Semitism a large problem. Looking back, he reflected that while there may have been frictions between certain minority groups, he did not believe they involved Jews more than any other group.[61]

Nonetheless, the Rosenthals may have been disappointed with their venture in other ways. They had probably not encountered Indian Time before agreeing to build a factory on Indian land, and Indian leaders had assured them that enough Indian workers could be found to staff the facility. The Texans could logically have expected a desperate and eager work force—a bit rough-hewn, perhaps, but trainable. Their disillusionment, however, could not have been greater than that of the Yanktons, who watched the erosion of a promised lifeline out of a century of dire poverty. The Rosenthals, in fact, had other sources for employees, especially in an era when family farmers, like independent meat-packers, began to suffer from the consolidation of agribusiness. Many whites, women in particular, began seeking second jobs in town. Wipf explained that the management gave Indian employees a fair chance but could not continue to function profitably with positions frequently vacant. Indians became a minority in a workforce made up of whites, Hispanics, and African-Americans. Indeed, by November 1974, nine months after the plant opened, only twenty out of the fifty employees at Yankton Sioux Industries were Yanktons. Four months later, they constituted only six of forty employees there. These few Indian workers, who were often new employees due to the frequent turnover, tended to work scrubbing cans for the minimum wage of $2.20 per hour, while non-Indians generally got better posts at up to $3.25 per hour. Meanwhile, Melvin Rosenthal was rumored to pay himself a salary of forty-five thousand dollars per year.[62]

Percy Archambeau, the only Yankton tribal member on the pork plant's corporate roster, attempted to effect a compromise between the management style of the Rosenthals and the working style of the Yanktons. Steve Cournoyer, Jr., recalled that Archambeau sought to create an office in the plant for Cournoyer, who could then help Indian workers adjust and stay employed. The Rosenthals strongly opposed the idea. By contract, the Rosenthals were required to share the plant's profits with the tribe, but this profit-sharing, which was to be a benefit secondary to Indian employment, never materialized. Some tribal members claimed that the plant made a lot of money, up to $361,000 in a year, while others judged that it was near bankruptcy. In any case, the Yankton Sioux Tribe was not kept well informed of the company's financial affairs. Because he was trying to attract other businesses to the Yankton Sioux Industrial Park, Archambeau was not in a position to challenge the investors, for fear of losing the potential $3-million beef-packing plant or the $2-million scrap-metal disposal plant he was courting.[63]

By March 1975, a number of people on the Yankton reservation had grown discontented with the lack of Indian employment and what they termed the "'ripoff' contract" at Yankton Sioux Industries.[64] Percy Archambeau, Steve Cournoyer, Jr., and other tribal leaders who were at least nominally responsible for the plant's management had been negotiating gingerly with the Rosenthals to correct its shortcomings, but others, especially members of rival families and factions, feared these individuals were selling them out.[65] Greg Zephier, a leader in the local AIM chapter, reported hearing that Melvin Rosenthal had told Percy Archambeau to get out of the plant because Rosenthal was in charge.[66] Whether or not Archambeau and others were nearing a compromise with the Rosenthals, other Yankton people lost their patience with negotiations and decided to act.

Greg Zephier's widow, Beverly, recalled that these tribal members, either plant employees or concerned shareholders, knew of his connections with AIM and began visiting their home in the Wagner Indian Housing section just north of the plant to discuss what might be done.[67] Occupations of various kinds had become a staple of Red Power protest since the Trail of Broken Treaties' week-long takeover of the BIA building in Washington, DC, in November 1972. In 1974 and early 1975, such occupations had been led by local Indian activist groups on reservations around the country. After a thirty-four-day takeover in January 1975 by the Menominee Warrior Society in Wisconsin and an eight-day takeover in late February by the Navajo Warriors Society in New Mexico, occupations formed part of the tactics of American Indian groups desiring action. The situation in New Mexico, where the tribally subsidized Fairchild Camera plant in Shiprock was laying off Navajo workers, carried overtones of events in South Dakota. One spokesman for the Navajo Warriors Society complained of corporations "coming in and using the Indian people for low wages." John Trudell, national AIM chairman at the time, called Fairchild "just one of many corporations which operates this way."[68]

Greg Zephier carefully planned a similar, nonviolent action for the Wagner pork plant. He and other local AIM members such as Sam Weddell assembled documents and files to support their claim that the tribe's deal with the Rosen-

Dissatisfied with the management of the Yankton Sioux
Industries plant, Greg Zephier (center) and others formed the
Eagle Warrior Society and made plans to occupy the facility in March 1975.
Photograph by Milo Dailey, *Yankton Daily Press & Dakotan*

thals was unfair and that the Yankton tribe would never be able to afford the estimated four hundred twenty-four thousand dollars to buy out the managers after ten years. Following the lead of the Indian takeovers in Wisconsin and New Mexico, the group called itself the "Eagle Warrior Society of the Yankton Sioux Tribe" rather than identifying officially with the pan-Indian AIM. Beverly Zephier recalled that, in contrast to the second Yankton event, conscientious planning went into the March takeover in order to avoid arrests. If anyone was taken into custody, the group anticipated that it would be Greg Zephier, who served as spokesman.[69]

According to the Reverend Robert McBride, a Methodist minister in Wagner and a friend of Greg Zephier and other Eagle Warrior Society members, Zephier faced dangers greater than getting arrested. McBride recalled that one of his parishioners warned him that a vigilante force of fifty white farmers and ranchers with guns stowed in their pickup trucks stood ready to silence an Indian uprising if called upon. McBride also feared that, in the aftermath of Wounded Knee, Attorney General Janklow, the highway patrol, and state or federal troops would use force to remove them from the plant.[70]

Thanks to Zephier's planning and leadership, and to the restraint exercised on both sides, the occupation occurred without either bloodshed or arrest. At about 7:30 on Monday morning, 17 March 1975, Zephier led a group of fifteen to twenty men, women, and children into the Yankton Sioux Industries plant. Members of the group, including Sam Weddell and his brother James Weddell, ushered Melvin and Joel Rosenthal and a few employees off the property at gunpoint and locked the gate behind them with a chain. Zephier then reminded the occupiers not to damage or deface the facility. Sam Weddell later recalled that no one even ate the ham stored in the plant's refrigerators.[71]

Zephier used the plant telephone to call the press and politicians and to issue the Eagle Warrior Society's demands. As a few BIA police blocked the three roads leading to the plant, the occupiers demanded that the tribe convene a general council meeting, which tribal law required if twenty-five of the tribe's forty-six hundred enrolled members requested it. Prepared for the worst, a spokesman for the group (probably Zephier) brazenly told the press, "We're here to die," and warned, "if they come out and start shooting at us, they are going to have to shoot our children, too." He also asked for an observation team at the general council that included national AIM leaders, white attorneys, and local clergymen.[72]

The Eagle Warrior Society had composed sixteen far-reaching demands to be presented to the tribe at the general council. Essentially, the occupiers sought termination of the Rosenthals' contract, training for tribal management of the pork plant, and a guarantee that 85 percent of the plant workforce would be Indian. They also included a few unrelated demands and some conditions concerning the occupation, such as a demilitarized zone around the plant and amnesty for themselves.[73] The group settled for a meeting the next day among their representatives, the Rosenthals, and the tribe's Business and Claims Committee. Percy Archambeau distanced himself from the Eagle Warrior Society and its methods but affirmed that he, too, wanted changes within Yankton Sioux Industries. "We don't go along with all of their demands, but we do want a better contract," he told the press. "We had this meeting set up a week ago to go over the contract, but they jumped the gun on us. We don't believe in their methods of resolving the issues. We believe in negotiating our differences." The occupiers' spokesman responded to these criticisms with defiant exasperation: "We know that the Indian people have been negotiating for the past 400 years and look what it's got us—nothing."[74]

Initially, the community of Wagner reacted to the takeover with panic. Schools closed as soon as students arrived in the morning, but, according to the *Wagner Post*, "by the end of the day people were going about the business of everyday living pretty much as usual."[75] A handful of BIA and state police loosely guarded the plant, but sympathizers easily came and went with food and supplies during the night. Some of the latecomers included Donald Cournoyer (the son of Steve Cournoyer, Jr., who opposed the occupation) and a few of his friends, who arrived on the scene just to find out what was happening. Greg Zephier's brother, John ("Zeph") Zephier, who also arrived late, recalled having to tell Donald Cournoyer and his companions to leave for violating the group's ban on drugs and alcohol during the occupation. Some of these young men would later create a different event at the pork plant. For now, the occupying force, which had grown to thirty or forty strong, took shifts sleeping and watching out for a police invasion that would never come.[76]

On the second day, the Yankton Sioux Industries board of directors, including the Rosenthals, met with tribal officials and representatives for the Eagle Warrior Society, including national AIM leader Ted Means of Pine Ridge and white attorney John Keller of Chamberlain. At midnight, after seven hours of negotiations, they reached a compromise that included a 15-percent pay increase for employees and a renegotiation of the tribe's contract with the Rosenthals. The agreement also paid employees for the days of work they missed during the occupation and stipulated that the tribe would not press charges against the occupiers provided they did not damage the plant. Even though he had displayed unbending bravado for the press, Greg Zephier accepted the

South Dakota highway patrolmen set up roadblocks to prevent anyone from
entering or leaving the pork-processing plant during the first takeover.
Photograph by Milo Dailey, *Yankton Daily Press & Dakotan*

compromise. The group had evidently sought only to catalyze improvements at the plant and not to impose its will on the rest of the Yankton people, as many critics had suggested. "They gave quite a bit," said Mark Meierhenry, the tribe's lawyer, impressed with the occupiers' flexibility, in contrast to the popular perception of AIM as an intransigent terrorist group. Zephier's only remaining demand was that the entire tribe consider the compromise for themselves.[77]

Early in the afternoon of 19 March 1975, the third day of the occupation, the protesters sent about six of their number out through the back fence with all of their weapons in two canvas bags. Approximately two hours later, a group of about forty American Indians, most of them men, emerged from the plant, unarmed and singing around a drum. Greg Zephier, his father Fred, and brothers Bill and Ted Means led them. The women and children walked in the center of the group for protection; Greg Zephier's lone fist in the air signaled victory and defiance as the group marched out.[78] Zephier called the takeover "a long overdue effort of self-determination by Indian people," and his image, complete with a revolutionary's beret, aviator sunglasses, and wrapped braids framing his unsmiling face, shot out over the news wires.[79]

Members of the white community around Wagner were not impressed with the militants' success. Many of them knew employees who had been forced out of the plant at gunpoint on Monday morning. Although the *Wagner Post* had published a statement from five local ministers urging "Christian patience" during the occupation, most white residents were outraged.[80] Many mistakenly believed that outside agitators like the Means brothers had directed the takeover. "What really ticked people off here in Wagner," noted former city councilman Alan Pirner, "was when they put the U.S. flag upside-down" above the pork plant in a trademark AIM gesture.[81] On the third and final day of the occupation, the *Mitchell Daily Republic* published an editorial, later reprinted in the *Wagner Post*, sharply criticizing government leaders for pandering to the AIM "criminals" inside the pork plant. In addition to calling a number of the group's demands "absurd and ridiculous" and "about as far fetched as the myth that the moon was made out of cheese," the writer bashed "government officials [who] cringe in some corner using meaningless words and excuses to support their action." The Eagle Warrior Society should be given one chance to surrender, the editorial concluded, and "then it's time to step in and put an end to this kind of revolutionary movement."[82]

On the evening the occupation ended, 19 March, Melvin Rosenthal looked over the plant and did not observe any damage or spoiled meat. Upon further inspection the next day, however, he reported discovering damaged equipment and between one and two tons of spoiled meat. Estimating the losses at fifty thousand dollars, Rosenthal stated that he would press charges.[83] Greg Zephier retorted, "He's a liar and he's going to have to prove it."[84] One week later, Rosenthal had not followed through on his threat. Two weeks after the take-over, the tribe held a general council meeting to consider the agreement that had ended the occupation. When only two hundred of the forty-six hundred registered tribal members attended, the group decided to refer the agreement to voters. The council set no official date for this referendum, and there is no evidence that a vote was ever held.[85] The take-over that had seemed so momentous appeared destined to pass into memory without either criminal or administrative consequences.

Then, beginning 21 April 1975, a federal grand jury convened in Sioux Falls. The United States attorney for South Dakota, evidently fearing another protest, refused to confirm or deny speculation that the jury would examine the Wagner pork-plant takeover. The following week, on 1 May, Greg Zephier was arraigned before a federal magistrate, charged with interfering with commerce by threats or violence, and released. The news media in the state got little chance to report this judicial victory against AIM. In the early hours of the next morning, the actions of the Yankton Seven at Yankton Sioux Industries sparked a much bigger story. James Weddell later claimed that the traditional chief of the tribe had directed him to lead a second invasion of the pork plant to divert attention from Zephier and other elder tribal members.[86]

Whether or not that was the case, it is safe to say that for the other six young men the action expressed a more shapeless anger. The reasons behind the second action, which the state government squelched with quick force, were fuzzy and complicated. Most of those involved had an uninformed, immature political consciousness, and their short, violent occupation of the Wagner pork plant was, to some degree, a copycat action. They certainly had not researched the shortcomings of the plant's contract as the first occupiers had done. Reverend McBride theorized that the Yankton Seven saw what Zephier and the Eagle Warrior Society had done and borrowed from it, perhaps, in part, out of jealousy. McBride also went on to say, however, that a general feeling existed that the time had come for Indians to stand up for their rights.[87]

On 26 July 1975, in another display of rash decision-making, five of the seven young men escaped from the Charles Mix County jail and were quickly recaptured. All seven eventually stood trial and were convicted in state court for the burglary of the Coast to Coast store. Despite the large American Indian population in Charles Mix County, the jury was all white. The Yankton Seven served their three-year burglary sentences concurrently with federal sentences for the takeover itself. Reacting as if the takeover had been a well-organized

AIM action, the state of South Dakota invested many resources in the Coast to Coast burglary case, hiring, for example, a special prosecutor.[88] The American Indian Movement had proved an elusive quarry for Attorney General Janklow and other state authorities; many of the movement's unlawful actions had occurred on Indian reservations outside state jurisdiction. During the first pork-plant takeover and numerous other incidents involving AIM, federal authorities had acted with restraint to avoid a repeat of the 1890 Wounded Knee Massacre or the more recent killings of civilians at Kent State University in Ohio. One FBI memorandum regarding the second pork-plant takeover emphasized that personnel were "not going to panic or stampede in response to the situation."[89] The state of South Dakota, on the other hand, moved quickly to appease those who demanded, like the *Mitchell Daily Republic*, that government act swiftly for their safety. Yet, it was precisely because the Yankton Seven had no affiliation with AIM (other than inspiration) that the state could prosecute them so strongly. Without the powerful AIM organization behind them, with its knack for shaping publicity and its corps of brilliant lawyers, the unknown young Yankton Sioux men became a kind of substitute for AIM.

Once the second takeover at the pork plant had ended, some South Dakotans responded with public gratitude, especially to Attorney General Janklow, for the symbolic victory over AIM. A letter to the editor published in the *Rapid City Journal* following the takeover declared, "[Janklow] is one politician who is fulfilling his campaign promises."[90] The *Sioux Falls Argus-Leader* editorialized, "The ending to this latest episode was as quick and clean as anyone could ask, or expect. Janklow deserves the credit."[91] Such praise helped to make the young attorney general a celebrity across the state and prompted a reaction from the FBI, which indicated in an internal memorandum that "we would review our policies and would unquestionably through this be able to respond in the future with a more definite response. . . . Our plans must be expedited so that we do not wait too long before execution."[92] The more forceful approach, however, met with tragedy when the FBI raided an AIM compound at Oglala on the Pine Ridge Indian Reservation less than two months later; two FBI agents and one Indian activist died in the shoot-out that ensued.[93]

In many ways, the first and second takeovers of the Yankton Sioux Industries pork plant in Wagner represented some of the best and worst of the Red Power movement. The first occupation was essentially a nonviolent action led by local activists. Although a number of their initial demands were unrealistic, the Eagle Warrior Society negotiated a modest but significant settlement that at least strengthened the Yanktons' voice with the Rosenthals, whose management of the plant, in the Indians' view, was conducted with little regard for the tribe. While the terms of this settlement never truly materialized, Greg Zephier and his group acted for the tribe's interests and gave the negotiating process impetus. At its best, the Red Power movement, including AIM, also gave American Indian people throughout the country a sense of pride that had been missing for the previous generation. Sociologist Joane Nagel argues that political actions like the pork-plant takeover "put forth an image of American Indians as victorious rather than victimized, confronting an oppressive federal bureaucracy, demanding redress of long-standing grievances, [and] challenging images of Indians as powerless casualties of history."[94] Eagle Warrior Society members gave their tribe a symbolic and significant place in Charles Mix County, where they had too long been "looked down upon," as Zephier contended when he started the local AIM chapter.[95] Elsie McBride explained, "Part of the problem [with economic development] was that it was always from the top down. And at least the AIM movement did come from the bottom."[96] The American Indian Movement gave some of the Yankton people a voice to vent their dissatisfaction with the latest in a long line of top-down impositions.

The drawback to this new Indian voice was that it often spoke the language of the bottom, which caused the alliances to self-destruct even before white authorities intervened. The first symbolic victory of the Red Power movement, the nineteen-month reclamation of Alcatraz Island beginning in 1969, tore itself apart when idealistic activists, a thuggish "security" corps, and a drug-dealing gang called the Thunderbirds found themselves pitted against one another.[97] The second takeover of the Yankton Sioux Industries pork plant epitomized this side of Red Power activism. Disorganized, violent, and alcohol-induced, the second action overshadowed the more carefully laid plans for change that characterized the first takeover.

Members of the Eagle Warrior Society, of course, had exhibited some rashness of their own, proclaiming, "We're here to die," during the first takeover, and Greg Zephier apparently had some regrets about his actions,[98] but in the end, the demanding, in and of itself, produced a change in many American Indian people. For all of their weaknesses, AIM and the Red Power movement provided some valuable, if often intangible, benefits. As Russell Means told a *New York Times* reporter from jail around the time of the two pork-plant takeovers: "The children are growing their hair long, wearing sacred eagle feathers. . . . I count that an immeasurable plus. First, one has to have self-pride, then you have to have political change and then follows economic change."[99] Some would point out that, thirty years after these occupations, little has changed on many reservations. Nevertheless, the renewed identity and "self-pride," as Means put it, created in the midst of the political turmoil of the 1970s, represented a complex but indeed "immeasurable plus" for many American Indians.

NOTES

1. The Red Power movement has been the subject of numerous works. See, for example, Paul Chaat Smith and Robert Allen Warrior, *Like a Hurricane: The Indian Movement from Alcatraz to Wounded Knee* (New York: New Press, 1996); Troy R. Johnson, *The Occupation of Alcatraz Island: Indian Self-Determination and the Rise of Indian Activism* (Urbana: University of Illinois Press, 1996); and Joane Nagel, *American Indian Ethnic Renewal: Red Power and the Resurgence of Identity and Culture* (New York Oxford University Press, 1996).

2. South Dakota, Circuit Court, First Judicial Court, State of South Dakota v. Mark Winckler, Mike Weston, Jesse Costello, Mike Honomichl, Jim Weddell, Donald Cournoyer, and Godwin Weston, official court transcript, 991, Charles Mix County Clerk of Courts Office, Lake Andes, SD (hereafter cited as Transcript); *Mitchell Daily Republic*, 3 May 1975; James Weddell, interview, Sioux Falls, SD, 18 Jan. 2002.

3. Transcript, 816–18.

4. Ibid.; James Weddell, interview.

5. Transcript, 827, 849–51.

6. Ibid., 822.

7. Ibid., 865–66. See also *Rapid City Journal*, 3 May 1975; "Report on Yankton Sioux Industries Break-in, Investigative Period: 2 May 1975–12 May 1975," 14 May 1975, 10, Federal Bureau of Investigation (FBI), Washington, DC. A copy of this document was obtained under the Freedom of Information (FOI)/Privacy Acts (PA). The author name and case title were deleted from the copy.

8. Transcript, 981–82; *Mitchell Daily Republic*, 3 May 1975.

9. Vine Deloria, Jr., and Clifford M. Lytle, *American Indians, American Justice* (Austin: University of Texas Press, 1983), 29–33, 170–72.

10. Dennis Eisnach, interview, New York, NY, 3 Feb. 2002.

11. *Sioux Falls Argus-Leader*, 2 May 1975.

12. *Mitchell Daily Republic*, 2 May 1975.

13. "South Dakota Troopers Invade Indian Land to End Meat Plant Sit-In," *Akwesasne Notes* 7 (Summer 1975): 19.

14. SAC, Minneapolis (70–9926), to Director, memorandum, "Attention: Laboratory, Latent Fingerprint Section, [subject deleted]," 7 May 1975, 3, FBI, FOI/PA.

15. *Rapid City Journal*, 4 May 1975.

16. Donald Cournoyer, interview, Wagner, SD, 14 Jan. 2002. See also *Mitchell Daily Republic*, 3 May 1975.

17. *Rapid City Journal*, 4 May 1975.

18. *Mitchell Daily Republic*, 3 May 1975.

19. Alan Pirner, interview, Wagner, SD, 15 Jan. 2002.

20. Lynwood E. Oyos, ed., *Over a Century of Leadership: South Dakota Territorial and State Governors* (Sioux Falls, SD: Center for Western Studies, Augustana College, 1987), 211–12; *Mitchell Daily Republic*, 3 May 1975.

21. Eisnach, interview.

22. Director, FBI, to SACs, Deputy Attorney General et al., message relay, 3 May 1975, 3, FBI, FOI/PA.

23. Transcript, 965–81.

24. Director, FBI, to SACs, Deputy Attorney General et al., message relay, 3 May 1975, 2. See also *Mitchell Daily Republic*, 3 May 1975.

25. Ibid., 4.

26. *Sioux Falls Argus-Leader*, 3 May 1975.

27. Herbert T. Hoover, "Yankton Sioux Tribal Claims against the United States, 1917–1975," *Western Historical Quarterly* 7 (Apr. 1976): 127–28. See also Reneé Sansom-Flood and Shirley A. Bernie, *Remember Your Relatives: Volume 1, Yankton Sioux Images, 1851–1904,* ed. Leonard R. Bruguier (Marty, SD: Marty Indian School, 1985), 7. For a complete accounting of Yankton Sioux land ownership, see Beth R. Ritter, "Dispossession to Diminishment: The Yankton Sioux Reservation, 1858–1998" (PhD diss., University of Nebraska, 1999).

28. See Article 5, Treaty of 1858, reprinted in Sansom-Flood and Bernie, *Remember Your Relatives: Volume 1,* 50. See also 7–11.

29. Ritter, "Dispossession to Diminishment," 113–14. See also Reneé Sansom-Flood, Shirley A. Bernie, and Leonard R. Bruguier, *Remember Your Relatives: Volume 2, Yankton Sioux Images, 1865–1915* (Marty, SD: Yankton Sioux Elderly Advisory Board, 1989), 27–42.

30. Vine Deloria, Jr., "The Evolution of Federal Indian Policy Making," in *American Indian Policy in the Twentieth Century,* ed. Vine Deloria, Jr. (Norman: University of Oklahoma Press, 1985), 247–52.

31. Percy Archambeau, interview by Joseph H. Cash, Greenwood, SD, 19 Aug. 1968, American Indian Research Project (AIRP), Manuscript 14, 5, 21, Institute of American Indian Studies (IAIS), University of South Dakota (USD), Vermillion.

32. U.S. Bureau of the Census, *1980 Census of Population: Volume 1, Characteristics of the Population,* chap. C, *General Social and Economic Characteristics,* part 43, South Dakota, PC80-1-C43, 234, 239.

33. Archambeau, interview, 12.

34. Pirner, interview.

35. *Wagner Post*, 18 Mar., 6 May, 15 July 1971; interview of Melvin Rosenthal, by Orlando and Violet Goering, n.p., Summer 1981, South Dakota Oral History Project, Manuscript 2251, 3, IAIS, USD.

36. *Wagner Post*, 10 June, 25 Nov. 1971, 28 June 1973.

37. Herbert T. Hoover, "Sioux Country: The Nakota Yankton Tribe," (2000), 529, 545,

copy in author's possession; Yankton Sioux Industries, Inc., Certificate of Incorporation (10 July 1972), *1972 Annual Report* (30 Apr. 1973), and *1973 Annual Report* (6 May 1974), Office of the South Dakota Secretary of State, Pierre.

38. *Wagner Post*, 13 Apr. 1972.

39. Ibid., 7 Feb. 1974.

40. Ibid., 31 Jan., 7, 28 Feb. 1974; Hoover, "Sioux Country," 528–29.

41. *Wagner Post*, 28 Feb. 1974.

42. AIM, the national organization that dominated Indian activism in the 1970s, received funding from the federal Office of Economic Opportunity as well as corporate and religious charities in its early days as an antipoverty organization. See Rolland Dewing, *Wounded Knee II* (Chadron, NE: Great Plains Network, 1995), 21, and Peter Matthiessen, *In the Spirit of Crazy Horse* (New York: Penguin Books, 1992), 36.

43. Nagel, *American Indian Ethnic Renewal*, 131; Smith and Warrior, *Like a Hurricane*, 183–86.

44. *Wagner Post*, 22 Feb., 8 Mar. 1973.

45. Ibid., 22 Feb. 1973.

46. Ibid., 8 Mar. 1973.

47. *Sioux Falls Argus-Leader*, 17 May 1975.

48. Elsie McBride, interview, Howard, SD, 20 Jan. 2002.

49. Owen Ray Wipf, interview, Wagner, SD, 15 Jan. 2002; *Wagner Post*, 23 Nov. 1972.

50. Ibid., 22 Mar. 1973.

51. Ibid.

52. Todd Morrow, interview, Marty, SD, 10 Jan. 2002; Richard Leasure, interview, Marty, SD, 9 Jan. 2002; Wipf, interview.

53. See, for example, the account of the Wagner Chamber of Commerce meeting in the 7 February 1974 issue of the *Wagner Post*.

54. Wipf, interview; Herbert T. Hoover and Leonard R. Bruguier, *The Yankton Sioux*, Indians of North America Series (New York: Chelsea House Publishers, 1988), 66.

55. Morrow, interview; Marlita A. Reddy, ed., *Statistical Record of Native North Americans* (Detroit, MI: Gale Research, 1993), 895; Sam Weddell, interview, Marty, SD, 14 Jan. 2002.

56. Steve Cournoyer, Jr., interview, Pickstown, SD, 15 Jan. 2002; Wesley R. Hurt, Jr., "The Urbanization of the Yankton Indians," *Human Organization* 20 (Winter 1961-1962): 226–31; Ethel Nurge, ed., *The Modern Sioux: Social Systems and Reservation Culture* (Lincoln: University of Nebraska Press, 1970); Steve Cournoyer, Jr., interview.

57. Morrow, Leasure, interviews.

58. Eric Schlosser, *Fast Food Nation: The Dark Side of the All-American Meal* (Boston: Houghton Mifflin, 2001), 172–73; Rosenthal, interview, 3; Morrow, interview.

59. Leasure, Morrow, and Steve Cournoyer, Jr., interviews.

60. Sam Weddell, interview.

61. Rosenthal, interview, 6.

62. Wipf, interview; Hoover, "Sioux Country," 529, 545–46; Herbert T. Hoover, interview, Vermillion, SD, 11 Jan. 2002; *Mitchell Daily Republic*, 18 Mar. 1975; "Yankton Seven Trials to Start," *Akwesasne Notes* 7 (Autumn 1975): 8.

63. "Yankton Seven Trials to Start," 8; Wipf, Steve Cournoyer, Jr., interviews; Hoover, "Sioux Country," 529, 545; "Transcription of General Council, 4/26/78," *Yankton Sioux Indian Small Business Investment Company Journal* 1 (Aug. 1978): 34.

64. *Yankton Daily Press & Dakotan*, 18 Mar. 1975.

65. *Mitchell Daily Republic*, 17 Mar. 1975.

66. Robert McBride, interview, by Herbert T. Hoover, n.p., 26 May 1976, AIRP, Manuscript 1032, 11, IAIS, USD.

67. Beverly Zephier, interview, Marty, SD, 9 Jan. 2002.

68. "Navajos Occupy Fairchild Plant," *Akwesasne Notes* 7 (Spring 1975): 34. See also *Rapid City Journal*, 11 Jan., 4 Feb. 1975.

69. McBride, interview, 11; Hoover, "Sioux Country," 545; Sam Weddell, interview; *Yankton Daily Press and Dakotan*, 19 Mar. 1975; Beverly Zephier, interview.

70. McBride, interview, 12. See also 15.

71. *Yankton Daily Press and Dakotan*, 18 Mar. 1975; *Wagner Post*, 20 Mar. 1975; Sam Weddell, interview.

72. *Mitchell Daily Republic*, 17, 19 Mar. 1975.

73. *Wagner Post*, 20 Mar. 1975.

74. *Mitchell Daily Republic*, 18 Mar. 1975.

75. *Wagner Post*, 20 Mar. 1975.

76. Donald Cournoyer, interview; John ("Zeph") Zephier, interview, Wagner, SD, 9 Jan. 2002.

77. *Mitchell Daily Republic*, 19, 21 Mar. 1975.

78. Ibid., 20 Mar. 1975; *Wagner Post*, 27 Mar. 1975; *Yankton Daily Press and Dakotan*, 19 Mar. 1975.

79. *Mitchell Daily Republic*, 20 Mar. 1975.

80. *Wagner Post*, 20 Mar. 1975. See also *Yankton Daily Press and Dakotan*, 18 Mar. 1975.

81. Pirner, interview.

82. *Mitchell Daily Republic*, 19 Mar. 1975.

83. Ibid., 20 Mar. 1975.

84. Ibid., 21 Mar. 1975.

85. *Wagner Post*, 27 Mar. 1975; *Mitchell Daily Republic*, 5 Apr. 1975; *Rapid City Journal*, 7 Apr. 1975.

86. *Sioux Falls Argus-Leader*, 19 Apr., 2 May 1975; "South Dakota Troopers Invade Indian Land," 19; James Weddell, interview.

87. McBride, interview, 18.

88. *Mitchell Daily Republic*, 28 July 1975; Transcript, 429; Carl Haberstick, interview, Huron,

SD, 22 Jan. 2002; "South Dakota v. Winckler et al.," *North Western Reporter*, 2d series, 260 (1977):356.

89. N. P. Callahan to Director, undated memorandum, "Yankton Sioux Industries, Inc., Yankton Indian Reservation, Wagner, South Dakota, Takeover of Pork Plant, May 2, 1975," 2, FBI, FOI/PA.

90. *Rapid City Journal*, 9 May 1975.

91. Reprinted in *Rapid City Journal*, 10 May 1975.

92. Clarence Kelly, Director, to Mr. Callahan, Mr. Jenkins, and Mr. Adams, memorandum, "Takeover of Yankton Sioux Industries, Yankton Indian Reservation, Wagner, South Dakota, May 2, 1975," 8 May 1975, 1–2, FBI, FOI/PA.

93. *Sioux Falls Argus-Leader*, 27–30 June 1975; Matthiessen, *In the Spirit of Crazy Horse*, 154–90.

94. Nagel, *American Indian Ethnic Renewal*, 140. For a history of the Yankton tribe, see Hoover, *The Yankton Sioux*.

95. *Wagner Post*, 22 Feb. 1973.

96. Elsie McBride, interview.

97. Johnson, *Occupation of Alcatraz Island*, 154–58.

98. Beverly Zephier, interview.

99. *New York Times*, 22 Apr. 1975, 18.

AFTERWORD

. . .

Mapping the terrain of twentieth-century northern plains tribal life is often an illusory undertaking, for Iktomi still stalks this land. A dearth of both primary sources and published materials makes it important to persevere in the search, for, as the essays in this anthology reveal, the rewards are immense. While it is not possible to cover every important topic or event in a volume of this size, the authors have crafted strong stories that illuminate numerous facets of the complex and compelling history of the twentieth-century Sioux on the northern plains.

As the Wounded Knee II and Wagner pork-plant occupations ended, President Richard M. Nixon was beginning his second term. Nixon and his predecessor, Lyndon B. Johnson, were the first chief executives since Franklin Roosevelt to give tribal issues a greater role in the national agenda. In response to Nixon's contention that the termination of tribes was morally wrong, Congress passed the 1972 Indian Education Act to improve tribal education, and the 1975 Indian Self-Determination and Educational Assistance Act created opportunities for reservation leaders and communities to assume more control over their own affairs. That same year, Congress created the American Indian Policy Review Commission in an attempt to emulate the efforts at Indian policy reform that had resulted in the Indian Reorganization Act.[1] Five years later, the United States Supreme Court awarded the Sioux monetary compensation for the taking of the Black Hills. The Sioux, however, refused the settlement, claiming the Black Hills had never been for sale. The issue remains unresolved today.[2]

The tumultuous first half of the 1970s presented many Sioux people with hope for a better future. Even if they could not escape the violence and poverty that stalked their communities during the era, their experience with home rule and federal programs like those of the Office of Economic Opportunity made a return to the days when the Indian superintendent ran the reservation impossible. Tribal leaders now demanded a seat at the table where they would participate in shaping their own destinies.

The cause of greater Sioux self-determination had taken a step forward with the decision of the Oglala Sioux Tribal Council to impose a tribal lease tax on outside lessees in 1949. Some stock growers then leasing reservation lands claimed that tribal governments had no authority to impose a land tax and refused to pay.[3] This challenge led to court proceedings that culminated in 1956 with the decision of the Eighth Circuit Court of Appeals upholding the tribe's civil jurisdiction over all persons, Indian and non-Indian, on the reservation. The court's ruling defined tribal sovereignty for the twentieth century by recognizing "the existence of Indian tribes as quasi-sovereign entities possessing all the inherent rights of sovereignty except where restrictions have been placed thereon by the United States."[4] This case spoke to the strength of tribal sovereignty and emerged as a leading precedent for subsequent cases such as *Williams v. Lee*, which denied Arizona courts jurisdiction in civil cases brought by non-Indians against Indians on reservations.[5]

Tribal-state conflicts escalated during the 1960s as tribal rights issues, including civil rights, treaty rights, and sovereignty, spread across the northern plains. Robert Burnette, a political leader and activist from the Rosebud reservation, came to the forefront on both the state and national scenes in demanding that tribal members imprisoned in local jails be guaranteed their civil rights and that tribal governments retain their sovereignty.[6] At the same time, tribal leaders created an entity called the United Sioux Tribes to fight an attempt by the South Dakota Legislature to assume jurisdiction over the reservations. United Sioux Tribes spearheaded a statewide referendum to block the legislature's action, and voters approved the referendum in November 1964, mainly out of concern over the high cost to taxpayers if the state were to assume jurisdiction over the reservations.[7]

The 1964 referendum formed only part of an ongoing and escalating legal battle over jurisdiction. In several cases brought on behalf of Sioux plaintiffs, the state claimed that late nineteenth- and early twentieth-century acts opening all or portions of reservations to homesteading indicated congressional intent to diminish reservation boundaries, the legal standard for deciding jurisdiction over civil matters. In a 1975 child custody case, the United States Supreme Court affirmed the state's jurisdiction, ruling that the 1891 act opening the Lake Traverse reservation to homesteading was, in fact, intended to reduce the reservation's boundaries. Two years later, in a case involving the boundaries of the Rosebud reservation, the Supreme Court ruled that the 1904, 1907, and 1910 acts opening the counties of Gregory, Tripp, and Mellette had indeed been meant to remove some reservation lands from tribal jurisdiction.[8]

The favorable rulings for the state contributed to racial tensions in South Dakota over the decades. In 1999, the United States Commission on Civil Rights conducted hearings in South Dakota and made fifteen recommendations designed to address its findings that the Sioux lacked confidence in the state's law enforcement and the judicial system, suffered from chronic underemployment, and did not participate in the electoral process despite the creation of tribal legislative districts, among other matters.[9]

Race relations constitute just one of a wealth of areas for further study of the Sioux in South Dakota in the last decades of the twentieth century. Legal history, ethnicity, mascot battles, and the gaming industry offer other possibilities. The Flandreau Royal River Casino, which began as a bingo hall just north of the state's largest city, Sioux Falls, is one example of a successful Sioux economic undertaking. Using the provisions of the 1988 Indian Gaming Regulatory Act, leaders of the Flandreau Sioux negotiated successful tribal gaming compacts. The tribe and the city of Flandreau have also worked together to minimize jurisdictional disputes by negotiating a tribal-city police agreement to reduce the social divide that has often characterized tribal and nontribal law enforcement.[10]

The new influx of capital from casino revenues is one sign of success on some Sioux reservations. Another symbol of the evolution and resurgence of tribal identity is the return of the bison, which can now be found on several South Dakota reservations, creating new experiences and stories for the future. For the last century, the Sioux have shared with the nontribal population of South Dakota a history filled with experiences both good and bad. Today, as tribal governments and their constituents redefine the contemporary meaning of tribal sovereignty, new debates, issues, and relationships are leading us into the next century of the Sioux in South Dakota.

NOTES

1. Francis Paul Prucha, *The Great Father: The United States Government and the American Indians*, 2 vols. (Lincoln: University of Nebraska Press, 1984), 2:1140–42, 1144–46, 1162–64.

2. For a slightly biased history of the Black Hills land claim, see Edward Lazarus, *Black Hills/White Justice: The Sioux Nation versus the United States, 1775 to the Present* (New York: HarperCollins, 1991).

3. Edward Charles Valandra, *Not Without Our Consent: Lakota Resistance to Termination, 1950–59* (University of Illinois: Urbana and Chicago, 2006), 129–35.

4. Iron Crow v. Oglala Sioux Tribe of Pine Ridge Reservation South Dakota, 231 F2d 89.

5. Native American Rights Fund, National Indian Law Library, *Landmark Indian Law Cases* (William S. Hein & Co.: Buffalo, 2002), p. 432.

6. Regan A. Lutz and Benson Tong, eds., *The Human Tradition in the American West* (Wilmington, DE: SR Books, 2002), 193–208.

7. For a study of this important state vote, see Richmond L. Clow, "State Jurisdiction on Sioux Reservations: Indian and Non-Indian Responses, 1952–1964," *South Dakota History* (Summer 1981): 171–84. Senator Karl Mundt of South Dakota described the costs of jurisdiction in his essay titled "Indian Autonomy and Indian Legal Problems," *University of Kansas Law Review* 15 (1967): 505–11.

8. DeCoteau v. District County Court, 420 US 425 (1975); Rosebud Sioux Tribe v. Kneip, 430 US 584 (1977). See also Thomas Biolsi, *"Deadliest Enemies": Law and the Making of Race Relations on and off Rosebud Reservation* (Berkeley: University of California Press, 2001).

9. *Indian Country Today*, 5 Apr. 2000.

10. Pub. L. No. 100-497, 17 Oct. 1988; "Flandreau Police Departments," http://www .innovations.harvard.edu/awards.html?id=16856, accessed 1 June 2007.

CONTRIBUTORS

HARRY H. ANDERSON is a retired historian and agency administrator from Whitefish Bay, Wisconsin. He has published studies on Teton Sioux history for more than five decades and has also served as an expert witness for the Lakota tribes in Sioux Docket 74a before the United States Indian Claims Commission.

ROGER BROMERT earned his BA from the University of South Dakota and his PhD from the University of Toledo. He taught at Huron College before joining the faculty at Southwestern Oklahoma State University, Weatherford, where he is a professor of Oklahoma and American Indian history. Bromert serves on the Board of Directors of the Oklahoma Historical Society.

RICHMOND L. CLOW is professor of Native American Studies at the University of Montana in Missoula. He has contributed several articles on Lakota history and other topics to *South Dakota History* over the years and is the author of *Chasing the Glitter: Black Hills Milling, 1874–1959*, published by the South Dakota State Historical Society Press in 2002.

JOSHUA GARRETT-DAVIS is a graduate of Amherst College and currently lives in New York City, where he is pursuing an MFA in nonfiction writing at Columbia University. His article is adapted from his undergraduate thesis in American Studies, which won the George Rogers Taylor Prize and the Doshisha American Studies Prize in 2002.

FREDERICK E. HOXIE is Swanlund Professor of History at the University of Illinois. He is the author of *A Final Promise: The Campaign to Assimilate the Indians, 1880–1920* and *Parading through History: The Making of the Crow Nation in America, 1805–1935* and coauthor of *The People: A History of Native America.*

MICHAEL L. LAWSON is a historical consultant with Morgan, Angel & Associates in Washington, DC. After earning degrees from the University of Nebraska at Omaha and the University of New Mexico, he served as historian for the National Park Service, the Smithsonian Institution, and the Bureau of Indian Affairs.

ALLISON FUSS MELLIS received her PhD from the University of Notre Dame and is a former assistant professor of history at the United States Naval Academy in Annapolis, Maryland. She is the author of *Riding Buffaloes and Broncos: Rodeo and Native Traditions in the Northern Great Plains.*

AKIM D. REINHARDT is author of a twentieth-century political history of the Pine Ridge Reservation entitled *Ruling Pine Ridge: Oglala Politics from the IRA to Wounded Knee* and a forthcoming collection of political documents in Lakota political history. He is an associate professor of history at Towson University, Towson, Maryland.

SCOTT RINEY is a historian of the American Indian and the American West. He earned his B.A. at Colorado College and his Ph.D. at Arizona State University. His most recent book, *The Rapid City Indian School, 1898–1933*, focuses on Indian boarding schools.

STEVEN C. SCHULTE is professor of history at Mesa State College in Grand Junction, Colorado, where he has taught since 1989. Schulte is the author of *Wayne Aspinall and the Shaping of the American West* and is finishing another book on Colorado's water wars. He received his PhD in history from the University of Wyoming in 1984.

DON SOUTHERTON, whose maternal grandparents homesteaded near the Pine Ridge Indian Reservation in the early twentieth century, has had a lifelong interest in history. He currently writes on entrepreneurialism, globalization, and early United States-Korea business ventures.

LAURA WOODWORTH-NEY is associate professor and chair of the Department of History at Idaho State University. She is the author of *Mapping Identity: The Creation of the Coeur d'Alene Indian Reservation, 1805–1902*, and *Women in the North American West*. She is also the award-winning editor of the peer-reviewed journal *Idaho Yesterdays*.

INDEX

Page numbers in **bold** indicate illustrations

Indian New Deal. *See* Indian Reorganization Act of 1934 (IRA)
Indian Reorganization Act of 1934 (IRA), 2, 58–59, 70, 98, 102–3, 207–9; Berry's criticism of; goals of, 181–82, 185, 208; opposition to, 182–84, 207–9
Indian reservations: creation of, in SD, 1–2, 11–12. *See also* specific reservations
Indian Rights Association (IRA), 18
Indian Self-Determination and Educational Assistance Act, 301
Indian Time, 283
Individual Indian Money (IIM) accounts, 55, 62, 243
Inheritance. *See* Heirship
Interior Board of Indian Appeals (IBIA), 66
Iron Cloud, Paul, 71
Iron Lightning, 15
Irving, Chester, 72
Irving, Mary, 71–72
Irving v. Clark, 74–75

Jackson, Henry M., 65
Jane E. Waldron v. The United States of America, Black Tomahawk, and Ira A. Hatch, 30, 41
Janis, Ben, 94
Janklow, William J., 275–76, 289, 293
Jermark, E. W., 97
Jewett, Charles, 22
Jicarilla Sanitarium, 171
Johnson, Lyndon B., 277, 301
Johnson-O'Malley Act (1934), 103
Jones, Guy W., 192
Juffer, Don, 279

Kash, Reese, 262, 263
Keller, John, 290
Kennedy, John F., 198
Kent State University, 294
Kershner, Nurse, 171
Kills Straight, Birgil, 264
King, A. E., 96
King, Thomas J., 24
King Brothers Rodeo Circus, 93
Kinney, J. P., 104

Kirk, Simon J., 185
Kneip, Richard F., 275
Kranz, Henry, 198

Lake Andes, SD, 226, 230, 233, 236–37, 275, 280
Lake Francis Case, 223, **225**, 234
Lake Traverse Indian Reservation, 49, 61, 67–68, 73
Lakota Sioux, 1, 160; pre-1889, 12–13; and ranching, 88, 98; and rodeo, 87–98, **91**, **95**. *See also* Teton Sioux; specific bands
Land allotment: cultural influences shaping, 46, 48; early program failures, 48–49; eligibility for, 30–42; entitlements, 48, 49, 51; farming affected by, 51; and leasing, 52–53; purpose of, 15, 49, 53; and trust period, 48, 55–56. *See also* General Allotment Act (1887); Land allotments, inheritance of
Land allotments, inheritance of: administrative burden of, 53–55, **54**, 62–64, **63**, 67–68, 76–77; and approval of wills, 57; decedent's rights in, 71–72, 74–75; escheat provisions, ICLA, 46, 69–77; fee property, 50, 55, 66; fractionated interests with, 50–51, 53, 57; and Indian Reorganization Act reforms, 58–59; probate administration of, 45, 49–50, 57, 60, 66–67; selling of, 51, 53–55, **54**, 57, 214; tribal purchase consent requirements for, 65, 70, 73. *See also* Heirship; Trust allotments
Langone, Stephen, 65
La Plant, Charles, 20
LaPlant, Fred, **21**
La Point, Sam, 182
La Pointe, James, 94
Larrabee, Charles F., 147, 149
Last Man, John, 20
Law enforcement: pre-1930, 13, 15, 23–24; state jurisdiction over, 215–17, 273
Leasure, Richard, 285
Leasing, 52–54, 92, 180, 181, 195, 208, 301
Leech Lake, MN, 142, 166

CPSIA information can be obtained at www.ICGtesting.com
Printed in the USA
LVOW11s0323230914

405339LV00003B/11/P